Nostra Aetate

Celebrating Fifty Years of the
Catholic Church's Dialogue with
Jews and Muslims

Nostra Aetate

Celebrating Fifty Years of the Catholic Church's Dialogue with Jews and Muslims

Edited by Pim Valkenberg and Anthony Cirelli

The Catholic University of America Press
Washington, D.C.

Library of Congress Cataloging-in-Publication Data

Valkenberg, Pim.
  Nostra aetate : celebrating fifty years of the Catholic Church's dialogue with Jews
and Muslims / edited by Pim Valkenberg and Anthony Cirelli.
  pages cm
  ISBN 978-0-8132-2878-5 (pbk. : alk. paper)
  1. Catholic Church—Relations. 2. Vatican Council (2nd: 1962–1965 : Basilica
di San Pietro in Vaticano). Declaratio de ecclesiae habitudine ad religiones non-
Christianas. 3. Catholic   Church—Relations—Judaism. 4. Judaism—Relations—
Catholic Church. 5. Catholic Church—Relations—Islam. 6. Islam—Relations—
Catholic Church. I. Title.
  BX1784 .N67 2016
  261.2—dc23   2016010915

Contents

Editors' Note

The contents of this book originate from a conference *"Nostra Aetate*: Celebrating Fifty Years of the Catholic Church's Dialogue with Jews and Muslims" organized in May 2015 by The Catholic University of America (CUA) School of Theology and Religious Studies and the Secretariat for Ecumenical and Interreligious Affairs of the United States Conference of Catholic Bishops (USCCB).

Almost all speeches and lectures at this conference have been edited for this book, but we have tried to keep the original style of some of the major addresses intact. As was the case at the conference, the book focuses on the relationships of the Catholic Church with the other "Abrahamic" faiths, Islam and Judaism, but useful essays on Asian religions are included as well. For the printed book, we added contributions by a Hindu scholar and a Catholic scholar of Buddhism in Part II and by an additional Muslim scholar in Part III to further represent the reception of *Nostra Aetate* in these religions. We should add that this book represents a snapshot of an ongoing process. For instance, "A Reflection on Theological Questions Pertaining to Catholic-Jewish Relations" from the Vatican and the "Orthodox Rabbinic Statement on Christianity," both issued in December 2015, can be seen as further developments of the documentation in Part IV of this book.

In structuring this book we decided to follow loosely the order of the document *Nostra Aetate* itself. The first part of this volume gives a broad view of the document and its importance, including a fresh English translation completed by one of the persons related to its development from the very beginning and a couple of theological essays from Catholic University of America scholars on its history and its context. The second part concentrates on the relationship between the Catholic Church and the Asian religions (see the second paragraph of *Nostra Aetate*). The third and fourth parts concentrate on the relationships with the Muslims (*Nostra Aetate* 3) and the Jews (*Nostra Aetate* 4) that were the main focus of the conference in May 2015. Finally, just as *Nostra Aetate* 5 focuses on the practical implications of the previous paragraphs, the fifth and final section of the book gives a survey of the different forms of reception of the document in various ecclesial and academic contexts with special attention to the situation in the United States.

We are fortunate to have had the participation in the symposium and the book of Thomas P. Stransky, CSP, who was present for the drafting of *Nostra Aetate* and who provided his own English translation for the symposium. We have included that translation in this book along with Fr. Stransky's explanation of why he undertook it, and most essays in the book quote from his translation. A few contributors preferred to use the official Vatican translation or their own; the first citation of *Nostra Aetate* in each essay will indicate which translation is being used for it.

We want to thank both John Martino of CUA Press for his great help in producing this book and Niki Creamer for her assistance.

Pim Valkenberg, PhD, School of Theology and Religious Studies, CUA

Anthony Cirelli, PhD, Secretariat for Ecumenical and Interreligious Affairs, USCCB

Foreword

BISHOP MITCHELL T. ROZANSKI

When Pope St. John XXIII announced his plans for an ecumenical council on January 25, 1959, at the Basilica of St. Paul outside the Walls, few could have imagined the implications of this beloved pope's intentions. Over the next six years, both in the preparative phase and in the sessions of the Council fathers, the sixteen documents that were promulgated had far-reaching effects in the life of the Church. *Nostra Aetate*, the shortest in length of the conciliar documents, initiated a new era of reaching out in friendship with members of non-Christian religions. When *Nostra Aetate* was proclaimed on October 28, 1965, by Blessed Pope Paul VI, this document not only affected Catholics *within* the Church, it also opened doors and built bridges to members of the Jewish, Muslim, and other non-Christian religious communities.

Few areas of the world were so fertile for sowing the seeds of mutual cooperation and dialogue than the United States, the world's melting pot. The bishops of this country quickly established an Office of Ecumenical and Interreligious Affairs in their conference and began a series of dialogues with members of the Jewish and Muslim faiths. Over the past fifty years, these dialogues have borne much fruit as we seek to understand one another in a more profound way and cooperate in seeking the common good for our people. They have also served us well when misunderstandings have surfaced, since opportunities for candid discussion had already been well established.

Commemorating this ground-breaking document's fiftieth anniversary, the conference "*Nostra Aetate*: Celebrating Fifty Years of the Catholic Church's Dialogue with Jews and Muslims" was held at The Catholic University of America in Washington, D.C., from May 19 to 21, 2015. This landmark symposium was cosponsored by The Catholic University of America School of Theology and Religious Studies and the Secretariat of Ecumenical and Interreligious Affairs of the United States Conference of Catholic Bishops. Signifying the importance of this event, Cardinal Jean-Louis Tauran, president of the Pontifical Council of Interreligious Dialogue; Cardinal Kurt Koch, president of the Pontifical Council for Promoting Christian Unity; and Cardinal Timothy Dolan, archbishop of New York, joined us and delivered keynote addresses. We were also graced by the presence of Professor Seyyed Hossein Nasr, Rabbi Irving "Yitz" Greenberg, and Rabbi Noam Marans as respondents, respectively, to our keynotes. Adding to the joy of this symposium, we were honored to have

Reverend Thomas Stransky, CSP, who was present during the crafting of *Nostra Aetate* at Vatican II.

As we met over those three days, much reflection was given on the progress of the past fifty years in our dialogues with one another. It was encouraging for all the participants that, at this point, we take the fact of our interreligious dialogues for granted. Only those who remember the pre–Vatican II days could fully appreciate the progress that has been made and the goodwill that has been engendered by responding to the challenge of *Nostra Aetate*. But our symposium not only reflected on the progress of these intervening years, we also were encouraged by the words of hope in speaking of future directions for our dialogues.

Just as the Council fathers viewed the documents of Vatican II to be breathing life into the Church for generations that follow, so, too, do we seek the dialogues in which we engage to be organic, dynamically developing to nurture our lives of faith. The spirit of *Nostra Aetate* was palpable throughout the presentations, responses, and questions that were raised during our conference.

This compendium of the presentations and responses from the "*Nostra Aetate*: Celebrating Fifty Years of the Catholic Church's Dialogue with Jews and Muslims" symposium has been composed to commemorate this historic meeting and to uplift people of all faiths to the good will that has resulted from our dialogues. Ultimately, the source of our faith in the creator and divine providence is based in hope. This hope spurs us on in seeking the common good and allowing faith to become a leaven for the world. Section V of *Nostra Aetate* challenges us: "We cannot truly call upon God, the Father of all, if we refuse to behave as sisters and brothers with anyone, created as all are in the image of God. The relation of man and woman to God the Father and their relation to their fellow human beings are linked to such a degree that Holy Scripture says, 'Whoever does not love does not know God' (1 Jn 4:8)."[1]

---

1. *Nostra Aetate* 5, trans. Thomas F. Stransky, CSP.

Introduction

John Garvey

As the president of The Catholic University of America (CUA), I had the pleasure to host a celebration of the golden jubilee of *Nostra Aetate*, the Second Vatican Council's Decree on the Relation of the Church to Non-Christian Religions. And it is a privilege for our university press to make the key contributions and insights of that event available to a wider audience.

We had many distinguished speakers at our gathering in May 2015: rabbis, professors from top universities, and leaders of key organizations and local communities from the Catholic, Jewish, and Muslim faiths, including three cardinals of the Catholic Church. The cardinals' presence speaks to the great significance the Church places on dialogue with other faiths and—together with their distinguished respondents—marked another public instance of that dialogue in action.

The following reflections are adapted from the welcome I gave to the conference, along with the introductions I offered for Jean-Louis Cardinal Tauran, Kurt Cardinal Koch, and CUA alumnus and trustee Timothy Cardinal Dolan, whose remarks received replies from Dr. Seyyed Hossein Nasr, Rabbi Irving Greenberg, and Rabbi Noam Marans, respectively. They cover the topics of interreligious dialogue in general, the Catholic-Muslim dialogue, the Catholic-Jewish dialogue, and the latter dialogue as it has been lived locally in the United States.

The Goal of Dialogue

Nostra Aetate is the shortest of the sixteen documents promulgated by the Second Vatican Council. It is just five sections long—no longer than the essays we learned to write in grammar school. But the impact of those five paragraphs over the last five decades has been extraordinary. Perhaps the greatest sign of this is that to young people, like the undergraduates at Catholic University, *Nostra Aetate* does not seem extraordinary at all.

To our undergraduates it is obvious that Catholics should work sincerely with Muslims "for mutual understanding."[1] It is clear that we should esteem their example of prayer, almsgiving, and fasting. They do this every day. Nor do young people find anything strange in the idea that "God holds the Jews most dear for the sake of their Fathers."[2] Before they were born, Pope St. John Paul II became the first pope, perhaps since St. Peter,

---

1. *Nostra Aetate* 3, trans. Thomas F. Stransky, CSP.
2. *Nostra Aetate* 4.

to visit the Roman synagogue to pray with the Jewish community. He taught us to recognize the Jewish people as our beloved "elder brothers" in the faith of Abraham. Pope Benedict XVI drew on scripture and the tradition of the Church to argue that "Israel is in the hands of God, who will save it, 'as a whole,' at the proper time."[3] Before his election to the papacy, Pope Francis coauthored an interfaith reflection on faith and family with his friend Rabbi Abraham Skorka. In 2013, Rabbi Skorka celebrated Sukkot with Pope Francis in the Vatican.

It would be tempting to pat ourselves on the back and call the mission of *Nostra Aetate* a fait accompli. But the first words of the declaration—from which it takes its name—tell us not to do so. "In our time," the declaration begins, "the Church examines with greater care her relationship to non-Christian religions."

Fifty years after the promulgation of *Nostra Aetate*, we must continue to examine closely the Church's relationship to other faiths. That is what we set out to do at the symposium. Perhaps the best way to approach the contributions on the topic is first to ask ourselves what we aim to accomplish in interfaith dialogue. That we should foster dialogue with people of other faiths is now almost universally accepted. Why we should foster dialogue is a question still worth exploring.

The goal of some dialogues, like treaty negotiations, is for each party to rationally maximize its own satisfaction through a series of compromises. When the United States and Mexico signed the 1944 Water Treaty, the United States gave up some of its water rights in the Colorado River to Mexico. In exchange it received a favorable apportionment of the Rio Grande for Texas.[4] In interreligious dialogue, the tenets of faith are not on the table for bargaining. Catholics won't give up the Incarnation, for example, in exchange for a confession of the Trinity by Muslims or Jews.

As silly as this comparison may be, it gets at something important. We can trade water rights because they are means to some end—the production of crops or the flourishing of a city. We cannot trade truths because they are the end. As *Nostra Aetate* observed, we are drawn to fellowship by our desire to understand "the profound enigmas of the human condition."[5]

A better example might be the free exchange of ideas that takes place in the academic community. Academics publish their ideas and read their peers' because they have a desire to know, and they believe their peers can

3. Benedict XVI, "Prophecy and Apocalyptic in the Eschatological Discourse," in *Jesus of Nazareth: Holy Week* (Vatican City: Libreria Editrice Vaticana, 2011), 46.
4. Colorado River Water Users Association, "Law of the River," http://www.crwua .org/colorado-river/uses/law-of-the-river.
5. *Nostra Aetate* 1.

help them satisfy this. Pope Francis said something like this about interfaith dialogue. "Dialogue," he observed, "is born from a respectful attitude toward the other person, from a conviction that the other person has something good to say."[6]

But this example, too, falls short of the mark. In a normal exchange of ideas I have my own opinions and convictions, but I am open to being persuaded otherwise. To give an example from my own intellectual history, I used to think that freedom was a right to choose, which is a fairly common notion in contemporary culture. Through many conversations with others, in person and in writing, I became convinced that freedom is rather a right to *act* in certain ways that are good. Interreligious dialogue is not quite like this. We come to our conversations with the certitude of faith. Less than two months after the promulgation of *Nostra Aetate*, for example, the Council released the Pastoral Constitution on the Church in the Modern World, *Gaudium et Spes*. It affirmed that only Christ "fully reveals man to himself and makes his supreme calling clear."[7] Catholics are not going to change their minds about that.

Consider a third example. In the days after the resurrection, two of Jesus's disciples were walking along the road to Emmaus. While they walked, they talked about all the things that had happened. And as they went along Jesus came to them and interpreted the scriptures for them.[8]

There are a few things I like about this example. First, the disciples are companions on a journey. They are able to talk with one another because they are going the same way. In interreligious dialogue we are traveling together toward the truth. We don't stop short at any other goal. Second, the journey to Emmaus from Jerusalem is about seven miles. That's a long time to be talking. It suggests that the companions were intimate friends, who had the habit of looking at the world together. Interreligious dialogue is also an act of friendship. We engage in dialogue not just to glean insights from others or to win arguments but to share what we have found to be the greatest source of joy. Third, the companions didn't arrive at truth. Truth came to them. Faith is a gift from God. We can't force others to believe any more than we can force ourselves. But truth did come to them as they were discussing. In fact, he inserted himself in the conversation.

I think this gets at the heart of interreligious dialogue, whether with Muslims, Jews, or adherents of any other religious tradition. We pray that in our conversations, God will make himself better known to all of us.

---

6. Jorge Mario Bergoglio and Abraham Skorka, *On Heaven and Earth: Pope Francis on Faith, Family, and the Church in the Twenty-first Century*, xiv (New York: Image, 2013).

7. Vatican Council II, *Gaudium et Spes*, December 7, 1965, par. 22.

8. Lk 24.

Dialogue with Muslims

At the time of Vatican II, as the bishops were developing theological principles for dialogue with other faiths, Thomas Merton, a Trappist monk at the Abbey of Gethsemani in Kentucky, was already putting those principles into practice. In a letter written a year before the promulgation of *Nostra Aetate*, Merton asked: "How can one be in contact with the great thinkers and men of prayer of the various religions without recognizing that these men have known God and have loved Him because they recognized themselves loved by Him?"[9]

The letter was addressed to Merton's friend Abdul Aziz, a Pakistani Muslim and student of Sufism. The two were correspondents throughout the 1960s. (Merton died in 1968.) They prayed for each other and swapped reading lists. They talked about their common faith in the Creator and their differences on dogmas like the Trinity and the Incarnation. Merton considered their friendship a blessing from God, through which God made himself known to them.[10]

Correspondence did not mean compromise. Merton acknowledged "enormous" differences in some matters.[11] But the more familiar he became with Islam, the more he found something familiar. In Islam he encountered a voice from his "own country, so to speak."[12]

Perhaps today more than ever, Christians can find a familiar voice in their dialogue with Muslims. We stand together in defense of religious liberty and the unborn. We strive to teach our children virtues like courage, chastity, honesty, and charity. Most important, we share a fundamental orientation toward God and strive to honor God as our source and our end. Merton's example reminds us that finding this common ground begins with a sincere act of friendship by deepening our understanding of Islam as lived by Muslims while sharing an uncompromised witness to our own faith.

Dialogue with Jews

In 1974—nearly a decade after the promulgation of *Nostra Aetate*—Pope Paul VI established the Commission for Religious Relations with the

---

9. Thomas Merton, *The Hidden Ground of Love: The Letters of Thomas Merton on Religious Experience and Social Concerns*, ed. Thomas H. Shannon, 55–58 (letter of June 28, 1964) (New York: Farrar, Straus and Giroux, 1985), 58.

10. Ibid., 57 (letter of October 18, 1963).

11. Ibid.

12. Ibid., 56.

Jews within the Pontifical Council for Promoting Christian Unity. This may seem a peculiar place for the commission to reside. What does inter-religious dialogue with the Jews have to do with Christian unity?

An answer can be found in paragraph four of *Nostra Aetate*. The Jewish people, it says, are the root of the well-cultivated olive tree onto which the Church is grafted. It's a vivid image. It suggests that the health of the Church depends on her bond with the Jews. "[T]he Jewish religion is not 'extrinsic' to us," John Paul II told the Roman Jewish community in 1986, "but in a certain way is 'intrinsic' to our own religion."[13]

In the fifty years since the promulgation of *Nostra Aetate*, this bond has been strengthened. Consider the strain it has withstood. *Nostra Aetate* did not instantaneously remove every impediment to Catholic-Jewish relations. In 1984, for example, a community of Carmelite nuns came to live on the grounds of Auschwitz. The nuns understood their presence as an act of love. Like St. Teresa Benedicta of the Cross and St. Maximilian Kolbe, who both died at Auschwitz, they wanted to suffer in solidarity with those who suffered and died there. But for many Jews their presence was a painful offense. And in 1993 John Paul II directed the nuns to remove their community from Auschwitz. It was a moment of tension. But it did not destroy the bond between the Church and the Jewish people. It became, instead, an opportunity for fraternal respect and care.

The intrinsic relationship of Judaism to Christianity is also an idea worth remembering as we see a resurgence of anti-Semitism, especially in Europe. Any gardener knows that when you attack the root, you attack the entire plant. In the same away, acts of violence and hatred directed toward the Jews are in this way also an attack on the Church. *Nostra Aetate* suggests this when it reminds us that, mindful of the patrimony she shares with the Jews, the Church must condemn all "hatreds, persecutions, and manifestations of antisemitism directed against Jews at any time and by anyone."[14]

This is the olive tree onto which we Gentile believers, the wild shoots, have been grafted. Good relations are the key to our own integrity.

American Catholic-Jewish Relations

In the United States we have been blessed by a particularly fruitful history of Catholic-Jewish relations over the past fifty years.

John Paul II was fond of reminding Catholics that the Jews are our elder brothers in the faith. He saw it as a natural implication of *Nostra*

---

13. John Paul II, "Allocution in the Great Roman Synagogue" (April 13, 1986).
14. *Nostra Aetate* 4.

Aetate.[15] Over the last five decades American Catholics have had ample reason to appreciate what it's like to have an older brother.

Like brothers who stand up for each other on the playground, Catholics and Jews have stood together to defend the values we share: the dignity of the human person, the sanctity of marriage, and religious freedom. When the Department of Health and Human Services announced that employers would have to provide insurance for abortion-inducing drugs, sterilizations, and contraception, many Jews defended the freedom of Catholic institutions (like Catholic University) to operate in accordance with our beliefs. When San Francisco proposed banning circumcision, Catholics defended the rights of Jewish parents to raise their children in accordance with their faith.

Older brothers also blaze a trail for younger ones. They show them how to ride a bike or throw a baseball. American Catholics have much to learn from our elder brothers in the faith about how to live faithfully when our beliefs are no longer deemed essential, or acceptable, by an increasingly secular majority.

This is a relatively new experience for American Catholics. Sixty years ago Archbishop Fulton Sheen (the Timothy Dolan of his time) beat out Edward R. Murrow and Lucille Ball to win the Emmy for Most Outstanding Television Personality. But the religious landscape has changed a lot since then. The Pew Forum reported once again in 2015 that the Christian share of the U.S. population is declining, and the number of self-identified "nones" is on the rise.[16]

Jews have known what it is to be a creative minority since the Babylonian exile. As Rabbi Lord Jonathan Sacks has observed, for more than two millennia the Jewish people have shown that "you can be a minority, living in a country whose religion, culture, and legal system are not your own, and yet sustain your identity, live your faith, and contribute to the common good."[17] Catholics are blessed to have in our older brothers courageous witnesses of faithfulness to the Lord.

The essays in this volume provide an opportunity to reflect with profound gratitude on the remarkable strides the Church has made in her dialogue with Muslims and Jews since the promulgation of *Nostra Aetate* fifty years ago. As we contemplate the fruits this dialogue has borne and consider the future of these conversations, we can say with the Psalmist, "How good and pleasant it is when brothers dwell in unity!"[18]

---

15. John Paul II, "Allocution in the Great Roman Synagogue."
16. Pew Research Center, "America's Changing Religious Landscape" (May 12, 2015), 4.
17. Jonathan Sacks, "On Creative Minorities," *First Things* (January 2014).
18. Ps 133:1.

Translation of *Nostra Aetate*

Thomas F. Stransky, CSP

DECLARATION ON THE RELATION OF THE CHURCH TO NON-CHRISTIAN RELIGIONS
NOSTRA AETATE

PROCLAIMED BY HIS HOLINESS
POPE PAUL VI
ON OCTOBER 28, 1965

1. In our time, when day by day humankind is being drawn ever closer together and the ties between different peoples are being strengthened, the Church examines with greater care her relation to non-Christian religions. In her task of fostering unity and love among individuals, indeed among peoples, she considers above all in this Declaration what human beings have in common and what draws them to live together their destiny.

One is the community of all peoples, one their origin, for God made the whole human race to live on all the face of the earth.[1] One also is their final goal, God. God's providence, manifestation of goodness, and saving designs extend to all,[2] until that time when the elect will be united in the Holy City, the city ablaze with the glory of God, where the peoples will walk in its light.[3]

One expects from the various religions answers to the profound enigmas of the human condition, which today, even as of old, deeply stir human hearts: What is the human being? What is the meaning, the purpose of our life? What is moral good, and what is sin? Whence suffering and what purpose does it serve? Which is the way to genuine happiness? What are death, judgment, and retribution after death? What, finally, is that ultimate inexpressible mystery which encompasses our existence: whence do we come, and where are we going?

2. Already from ancient times down to the present, there is found among various peoples a certain perception of that mysterious power abid-

---

1. See Acts 17:26.
2. See Wis 8:1; Acts 14:17; Rom 2:6–7; 1 Tm 2:4.
3. See Apoc 21:23f.

ing in the course of nature and in the happenings of human life; at times some indeed have come to the recognition of a Supreme Being or even a Father. This perception and recognition penetrate their lives with a profound religious sense. However, religions that are intertwined with a developing culture have struggled to answer the same questions by means of more refined concepts and a more developed language. Thus, in Hinduism, men and women contemplate the divine mystery and express it through an inexhaustible abundance of myths and through searching philosophical inquiries. They seek freedom from the anguishes of our human condition through ascetical practices or through profound meditation or through a flight to God with love and trust. Buddhism, in its various forms, realizes the radical insufficiency of this changeable world; it teaches a way by which persons, in a devout and confident spirit, may be able either to acquire the state of perfect liberation or to attain, by their own efforts or through higher help, supreme illumination. Likewise, other religions found everywhere try to counter the restlessness of the human heart, each in its own manner, by proposing ways, comprising teachings, rules of life, and sacred rites.

The Catholic Church rejects nothing that is true and holy in these religions. She regards with sincere reverence those ways of acting and of living, those precepts and teachings which, though differing in many aspects from the one she holds and sets forth, nonetheless often reflect a ray of that truth which enlightens all. Indeed, she proclaims, and ever must proclaim, Christ as "the Way, the Truth, and the Life" (Jn 14:6), in whom men and women may find the fullness of religious life, and in whom God has reconciled all things to Himself.[4]

The Church therefore exhorts her sons and daughters to recognize, preserve, and foster the good things, spiritual and moral, as well as the socio-cultural values found among the followers of other religions. This is done through conversations and collaboration with them, carried out with prudence and love and in witness to the Christian faith and life.

3. The Church also regards with esteem the Muslims. They adore the one God, who is living and subsisting in himself, merciful and all-powerful, the Creator of heaven and earth,[5] who has spoken to humans; they strive to submit wholeheartedly even to His inscrutable decrees, just as Abraham, with whom the faith of Islam is gladly linked, submitted to God.

Though they do not acknowledge Jesus as God, they revere him as a prophet. They also honor Mary, his virgin mother; at times they even call on her with devotion. Moreover, they look forward to the day of judgment when

4. See 2 Cor 5:18–19.
5. See St. Gregory VII, "Letter XXI to Anzir (Nacir), King of Mauritania" (Migne, P.L. 148, col. 450f).

God will reward all those raised up. For this reason, they value the moral life and worship God, especially through prayer, almsgiving and fasting.

In the course of centuries there have indeed arisen not a few quarrels and hostilities between Christians and Muslims. But now this Sacred Synod pleads with all to forget the past, to make sincere efforts for mutual understanding, and so to work together for the preservation and fostering of social justice, moral welfare, and peace and freedom for all humankind.

4. As this Sacred Synod searches into the mystery of the Church, it remembers the bonds that spiritually tie the people of the New Covenant to the offspring of Abraham.

Thus the Church of Christ acknowledges that, according to God's mysterious saving design, the beginnings of her faith and her election are already found among the Patriarchs, Moses and the Prophets.

She professes that all who believe in the Christ, Abraham's children by faith,[6] are included in this Patriarch's call and, likewise, that the salvation of the Church is symbolically prefigured in the exodus of the chosen people from the land of bondage. The Church, therefore, cannot forget that she received the Revelation of the Old Testament through that people with whom God in His ineffable mercy was pleased to enter into the Ancient Covenant. Nor can she forget that she draws sustenance from the root of that well-cultivated olive tree onto which have been grafted the wild shoots, the Gentiles.[7] Indeed, the Church believes that by his cross Christ, who is our peace, reconciled Jews and Gentiles, and in Himself making the two one.[8]

As Holy Scripture testifies, Jerusalem did not recognize the time of her visitation,[9] nor did the Jews, in large numbers, accept the Gospel; indeed, not a few of them opposed its dissemination.[10] Nevertheless, now as before, God holds the Jews most dear for the sake of their Fathers; he does not repent of the gifts he makes or revoke the call he issues—such is the witness of the Apostle.[11] In company with the Prophets and the same Apostle, the Church awaits that day, known to God alone, on which all peoples will address the Lord with a single voice and "serve him with one accord" (Zeph 3:9).[12]

6. See Gal 3:7.
7. See Rom 11:17–24.
8. See Eph 2:14–16.
9. See Lk 19:44.
10. See Rom 11:28.
11. See Rom 11:28–29; dogmatic constitution, *Lumen Gentium* [Light of Nations] AAS, 57 (1965): 20.
12. See Is 66:23; Ps 65:4; Rom 11:11–32.

The Church keeps ever in mind the words of the Apostle about his kinsfolk: "To them belong the adoption as children, and the glory, and the covenant, and the giving of the law, and the worship, and the promises; to them belong the fathers and from them is the Christ according to the flesh" (Rom 9:4–5), the Son of the Virgin Mary. She also recalls that the Apostles, the Church's foundation stones and pillars, as well as most of the early disciples who proclaimed the Gospel of Christ to the world, sprang from the Jewish people.

Since the spiritual heritage common to Christians and Jews is thus so rich, this Sacred Synod wishes to foster and commend mutual understanding and esteem. This is the fruit, above all, of biblical and theological studies and of friendly conversations.

True, the Jewish authorities and those who followed their lead pressed for the death of Christ;[13] still, what happened in His passion cannot be charged against all the Jews, without distinction, then alive, nor against the Jews of today. Although the Church is the new people of God, the Jews should not be represented as rejected by God or accursed, as if this followed from Holy Scripture.

May all, then, see to it that in catechetical work and in preaching of the Word of God they teach nothing save what conforms to the truth of the Gospel and the spirit of Christ.

The Church, moreover, rejects all persecutions against any person. Mindful of the inheritance she shares with the Jews, the Church decries hatreds, persecutions, and manifestations of anti-Semitism directed against Jews at any time and by anyone. She does so not impelled by political reasons but moved by the spiritual love of the Gospel.

Besides, Christ underwent his passion and death freely, out of infinite love, because of the sins of humans in order that all might reach salvation. This the Church has always taught and teaches still; it is therefore the duty of the Church to proclaim the cross of Christ as the sign of God's all-embracing love and as the fountain from which every grace flows.

5. We cannot truly call upon God, the Father of all, if we refuse to behave as sisters and brothers with anyone, created as all are in the image of God. The relation of man and woman to God, the Father, and their relation to their fellow human beings are linked to such a degree that Holy Scripture says, "Whoever does not love does not know God" (1 Jn 4:8).

No foundation therefore remains for any theory or practice that leads to discrimination between person and person and between people and people insofar as their human dignity and the rights flowing from it are concerned.

13. See Jn 19:6.

The Church reproves, as foreign to the mind of Christ, any discrimination or harassment against men or women because of their race or color, condition in life or religion. On the contrary, following the footsteps of the Holy Apostles Peter and Paul, this Sacred Synod ardently implores the Christian faithful to "maintain good conduct among the peoples" (1 Pt 2:12), and, if possible, to live for their part in peace with all,[14] so that they may truly be sons and daughters of the Father who is in heaven.[15]

14. See Rom 12:18.
15. See Mt 5:45.

Part I

Historical and Theological Context

In our time, when day by day humankind is being drawn ever closer together and the ties between different peoples are being strengthened, the Church examines with greater care her relation to non-Christian religions.

—*Nostra Aetate* 1, trans. Thomas F. Stransky, CSP

Why Fifty Years after the Promulgation of *Nostra Aetate*, One More English Translation, My Own?

Thomas F. Stransky, CSP

The only *official* text is the Latin, declared as such and published by the General Secretariat of Vatican II: *Constitutions, Decreta, Declarationes*.[1] *All translations are unofficial*, including the English on the same Vatican website, which one presumes is recommended. English-speaking hierarchies have not endorsed a translation, unlike the German bishops who in 1966 adopted one and have never withdrawn their approval.

Nostra Aetate has a cluster of successive English translations. They offer borrowed similarities more than serious differences.

1. The first, in French and Arabic, was prepared by some in the Secretariat for Promoting Christian Unity (SPCU) for distribution to the media shortly before the October 26, 1965, promulgation.
2. This original version was copied with very few changes in the almost one million copies of Walter Abbott, SJ, and Joseph Gallagher, *Documents of Vatican II*,[2] which some still cite as their source.
3. Austin Flannery, OP, published new translations in *The Conciliar and Post Conciliar Documents*[3] and a revised edition in 1996 that principally used more inclusive language; for example, humankind, men and women, sisters and brothers, fellow human beings.
4. I wanted the same inclusiveness, and some other changes, in my 1985 translation,[4] which some Protestant missiologists still use.
5. In 1990 Norman Tanner, SJ, published in *The Decrees of the Ecumenical Councils*, the original official text and its English translation by Leo Arnold.[5]

---

1. "Declaration on the Relation of the Church to Non-Christian Religions Nostra Aetate" (Vatican City: Vatican Polyglot Press, 1966), http://www.vatican.va.
2. New York: Herder and Herder Association Press, 1966.
3. Northport, N.Y.: Costello Publishing Co., 1975.
4. *International Bulletin of Missionary Research* 9 (1985): 157.
5. *The Decrees of the Ecumenical Councils*, vol. 2, 968–71 (Washington, D.C.: Georgetown University Press, 1990).

Beginning in October 1960, SPCU's president, Cardinal Augustin Bea, assigned me the staff portfolio, among others, for *De Iudaeis* and, unknown then, for its enlargement to include all non-Christian religions. This responsibility required channeling correspondence and gathering texts and minutes of drafting subcommittees for their own and the SPCU plenary use. I supervised the proper order of all the oral and written interventions of the Council fathers. Perhaps I have become overfamiliar with the successive Latin schemata and their translations.

When I was commissioned a few years ago to write an insider's story on the genesis of *Nostra Aetate*, I decided to add my fresh translation to the list of others. I try not to betray the literal intent of the Latin, although there is a fine line between translation and interpretation. And I do not ignore the attempts by other translators in many languages. I offer an outline of my own criteria and judgment. I recognize some criteria are subtle.

1. *Nostra Aetate* was a pastoral act of Vatican II, thus a solemn magisterial act of the Church. The pastoral magisterial Latin should reign also in translation.
2. The declaration has only 1,141 words in forty-one sentences. One finds no wasted Latin words or phrases, and a translation should not mar that sparseness. I have broken up a few long sentences. Bald and bold.
3. The final version in fact brought together five different texts: first, the longer *De Iudaeis* (4), then on the Muslims (3), then on other religions (2), then the conclusion (5), then the preface (1). A translation should make smoother transitions and catch the obvious unity to the whole declaration.
4. To be wherever possible literal does not cross out choices. "In our time"? Or "In our age"?
5. The Latin usually avoids the customary lazy passive voice, which hides the agent. When the passive is used, almost always I found a way to change to the active without awkwardness.
6. The literal Latin deliberately refrains from using new, still unclear words. Emilio Springhetti, SJ, assigned to the SPCU as its Latinist from the pool in the secretariat of state, insisted that the term *dialogue* not be used. *Dialogue*, the word that Paul VI used more than seventy times in his first encyclical,[6] was too new, unclear, "unLatin." So best to use the term *conversations*[7] and avoid the word *discussion*.[8]

---

6. *Ecclesiam Suam* (1964).
7. *Nostra Aetate* 2.
8. Flannery translation.

7.   The graceful, literary list of questions that deeply stir human hearts are
      "enigmas of the human condition," but translators had a penchant for
      avoiding the word and settled for weaker "obscure riddles,"[9] "unre-
      solved riddles,"[10] or "die ungelösten Rätsel."[11] Latin drafts would resist
      changing *aenigmatibus*. One tries to solve riddles, one tries to live
      enigmas.

9. Arnold translation.
10. Flannery translation.
11. German bishops.

Nostra Aetate: Historical Contingency and Theological Significance

PIM VALKENBERG

To properly celebrate the document *Nostra Aetate*, it may be helpful to begin by remembering its drafting history and its formative influences. In the first place, I want to suggest that *Nostra Aetate* is a document situated in a specific geographic and historical context: post-Holocaust (or post-*Shoah*) Europe. This context explains the specific attention to the Church's teaching about Jews and Judaism in the final document and its history of drafting. In fact, the document that we know as *Nostra Aetate* originated as *De Iudaeis* from its early beginnings before the Council in 1960 until well into the third session of the Council in 1964. However, the influence of non-Western bishops from the Middle East, Africa, and Asia widened the scope of this document to include other religions as well, so that its name changed into *De non-Christianis* in the last year before its proclamation in October 1965.

In the second place, I want to suggest that this change from a document on the Jews to a document about all non-Christian religions not only is a matter of politics but also has deep theological roots. To show these roots, I will connect *Nostra Aetate* with the "dialogue encyclical" *Ecclesiam Suam* by Pope Paul VI from 1964 and with Vatican II's dogmatic constitution about the Church, *Lumen Gentium*, from the same year. I argue that a proper hermeneutical approach to the document *Nostra Aetate* can only be given by the combination of these historical and theological analyses.[1]

Historical Contingencies: From *De Iudaeis* to *Nostra Aetate*

When we look back at the document *Nostra Aetate* after fifty years, we notice that much has changed between 1965 and 2015, not the least in the relation between the Roman Catholic Church and the other religions. So much has in fact changed that Gerald O'Collins in his book about *The Second Vatican Council on Other Religions* suggests that the document cer-

---

1. For an insightful discussion of such a hermeneutics of the Council with application to the relations between the Church and Jews and Muslims, see chapter 1, "Interpreting the Interpreters" in Gavin D'Costa, *Vatican II: Catholic Doctrines on Jews and Muslims*, 10–58 (Oxford: Oxford University Press, 2014).

tainly would have been written differently even thirty years after its prom-ulgation.[2] For instance, the title of the declaration: "The Relationship between the Church and Non-Christian Religions" would nowadays no longer be considered an adequate description of these other religions. In interreligious encounters, we have experienced that we cannot characterize our partners in dialogue by what they are not, but, rather, we should take seriously how they describe themselves. This has, for instance, occasioned the change of name of the Vatican institution responsible for contacts with other religious from "Secretariat for Non-Christians" to "Pontifical Coun-cil for Interreligious Dialogue" in 1988. This is indeed quite a different name, indicating a different approach: the church no longer takes itself as point of departure in thinking about its relationship with others, but it now actively promotes dialogue between religions.

This shift is not, however, as large as the difference between the doc-ument *Nostra Aetate* and the attitude of the Church toward other religions in the centuries before that. In a time in which members of other religions were considered as unbelievers, the Church's task was to bring them to faith. Therefore they would be addressed in an endeavor to promote the Catholic faith, as was the objective of the *sacra congregatio de propaganda fide* between 1622 and 1988. Since then, the congregation has been renamed *congregatio pro gentium evangelisatione*. Even though its aim is still the proclamation of the Gospel, the distinction between faith and unbelief is no longer that stark.

I do not want to go too far back in history, but I want to give a few observations concerning the immediate pre-history of this unprecedented text. *Nostra Aetate* was really something new, and even those who were working on it were surprised by some developments.[3] Working as a Euro-pean theologian at The Catholic University of America, I am aware of the fact that the Second Vatican Council was still very much a European coun-cil in which almost all of the protagonists were European bishops and the-ologians. Alternatively, the influence of the world church has made *Nostra Aetate* the document that it has become.

---

2. Gerald O'Collins, SJ, *The Second Vatican Council on Other Religions* (Oxford: Oxford University Press, 2013), 84.

3. These developments can be traced in the diaries of some of the bishops and theologians working for the Secretariat for (the Promotion of) Christian Unity that was responsible for the text of *Nostra Aetate*. Among them are Bishop (later cardinal) Johannes Willebrands and the-ologian Yves Congar. See Theo Salemink, *You Will Be Called Repairer of the Breach: The Diary of J.G.M. Willebrands 1958–1961* (Leuven: Peeters, 2009); Leo Declerck, *Les agendes conciliaires de Mgr. J. Willebrands, secrétaire du secretariat pour l'unité des Chrétiens,* traduction française annotée (Leuven: Peeters, 2009); and Yves Congar, OP, *Mon journal du Concile*, Paris 2002 [available in English as *My Journal of the Council* (Collegeville, Minn.: Liturgical Press, 2012)].

In fact, the document was not named *Nostra Aetate* and did not relate
to other religions in general until the very last phase of its conception.
During the preparations and the first three sessions of the Council, the document was generally referred to as *De Iudaeis*, and those who contributed
much to its present form, such as the French Dominican theologian Yves
Congar and the Dutch bishop Johannes Willebrands, kept referring to it as
a document about the Jews until October 1964. The change was quite
sudden and quite drastic, as can be seen in Congar's journal.[4] In fact, one
can still say that the text "on the Jews" (*de Iudaeis*) that had been the focus
until that time and finally became the fourth and longest section of the document on non-Christian religions still retained a unique identity as almost
a document within the document. This fourth section has a separate history
of its reception, since most of the literature about *Nostra Aetate* concentrates
on this specific section. Consequently, if we want to go back to the origins
of *Nostra Aetate*, we need to focus on Catholic-Jewish relationships.

The complicated origins of the document *Nostra Aetate* have been told
many times, but recently John Connelly added a new chapter to the inves-
tigation into these origins.[5] The direct origin of the document seems to be
a visit of the French Jewish historian Jules Isaac to Pope John XXIII in
early summer 1960. Isaac, who had made a name in France and the rest of
Europe with his book on Jesus and Israel in 1948, was one of the develop-
ers of a number of theses accepted at the second meeting of the International Council of Christians and Jews in Seelisberg, Switzerland, in 1947.[6]
But Isaac was not on his own: behind him was a group of Catholics, almost
all of them converts from either Judaism or Protestantism, who wanted the
Church to speak out on behalf of the relationship with Judaism after the
atrocious experiences of the Holocaust. Some of them had started this
rethinking of the relations between the Catholic Church and the Jewish
people already before the National Socialist regime; for instance, the group
Amici Israel (friends of Israel) in 1928. It is interesting to know that the
first condemnation of anti-Semitism by Pope Pius XI in 1928 was a sort of
compensation for banning this group from the Church.[7] As Connelly
made clear, the awareness that the Church needed to rethink its relation
with the Jewish people was mainly emphasized by a group of middle-Euro-

---

4. See Yves Congar, *My Journal of the Council*, 634 (entry of October 20, 1964). In the
case of Jo Willebrands, see *Les agendes conciliaires de Mgr. J. Willebrands*, 137–43, covering the
period of October 9 to 17, 1964.

5. John Connelly, *From Enemy to Brother: The Revolution in Catholic Teaching on the
Jews 1933–1965* (Cambridge, Mass., and London: Harvard University Press, 2011).

6. Ibid., 176–78.

7. Ibid., 97.

pean converts among whom Dietrich von Hildebrand, Johannes Oesterre-icher, and Karl Thieme were the most prominent.

The immediate prehistory of the document *Nostra Aetate* begins with Pope John XXIII, who was willing to include a statement about the Jews in the documents to be written in preparation of the Second Vatican Council. As John Oesterreicher makes clear, the pope had already ordered a change in the infamous prayer *pro perfidis Iudaeis* in the liturgy for Good Friday in 1959, and so the visit from Jules Isaac should be seen as a catalyst rather than as an absolute beginning for the pope's involvement.[8]

After Isaac's visit, the pope asked the newly instituted Secretariat for Promoting Christian Unity in September 1960 to prepare a document about the relationship between the Church and the Jewish people.[9] This was a decision with far-reaching consequences since it built a theological bridge between ecumenism and what we now call interreligious dialogue at a time when this dialogue was not yet envisaged as a real possibility. Because of the position of the Jewish faith in the Christian history of salvation and because he trusted his friend, German Jesuit scholar Augustin Bea, rector of the Pontifical Biblical Institute in Rome, the pope decided to entrust this new secretariat with the task of developing this document.[10]

It is a fact that Pope John's engagement in interreligious dialogue originated in a personal feeling of connectedness with Jewish friends—as has often been observed about Pope John Paul II as well.[11] Between 1925 and 1935 Angelo Giuseppe Roncalli served under Pope Pius XI as apostolic visitor in Bulgaria, and later he became the papal nuncio in Turkey and Greece. In this period he had many contacts with Jews and helped many of them escape the Nazi regime. This familiarity with the Jews and their plight explains the spontaneous words that the pope directed to a number of American Jews who visited him in October 1960: *Son io, Giuseppe, il fratello vestro*: "I, Joseph [his proper name] am your brother."[12] Oesterreicher mentions a number of others sources for this document as well: for instance, the request by the Pontifical Biblical Institute to explicitly refute anti-Semitism.[13] Also, some bishops from the United States and some institutes for Christian-Jewish dialogue in Europe wanted the Coun-

---

8. See Johannes Oesterreicher, "Kommentierende Einleitung," in *Das zweite Vatikanische Konzil: Konstitutionen, Dekrete und Erklärungen Lateinisch und Deutsch, Kommentare II* (*Lexikon für Theologie und Kirche*, XIII) (Freiburg i. Br.: Herder, 1967) 406–78.

9. See *Diary Willebrands 1958–1961*, 206 (September 8, 1960).

10. Oesterreicher, 406.

11. See Byron L. Sherwin and Harold Kazimow, eds., *John Paul II and Interreligious Dialogue* (Maryknoll, N.Y.: Orbis Books, 1999).

12. Oesterreicher, 408.

13. Ibid., 409.

cil to talk about its relationship with the Jews, mainly because they thought it was necessary for the Church to openly distance itself from the tradition of blaming the Jews for the death of Jesus and consequently determining their dispersion and their near-extinction as a penalty from God.

Pope John XXIII wanted to take this request very seriously and therefore he entrusted this task to the Secretariat for Promoting Christian Unity that prepared under the leadership of Cardinal Augustin Bea a number of versions during the years 1961–1965.[14] It is of course noteworthy that the origins of the text on non-Christian religions came out of the context of the reflection on ecumenism. This is interesting not only because of the relations between ecumenical and interreligious dialogues but also because it took some time before the Secretariat for Promoting Christian Unity was allowed to prepare texts alongside the central preparatory committee of the Council. Yet the texts that they prepared ended up to be among the most important and certainly the most renewing texts of the Council: not only the decree *Unitatis Redintegratio* on Ecumenism and the declaration *Nostra Aetate* on non-Christian religions but also the declaration *Dignitatis Humanae* on human dignity and freedom of religion and finally coauthorship of the constitution *Dei Verbum* on divine revelation.[15] As it turned out, the two texts on non-Christian religions and on human dignity are often seen as the most revolutionary texts of the Council, and consequently they are not accepted by those who think that the Council broke away from the established tradition of the Church.[16]

The first version of *De Iudaeis* was the result of the work of the Secretariat for Promoting Christian Unity between fall 1960 and fall 1961, more specifically of the Canadian theologian Gregory Baum (of German origin) and the American abbot Leo Rudloff, OSB, who, together with John Oesterreicher, came up with the concept for a first decree on the Jews. While this obviously was meant as a pastoral document that would underscore the lasting significance of the Jewish people according to chapter 11 of Paul's Letter to the Romans, some governments in the Middle East began to formulate objections because they saw its potential proclamation as a political move toward the recognition of the State of Israel by the Vatican.[17] When

14. The documentation is largely taken from the website of the Institute for Jewish-Christian Relations at Saint Joseph's University in Philadelphia, directed by Philip Cunningham; see http://www.ccjr.us/ dialogika-resources.

15. See Declerck's introduction in Leo Declerck, trans., *Les agendes conciliaires de Mgr. J. Willebrands*, xxv–xxxii.

16. See, for instance, the objections brought forward by the Priestly Confraternity of Saint Pius X.

17. Oesterreicher, 415.

the Jewish World Congress appointed a new delegate to the Vatican in summer 1962, many thought that such a recognition of the Jewish state would be imminent, and they started to voice objections. Because of these political tensions, the preparatory committee of the Council decided to remove the decree on the Jews from the agenda of the Council.

That early text contains a number of interesting points that recur in the final text of *Nostra Aetate*, as well as some points that do not recur.[18] The first of its four paragraphs underlines the continuity between the people of Israel and the Church; the second describes the Church as consisting of Jews and Gentiles and tells in strong words that it would be wrong to call the Jews an accursed people and adds: "The Church loves this people." The third paragraph talks about the union with the Jewish people as an integral part of the hope of the Church, with reference to Romans 11. The final paragraph says that the Church "raises her voice in loud protest against all wrongs done to the Jews."

As said, this text never reached the Vatican Council because of the political protests. The first text that did reach the fathers of the Council was distributed during the second session in November 1963 as the fourth chapter of the Decree on Ecumenism. While the body of the text remains more or less the same as in the 1961 version, the introductory paragraph gives two statements of great importance. First, the principles of ecumenism hold true for interreligious relationships as well; second, people who are not Christians can be related to the Church insofar as they worship God or observe basic moral principles. I will come back to these two crucial guidelines later since they connect *Nostra Aetate* to the dogmatic constitution *Lumen Gentium* about the Church. In fact, as I will show later, some of the basic principles from the texts on ecumenism and on the Church, in addition to the new Pope Paul VI and his "dialogue" encyclical *Ecclesiam Suam*, influenced some of the principles of this second version.

There was some opposition against including a text on other religions in the larger text on ecumenism since it would suggest that other religions are more or less at the same level as Christian churches.[19] In these days, Pope Paul VI founded a separate Secretariat for Non-Christians, but he wanted the text on the Jews to remain the responsibility of the Secretariat for Promoting Christian Unity.[20] Congar did not know what to think of it,

---

18. Miikka Ruokanen, *The Catholic Doctrine of Non-Christian Religions according to the Second Vatican Council* (Leiden: Brill, 1992), gives the texts of the different versions in an appendix.

19. See Congar, *My Journal of the Council*, 316 (entry for September 18, 1963).

20. Congar, *My Journal*, 331. This new secretariat was officially announced in September 1963, but it was not yet active in spring 1964.

as the entry in his journal of the Council for February 3, 1964, makes clear: "I made a note, too, on the Secretariat for non-Christian Religions, the creation of which has been officially announced. It seems that there is not a clear view of WHAT TO DO. Will there perhaps be a DIALOGUE between Catholicism and Buddhism, or Confucianism? There does not seem to have been progress towards anything specific. And, Mgr. Willebrands said, where will we get suitable MEN?"[21]

At the same time, the Doctrinal Commission worked on the Declaration on the Church, and it decided to add a chapter "on the People of God," which would become the first place to mention non-Christian religions in the documents of the Council.[22] Congar—who worked for the secretariat and the Doctrinal Commission at the same time—related that he wanted to mention the Jews in this chapter, but representatives of Middle Eastern churches and of non-Latin rites told him that they were against doing so.[23] In their interventions at the Council (November 18, 1963), some of the patriarchs of the Eastern churches warned against having a chapter on the Jews but added that if something would be included, a paragraph on the Muslims should certainly be included.[24] In these days, Pope Paul VI announced that he would go as a pilgrim to the Holy Land in January 1964 and pray there for unity among Christians, but some also saw this as an opportunity to address the situation of Jews and Muslims. The pope meanwhile began to talk more about dialogue as an essential characteristic of the Church (dialogue with other Christians, with other religions, and with the world), and this caused the Secretariat for Promoting Christian Unity to think that maybe the other religions should be addressed more specifically. Congar gives the following summary in February 1964: "The chapter on the Jews will form an appendix to *De oecumenismo* (I said that, in my opinion, it should be put back into the *De populo Dei*); there will also be a text on the Muslims, and perhaps on non-Christian religions."[25] Members of the Secretariat for Promoting Christian Unity, such as Bishop Willebrands, did explore the idea of an incomplete membership of the Church for Protestants that would be the core of *Lumen Gentium* 15, but Congar extended this idea to include the Jews as well.[26]

---

21. Congar, *My Journal*, 482. Capitals in original.
22. Ibid., 356.
23. Ibid., 363; see also 473.
24. Ibid., 430. Willebrands (*Les agendes conciliaires*, 73) mentions "sensational articles in the Arab press" in November 1963.
25. Congar, *My Journal*, 481 (entry for February 3, 1964).
26. Willebrands, *Diary 1958–1961*, 244 (entry for December 3, 1960).

In the meantime, Willebrands's diaries make clear that this new type of thinking about the Church became one of the major bones of contention between the Secretariat for Promoting Christian Unity and more conservative cardinals, including Cardinal Felici who was appointed the secretary general of the central preparatory committee in 1960.[27] In this period, the Secretariat for Promoting Christian Unity began considerations about adding a text on Muslims after the text on Jews, both in appendix to the document on ecumenism. A special subcommittee was appointed with the French White Father Jean-André Cuoq, who was a specialist on African Islam, and a Lebanese and an Iraqi bishop.[28] A few days later, a new subcommittee *De ceteris religionibus* (on other religions) was added.[29] Finally, the different subcommittees placed their texts together in one text on the Jews and the other religions, thus forming the basic structure of the document *Nostra Aetate* as we know it.[30] This does not mean, however, that this beginning had as positive a tone as *Nostra Aetate* would later take. Judging by their diaries, Willebrands and Congar seemed open to dialogue with Jews, but not so much with others and certainly not with Muslims. Congar wrote the following in his diary for April 25, 1964:

> We were invited by Mgr. Willebrands to work on the drafting of an ENLARGED text in which the Declaration on the Jews would be included. Mgr. Willebrands told us about his journey to Constantinople, from which he had just returned. The situation of the Christians, and especially of the Greeks, is difficult and very distressing. . . . According to Mgr. Willebrands, there should not be any specific reference to Muslims. All the experts and the missionary bishops say that an attitude like that of Massignon is, in practical terms, contrary to the realities. We are at peace with the others everywhere else, except the Muslims, who fight against us.[31]

---

27. Ibid., 263 (entry for February 1, 1961).

28. Willebrands, *Agendes conciliaires*, 91 (entry for March 3, 1964). It is interesting to note that Willebrands first speaks about *De Mahometanis* ("Muhammadans," 91, 93) but later corrects himself and speaks about *De Iudaeis et de Musulmanis* (93, twice).

29. Willebrands, *Agendes conciliaires*, 94 (entry for March 6, 1964).

30. Ibid., 109 (entry for April 18, 1964).

31. Congar, *My Journal*, 521 (entry for April 25, 1964). Capitals in original. When Congar later tallies the count of a preliminary vote on the second chapter of *Lumen Gentium* on the people of God, he gives the number of 553 *placet iuxta modum* and adds "= the Muslims!!!" So apparently the relation with the Muslims explains for him the great number of unsatisfied voters on this text for which Congar was responsible to a large extent, but it appears that he did not like the inclusion of Muslims while he did like the inclusion of Jews (*My Journal*, 580, entry for September 18, 1964).

This sounds like almost the opposite of the final statements in *Lumen Gentium* 16 and *Nostra Aetate* 3 about the Muslims, which include an implicit reference to the work of Louis Massignon.[32]

While a more positive tone toward other religions was contemplated at the request of the central coordinating committee (Cardinals Cicognani, Felici), the text on the Jews was watered down, and a passage about possible conversion of the Jews was added by Cardinal Felici, who said that the pope wanted it. Willebrands reacted by saying: "only Cardinal Bea can save us now" by intervening with the pope.[33] And Congar wrote the following: "I come back to this question of the Jews. Really, it is quite scandalous and unacceptable that the Church, in order to please some Arab governments that obey no other reason than just an instinct that is simplistic and all-inclusive, should have to refrain from saying what should be said on a question that comes within its province, and on which it has a duty to speak. I believe that the WHOLE of the Secretariat's text should be retained, while removing only the word 'deicide', and expressing the idea in some other way."[34] So it would be quite beside the truth to think that, at the outset, the dialogue with Jews and the dialogue with Muslims were brought together in a way in which we try to do so fifty years after the Council. Quite the contrary was the case: the members of the Secretariat for Promoting Christian Unity tried to defend the theological relation with the Jews; the members of the central coordinating committee tried to defend the Christian interests in the Muslim world. These were clearly opposed interests.

In September 1964 the Council began a debate on the third version of the text, which contained, as indicated, a number of elements that were seen as watering down the positive attitude toward the Jews. Some of these changes were widely published in the United States, and quite a few Jews (plus some Protestants) reacted with anger on the suppression of a condemnation of accusing Jews of "deicide" in the text, suggesting that the Church now allows the possibility to continue such accusations.[35]

---

32. On the latter, see Sidney Griffith, "Sharing the Faith of Abraham: The 'Credo' of Louis Massignon," *Islam and Christian-Muslim Relations* 8 (1997): 193–210.

33. Willebrands, *Agendes conciliaires*, 125 (entry for May 30, 1964).

34. Congar, *My Journal*, 522 (entry for April 25, 1964).

35. See Willebrands, *Agendes Conciliaires*, 131 (entry for June 12, 1964), on his phone conversation with Robert Doty, journalist of the *New York Times* who had published a front-page article the day before. Willebrands feels betrayed because Doty had promised to remain silent. Congar (*My Journal*, 559) talks about "a certain Heschel" as representing this overreaction, and he adds: "Truly, one cannot allude, even distantly, to the Jews without a violent reaction of offended protest on their part! Even to speak well of them evokes a violent reaction of offended and accusatory protest on their part. . . . [T]he Protestants of the USA have voiced their agreement with the Jews: they are saying that, since John XXIII, nothing is going forward any more" (559, entry for July 31, 1964).

From the perspective of the dialogue with Judaism, the text was much weakened. We still find the four elements from the first text, but in a somewhat different order. Again the text begins with talking about the continuity between the Jewish people and the Church, but then it goes on to mention the third element of the old text (future hope of unity) by adding a formulation that would stir up a lot of emotion: "the Church expects . . . the entrance of that people into the fullness of the people of God established by Christ." Many observers said that the idea of mission to the Jews, while it had disappeared in earlier versions, came back here. In the new third part of the text, the element of brotherly behavior is now connected to the idea of God as Father of the whole of humankind, and a separate paragraph on the Muslims is added. The final element, against discrimination, is still there but considerably weakened.

This third version was debated at the Council in September 1964, and one can distinguish a pattern in the interventions of the bishops.[36] On the one hand, most bishops from America and the middle of Europe deplored the loss of the strong texts about Judaism; on the other hand, some bishops from southern Europe and many bishops from Arab countries pleaded for a further weakening of the texts on the Jews. So the "Jewish question" was still central here, and barely any attention was paid to other religions, even though there were some bishops who said that the latter needed to be addressed as well.

However, ten days after this debate, the central coordinating committee asked the pope to give permission to cut back the entire declaration *De Iudaeis* (as it was still called in this stage by both Congar and Willebrands) to a few lines, to include it in the chapter on the People of God in *Lumen Gentium*, and to let it be revised by a number of bishops who were among its opponents. Willebrands describes this as an impossible situation that created quite some anger and indignation.[37] Congar tells that he was summoned to the sacristy of St. Peter's on October 20, 1964, to preview a new text, still named *De Iudaeis*, but the scholars he mentions are specialists in Japanese religion (Paul Pfister, SJ) and Hinduism (Joseph Neuner, SJ). This text was to be added as a corollary or an appendix to the chapter on the People of God in *Lumen Gentium*. Congar thought that this would be a good idea since it would make clear that the text about the other religions was a theological and not a political text.[38] He gives us the names of the scholars responsible for the section on Asian religions: Tom Stransky,

36. See "Dialogika," Council of Centers on Jewish-Christian Relations, http://www.ccjr.us/dialogika-resources/ (accessed May 15, 2015).

37. Willebrands, *Agendes conciliaires*, 137–43 (entry for October 9–17).

38. Congar, *My Journal*, 634 (entry for October 20, 1964).

Charles Moeller (Louvain), Neuner, Pfister, and Congar himself.[39] He also gives the structure of the future document: it begins with the unity of the human race, goes on to talk about the great religions and the desire for dialogue, and finishes with separate paragraphs on the Muslims and the Jews. A few months later, a final and fifth section, condemning anti-Semitism, was added.[40] There was some struggle about whether parts of the text should be written by the Secretariat for Non-Christians, but in the end the Secretariat for Promoting Christian Unity prevailed. Willebrands mentions the same names as Congar, plus Gregory Baum, Abbott von Rudloff, and John Oesterreicher for the relation with the Jews, and White Fathers Cuoq and Robert Caspar for Islam.[41] From other writers, we know that at least the name of Georges Anawati, OP, must be added to this list.[42]

In November 1964 a new text that contained most of the text of *Nostra Aetate* as we know it now was discussed in the doctrinal committee of the Council. Congar, who was present, notes that the famous theologian Jean Daniélou "was furious . . . about the text from the Secretariat for Non-Christian Religions, which, he said, made Christianity one religion among others." Congar defended himself by saying that he had included phrases about the absolute truth of the Gospel and the duty to proclaim it.[43] A few days later, a general vote was taken in the General Congregation of the Council on the proposed text: 1,651 of the Council fathers voted in favor, 99 voted against the text, while 242 voted *placet iuxta modum*—"I agree, but with restrictions."

Yet again, in spring 1965 quite some opposition arose on this text. Part of it originated in resistance to the work of the Secretariat for Promoting Christian Unity inside the Council, part of it in political reactions in countries of the Middle East. Willebrands was sent by the pope to a number of ecclesial dignitaries in the Middle East to explain the theological, not political, nature of the document. Yet the work of the secretariat seemed to reach an impasse in the middle of May 1965. Cardinal Bea proposed an alternative text, and Bishop Willebrands suggested that maybe the text should be withdrawn after all. Congar gave the following report of what Willebrands had to say after his trip to Egypt, Lebanon, and Jerusalem: Everyone will

---

39. Ibid., 638.

40. Willebrands, *Agendes conciliaires*, 158 (entry for March 4, 1965).

41. Ibid., 155 (entry for February 1965).

42. See Gavin D'Costa, "Continuity and Reform in Vatican II's Teaching on Islam," *New Blackfriars* 94 (2013): 208–22, cited at 212.

43. Congar, *My Journal*, 673 (entry for November 12, 1964). Note that Daniélou refers to the Secretariat for Non-Christian Religions and not to the Secretariat for Christian Unity. Were both secretariats responsible for parts of the texts?

take the declaration in a sense in which it was not meant. The Jews "will exploit the text, as they have done already"; Muslims will react violently and "the orthodox will reproach us bitterly ... for having sold out the possibilities for a Christian presence in the Middle East."[44] It is clear that he was quite depressed, and he was ready to revoke the entire document while Bea wanted to suppress texts not only about deicide but also about anti-Semitism.[45] In sum, exactly fifty years before our May 2015 celebration of *Nostra Aetate*, the writers of *De Iudaeis* were ready to let the entire project go.

Yet the pope decided that the text, instead of being scrapped, should be explained better both to the Catholics and to the Muslims in the Middle East. So Willebrands went on another tour of the Middle East, together with the influential Belgian bishop De Smedt. This trip, from July 16 to 24, was meant to share the new text (with some alterations, meant to pacify the patriarchs of the Middle East) and to discuss its implications. Some of the patriarchs proposed a few changes in the text themselves, and a final press offensive with letters to embassies of Muslim countries and texts delivered personally helped clear the air further. Ultimately the final text was voted on (2,221 in favor; 88 against) and officially promulgated on October 28, 1965. It had come to pass that, at the very time in which the bishops and the theologians were expressing despair, the pope was successful in his decision to go forward. I contend he did so because the text of the final version, *Nostra Aetate*, was totally in line with his own ideas about dialogue and with the teaching of the Church.

Theological Continuity: *Ecclesiam Suam* and *Lumen Gentium* (1964)

The first part of my essay was about historical contingencies: there have been a number of moments, as late as May 1965, on which it looked as if there would be no *Nostra Aetate* document. But ultimately it became an official document of the church, and I think that this is mainly due to the personal engagement of Pope Paul VI in interreligious dialogue. I want to show this first by discussing some characteristics of his encyclical *Ecclesiam Suam*. Next I want to show how the document is, in spite of its historical contingency, solidly grounded in the self-awareness of the Catholic Church as evidenced by the second chapter of the document on the Church, *Lumen Gentium*.

When Pope Paul VI succeeded Pope John XXIII in 1963, he did a couple of things that established interreligious dialogue as an important

44. Congar, *My Journal*, 755 (entry for May 3, 1965).
45. This happened at the meeting of the secretariat on May 3. See Congar, 756, and Willebrands, 181.

task for the Roman Catholic Church. First, he announced the establishment of the Secretariat for Non-Christians in September 1963; this new
unit was officially created in a message on Pentecost, May 17, 1964.[46] As
the goal of this secretariat, the pope established "a means by which to arrive
at a sincere and respectful dialogue with those who 'still believe in God and
worship him.'"[47] The notion of dialogue is central here right from the
beginning, and this is confirmed by the important role it played in the
pope's encyclical that was published a few months later, in August 1964—
that is, before the debate about the declaration *De Iudaeis et de non-Christianis* during the third session of the Council in September 1964. This
encyclical (dated August 6, 1964) has a section on dialogue in which the
pope says: "The Church should enter into dialogue with the world in
which she exists and labors."[48] Dialogue should be the characteristic of the
Church in all of its communication with the world, even though the pope
thinks about the Church speaking to the world rather than listening to the
world. An interesting theological foundation comes in number 72 of the
same encyclical, in which he says: "The transcendent origin of the dialogue
… is found in the very plan of God."[49] He sketches the history of salvation
as a dialogue between God and human beings, initiated by God, culminating in the incarnation, but interrupted by human sinfulness. He talks about
the dialogue of salvation that is ultimately grounded in the love of the
Trinitarian God. Later on the encyclical suggests that dialogue be the
method of accomplishing the apostolic mission of the church.[50] Clarity,
meekness, trust, and prudence are characteristics of this dialogue. But
preaching remains important as well. Finally, the encyclical discusses the
question about dialogue partners, and it distinguishes a number of concentric circles in an approach that we find in *Nostra Aetate* as well.[51] Dialogue
with the entire humankind forms the first circle; dialogue with those who
believe in God is the second circle. Here the encyclical says that there is
but one true religion, the religion of Christianity, but that the church recognizes and respects the moral and spiritual values of the non-Christian
religions and that it wishes to join with them "in promoting common
ideals of religious liberty, human brotherhood, good culture, social welfare,

46. See Francesco Gioia, ed., *Interreligious Dialogue: The Official Teaching of the Catholic
Church from the Second Vatican Council to John Paul II (1963-2005)*, no. 194 (Mahwah, N.J.:
Paulist Publications, 2006), 161.
    47. Ibid., no. 196.
    48. Pope Paul VI, *Ecclesiam Suam* (August 6, 1964), par. 67; Gioia, 72.
    49. Ibid., 72; Gioia, 74.
    50. Ibid., 83; Gioia, 76.
    51. See *Ecclesiam Suam* 100.

and civil order."[52] More specifically, Pope Paul VI explicitly mentions the Jewish and Muslim forms of monotheism, referring to them as *religiones*.[53] About the Jews, the encyclical has the following to say: they "retain the religion of the Old Testament and . . . are indeed worthy of our respect and love." About the Muslims, the document says that they adhere to monotheism and that "we do well to admire these people for all that is good and true in their worship of God."[54] These are remarkably positive statements that seem to usher in a new era of dialogue.

Another important initiative undertaken by Pope Paul VI was his journey to the Holy Land in January 1964, where he met with the Eastern Orthodox patriarch to pray for the unity of Christians. According to Gavin D'Costa, he also gave a very important speech in Bethlehem. D'Costa writes:

> Paul visited the Holy Land prior to the document being discussed at the Council, and made a very memorable speech at Bethlehem, affirming the Church's deep spiritual connection with both Jews and Muslims. The wording of his speech was to enter the Council as the basis of *Lumen Gentium*'s text on Islam. Paul was walking a tightrope in attempting to show both Jews and Muslims that the Council was not being partisan. Paul was also a member of a small prayer group, the Badaliya, which was dedicated to praying for Muslims. Paul had been deeply influenced by Louis Massignon's views on Islam. It is reported that Paul directed Cardinal Bea to make sure that every time the Jewish people were mentioned so were the Muslims. If it was not for the personal initiatives taken by these two popes we might not have had the positive statements on Judaism and Islam. If it was not for a statement on the Jews, there may have never been a statement on Muslims.[55]

This brings us to the document *Lumen Gentium* and its teaching about the relationship between the Catholic Church and Judaism and Islam. It is

52. *Ecclesiam Suam* 111–12; Gioia, 84–85.

53. *Ecclesiam Suam* 107; Latin text quoted from the Vatican website (http://w2.vatican .va/content/paul-vi/la/encyclicals/documents/hf_p-vi_enc_06081964_ecclesiam.html): *Mentionem scilicet inicimus de filiis gentis Iudaeae, reverentea et amore nostro sane dignis, qui eam retinent religionem, quam Veteris Testamenti propriam esse dicimus; deinde de iis, qui Deum adorant religionis forma, quae monotheismus dicitur, maxime ea qua Mahometani sunt astricti, quos propter ea quae in eorum cultu vera sunt et probanda, merito admiramur.*

54. Translation according to the Vatican website (http://w2.vatican.va/content/paul-vi/en/encyclicals/documents/hf_p-vi_enc_06081964_ecclesiam.html).

55. Gavin D'Costa, "Vatican II on Muslims and Jews: The Council's Teachings on Other Religions," in *The Second Vatican Council: Celebrating Its Achievements and the Future*, ed. Gavin D'Costa and Emma Jane Harris, 105–20 (London: Bloomsbury T&T Clark, 2013), text from footnote 6, page 108. In the first part of this footnote, D'Costa describes the development of the document on the Jews and its unfinished nature at the death of Pope John XXIII.

important to mention this document here since it gives the theological foundation of the Church's teaching about other religions in *Nostra Aetate*.[56] Moreover, it serves as a reminder that the teaching in *Nostra Aetate*, it being a declaration and thus the lowest level of the Council documents, should be subordinated to a dogmatic constitution such as *Lumen Gentium*. In this aspect, I agree with conservative interpreters of the Second Vatican Council that one cannot consider declarations such as *Nostra Aetate* on its own, but that they need to be related to dogmatic constitutions such as *Lumen Gentium*. In a book on *Catholic Engagement with World Religions*, Ilaria Morali, for instance, states: "The most common trend among today's theologians is in fact to assign *Nostra Aetate* a dogmatic value superior to that of *Lumen Gentium* 16 and of *Ad Gentes* . . . and often to omit so much as a mention of these last."[57]

As Dr. Michael Root has observed about ecumenical relationships, the Catholic Church sees itself as a center with different relationships to "others," both other Christian churches and other religions. This relationship is characterized by a word, *ordinari*, that indicates a relation and a hierarchy at the same time.[58] According to *Lumen Gentium*, the Church is central and others are related to her in a certain way. As Gerald O'Collins indicates, the origin of this idea of "ordering towards the Church" can be found in the encyclical *Mystici Corporis* by Pope Pius XII in 1943 that exhorts the faithful to pray for "those who have not yet received light from the truth of the Gospel."[59] The encyclical continues to discuss the relationship between the Mystical Body of Christ and those who are outside as follows: "Although they may be ordered (*ordinentur*) to the Mystical Body of the Redeemer by some unconscious yearning and desire . . . they are deprived of those many great heavenly gifts and aids which can be enjoyed only in the Catholic Church."[60] The language of a hierarchical relationship is present in 1943, but it is formulated in negative terms: they have not yet received the light, they are deprived of the heavenly gifts. In *Lumen Gentium*, on the contrary, the relationship is formulated in terms of a threefold difference. First, the Catholic faithful belong to the Church in different

---

56. See Joachim Zehner, *Der notwendige Dialog: die Weltreligionen in katholischer und evangelischer Sicht* (Gütersloh: G. Mohn, 1992).

57. Ilaria Morali, "Salvation, Religions, and Dialogue in the Roman Magisterium: From Pius IX to Vatican II and Postconciliar Popes," in *Catholic Engagement with World Religions*, ed. Karl J. Becker and Ilaria Morali, 122–42 (Maryknoll, N.Y.: Orbis Books, 2010), 126.

58. For a somewhat different analysis of this word in this context, see D'Costa, *Vatican II: Catholic Doctrines on Jews and Muslims*, 89–99.

59. Pope Pius XII, *Mystici Corporis* (1943), 101, quoted in O'Collins, *The Second Vatican Council on Other Religions*, 48.

60. *Mystici Corporis*, 102, in O'Collins, 49.

ways (*Lumen Gentium* 14). Second, the Church is in many ways related to those who are baptized but do not profess the Catholic faith.[61] Third, "those who have not yet received the Gospel are related in various ways to the people of God."[62] Notice how the old language is still there ("they have not yet received the Gospel") but at the same time the positive relationship is now highlighted.

Interestingly, the text of *Lumen Gentium* 16 here has a footnote that contains one of the few references in the documents of the Council to Thomas Aquinas, namely to the third part of the *Summa theologiae* where Aquinas discusses the grace of Christ as head of the Church and wonders whether Christ is *caput omnium hominum*. Answering the objection that unbelievers are not members of the Church, Aquinas states that unbelievers might not be actual members of the Church, yet they may be potential members.[63] He adds that there are two reasons for this potentiality: the principal reason is the power of Christ (*in virtute Christi*) whose grace (the context of the *Summa theologiae* III.8) is sufficient for the salvation of the whole of humankind; the second reason is human freewill. So Aquinas suggests that this "ordering toward" the Church is not only a preparation for the Gospel, as is often suggested, but that there is already a potential relationship thanks to the power of the grace of Christ. Christ is somehow potentially present in these relationships. One can see here a possible influence of two major models in the inclusivist theology of religions at that time, as represented by Jean Daniélou and Karl Rahner in which other religions were seen as preparations for the Gospel and containing a hidden presence of Christ.[64]

According to Gérard Philips, "who perhaps more than any other single theologian was involved in the crafting of *Lumen Gentium* from its very beginnings,"[65] the new texts that discuss the relationship between the Church as the people of God and those who are differently ordered toward the Church tried to show the universality of God's saving will on

61. *Lumen Gentium 15: Ecclesia semetipsam novit plures ob rationes coniunctam*. For the Latin text of *Lumen Gentium*, see *Lexikon für Theologie und Kirche* XII, 202. For English paraphrases, see the official translation on the Vatican website, http://w2.vatican.va.

62. *Ii tandem qui Evangelium nondum acceperunt, ad Populum Dei diversis rationibus ordinantur. Lumen Gentium* 16; *Lexikon für Theologie und Kirche* XII, 204.

63. *Illi qui sunt infideles, etsi actu non sint de Ecclesia, sunt tamen de Ecclesia in potentia.* Thomas Aquinas, *Summa theologiae* III.8.3 ad 1um.

64. See Jacques Dupuis, *Toward a Christian Theology of Religious Pluralism*, 133–57 (Maryknoll, N.Y.: Orbis Books, 1997).

65. Ralph Martin, *Will Many Be Saved? What Vatican II Actually Teaches and Its Implications for the New Evangelization* (Grand Rapids, Mich.; Cambridge: William B. Eerdmans, 2012), 19.

the one hand, and the necessity of missionary endeavors on the other.[66] As Philips indicates, articles 13-16 of *Lumen Gentium* followed quite naturally from the idea that human beings are ordered differently to God's universal saving will according to their different spiritual positions. As Msgr. Garrone mentioned in his *relatio* to the fathers of the Council on September 17, 1964, the main idea was to prevent an extreme individualism and to clearly distinguish between the different non-Christians.[67] One of the consequences was that *Lumen Gentium* 16 contains separate references to four different groups: the Jews, the Muslims, those who are seeking the unknown God, and those who do not know the Gospel of Christ.

What unites the first and second groups (Jews and Muslims) in being ordered toward the Church is their relation with the one true God. In the case of the Jews, the relation is characterized by the idea of the covenant and the promises (*promissa*) that God keeps; in the case of the Muslims, it is characterized by a faith like that of Abraham, a faith (*fides*) in the one and merciful God.[68] The third group mentioned is those who search for God in shadows and images. These words, *in umbris et imaginibus*, are used here to refer to other religions that are not mentioned by name but characterized in words that remind us of St. Paul's famous speech at the Areopagus in Athens: "What therefore you unknowingly worship, I proclaim to you" (Acts 17:23). The fourth group consists of those who do not know God but live a good life, and it is said that God's providence will assist them as well to reach salvation. This is a very complicated text about which much has been said, but for our purposes today it is enough to concentrate on the nexus between the relationship with Jews and the relationship with Muslims.

As Ralph Martin reminded us in his recent monograph on *Lumen Gentium* 16, these paragraphs were relatively uncontroversial, at least in comparison to the big debates about the idea of episcopal collegiality expressed in the third chapter of the document.[69] The text about the first

---

66. Philips's, "Die Geschichte der dogmatischen Konstitution über die Kirche 'Lumen Gentium,'" in *Lexikon für Theologie und Kirche* XII, 151.

67. Msgr. Garrone's *relatio* to the Council fathers in St. Peter on *Lumen Gentium* 16 is reproduced in Martin, *Will Many Be Saved?*, 211–12; English translation, 213–14.

68. In his commentary on this paragraph, Alois Grillmeier in *Lexikon für Theologie und Kirche* XII (Freiburg i. Br.: Herder, 1966), 206, remarks that an earlier version of this paragraph drew a parallel between Jews and Muslims by talking about the "sons of Ishmael." This version underscores the faith in one God as defining characteristic of Muslims, and in doing so it singles out what unites Catholics and Muslims: their stress on Abraham's faith.

69. Martin (2012), 11, with reference to both Karl Rahner and the most recent comprehensive account by Richard Gaillardetz, *The Church in the Making* (Mahwah, N.J.: Paulist Press, 2006).

of the groups ordered toward the church is relatively short and unremarkable since the big debates about the relationship with the Jewish people were to be held with reference to the fourth chapter of *Nostra Aetate* (at that point still on the table as *De Iudaeis*).[70] So the text of *Lumen Gentium* 16 limits itself to stating the theological nature of the relationship with the Jews, namely that they are "the people to whom the covenants and the promises were given and from whom Christ was born according to the flesh." Furthermore, this people "remains most dear to God, for God does not repent of the gifts He makes nor of the calls He issues."[71] This theology of Judaism is basically derived from Paul's letter to the Romans, chapters 9 to 11.[72]

The second group consists of the Muslims, the only group mentioned here by name (*Musulmani*). The text about them from *Lumen Gentium* 16 is arguably the most remarkable one, since for the first time in history the Church describes this religion in positive terms, which is quite a change from the historically dominant approach.[73] Islam gets a remarkably full theological description, even though the description in *Nostra Aetate* 3 one year later would be a bit more comprehensive. Four elements can be distinguished in the text. The first element is of a more generic nature: the acknowledgment of God as creator. The second element is the claim to possess the faith of Abraham, a claim that is acknowledged. The third element adds that Muslims adore, together with the Christians, the one and merciful God. One hears here an echo of the first verse of each *surah* in the Qur'an, the *basmala* in which the oneness and the mercifulness of God are mentioned. The fourth element is the faith in the last day (*al-āchira*) when God will pass judgment.[74]

70. See the Council journals by Congar and Willebrands.

71. . . . *populus ille cui data fuerunt testamenta et promissa et ex quo Christus ortus est secundum carnem (Rom 9:4–5), populus secundum electionem carissimus propter patres: sine poenitentia enim sunt dona et vocatio Dei* (Rom 11:28–29). Text according to *Lexikon für Theologie und Kirche* XII, 204.

72. See Matthew Tapie, *Aquinas on Israel and the Church: The Question of Supersessionism in the Theology of Thomas Aquinas* (Eugene, Ore.: Pickwick, 2014); for the important part of these Pauline chapters in the change in Catholic thinking about the Jews, see Connelly, *From Enemy to Brother*.

73. Congar, in his *Journal of the Council* (580), wrote that the 553 votes with reservations (*placet iuxta modum*) were related to this paragraph on the Muslims.

74. The plan of salvation also includes those who acknowledge the Creator, in the first place among them the Muslims who, professing to hold the faith of Abraham, along with us adore the one and merciful God, who on the last day will judge humankind. *Sed propositum salutis et eos amplectitur, qui Creatorem agnoscunt, inter quos imprimis Musulmanos, qui fidem Abrahae se tenere profitentes, nobiscum Deum adorant unicum, misericordem, homines die novissimo iudicaturum.* Text in *Lexikon für Theologie und Kirche* XII, 204.

It is important to see what is said here and what not. Positively, the Council acknowledges that the Muslims adore the One and Merciful God together with the Christians. But with reference to the faith of Abraham, there seems to be an intentional ambiguity here. The text does not state that Muslims share the faith of Abraham, but it states that they claim to do so. The text in *Nostra Aetate* 3 is similar, so this cannot be a coincidence. It acknowledges that Muslims adore the One God, but it is circumspect with reference to the faith of Abraham: Muslims try to submit to God as Abraham, to whom the Muslim faith likes to refer, submitted to God.[75] Twice the Council mentions the connection between the faith of Abraham and the Muslim faith, and it uses the term *fides* in both cases, but it does not directly state that Muslims have the faith of Abraham; it only states that they like to refer to Abraham and his faith.

This indirect recognition of the faith of Muslims seems to reflect a position halfway between the default historical approach to Muslims as unbelievers and our present-day inclination to recognize their faith as true faith in the One God whom they adore together with us, as the Council affirms twice. In his commentary on these two texts on the Muslims, Georges Anawati, OP, mentions that the Council fathers said something that was really new, so they had to proceed very carefully.[76] But where did this new language come from? Almost all scholars seem to indicate that it originated with Pope Paul VI, who was influenced in his view on Islam by Louis Massignon's explicitly affirmation of Islam as "the faith of Abraham."[77] Even though the Second Vatican Council did not follow Massignon exactly in his tendency to accept the questionable historical claim of the Arab people to partake of the Abrahamic heritage through Ishmael as proposed in an earlier version of the text, it seemed cautiously to endorse the idea that the Islamic faith shares theologically in the faith of Abraham.[78]

---

75. *Ecclesia cum aestimatione quoque Muslimos respicit qui unicum Deum adorant, viventem et subsistentem, misericordem et omnipotentem, Creatorem caeli et terrae, homines allocutum, cuius occultis etiam decretis toto animo se submittere student, sicut Deo se submisit Abraham ad quem fides islamica libenter sese refert.* Text in *Lexikon für Theologie und Kirche* XIII, 490.

76. See Georges Anawati, "Exkurs zum Konzilstext über die Muslim," in *Lexikon für Theologie und Kirche (zweite Auflage)*, XIII, 485–87 (Freiburg i. Br.: Herder, 1967), who speaks about "äußerste Vorsicht" (486).

77. See Griffith (1997); Karl-Josef Kuschel, *Juden—Christen—Muslime: Herkunft und Zukunft*, 606–7 (Düsseldorf: Patmos, 2007); D'Costa, "Continuity and Reform in Vatican II's Teaching on Islam," 217.

78. Anawati, 486. Also, D'Costa, *Vatican II: Catholic Doctrines on Jews and Muslims*, 186.

Nostra Aetate, Moving Forward

As we noted at the beginning of this contribution, the proper hermeneutics of the Second Vatican Council has been the focus of quite a few recent debates. Gavin D'Costa, who has recently published a number of studies about the Council's approach to other religions, and to Judaism and Islam in particular, comes to the conclusion that there is a strong continuity in the doctrinal teaching about Judaism and Islam, while at the same time there is a revolutionary discontinuity in the ethos and the practices that accompany the doctrinal teaching.[79] While this sounds rather cautious, he also comes to the conclusion that the Second Vatican Council acknowledged more than simply natural knowledge in Islam, and that it even might have affirmed a partial truth of the claim that the Qur'an and Muhammad would have mediated some knowledge of the true God.[80] Yet in all Vatican documents the positive statements are balanced by other statements—usually in the same paragraph—that underline the differences between the Catholic faith and the faith of others and that stress the necessity to bring God's revelation in Christ to the attention of the others as well. In other words: dialogue and proclamation are two aspects of the universal mission of the Church.[81]

Nostra Aetate may be so popular among dialogue-minded people and in the academy because the mission-oriented language is toned down in that specific document. Historically, this de-emphasis on mission is why Jean Daniélou did not like the document and why Yves Congar hastened to say that he had included a reference to the duty to proclaim Christ. The juxtaposition between dialogue and proclamation—between a new, positive valuation of other religions and the constant Christian claim of uniqueness—is evident in the last phrases of *Nostra Aetate* 2 that might be the most famous of the entire document:

> [T]he Catholic Church rejects nothing that is true and holy in these religions. She regards with sincere reverence those ways of acting and of living, those precepts and teachings which, though differing in many aspects from the one she holds and sets forth, nonetheless often reflect a ray of that truth which enlightens all. Indeed, she proclaims, and ever must proclaim, Christ as "the Way, the Truth, and the Life" (Jn 14:6), in whom men and women may find the fullness of religious life, and in whom God has reconciled all things to Himself.[82]

79. See D'Costa, *Vatican II: Catholic Doctrines on Jews and Muslims*, 212.
80. D'Costa, "Continuity and Reform in Vatican II's Teaching on Islam," 221–22.
81. See the last part of *Lumen Gentium* 16, but also the second half of *Ecclesiam Suam* 107. D'Costa and Morali add *Ad Gentes* 7 to the picture as well.
82. *Nostra Aetate* 2, trans. Thomas F. Stransky, CSP.

On the one hand there is reverence and respect for all religions; on the other hand there is the affirmation of truth and the fullness of religious life in Christ.

These two elements lead to a rather specific form of dialogue, balanced for some, ambiguous for others.[83] Let me finish by quoting the next and final sentence of *Nostra Aetate* 2: "The Church therefore exhorts her sons and daughters to recognize, preserve and foster the good things, spiritual and moral, as well as the socio-cultural values found among the followers of other religions. This is done through conversations and collaboration with them, carried out with prudence and love and in witness to the Christian faith and life."[84] This combination of dialogue ("conversations and collaboration") and witness ("proclamation") has created a tension in the academic reception of the document, as I hope to show in the last part of this book. But, more importantly to the document's aims, it has characterized the reception of *Nostra Aetate* by both the Catholic Church and the religious partners with whom it has joined meaningful dialogues over the last fifty years, dialogues that will likely continue for the next fifty years, and whose current contents and directions are discussed in the remainder of this book.

---

83. For a somewhat stronger dialogue-oriented interpretation of this text, see Francis X. Clooney's contribution to this volume.

84. *Nostra Aetate* 2, trans. Thomas F. Stransky, CSP.

Nostra Aetate and Ecumenism

Michael Root

As is well known, the text that became *Nostra Aetate* began its life under the aegis of the Secretariat for the Promotion of Christian Unity and its able head, Cardinal Augustin Bea. A common incubator, so to speak, sheltered *Nostra Aetate* and *Unitatis Redintegratio*, the Council's declaration on ecumenism, on the intra-Christian pursuit of greater unity. As I hope to show, the two texts, while obviously different, share a common logic and rhetoric and represent similar shifts in official Catholic attitudes toward, respectively, other religions and other Christian communities. They are of a piece. Oddly enough, however, there is almost no literature on the how the contents of these two texts interrelate.

In this essay, I will, necessarily briefly, take up that analytic task and then explore the differences and similarities between ecumenical and interreligious dialogue. Are interreligious and ecumenical dialogue two species of the same genus, religious dialogue, or are they radically distinct in their foundations, methods, and goals? Can interreligious dialogue be understood as "the wider ecumenism," as some have argued, or is such a term misleading? More practically, what might either dialogue learn from the other? Again, I was surprised to find that the literature on this larger question of the interrelation of ecumenical and interreligious dialogue is also surprisingly meager. This whole presentation is thus somewhat exploratory and tentative.

I should note at the beginning that my experience of dialogue is entirely in the ecumenical sphere. I have no expertise or experience in interreligious dialogue and only a nonspecialist's knowledge of other religions. I therefore ask your indulgence for any interreligious faux pas that I may commit.

Let me preface my remarks with some speculative questions. The similarities that link *Nostra Aetate* and *Unitatis Redintegratio* show that the Council approached other religions and other churches with a comparable set of categories and questions. For the Council, ecumenical and interreligious questions are treated in similar ways. Can the same be said about other religions? Do Muslim or Buddhist or Jewish understandings of their relations with other religions run parallel to their understandings of the commonalities and differences that exist within their own internal unity? There have been parallels to modern Christian ecumenism in other religions. The Sunni-Shia divide has been an important feature of Islam and the pursuit of *taqrib*, rapprochement or reconciliation, has been a significant project for some Muslims in the twentieth century. In 1967, the World Buddhist Sangha Council put forward a statement titled "The Basic Points Unifying the Theravada and the Mahayana" that sought to enunciate a shared doctrinal foundation common to all (or at least most) Buddhists.[1] Internal unity is not understood in the same way among religions, however. The Catholic understanding of unity in governance as one aspect of Christian unity seems foreign to a Buddhist understanding of Buddhist unity. At least in the twentieth century, the pursuit of greater Islamic unity had complex relations with questions of Islamic political unity in a way not paralleled among Christians or Buddhists. Do the varying understandings of their own internal unity affect, or at least align with, the way different religions understand the nature and purpose of interreligious relations and dialogue? I do not have the answer to this question, although I strongly suspect that a religion's understanding of its internal and external relations do form a whole, but perhaps in quite varying ways. An answer to this question would first require the exploration of what one might call a "comparative ecumenics," a study of how various religions understand their own identity and unity, how important such unity is in their self-understanding, and how they deal with internal disagreements that threaten this unity. Such a study would be fascinating, but it would be a daunting task and, as far as I know, no one has even begun it. I can only note that larger question here. (I should add that, for simplicity's sake, I will continue to follow usual practice and use the term *ecumenism* and its cognates to refer to the intra-Christian pursuit of unity, although there are parallel phenomena within other religions.)

Formal Similarities: The Shift to More Complex Judgments

Nostra Aetate and *Unitatis Redintegratio*, interreligious and ecumenical relations, were two areas in which the Second Vatican Council introduced obvious changes in Catholic practice. The significance of these changes makes it all the more important to understand the inner logic of the theology involved in the changes. In both cases, a similar pattern emerges. Judgments prominent in earlier official statements were not rejected but placed in a new context, as they were linked with judgments of a different logical sort.

---

1. World Buddhist Sangha Council, "The Basic Points Unifying the Theravada and the Mahayana" (1967), http://www.buddhisma2z.com/content.php?id=432 (accessed September 8, 2015).

What is distinctive in both texts is a move toward a nuanced combination of two sorts of categories: all-or-nothing binary categories, which I will call nonscalar, and more-or-less categories, which I will call scalar. The first set, all-or-nothing categories, either applies or does not apply. These categories are not matters of degree; there is no scale for them (hence, they are nonscalar). I am afraid there is always the same standard example of a nonscalar predicate: one cannot be a little bit pregnant. There are many other examples, however. For example, in an American court of law, one cannot be fifty-five percent guilty. The jury must pronounce guilty or not guilty. The central soteriological categories of Christian faith are nonscalar. One is either redeemed or not redeemed; justified before God or not justified.

By contrast, a more-or-less, or scalar, category is one that does allow for a scale—categories such as tall, fat, smart, mature, holy, righteous. It is not the case that a person simply is or is not tall; one can be "sort of" tall, and one person can be taller than another. A person can be a better or worse disciple, more or less holy, more or less attached to particular sins.

Both scalar and nonscalar, more-or-less and all-or-nothing categories have their place. Theological judgments require both. In the area of ecumenism, official Catholic teaching about non-Christian communities prior to Vatican II tended to emphasize nonscalar, all-or-nothing judgments. A community is or is not a church. A person is or is not a member of the church. In such nonscalar terms, judgments about non-Catholic communities were often negative. In *Unitatis Redintegratio*, the use of such nonscalar categories is not rejected, but it is supplemented by the use of scalar, more-or-less categories. A Protestant church may not, according to Catholic theology, be a "church" in the proper sense of that word,[2] but that judgment can be supplemented by the more nuanced judgment that such a community is truly ecclesial, that is, that it realizes authentic elements of the reality of the Church and can do so in a way that mediates salvation.[3] Rather than simply ask if a Protestant is or is not a member of the one church, *Unitatis Redintegratio* states that anyone truly baptized is in a real but imperfect communion with the one church.[4] "Communion" is applied as a scalar predicate; it admits of degrees. Communion can be full, but it can also be relatively close or relatively distant.

The shift represented by *Nostra Aetate* seems similar (with the exception noted below of the text's approach to Judaism). While earlier discussions of other religions tended to operate with nonscalar categories, especially the category "true religion," *Nostra Aetate* shifts the discussion to

2. Vatican Council II, *Unitatis Redintegratio*, November 21, 1964, par. 22.
3. Ibid. 3.
4. Ibid. 3.

elements of the holy and the true that can be found in religions or the ways a religion reflects a ray of the truth that illumines all men.[5] These ways of speaking are scalar. A religion may embody more or less of the true and the good or reflect more clearly or more obscurely the light that enlightens all men. The absolute, nonscalar category does not disappear. As *Nostra Aetate* states, only in Christ is to be found "the fullness of religious life," but that judgment does not stand alone.[6]

The kinds of scalar categories used in both *Unitatis Redintegratio* and *Nostra Aetate* are of the same general sort; they focus on the presence or absence of discrete items or elements. In non-Catholic Christian communities, these elements are the sacraments (especially baptism, the Eucharist, and ordination); the Scriptures; a life of faith; the virtues of faith, hope, and love; interior gifts of the Holy Spirit.[7] The more such elements are shared between the Catholic Church and another Christian community, the closer the communion between the Catholic Church and that community and its members (although it must be immediately added that some elements are more foundational than others, most notably baptism).

Nostra Aetate operates in a similar way, noting certain elements of truth and holiness in other religions. These elements establish commonalities between these religions and Catholic Christianity: for example, a focus on basic questions of human existence, a perception of an unseen power at work in the world, a reliance on God.[8] With Islam and Judaism, these elements are extensive, many relating to a common historical heritage flowing ultimately from God's promises to Abraham.[9] This greater range of common elements means that Islam is closer to Catholic Christianity than is, say, Buddhism.

This emphasis on shared elements does have its drawbacks. The emphasis on "ecclesial elements" in *Unitatis Redintegratio* has been criticized as leading to an overly quantified or check-list approach to ecclesiology, without attending to what binds such elements together into a truly ecclesial life. One is tempted simply to verify whether certain essential elements are or are not present, without looking at the true inner life of a community. It should be noted, however, that the text explicitly lists such

5. *Nostra Aetate* 2.

6. Ibid., trans. Thomas F. Stransky, CSP. "Fullness" is used in *Nostra Aetate* in a nonscalar way. Something either is full or it is not. Of course, "fullness" could also be used in a scalar sense, in which something is more or less full. At least in the past, "perfect" also could be used in its present, nonscalar sense, as it usually is today, and in a scalar sense, as in the U.S. Constitution: "in order to form a more perfect union."

7. *Unitatis Redintegratio* 3.

8. *Nostra Aetate* 2.

9. Ibid. 3–4.

elements as faith, hope, and love and the interior gifts of the Spirit, not simply externally verifiable items such as the use of a common canon of scripture.

The elements approach can make it seem that the Council saw other Christian communities and other religions as taking form as a series of concentric circles around the Catholic Church. The Orthodox would form the circle closest to the Catholic Church. Then would come Western communities, with the Anglicans just beyond the Orthodox and other communities at an increasing distance as one moved toward, say, Baptists or Quakers. Beyond them would lie other religions, with Judaism closest, followed by Islam and then Buddhism and Hinduism.

Such a concentric circles approach, while not simply false, is obviously inadequate and tends to ignore the specificity of each Christian community and other religion. Again, the danger arises of treating religious similarities and differences in an overly quantitative rather than qualitative way. In addition, such an approach does not fit with the actual experience of religious encounter. A Catholic contemplative monk may find far more in common with a Buddhist monk than with a Christian Pentecostal street preacher. Most important, the Council's understanding of the particular relation of Christianity to Judaism is not merely a matter of common elements shared but more fundamentally is based on the Christian belief in God's irrevocable covenant with the people of Israel.[10] The Catholic Church shares a greater range of common elements with Presbyterians than with Jews, but Judaism and the Jewish people have a kind of importance for the Catholic Church and Catholic theology that Presbyterian churches and Reformed theology do not. (I would note that the section on Judaism and the Jewish people in *Nostra Aetate* is the one section that to an extensive degree does not fit the analysis here given. What makes *Nostra Aetate*'s discussion of Judaism distinctive is not the move to scalar categories but the emphasis on God's irrevocable commitment to his covenant promises.)

The Council thus shared a common logic as it approached ecumenism and interreligious relations. In each case, a former emphasis on absolute, nonscalar judgments is supplemented and recontextualized by scalar, more-or-less judgments. In both cases, the more-or-less judgments are expressed in terms of discrete shared elements. In both cases, however, the nonscalar, all-or-nothing judgments are not abandoned; they are supplemented. Both Catholic ecumenism and Catholic interreligious relations are misjudged in a way that can lead only to disappointment when the continuing presence of these nonscalar judgments is ignored.

10. Ibid. 4.

This common logic embodied in the two documents permits a shared rhetoric. *Unitatis Redintegratio* and, more clearly, *Nostra Aetate* tend to begin their comments on other Christian communities or other religions with an emphasis on what is shared and affirmed rather than on what is different. In *Nostra Aetate*, the first comments about Hinduism, Buddhism, Islam, and Judaism are in each case a reference to something shared and thus affirmed. Such a positive beginning is only possible because of the shift toward scalar judgments focused on shared elements. In *Unitatis Redintegratio*, the emphasis on the shared is less evident since the text begins with an extensive discussion of the nature of the unity of the Church, which is attested to subsist in a unique way in the Catholic Church.[11] Nevertheless, in chapter 3 of the text, where other churches are discussed in their specificity, more space is given to what unites than to what divides. More than is the case in *Nostra Aetate*, however, the ecumenical text qualifies the affirmation of shared elements by noting some divisive element related to what is shared. For example, after noting the Scripture shared by Protestants and Catholics, *Unitatis Redintegratio* adds that Protestants and Catholics understand scriptural authority in relation to the Church's teaching authority in different ways.[12] *Unitatis Redintegratio* seems to manifest a greater concern that its positive remarks not be overread. In both texts, however, a common logic has opened the way to a common, more positive rhetoric in a significant shift from earlier official texts on other churches and other religions.

Material Differences: The Importance of Different Elements Shared

So far, I have been looking at formal aspects of *Unitatis Redintegratio* and *Nostra Aetate*, the types of categories that form their judgments, and the ways they develop those judgments. From this formal perspective, the texts are strikingly similar and manifest a common outlook. When we turn from these formal aspects to what can be called the material aspects—in particular to the sorts of shared elements or commonalities that each text picks out and the significance of those elements—then the differences between ecumenical and interreligious relations become more pronounced.

What are the common elements that *Nostra Aetate* picks out among the various religions and *Unitatis Redintegratio* picks out among the various churches? *Nostra Aetate* begins with a theological assertion—humanity has a common origin and end in God. This common origin and end finds expression in certain universal human questions: What is man? What is the meaning, the aim of our life? What origins and purposes do sufferings

---

11. *Unitatis Redintegratio* 4.
12. Ibid. 21.

have? Which is the road to true happiness? Religions share a common function: they seek to answer certain basic questions about the origin, nature, and point of human existence.[13] (The text's implicit definition of what constitutes a religion seems to be that a religion is a means of addressing these fundamental questions theoretically and practically.)

This general description is then followed by a series of comments on specific religions in which various common elements are mentioned. On the one hand, these common elements are put forward descriptively. They are shared beliefs and practices: for example, a common perception of an unseen force and a sense of "the radical inadequacy of this changeable world" in the cases of Hinduism and Buddhism;[14] a shared belief in God as "living and subsistent . . . merciful and all-powerful, the Creator of heaven and earth" in the case of Islam;[15] a shared appeal to God's calling of Abraham and to the tradition of Moses and the prophets in the case of Judaism.[16] On the other hand, commonalities are also put forward more normatively. Other religions contain things that are "true and holy" and they not infrequently (*haud raro*) "reflect a ray of that truth which enlightens all."[17]

The commonalities among the Christian churches noted in *Unitatis Redintegratio* focus on elements of Christian life. As noted, they include not only public, visible realities, such as the Scriptures and the sacraments, but also interior gifts. Of greatest importance for *Unitatis Redintegratio* is a common baptism. "Those who believe in Christ and have been truly baptized are in a kind of communion with the Catholic Church, even if imperfect. . . . All who have been justified in baptism by faith are incorporated into Christ and have a right to be called Christians and so are deservedly recognized as brothers and sisters in the Lord by the children of the Catholic Church."[18] Christians in divided communities share a common communion or participation in the one Church, although the Catholic Church is understood to do so in a perfect way (at least, perfect under the conditions of history) and the non-Catholic communities in an imperfect way, to varying degrees.

These differing sets of particular commonalities, with their related differences, set up different kinds of theoretical and practical challenges for ecumenism and interreligious relations. *Nostra Aetate* makes no reference, even implicitly, to the theoretical, conceptual, or theological challenges

13. *Nostra Aetate* 1.
14. Ibid. 2.
15. Ibid. 3.
16. Ibid. 4.
17. Ibid. 2.
18. *Unitatis Redintegratio* 3.

that the reality it considers presents to Catholic thought, although the challenge is quite clear in other texts from the Council, most notably *Lumen Gentium* 16, and is more explicitly discussed in various postconciliar official texts. If God, in some sense, wills the salvation of every person,[19] if grace sufficient unto salvation is offered to every person, and if every person is in some way united to Christ by the eternal Word's assumption of human nature, then how is this universal offer of saving grace in Christ to be understood, and what role do non-Christian religions, their beliefs and rites, play in the mediation of grace and the formation either of a life preparatory for grace or of a life that embodies a right response to such grace? Although perhaps not mentioned in official Catholic texts (I at least have not been able to find it), a deeper theological question is how to understand the diversity of religions in the light of God's overarching intentions and providence? As the World Council of Churches' Baar Statement on "Theological Perspectives on Plurality" asks: "what is the relation of the diversity of religious traditions to the mystery of the one Triune God?"[20]

I would note that these are not so much questions for interreligious dialogue as they are challenges to a Catholic understanding of Christian doctrine about Christ, salvation, and history. The combination of a belief in the universality of God's saving will and action and the reality of non-Christian religions creates a certain perplexity for Christian theology, a perplexity that calls for more careful thought and exploration.

The commonalities noted in *Nostra Aetate* also throw up practical challenges. Most notably, Christians must find ways of respecting and valuing what is true and holy in non-Christian religions.[21] All unjust forms of religious discrimination are rejected,[22] and anti-Semitism is explicitly deplored.[23]

The commonalities and related differences among the Christian communities noted by *Unitatis Redintegratio* call forth a different sort of theoretical and practical challenge. The theoretical/theological challenge is less a perplexity about how to interrelate various beliefs and realities and more an apparent internal contradiction between what Christians know must be the case and what stares them in the face. There can only be one Church of Christ, and yet there is a diversity of Christian communities, many not in communion with one another. As *Unitatis Redintegratio* states, the shared

19. Vatican Council II, *Lumen Gentium*, November 21, 1964, par. 16.
20. World Council of Churches, "Baar Statement: Theological Perspectives on Plurality" (1990), https://www.oikoumene.org/.
21. *Nostra Aetate* 2.
22. Ibid. 5.
23. Ibid. 4.

reality of baptism "is only a beginning, an inauguration wholly directed toward the fullness of life in Christ," a fullness that includes "a complete inclusion [*insertionem*] in eucharistic communion."[24] And yet, Catholic teaching asserts that for many communities, that complete inclusion does not occur. John Paul II asked in his encyclical on ecumenism, *Ut unum sit*: "How is it possible to remain divided, if we have been 'buried' through Baptism in the Lord's death, in the very act by which God, through the death of his Son, has broken down the walls of division?"[25] As Bruce Marshall has argued, the Christian theologian should take Christian division as one of the strongest arguments against the truth of Christianity.[26]

The Catholic theologian and *Unitatis Redintegratio* do have arguments—I believe good arguments—for why the division of Christians does not constitute such a fatal self-contradiction. The unity Christ wills for his Church "subsists in the Catholic Church as something she can never lose, and we hope that it will continue to increase until the end of time."[27] The Church cannot be divided. Christ does not have multiple bodies. But that assertion, true as it is, does not change the division that exists among those whom the Council states are rightly called Christian brothers and sisters. This division remains a scandal, a stumbling block, as *Unitatis Redintegratio* states[28]—a stumbling block not just for Christian practice but for Christian thought. Even if the unity Christ wills for his Church continues to exist in the Catholic Church, this division that exists among Christians significantly damages her. "The divisions among Christians prevent the Church from attaining the fullness of catholicity proper to her, in those of her sons and daughters who, though attached to her by baptism, are yet separated from full communion with her. Furthermore, the Church herself finds it more difficult to express in actual life her full catholicity in all her bearings."[29] The disunity of Christians cannot destroy the unity of the Church, but it constrains the Church in one of her essential marks, her catholicity. As the Congregation for the Doctrine of the Faith would later say, division "wounds" not just others, but the Catholic Church herself in her catholicity. While other religions are an external reality, presenting Catholic theology with a perplexity, the division of Christians is more an

---

24. *Unitatis Redintegratio* 22.

25. John Paul II, Ut unum sint: *On Commitment to Ecumenism* (Vatican City: Libreria Editrice Vaticana, 1995).

26. Bruce D. Marshall, "The Disunity of the Church and the Credibility of the Gospel," *Theology Today* 50 (1993): 78–89.

27. *Unitatis Redintegratio* 4.

28. Ibid. 1.

29. Ibid. 4.

internal reality that presents something close to a contradiction of basic Christian claims.

The difference in theoretical, conceptual, or theological challenges raised by ecumenical and interreligious relations is paralleled by a difference in practical challenges. *Nostra Aetate* does not call for a "restoration of unity," a *unitatis redintegratio*, among the religions, but the ecumenism text in its very title lays out the challenge of Christian unity as "one of the principal concerns of the Second Vatican Council."[30] *Unitatis Redintegratio* goes on to spell out more concrete challenges: reconciling the memories of a painful history in which all sides bear blame,[31] seeking and offering forgiveness,[32] recognizing legitimate diversity,[33] and, most profoundly, renewing Catholicism itself through the pursuit of holiness, interior conversion, "self denial[,] and an unstinted love that desires unity."[34] These challenges are all oriented, however, to the overarching challenge of the call to unity.

Both *Nostra Aetate* and *Unitatis Redintegratio* call for action, but the actions they call for are of different natures.

Ecumenical and Interreligious Dialogue

As I have shown, *Nostra Aetate* and *Unitatis Redintegratio* apply similar strategies to similar but also significantly different realities. In each case, they broke with aspects of the Catholic past by supplementing previous assertions with assertions framed in categories that had been neglected in addressing other churches and other religions. The different realities these texts address present different challenges. These challenges lead to the significant similarities and significant differences between ecumenical and interreligious dialogue.

The significant similarities and differences between ecumenical and interreligious relations affect the specific activity of interreligious and ecumenical dialogue. In each case, dialogue takes similar forms: a dialogue of life, in which persons seek understanding and harmony in daily life; a dialogue of engagement, in which representatives of communities come together around congruent concerns in local, national, or global life; and a dialogue of experts, in which those particularly well versed in the understanding of their own and other traditions come together to explore similarities and differences. The relative emphasis given to these forms of dia-

---

30. Ibid. 1.
31. Ibid. 3.
32. Ibid. 7.
33. Ibid. 17.
34. Ibid. 7.

logue may vary, however, between ecumenical and interreligious dialogue. The dialogue of experts has been decisive for ecumenical relations but has been far less prominent in interreligious relations.

The inner dynamics of dialogue will be similar in both cases. Getting to know one another personally is intertwined with getting to know another tradition in a particular embodied form. Islam or Lutheranism may look very different in the particular community engaged in dialogue than it does in standard textbook summaries. Prejudices must be overcome or at least nuanced. An appreciation has to develop for the way another community thinks and feels.

Significant similarities also exist in the goals of dialogue. All religious dialogue seeks greater mutual understanding, trusting that greater mutual understanding will lead to paths toward the lowering of tensions and the elimination of false and harmful preconceptions. Both interreligious and ecumenical dialogue are at times concerned with collaboration in efforts that serve the common good.

Both ecumenical and interreligious dialogue should have as an objective a genuine deepening of the religious life of all participants. Dialogue should be a common walk toward the truth, as the statement on "Dialogue and Mission" of the Pontifical Council for Inter-religious Dialogue states. In the case of ecumenism, division has often produced one-sided reactions on both sides of a divide, as each emphasizes what it believes the other has gotten wrong. Dialogue can confront each side with the challenge of doing justice to what is true in the other. Faith, theology, and witness are thus strengthened.

The dynamics of such an exchange in interreligious dialogue will be different but certainly also similar. Each side will encounter the example and questions of the other. For example, the Christian may be inspired by the prayer life of the Muslim and also challenged to explain just how belief in the Trinity is not a denial of the unity of God. Both may be to the Christian's profit. An excellent example of this dynamic has been the Scriptural Reasoning initiative, in which Christian, Jewish, and Islamic scholars have sat and worked together on the exegesis of their respective Scriptures. Those engaged have found not only that they have learned something new and valuable about the other but also that their own understanding of their own sacred text has been deepened by reading it carefully with scholars from the other religions. An ecumenical or interreligious dialogue that does not understand itself as a moment in the common pursuit of truth in thought and practice is impoverished.

Ecumenical dialogue, however, is set apart by a decisive additional goal, especially in the case of the "dialogue of experts." Ecumenical dialogue, often explicitly and almost always at least implicitly, is concerned with achieving what each side believes to be that unity in faith and life among Christians that is called for by the Christian faith itself. As John Paul II said in *Ut unum sint*: "The ultimate goal of the ecumenical movement is to re-establish full visible unity among all the baptized."[35] This goal forms the background of ecumenical dialogue. Bishop Michael Fitzgerald has stressed this point:

> What needs to be pointed out is that theological dialogue within an interreligious context differs radically from that which is conducted in an ecumenical context. Among Christians of different Churches and Confessions theological dialogue aims at achieving a common understanding and statement of the same faith. The purpose is to achieve a unity in belief sufficient to allow the members of different communities to recognize one another as being in communion.[36]

Interreligious dialogue has no parallel aim. Cardinal Edward Cassidy noted the difference in goal in relation to Catholic-Jewish dialogue: "There is a fundamental difference between ecumenical dialogue and Christian-Jewish dialogue. The aim of the first is to seek within the Christian communities a profound unity of faith, while that is simply impossible in the second."[37]

I would stress, out of my own experience, how thoroughly the goal of unity shapes and colors ecumenical dialogue. Even when the possibility of full communion is remote, unity forms an implicit criterion or goal. The question in the background on any topic tends to be: is this degree of shared belief and practice sufficient for unity, or should some specific difference in this area keep us apart? The common genre of the ecumenical dialogue statement is oriented toward that goal. One need only look at perhaps the two most prominent ecumenical statements—the World Council of Churches' statement on "Baptism, Eucharist and Ministry" and the Catholic-Lutheran "Joint Declaration on the Doctrine of Justification"—to see how the genre works. In each case, what can be said together is juxtaposed with what each community still says distinctively, with the question raised, implicitly or explicitly, whether the common statement is sufficient for unity, despite the remaining difference. In the case of the Catholic-Lutheran Joint Declaration, I can say as a member of the final

35. John Paul II, Ut unum sint: *On Commitment to Ecumenism.*
36. Michael L. Fitzgerald, "A Theological Reflection on Interreligious Dialogue," in *Catholic Engagement with World Religions: A Comprehensive Study*, ed. Karl Josef Becker and Ilaria Morali, 383–94 (Maryknoll, N.Y.: Orbis Books, 2010), section 4.
37. Edward Idris Cassidy, *Ecumenism and Interreligious Dialogue*: Unitatis Redintegratio, Nostra Aetate (Mahwah, N.J.: Paulist Press, 2005), 242.

drafting team that the structure was deliberately fashioned to meet the ecumenical goal.

I could imagine a common statement being produced by an interreligious group. Perhaps a group of Muslim, Jewish, and Christian scholars would produce a statement outlining what they can say together about God and where there beliefs conflict. That might very well be an interesting project. It might ask questions analogous to ecumenical questions; for example, could all say that they in fact worship the same god, even if they do not agree on how to worship that god rightly? Even so, such a text would not seem to serve the same function as the typical ecumenical common statement. Dialogues among the Abrahamic religions have not had as a goal the movement toward unity in belief and practice, and so a common statement would not function as a step on the way to such a goal.

These perhaps obvious differences need to be noted because tendencies exist to conflate ecumenical and interreligious dialogue. This conflation can occur from both sides, so to speak. That is, sometimes interreligious dialogue tends to be understood in terms more appropriate to ecumenical dialogue, and sometimes ecumenical dialogue tends to be understood in ways more appropriate to interreligious dialogue. The former can happen when the term *wider ecumenism* is used to describe interreligious relations. Sometimes this phrase is used only to urge those concerned with Christian division to attend also to the problems of religious division. But it is likewise used on occasion to advocate a concern for unity in interreligious relations similar to the concern of ecumenism, to make the goal of interreligious dialogue a unity such as the unity sought in ecumenical dialogue. Such a tendency is a concern in a variety of ways, but perhaps most notably it confuses the common walk toward the truth with a common conversion to a new religion inevitably different from any of those religions that enter the dialogue. As John Borelli noted: "Critics can easily shout 'compromise' whenever doctrine is taken up [in interreligious dialogue] as though there could be some negotiation in doctrine in interreligious relations. This is where the proximity of ecumenical dialogue, which involves efforts to find language to overcome differences keeping Christians apart, to interreligious dialogue can confuse those engaged in interreligious dialogue."[38]

A parallel but opposite danger arises in tendencies among ecumenists to drop the goal of unity from ecumenical dialogue. The goal of unity does put a particular kind of pressure on a dialogue. Could more be achieved if

---

38. John Borelli, "*Unitatis Redintegratio* and *Nostra Aetate*: Reception at the Fifty Year Mark in the New Era of Pope Francis," *Ecumenical Trends* 42 (2013): 113–21.

ecumenical dialogue became more 'no strings attached,' as Professor Clooney described interreligious dialogue in this conference? Allowing the goal of unity to recede and play a more background role has served in some cases to free dialogue for both a wider participation and a more lively engagement, as is shown by new institutions, such as the Global Christian Forum, and new tendencies, such as Receptive Ecumenism. Nevertheless, an ecumenism without the ultimate goal of unity would be an ecumenism that has forgotten the scandal that originally called forth ecumenism. If ecumenism were to give up that goal, something else would have to take it up.

For all their real similarities, ecumenical and interreligious dialogue are distinct, and neither is served is by confusing the two.

Conclusion

The Second Vatican Council broke new ground in both ecumenism and interreligious relations, following a similar logic of supplementing nonscalar, all-or-nothing categories with scalar, more-or-less categories. Nevertheless, when these same categories are applied to the different realities of the diversity of religions and the diversity of Christian communities, they produce not only similar judgments but also, on some topics, different kinds of judgments. The diversity of distinct religions that cannot with integrity live as one faith presents a different set of conceptual and practical challenges than does the diversity of distinct Christian communities, all claiming to be genuine realizations of the one Church of Christ, which nevertheless cannot live in communion one with another. As a result, ecumenical and interreligious dialogues have overlapping but not identical goals. Ecumenical dialogue is focused and perhaps constrained by the intra-Christian concern for a common life in Christ that should unite all those united with him in faith and baptism. In a sense, interreligious dialogue is more open-ended. Ecumenical and interreligious dialogues can learn from each other, but each will flourish when the specific character of each is preserved.

Part II

Asian Religions

The Catholic Church rejects nothing that is true and holy in these religions. She regards with sincere reverence those ways of acting and of living, those precepts and teachings which, though differing in many aspects from the one she holds and sets forth, nonetheless often reflect a ray of that truth which enlightens all.

—*Nostra Aetate* 2, trans. Thomas F. Stransky, CSP

Nostra Aetate and Pope Francis: Reflections on the Next Fifty Years of Catholic Dialogue with Buddhists

JAMES L. FREDERICKS

In this, the fiftieth year of *Nostra Aetate*, Pope Francis has called for a new form of interreligious dialogue: a dialogue of fraternity. In the final paragraph of *Nostra Aetate* 2, the declaration famously exhorts Catholics to engage those who follow other religious paths in "dialogue and collaboration" (*per colloquia et collaborationem*). In his call for a dialogue of fraternity, Francis is teaching us that the Church's ministry of interreligious dialogue only begins with theological exchange. After learning about our dialogue partners and coming to hold them and all that is "true and holy" in their religions in esteem, our dialogues fulfill their true purpose in collaborative efforts in the service of peace and justice.[1] This is what Francis means in calling us to a dialogue of fraternity as we begin the next fifty years of *Nostra Aetate*.

The impact this dialogue will have on the Church and on our dialogue partners is yet unclear, although Catholics and their friends who follow other religious paths are already in the process of putting such a dialogue into effect. In this essay, I offer some reflections on the roots of the pope's vision of interreligious dialogue, with special attention paid to our dialogue with Buddhists. In addition, I want to speculate, with the help of some of my Buddhist friends, on the basis within Buddhist tradition that might allow those who follow the Buddha's teaching to respond in depth to the pope's invitation. To accomplish these ends, I propose to do three things in this essay. First, I will offer an evaluation of our dialogues with Buddhists since the promulgation of *Nostra Aetate*. Second, I will investigate the roots of Francis's notion of fraternity in the teachings of Pope John Paul II. Third, I want to reflect on how Buddhists might respond to the invitation to engage in a dialogue of fraternity based on resources supplied by their own religious tradition.

---

1. See Pope Francis's comments on interreligious dialogue in his apostolic exhortation, *Evangelii Gaudium* 250.

Part One: Previous Dialogues with Buddhists

Jan van Bragt (1928–2007), who was at the center of Catholic engagement with Buddhism in Japan since the promulgation of *Nostra Aetate*,
made an insightful observation to me some years ago. Van Bragt said that,
in the case of Buddhism and Catholic Christianity, never were there two
religions so distantly separated by doctrine and yet so intimately related by
religious practice. Van Bragt's observation captures rather well the character of Buddhist-Catholic dialogue over the last fifty years.

Not surprisingly, since the promulgation of *Nostra Aetate*, a good deal
of Buddhist-Catholic dialogue has taken place through the good services
of monastics, Catholic and Buddhist, on matters of religious practice, or on
what Catholics more commonly refer to as *spirituality* and *asceticism*. The
efforts of the international Monastic Interreligious Dialogue, under the
guidance of Benedictines like Pierre-François de Béthune, William Skud-
larek, James A. Wiseman, Pascaline Coff, and Mary Margaret Funk, have
been complemented by the work of Buddhist monastics, not the least of
which is the Dalai Lama and Thich Nhat Hanh. The interfaith work of
these Buddhists and Catholics has borne fruit not only in the multiple
intermonastic exchanges (in which Buddhist and Catholic monks live for
a time in one another's monasteries) but also in meetings similar to the one
held in the Abbey of Our Lady of Gethsamani in 1996.[2] Since the promulgation of *Nostra Aetate*, Catholics have been engaged in a particularly
intense way by the various Zen lineages of Mahayana Buddhism in Japan.
Catholics like Robert Kennedy, SJ, Ruben and Maria Reis Habito, and J.
K. Kadowaki, SJ,[3] who have trained in Zen with Yamada Koun Roshi of
the Sanbō Kyōdan community in Kamakura, have made a remarkable contribution to Catholic spirituality.

Somewhat paradoxically, during this same fifty years, an equal amount
of dialogue among Buddhist and Catholics has been pursued by theologians and dharma teachers on the subtleties of doctrine. The appeal of
intermonastic dialogue, for both Buddhists and Catholics, lies in the
remarkably mutual concerns of monks and nuns who live the vowed life in
religious community. The dialogue of theologians and dharma teachers, in
contrast, rests in no small way on the remarkable differences that separate

---

2. The papers given at this historic meeting have been published in *The Gethsemani
Encounter: A Dialogue on the Spiritual Life by Buddhist and Christian Monastics*, ed. Donald
Mitchell and James K. Wiseman (New York: Continuum Publishing, 1999).

3. Robert Kennedy, SJ, *Zen Gifts to Christians* (New York: Continuum Publishing,
2004); Ruben Habito, *Zen and the Spiritual Exercises* (New York: Orbis Books, 2013); J. K.
Kadowaki, *Zen and the Bible* (Maryknoll, N.Y.: Orbis Books, 2014).

Buddhism and Christianity. Compared to the dialogue of monastics, the dialogue of experts has been painfully slow. This should not be taken as an indication that the comparisons of Buddhist and Christian teachings yield sheer difference. On the contrary, my point is that the often-astounding differences in doctrine have made dialogue with Buddhists particularly attractive to not a few Catholic theologians.

In addition, in the last fifty years of the dialogue of experts, Buddhist-Christian dialogue has had more appeal to Christian theologians than to Buddhist dharma teachers.[4] Reasons for this asymmetry certainly must include the theological component of Christianity's missionary effort. I also think it fair to say that most Catholic theologians, since the Second Vatican Council's call for an *aggiornamento*, have moved beyond their confinement in an inward-looking neo-scholasticism to embrace more correlational methods for doing theology. This can be seen in theological movements as diverse as the liberation theology and biblical scholarship. The correlational impetus of post-conciliar Catholic theology's engagement with Buddhist doctrine can be seen in the work of comparative theologians like Leo Lefebure, Don Mitchell, and me.[5] In contrast, very few Buddhist teachers in Asia have adopted correlationist methods for thinking about the dharma. This is somewhat the case with dharma teachers in the Buddhist diaspora in North America, Europe, and other parts of the world. This state of affairs is reflected in various Buddhist calls for a Buddhist theology in which "theology" is understood as a correlationist enterprise. In theory, at least, a Buddhist theology would be more supple in developing a revisionist understanding of its tradition in response to an encounter with Christianity.[6] Of course, *Nostra Aetate*'s call for dialogue and collaboration must be recognized, in no small way, as a motivation for Catholic theological engagement with Buddhists.

Van Bragt's insight into Buddhism and Christianity goes a long way in accounting for the twofold character of Catholic dialogue with Buddhists since the promulgation of *Nostra Aetate*. Now, Pope Francis is call-

---

4. For a reflection on this state of affairs by an American Buddhist, see Grace G. Burford, "Asymmetry, Essentialism, and Covert Cultural Imperialism: Should Buddhists and Christians Do Theoretical Work Together?" in *Buddhist-Christian Studies* 31 (2011): 147–57.

5. Leo Lefebure, *Life Transformed: Meditations on the Christian Scriptures in Light of Buddhist Perspectives* (Chicago: Acta Publications, 1997); Donald Mitchell, *Spirituality and Emptiness: The Dynamics of Spiritual Life in Buddhism and Christianity* (Mahwah, N.J.: Paulist Press, 1991); James L. Fredericks, *Buddhists and Christians: Through Comparative Theology to a New Solidarity* (New York: Orbis Books, 2004).

6. For a collection of essays reflecting on the prospect of a Buddhist theology, see Roger Jackson and John Makransky, eds., *Buddhist Theologies: Critical Reflections by Contemporary Buddhist Scholars* (London: Routledge, 2013).

ing for a new kind of dialogue that will take us beyond the parameters currently established by the arduousness of doctrinal dialogue and the relative ease of monastic dialogue.

Part Two: The Meaning of *Fraternity* in the Work of Pope Francis

Although it has not been given the attention that "culture of encounter"[7] has received, the principle of *fraternity*, as it is being developed in the documents of Pope Francis, can also claim to be a central theme in his teaching. *Fraternidad* and its adjectival cognates appear nine times in the Spanish version of *Laudato Si* and no less than nineteen times in the Spanish version of *Evangelii Gaudium*.[8] So far, however, the most extensive treatment Francis has given to this theme is in the 2014 "Message for the World Day of Peace," wherein *fraternidad* and its cognates appear no less than forty-eight times in a relatively short text.[9] Based on an analysis of the 2014 message, I will argue the following: "Fraternity" in the magisterium of Pope Francis is an appropriation of the principle of "solidarity" as it is articulated in the encyclical letter *Sollicitudo Rei Socialis* (1987), of John Paul II.

Sollicitudo Rei Socialis is a reflection on the moral demands of globalization that takes as its starting point Paul VI's landmark encyclical on the relationship between developed and developing nations, *Populorum Progressio* (1967). In an extended "survey of the contemporary world,"[10] John Paul reflects on the phenomenon of globalization under the rubric of "interdependence."

> At the same time, in a world divided and beset by every type of conflict, the conviction is growing of a radical interdependence and consequently of the need for a solidarity which will take up interdependence and transfer it to the moral plane. Today perhaps more than in the past, people are realizing that they are linked together by a common destiny, which is to

---

7. Richard Gaillardetz, "A Culture of Encounter: Francis Wishes to Release Vatican II's Bold Vision from Captivity," in *National Catholic Reporter* 50, no. 1 (October 11–24, 2013), cited at 9.

8. They appear six times in *Lumen Fidei*, all but one in the latter part of the text. The origin of the phrase "fraternal dialogue" may actually be *Nostra Aetate* itself, where, in section 4 of the declaration, the Council fathers called for "fraternal dialogues" (*fraternis colloquiis*) with Jews, which, along with biblical and theological studies, promote "mutual understanding and respect."

9. Pope Francis, "Message of His Holiness Francis for the Celebration of the World Day of Peace," January 1, 2014, http://w2.vatican.va/content/francesco/en/messages/peace/documents/papa-francesco_20131208_messaggio-xlvii-giornata-mondiale-pace-2014.html.

10. John Paul II, *Sollicitudo Rei Socialis* (1987): 11–26.

be constructed together, if catastrophe for all is to be avoided. From the depth of anguish, fear and escapist phenomena like drugs, typical of the contemporary world, the idea is slowly emerging that the good to which we are all called and the happiness to which we aspire cannot be obtained without an effort and commitment on the part of all, nobody excluded, and the consequent renouncing of personal selfishness.[11]

The cautious message of hope sounded here by John Paul is noteworthy. The modern world may be beset by a multitude of social, economic, and political problems, but an increasing sense of interdependence brings with it an emerging awareness of the need for solidarity among the peoples of the world.

Starting in section 35 of *Sollicitudo Rei Socialis*, John Paul develops his view of interdependence by providing a theological reading of it. He begins by asserting that social, political, and economic problems have an ethical dimension. This being the case, policies for addressing obstacles to the development of nations require moral discernment. The problems attending globalization are the result of a "moral evil" in which the "fruit of many sins" leads to the construction of "structures of sin." Then, John Paul quickly clarifies the practical purpose of this theological reading of the interdependence of people today: "To diagnose the evil in this way is to identify precisely, on the level of human conduct, the path to be followed in order to overcome it." The path John Paul has in mind involves personal conversion in the biblical sense of *metanoia*. This conversion is in response to the "demand of God's will," which is "the only true foundation of an absolutely binding ethic."[12]

In section 38e and 38f of *Sollicitudo Rei Socialis*, John Paul makes an important connection between our interdependence and "the virtue of solidarity." Above all, John Paul writes, we must learn how to think rightly about the fact of our increasing interdependence. Today, the interdependence of human beings is taking form as a global system with social, cultural, political, economic, and religious aspects. In keeping with the argument he has developed in the preceding sections of the encyclical, John Paul teaches that this interdependence must be seen as a "moral category."

When interdependence is recognized as a moral demand that confronts us all, our response to this challenge cannot be limited to "a feeling of vague compassion or shallow distress at the misfortunes of so many people, both near and far." Rather, what is required is "a firm and persevering determination to commit oneself to the common good; that is to say to the good of

---

11. *Sollicitudo Rei Socialis* 26e.
12. *Sollicitudo Rei Socialis* 38.

all and of each individual, because we are all really responsible for all." This commitment to the common good in response to the fact of our interdependence is what John Paul calls "the virtue of solidarity."

Human fraternity, as Pope Francis develops it in his 2014 "Message for the World Day of Peace," is an appropriation of John Paul's virtue of solidarity. There are several factors that point to this conclusion. Section 1 of the 2014 Message, for example, takes note of the "irrepressible longing for fraternity which draws us to fellowship with others and enables us to see them not as enemies or rivals, but as brothers and sisters to be accepted and embraced." He goes on to observe that this "fraternity is an essential human quality, for we are relational beings" and that "without fraternity it is impossible to build a just society and a solid and lasting peace." Then Francis comments on the "ever-increasing number of interconnections and communications in today's world" that make us "powerfully aware of the unity and common destiny of the nations." This language is clearly reminiscent of *Sollicitudo Rei Socialis* 26e, where John Paul observes that "the conviction is growing of a radical interdependence" and that "people are realizing that they are linked together by a common destiny." In response to this growing awareness, both Pope Francis and Pope John Paul recognize a need for solidarity among peoples. Francis goes on to claim that in this emergent awareness of interdependence "we see the seeds of a vocation to form a community composed of brothers and sisters who accept and care for one another." The pope laments the fact that "this vocation is frequently denied and ignored" in a world marked by "the globalization of indifference."

The point to be taken from all this is that Francis's "vocation to form a community composed of brothers and sisters" (i.e., this vocation of fraternity) corresponds to John Paul's "virtue of solidarity." John Paul employs the language of political science (interdependence) and of Christian ethics (virtue). Francis, without abandoning John Paul's language, appropriates John Paul's teaching on interdependence and solidarity with the pastoral language of Christian spirituality (vocation).

This distinction, however, can easily be overdrawn. An anticipation of Francis' understanding of fraternity as "vocation" can be found in John Paul's treatment of solidarity. This fact also supports the conclusion that the notion of "fraternity" grows out of "solidarity." In *Sollicitudo Rei Socialis* 40, John Paul connects his notion of solidarity with Christian discipleship. Solidarity is intimately connected with the practice of charity, "which is the distinguishing mark of Christ's disciples."[13] John Paul connects the virtue

13. Cf. Jn 13:35.

of solidarity to Christian discipleship. Francis, in appropriating the notion of solidarity, turns to the language of "vocation" in explaining what he means by fraternity.

Francis's appropriation of the virtue of solidarity can also be seen in the proximity of these two terms in the 2014 Message. For example, in section 1, Francis observes that "globalization . . . makes us neighbours, but does not make us brothers."[14] Since this is the case, "The many situations of inequality, poverty and injustice, are signs not only of a profound lack of *fraternity*, but also of the absence of a culture of *solidarity*" (emphasis added). To give another example, in section 4, Francis turns to *Populorum Progressio* of Paul VI and to *Sollicitudo Rei Socialis*, where John Paul discusses the principle of solidarity. These social encyclicals, Francis comments, "can be very helpful" in understanding how fraternity is "the *foundation* and *pathway* of peace" (emphasis in original). From this he concludes that peace is an *opus solidaritatis* and that "fraternity is its principal foundation." Also in section 4, Francis claims that our obligations to one another are rooted in "human and supernatural fraternity." This "spirit of fraternity" places on those who are privileged the duties of social justice and universal charity and also "the duty of solidarity." The proximity of these two terms in the 2014 Message makes them seem, at times, almost interchangeable.

There is yet another basis for affirming the kinship of fraternity and solidarity in Francis's thought. In *Sollicitudo Rei Socialis* 40, John Paul states that solidarity is "undoubtedly a Christian virtue." Guided by Christian faith, "solidarity seeks to go beyond itself" and to take on the specifically Christian characteristics of "total gratuity, forgiveness and reconciliation." Viewed through the lens of Christian faith, the practice of solidarity leads us to recognize that our neighbor is not only a human being with rights and equality but also "the living image of God the Father, redeemed by the blood of Christ and placed under the permanent action of the Holy Spirit." Thus, the fulfillment of the virtue of solidarity in Christian discipleship will bring about "a new model of the unity of the human race."

Francis understands fraternity in theistic terms as well. Turning to the New Testament in section 3 of the 2014 Message, Francis cites Mt 23:8–9, "For you have only one Father, who is God, and you are all brothers and sisters." The ultimate basis of fraternity, therefore, is to be found in God's fatherhood, which is a fatherhood that "effectively generates fraternity, because the love of God, once welcomed, becomes the most formidable means of transforming our lives and relationships with others, opening us

---

14. Francis cites Benedict XVI, *Caritatis in Veritate*, Encyclical Letter, June 29, 2009, par. 19.

to solidarity and to genuine sharing." Similarly, the vocation of fraternity requires a knowledge of divine providence. In section 2 of the 2014 Message, Francis writes, "To understand more fully this human vocation to fraternity, to recognize more clearly the obstacles standing in the way of its realization and to identify ways of overcoming them, it is of primary importance to let oneself be led by knowledge of God's plan, which is presented in an eminent way in sacred Scripture."

Finally, as is the case with the virtue of solidarity, there is a Christological dimension to human fraternity as well. In section 3 of the 2014 Message, Francis teaches that fraternity is revealed in a paramount way in the death and resurrection of Christ. The cross of Christ is the "definitive *foundational* locus" of human fraternity that human beings cannot supply for themselves. Christ has become a "*definitive and new principle* of us all," for in Christ we have all become "brothers and sisters." This text in the 2014 Message can be compared to a passage in section 40 of *Sollicitudo Rei Socialis* where John Paul writes of the "brotherhood of all in Christ" in whom we have an "awareness of the common fatherhood of God." Solidarity and fraternity, as specifically Christian practices, lead us beyond natural bonds based on political and social commitments to "a new model of the unity of the human race."

Part Three: Implications for a Dialogue of Fraternity with Buddhists

Francis, in calling for a dialogue of fraternity, is emphasizing *Nostra Aetate*'s call for cooperation as the logical step beyond dialogues focused on theological and monastic exchanges. But cooperative efforts on the part of Buddhists and Catholics aimed at promoting justice and resisting the structural and social causes of suffering cannot rest on Christian belief in God as the one Father of all. The theistic and, indeed, specifically Christological foundation and fulfillment of fraternity have implications for any dialogue of fraternity with Buddhists that is to lead to cooperative *praxis*. Monotheism, let alone Christology, cannot serve as a common language in a dialogue with Buddhists based on fraternity.

If Christians and Buddhists are to pursue a dialogue of fraternity as we begin the next fifty years of *Nostra Aetate*, perhaps the first item for discussion should be concerned with a Buddhist understanding of what Francis calls fraternity and with how Buddhist practitioners might contribute to such a dialogue. Is there a specifically Buddhist basis for something like what Francis means by "fraternity"? If so, what would a dialogue of fraternity look like from a Buddhist perspective?

At Castel Gandolfo, during the initial dialogue of fraternity with Buddhists in June 2015, I pointed out the roots of fraternity in Catholic social teachings. Several of the Buddhist participants responded informally to my comments, saying there is really no equivalent to the Roman Catholic social teachings in their religious tradition. The "engaged Buddhism" of the Vietnamese monk and social activist Thich Nhat Han and other Buddhists has been compared with the theology of liberation and the social gospel in Christian tradition.[15] But a developed set of social teachings, understood as a comprehensive vision of the human person in society, as well as the ethical responsibilities of individuals, groups, and governments as they relate to economics and political life, has yet to be articulated by Buddhists, either in Asia or in the Western Buddhist community.

This case is somewhat overstated. Theravada, Mahayana, and Vajrayana forms of Buddhism have contributed to social order and social solidarity in regions of Asia, however ambiguously, for many hundreds of years. Since the time of Emperor Ashoka (304–232 B.C.) and before, Buddhists have been reflecting on the responsibilities of kings and their subjects to the good of society.[16] In the 20th century, public intellectuals, like the Thai monks Buddhadāsa Bhikkhu (1906–1993) and more recently Phra Dhammapidok (b. 1938)[17] have produced significant writings on politics, economics, society, and ethics.

Buddhadāsa was one of the most important monastic reformers in the history of Thailand. As if this were not enough, he wrote voluminously on social ethics as well. His program for social ethics, what he calls "dhammic socialism," is a comprehensive view of the human person, society, the state, and the development of public policy with deep roots in the worldview of Theravada Buddhism.[18] Dhammic socialism has been praised as an indigenously Thai and authoritatively Buddhist critique of consumerism, colonialism, Marxism, and capitalism—to say nothing of the exploitation of women and children in Thailand's notorious sex industry, political corruption, and the influence of the military in Thai politics. Buddhadāsa's thought has also been criticized as idealistic, nostalgic, unworkable, and, in

---

15. For a useful introduction to engaged Buddhism in an Asian context, see Christopher S. Queen and Sallie B. King, eds., *Engaged Buddhism: Buddhist Liberation Movements in Asia* (Albany: State University of New York Press, 1996).

16. See *inter alia*, the *Kutadanta Sutta* on economic development as an antidote to crime, and the *Cakkavatti Sihananda Sutta* on the origins of immorality and crime in poverty.

17. This monk has received multiple titles in recognition of his contributions to Thai society. He is also known as Phra Prayudh Payutto.

18. Buddhadāsa Bhikkhu, *Dhammic Socialism,* trans. and ed. Donald K. Swearer (Bangkok: Thai Interreligious Commission for Development, 1986). For a French translation of Swearer's English text, see Buddhadāsa Bhikkhu, *Bouddhisme et socialisme*, trans. Marie-Charlotte Grandre (Paris: Deux Océans, 1987).

some important aspects, antidemocratic.[19] However, several Buddhists, all familiar with Pope Francis's social thought, have suggested dhammic socialism as a starting point for a Buddhist response to Francis's invitation to a dialogue of fraternity. I will offer only a sketch of Buddhadāsa's program for a Buddhist social ethics with the aim of pointing out how dhammic socialism might serve as a starting place for Buddhist engagement with Catholics in a dialogue of fraternity.[20]

Dhamma is the Pali equivalent of the Sanskrit word *dharma*, which normally refers to the teaching of the Buddha. In this case, *dhamma* means "the way things really are" or "the way in which phenomena naturally arise." The Thai word translated into English as *socialism* is *sungkomniyom*, which is derived from *sangha* (community) and *niyom* (restraint and patience).[21] Thus, *socialism*, as it is used by Buddhadāsa, has a different meaning than is usually associated with this word in the political discourse of the West. Rather than government control of institutions and companies that would be in the private sphere in liberal political economies, for Buddhadāsa, socialism refers to what is essentially a Buddhist practice of restraint or nonattachment and compassionate action by individuals for the benefit and welfare of the greater community. Dhammic socialism, therefore, brings with it important implications for social action by Buddhists and the development of public policy.[22]

Dhammic socialism is based on a type of natural law theory in a way that is both similar and different when compared with Catholic social teachings.[23] In Buddhadāsa's view, the entire universe is unified by the intimate interdependence of all things. Events transpire by means of what

19. For a critique of dhammic socialism, see Tavivat Puntarigyivat, "Dhammic Socialism: Political Thought of Buddhadāsa Bhikkhu," in *The Chulalongkorn Journal of Buddhist Studies* 2, no. 2 (2003): 189–207.

20. For Buddhadāsa's engagement of Christianity, see Donald K. Swearer, "The Ecumenical Vision of Buddhadāsa Bhikkhu and His Dialogue with Christianity" in *Buddhist Studies from India to America: Essays in Honor of Charles S. Prebish*, 270–85 (London: Routledge, 2006).

21. Buddhadāsa Bhikkhu, *Dhammic Socialism*, trans. and ed. Donald K. Swearer (Bangkok: Thai Interreligious Commission for Development, 1986), 14. For a comparative study of Buddhadāsa and a Roman Catholic engaged in the work of social justice with Buddhists in Sri Lanka, see In-gun Kang, *Buddhist-Christian Dialogue and Action in the Theravada Countries of Modern Asia: A Comparative Analysis of the Radical Orthopraxis of Bhikkhu Buddhadāsa and Aloysius Pieris* (London: Heythrop College, Doctoral Dissertation, 2012).

22. Donald K. Swearer, *Me and Mine: Selected Essays by Bhikkhu Buddhadasa*, 182–93 (Albany: State University of New York Press, 1989).

23. Sallie B. King, "From Is to Ought: Natural Law in Buddhadāsa Bhikku and Phra Prayudh Payyuto," in *Journal of Religious Ethics*, 3, no. 2 (2002): 275–93.

he calls a "socialist system." This can be seen, in a paramount way, in the harmonious ordering of the natural world where planets "are not so crazy to crash into one another." Human beings, in contrast, "are so crazy they bite each other and clash with each other because they adhere to an unrighteous (non-Dhammic) socialism, one that is not right according to the standards of nature, and do not know the truths of nature."[24]

Let me offer two observations. First, unlike the social teachings of the Catholic Church, Buddhadāsa's view of natural law appeals to a Buddhist, not an Aristotelian, metaphysics. Especially important in this regard is the law of causality as articulated in early Buddhist texts. All phenomena arise by means of the principle of dependent origination (*paṭiccasamuppāda*). When a certain set of causes are in place, a corresponding phenomenon arises. When these causes are no longer in place, the phenomenon ceases to exist. In consequence, nothing is either absolute or eternal. Nothing exists of itself, independently of causes that themselves have causes. Since this is the case, all things arise in the form of an interrelated, ever-changing, and harmonious whole. Therefore, the word *socialism* (*sungkomniyom*) for Buddhadāsa indicates the interdependence of all things on other things in the continuous arising of a community of beings.

Second, in keeping with the notion of natural law, dhammic socialism, as Buddhadāsa conceives of it, is not a human invention. This, too, is consonant with natural law theory in Catholic social teachings. Socialism is the natural state of the world that can be discerned with the proper use of reason. In a much quoted passage, Buddhadāsa writes: "Look at birds: they consume only as much as their stomachs can hold. They cannot take in more than that. They have no granaries for hoarding."[25] Rational reflection on the natural environment, in contrast to the unnatural world of human society, will reveal an original, "natural" law of harmony and restraint. Socialism is the human practice of harmony and restraint in keeping with the law of nature.

A number of implications for Buddhist engagement with Francis's notion of human fraternity flow from this. First, based as it is on the natural law of dependent origination, dhammic socialism has no difficulty in affirming, along with Catholic social teachings, the innate sociality of the human person. The Church's social teachings emphasize that human beings are naturally social and interdependent, not autonomous, and that human fulfillment and flourishing necessarily entails social existence.[26] The innate sociality of the human person should be taken as a background

24. *Dhammic Socialism*, 117–18.
25. *Dhammic Socialism*, 65–66.
26. Vatican Council II, *Gaudium et Spes*, December 7, 1965, par. 25.

concept to Francis's understanding of fraternity. Human fraternity is a concrete actualization of our sociality. The same must be said, of course, for any exercise of the virtue of solidarity. For Buddhadāsa, the assertion of autonomy by the individual is a sign of defilement (*klesha*) and a violation of the natural law of socialism. In accordance with the nature of all things, human beings are innately interconnected and interdependent with all other human beings. Thus, dhammic socialism provides a way for Buddhists to respond to Francis's notion of fraternity. As a pastoral practice, human fraternity implies that human beings—no matter how separated they may be by geography, economic resources, cultural outlook, or social class—can work together for the common good. The basis for this solidarity can be found in the innate sociality of the human person.

Second, the human sociality implicit in Buddhadāsa's natural law includes the interdependence of all phenomena, not just human persons. Seen from Buddhadāsa's perspective, human fraternity expands to include a fraternity of all beings, both sentient and inanimate. The world of human culture cannot be seen as something qualitatively separate from the natural world. Both are governed by the natural law of dependent origination. Human beings, therefore, naturally enjoy a radical intimacy with their environment.[27] This augurs well for a dialogue of fraternity with Buddhists regarding *Laudato Si*, Francis's encyclical on the environment, which he calls repeatedly "our common home."[28] In fact, some of the Buddhists who participated in the initial dialogue of fraternity at Castel Gandolfo have already proposed joint Catholic-Buddhist reading groups on the new encyclical.

Third, Buddhadāsa's dhammic socialism has a robust sense of the common good. This constitutes yet another convergence of his social ethics on the concept of fraternity. For Francis, the aim of the fraternal cooperation of individuals, groups, and nations is to promote the common good of their shared community. Social problems cannot be addressed apart from fraternal cooperation in seeking the common good. In section 8 of the 2014 Message, he states that fraternity "creates a balance between freedom and justice, between personal responsibility and solidarity, between the good of individuals and the common good." Buddhadāsa takes a similar position: "In a society that puts the interests of any one individual above those of the community, social problems cannot be addressed."[29] As

27. For a discussion of Buddhadāsa's view of environmental ethics, see Donald K. Swearer, "The Hermeneutics of Buddhist Ecology in Contemporary Thailand: Buddhadāsa and Dhammapitaka," in *Buddhism and Ecology: The Interconnection of Dharma and Deeds*, 21–44 (Cambridge, Mass.: Harvard University Press, 1997).

28. The subtitle of the encyclical is "On Care for Our Common Home."

29. *Dhammic Socialism*, 59.

is the case with Catholic social teachings, Buddhadāsa believes that the *ultimate* good of the individual does not conflict with the good of all. Thus, socialism, as Buddhadāsa uses the word, is to be distinguished from individualism in its various forms, including its modern Western form.

Fourth, Catholics who have gathered with their Buddhist friends for a dialogue of fraternity might explore Catholic commitment to the "preferential option for the poor"[30] in light of Buddhadāsa's dhammic socialism. Buddhadāsa believes that public policy and individual behavior should be based not on the attachments and immediate desires of the individual but on what he calls "social preference" in contrast to "individual presence." On the one hand, social preference refers to activities that promote the common good.[31] But beyond this, Buddhadāsa's notion of social preference may have positive correlations with the preferential option in Catholic social teaching. If this should prove to be the case, then here again is yet another positive correspondence between Francis's understanding of fraternity as a pastoral realization of the virtue of solidarity and Buddhadāsa's agenda for a Buddhist social ethics. Speaking from the Catholic side of the conversation, I am interested in more than whether or not a Buddhist preferential option for the social and a Catholic preferential option for the poor converge on one another. Catholics should explore, together with their Buddhist friends, how these preferential options can become a concrete praxis for realizing the common good in a world governed by an economics of winners and losers.

Fifth, Buddhadāsa promotes dhammic socialism as an alternative to both Marxist class struggle and the acquisitive individualism of neo-liberalism. Once again, the affinity of Buddhadāsa with certain themes in Catholic social teachings suggests ways in which Buddhists can affirm the principle of fraternity in the thought of Pope Francis. In regard to neo-liberal economics, the natural socialism of all phenomena, as argued by Buddhadāsa, contrasts starkly with the "war of all against all" and unrestrained freedoms envisioned by Thomas Hobbes in the "state of nature." For Hobbes, government is the result of a limited social contract entered into by unrestrained human beings for their own protection. The state, as constituted contractually, is responsible for the protection of life, the personal freedoms of the individual, and private property. For Buddhadāsa, human law is proceeded not by chaotic freedom but, rather, by the natural law of harmony and interdependence. Genuine human freedom and flourishing can only be found in what Buddhadāsa calls "social practice."

---

30. For John Paul II on the preferential option for the poor, see *Centesimus Annus*, Encyclical Letter, May 1, 1991, par. 57.

31. *Dhammic Socialism*, 95.

Buddhadāsa is also critical of Marxist totalitarianism. Marx placed his confidence in the empowerment of the working class and party control over civil society. The dialectical materialism of Marx's scientific socialism, however, is far removed from the Buddhist vision of interdependence that underlies dhammic socialism. From Buddhadāsa's perspective, Marx's class struggle is not in keeping with the natural socialism of all things. Once again, genuine human freedom and flourishing can only be found in social practice, but not of a totalitarian kind. Catholic social teachings, as they have developed since Leo XIII, are likewise critical of both totalitarian collectivism and laissez-faire economics.[32] Francis's "fraternity" and its relationship with John Paul's "solidarity" should be understood within this context.

There are a number of points on which Buddhadāsa and Catholic social teachings may be at odds. This state of affairs augurs well for a rewarding dialogue. Of salient importance is the question of human dignity. Time and again, in the social teachings of the Church, including the writing of Pope Francis on fraternity, the innate and inalienable dignity of the human person is based on the theological affirmation that every person is created in the image and likeness of the living God and redeemed through the death and resurrection of Christ. The theology of the human person as *imago dei*, however, is utterly foreign to Buddhism, which is silent regarding the existence of God and the soul. Instead of belief in an immortal soul, Buddhists hold up the teaching of the nonself (*anatta/anatman*). Of all the basic teachings of Buddhism, certainly this teaching must be counted among the least accessible to those who do not practice the Buddhist path. Explanations of this traditional teaching vary widely among Buddhist teachers today and in the past. For present purposes, let me observe that Buddhist rejection of the existence of an enduring self or soul makes a Buddhist affirmation of human dignity problematic. This, of course, is not to suggest that Buddhists do not recognize the human person as a reality that places absolute moral demands on us. However, the doctrine of the nonself, in fact, does form the basis of a widespread skepticism among Buddhist intellectuals about the appropriateness of human rights as a way of addressing social ills. Like Catholic social teachings, Buddhadāsa has much to say in regard to our responsibilities to others and society at large. As one would expect of a Buddhist, he articulates a virtue ethics of compassion and selflessness. However, in keeping with his Buddhist virtue ethics, Buddhadāsa finds the language of human rights uncongenial for

---

32. The moral inadequacy of both Marxism and neo-liberal capitalism is a major theme of *Centesimus Annus*.

addressing social problems. Human rights are about the assertion of a self to which rights accrue. Buddhism is about compassion born of selflessness, not the assertion of self and the rights that this self can legitimately demand.[33] Buddhist reticence on the question of human rights language becomes all the more interesting when we take note of the fact that, in the case of Buddhism, rights language is looked on with suspicion because Buddhist ethics is a virtue ethics. Catholic social teachings, like Buddhism, is a virtue ethics. How can it be that many Buddhists promote virtues like compassion in lieu of rights, while Catholics, in addition to their own virtue ethics, embrace rights?

Conclusion

Pope Francis's call for a dialogue of fraternity has deep roots in the social teachings of the Church, especially the principle of solidarity in the teachings of John Paul II. This means that Buddhists will look to their own tradition for resources in responding to fraternity as the pastoral praxis of the virtue of solidarity. My intention in this essay has not been to give the impression that Buddhadāsa's dhammic socialism is the only resource available to Buddhists in this regard. But many Buddhists will look to Buddhadāsa for guidance in responding to their Catholic friends.

Since the promulgation of *Nostra Aetate*, Francis sees the dialogue of fraternity as a necessary next step in our dialogues with those who follow other religious paths. This new form of dialogue is not intended to supplant the dialogues of theologians and monastics. During the last fifty years, however, Buddhists and Catholics have learned a good deal about one another and, as a result, have come to hold one another in esteem. Now, based on this fraternity, the time has come for Buddhists and Catholics to come together for cooperative efforts to alleviate the suffering that afflicts the global community they share.

---

33. For a discussion of Buddhism and human rights, see Damien Keown, Charles S. Prebish, and Wayne R. Husted, eds., *Buddhism and Human Rights* (Surrey: Curzon Press, 1998).

Nostra Aetate and the Catholic Way of Openness to Other Religions

FRANCIS X. CLOONEY, SJ

For several decades I have devoted myself to the theological study of Hinduism. In various ways, I have been enabled to do this—as a Catholic—because fifty years ago Vatican II opened up a new era in how Catholics and Hindus might relate to one another. The 1965 document *Nostra Aetate* ("In Our Age") looked with attentiveness at Hindu paths of action, wisdom, and love, and stated that, looking beyond Judaism and Islam, the Church "rejects nothing that is true and holy" in Hinduism and other religions: "Indeed, she regards with sincere reverence those ways of conduct and of life, those precepts and teachings which, though differing in many aspects from the ones she holds and sets forth."[1] How can this be? It is because they "by no means rarely reflect the radiance of that Truth which enlightens all people," because, as the Church ever announces, Jesus is "the way, the truth, and the life."[2] From a Catholic perspective, Jesus is radiant and alive in whatever paths lead to God, whatever is true, whatever is alive. The challenge then is getting to a still deeper level in the Catholic understanding of the other religions, including Hindu traditions.

All of these are remarkable claims, yet they are views deeply imbedded in the consciousness of many (though not all) Catholics today. During my four decades of studying Hinduism, I have found the second paragraph of *Nostra Aetate*—henceforth *Nostra Aetate 2*—to be most influential in setting the tone for the Catholic entrance upon interreligious openness and for the study of Hinduism. There is a great deal to learn from *Nostra Aetate* 2, but to understand what we read, we are required to understand *Nostra Aetate* in its contexts, noting what it does and does not say. Its effective meaning lies in the cultivation of a deep openness and attitude of learning. As the following analysis makes clear, dialogue meetings are only a part of what *Nostra Aetate* 2 enables and encourages. Made possible too is a deeper learning, a learning that changes us even apart from the dialogue. This learning is the primary focus of my reflections here. First I offer first a close reading of paragraph 2, the part of *Nostra Aetate* covering "non-Abra-

---

1. *Nostra Aetate* 2, author's translation.
2. Jn 14:6.

hamic" religions and most relevant to the study of Hinduism. I argue that the teaching of *Nostra Aetate* is genuinely open. I then argue that *Nostra Aetate* stands in continuity with tradition and yet, in a particular way, is a strikingly distinctive, even unique, document. Finally, I indicate how *Nostra Aetate*, properly understood, sets a direction in the study of religions and, in this regard, serves very well with respect to Hinduism.[3]

A Reading of *Nostra Aetate* 2

If, for the sake of simplicity and my own competence, we limit our topic to the Catholic engagement with the Hindu traditions, then the question is how this study is to proceed. Since it is not determined by a specific historical situation, many possibilities are open; indeed, understanding what is at stake and possible in Catholic-Hindu studies is hampered, in a way, by the sheer abundance of possibilities ungoverned by any single workable frame to control that plurality. My purpose is to focus on the deep and unrestricted openness of *Nostra Aetate* 2. It is important to understand it properly, without distraction by merely similar matters or by the complications arising in the conflation of multiple documents. If *Nostra Aetate* is seen as doctrine, primarily content, then it will be seen as understated, incomplete, and thus needing to be woven in with an array of other conciliar and ecclesial teachings. It always will be put in its place. If *Nostra Aetate* is read as a work of literature, it will be respected for what it says and how it says it. It will be allowed to stand on its own and respected for its silences, understatedness, and gaps. This is a robust openness, not a phase that is quickly passed through as the openness comes to an end. It is best characterized as an invitation to study. This openness is not by way of a doctrine open to conservative or liberal modifications. *Nostra Aetate* does

---

3. I must highlight two cautions before proceeding further. First, of course, *Nostra Aetate* 2 must be taken in context, studied in light of paragraphs 3–4, where the need to respect the other becomes still more urgent. The teachings on relations with Muslims (par. 3) and Jews (par. 4) are crucial even for our reading of *Nostra Aetate* 2, because they show not only an opening up of a continuing relationship with these two religions but also—for otherwise it would make no sense—a Church ready for dialogue for the long run. How Catholics relate to Hindus and Buddhists must be framed by our relationship to Jews and Muslims; what Jews, Christians, and Muslims learn from Hindus and Buddhists should affect how we relate to one another as well. Second, in these pages I present *Nostra Aetate* 2 as I have read it over the past forty years, noting how it has affected my study of Hinduism. (See also Francis X. Clooney, SJ, "The Study of Non-Christian Religions in the Post-Vatican II Roman Catholic Church," *Journal of Ecumenical Studies* 28, no. 3 (1991): 482–94.) I speak from my own experience and study, not as an ecclesiologist or a historian of the Council. And I certainly cannot speak for or in place of Indian Catholics and Christians, even if I have visited India many times and have many friends there.

not talk *about* salvation, does not judge the religions; rather, it creates a space for engagement and learning. Nor is it "just" dialogue, if that suggests encounters instigated primarily by occasions of formal encounter and diplomatic exchanges without a more regular, ordinary change of way of thinking and acting.

Right from the start, the descriptions are generous and comprehensive, without explicit evaluation. Large commonalities are held up for regard:

> From ancient times down to today, there is found among diverse peoples a certain perception of that hidden power which is present in the course of things and the events of human life, and indeed at times a recognition of a Supreme Power, or even a Father. This perception and recognition penetrate their lives with a deep religious sense. Religions, however, that are bound up with the advance of culture have struggled to answer the same questions by means of subtler concepts and a more developed language.[4]

Nostra Aetate 2 then describes Hinduism, attentively and without criticism:

> Thus in Hinduism, humans examine thoroughly the divine mystery and express it through an inexhaustible abundance of myths and through the acute efforts of philosophy; they seek freedom from the anguish of our condition either through forms of the ascetical life or profound meditation or a flight to God with love and trust.[5]

Buddhism too is given a respectful and positive description:

> In Buddhism, in its various forms, there is realized the radical insufficiency of this changeable world; a way is taught by which humans, in a devout and trusting spirit, may be able either to acquire the state of perfect liberation or, by their own efforts or through higher assistance, attain to supreme illumination.[6]

Both descriptions are minimal, sketches of broader and more complex traditions. Even more sweepingly, still other religions are noted:

> Thus too other religions found throughout the whole world strive to counter by various means the restlessness of the human heart, by putting forth ways, indeed doctrines and rules of life, as well as sacred rites.[7]

We are not meant to settle on these details as sufficient but, rather, to use these broad characterizations as guides to further study. That the religions

---

4. *Nostra Aetate* 2, author's translation.
5. Ibid.
6. Ibid.
7. Ibid.

are described in terms of human effort may by implication be contrasted unfavorably with the emphasis on divine initiative favored in Judaism, Christianity, and Islam. But such an implication is only that, a possible reading. *Nostra Aetate 2* then moves in a different direction, to a very positive affirmation:

> The Catholic Church rejects none of the things that are true and holy in these religions. She regards with sincere attentiveness those ways of acting and living, those precepts and doctrines which, though differing in many aspects from the ones she holds and sets forth, nonetheless by no means rarely reflect the radiance of that Truth which enlightens all people.[8]

This probable allusion to John 1:9 presents Christ as light and truth and through images of radiance and reflection. The explicit statement that follows, drawing specifically on John, likewise serves to undergird and justify, rather than narrow, the reverence with which the Church approaches religious traditions:

> Truly she announces, and ever must announce Christ "the way, the truth, and the life" (John 14:6), in whom humans may find the fullness of religious life, in whom God has reconciled all things to Himself.[9]

Building on the preceding insights and affirmations, enabled by the Church's commitment to the Johannine Jesus, *Nostra Aetate* 2 concludes with an appeal for colloquy and collaboration:

> The Church, therefore, exhorts her children that, with prudence and charity, through talking with and working with the followers of other religions, and witnessing to the Christian faith and life, they recognize, preserve and promote the good things, spiritual and moral, and even the socio-cultural values, found among these people.[10]

---

8. Ibid.

9. Ibid., borrowing from 2 Cor 5: 18–19; I have long thought that Phil 4:8 might well have been cited here: "Finally, beloved, whatever is true, whatever is honorable, whatever is just, whatever is pure, whatever is pleasing, whatever is commendable, if there is any excellence and if there is anything worthy of praise, think about these things." I am grateful to Dr. John Borelli, Georgetown University, for pointing out to me recently that Joseph Neuner's initial draft, the one he returned with to the meeting on October 25, 1964, begins the paragraph after the ones on religions, Hinduism, Buddhism, and Islam, with this sentence: "Ecclesia enim nihil eorum, quae in his religionibus ut vera et sancta sunt reicit (cf. Phil. 4:8)." He then continues, "[Ecclesia] credit enim Deum in Christo mundum sibi reconciliasse (cf. 2 Cor. 5:19)."

10. Author's translation.

Nostra Aetate 2 seems intent on not taking anything back from what is potentially a startlingly deep cooperation. It encourages, even mandates, a deepening of the interreligious learning process because of who Christ is. Specific learning is encouraged. Regarding Hinduism, for example, *Nostra Aetate* 2 sketches what is effectively a detailed list of areas for learning of and from the Hindu traditions: their "thorough examination of the divine mystery," their "inexhaustible abundance of myths," their "acute efforts of philosophy," their "forms of the ascetical life" and "profound meditation," and "a flight to God with love and trust."[11] Though brief, this list charts a wide area for study, topics introduced in a neutral fashion that does not prejudge what is to be learned.

Nostra Aetate 2: In Continuity and Distinct

Because *Nostra Aetate* 2 is consistent with tradition, its novelty is not limited simply to its positive tone. To show this, I now draw on several relevant examples from before and during the Council. A first exemplary document is Pius XII's 1951 *Evangelii Praecones*, in some ways a remarkably forward-looking text. In it Pius asserts that while humanity has fallen due to Adam's sin, "yet it has in itself something that is naturally Christian." This can by grace "eventually be changed into true and supernatural virtue."[12] For this reason, the Church "has neither scorned nor rejected the pagan philosophies. Instead, after freeing them from error and all contamination, she has perfected and completed them by Christian revelation." Similarly, the Church uplifts and perfects native art and culture and gives customs and traditions a new religious significance.[13] The language is positive, as in *Nostra Aetate*, while the mechanics of positive reception found in the former—freeing from error, perfecting, and completing—are not stated in the latter document.[14]

---

11. Ibid.
12. Pius XII, *Evangelii Praecones*, Encyclical Letter, June 2, 1951, par. 57.
13. Evangelii Praecones 58.
14. A large section of paragraph 58 of *Evangelii Praecones* is devoted to a rather beautiful and telling set of analogies. The pagan traditions are like the underlying dye on cloth, background that serves to accentuate the more beautiful dye applied last; they are like the sun's reflection in water, giving us a first sense of the brilliance of the sun; they are like the leaves on a tree, necessary and beautiful, even if not the fruit that is the tree's true glory. Indeed, Moses is evoked as a model: "Thus Moses, a man of the greatest renown for his wisdom, is said to have come to the contemplation of Him, Who is, only after being trained in Egyptian lore," and so too Daniel who learned from the Babylonians. All of these analogies vividly remind us of the positive heritage of the pre–Vatican II Church, and the genuine ways in which the Church sought to affirm non-Christian religions. But we must also note that in every instance Pius is working with a fulfillment model, the correction and perfection of the

My second example is taken from, during the years of the Council, Paul VI's adoption of an open and generous attitude toward the world's religions. At the start of the second session of the Council in 1963, Paul highlighted themes that would become familiar in conciliar and postconciliar statements on other religions. He affirmed that the Church has a universal interest in humans everywhere. The Church "directs her eyes beyond the Christian realm" and looks with interest toward those other religions that have in place certain features of faith: the preservation of a sense and concept of God as one, creator, providential, supreme, and transcending the nature of things; worship of God with acts of sincere piety; and the derivation from these practices and ideas of "precepts of morality and life in society." Paul went on to point out the Church's role as judge and corrector, admonisher, and perfector: "In these religions, the Catholic Church in fact discerns, not without sorrow, gaps, defects, and errors. But she cannot but still turn her mind to them, that she might make them more certain that the Catholic religion with proper respect discovers among them whatever is true, good, and human."[15] While this language of gap, defect, and error does not appear in *Nostra Aetate*, it is interesting that for Paul, noticing these problems enhances rather than undercuts the desire for positive exchange.

In his 1964 encyclical, *Ecclesiam Suam*, Paul first emphasizes the interconnectedness of monotheists—Jewish, Muslim, and Christian—who share in the worship of "the one supreme God." With more caution, he turns then to the "great Afro-Asiatic" religions. He asserts difference and rejects any hint of relativism: "Obviously we cannot agree with these various forms of religion, nor can we adopt an indifferent or uncritical attitude toward them on the assumption that they are all to be regarded as on an equal footing." The members of those religions are obliged to "enquire whether or not God has Himself revealed definitively and infallibly how He wishes to be known, loved, and served." While Catholics honestly and openly declare "our conviction that the Christian religion is the one and only true religion," even so "we do not wish to turn a blind eye to the spiritual and moral values of the various non-Christian religions." Rather, "we desire to join with them in promoting and defending common ideals in the spheres of religious liberty, human brotherhood, education, culture, social

---

non-Christian in the Christian. This framing of the non-Christian as prior, preparatory, and imperfect is largely missing from *Nostra Aetate* 2; only the image of reflected radiance makes its way into the conciliar document. That *Nostra Aetate* is positive toward the religious other is not in itself its distinctive feature; rather, we need also to note what it does not say.

15. Pope Paul VI, "Address at the Opening of the Second Session of the Council," September 29, 1963 (*Acta Apostolicae Sedis* 55 [1963], 858).

welfare, and civic order." The future will be marked by its dialogical commitments: "Dialogue is possible in all these great projects, which are our
concern as much as theirs, and we will not fail to offer opportunities for
discussion in the event of such an offer being favorably received in genuine,
mutual respect."[16] This is very much a near prefiguration of the spirit of
Nostra Aetate 2 even if, in still later documents such as *Evangelii Nuntiandi*
(1975), Paul manifests much greater hesitation.[17]

But we can profitably also consider several of Paul VI's statements on
the religions during his visit to the Eucharistic Congress in Bombay in
December 1964. On December 3, the feast of St. Francis Xavier, he gives
two speeches that quote from Hindu texts. First, at the end of the ordination of new bishops, Paul quotes from the *Mundaka Upanishad*:

> Let your words echo the message of the divine truths, which as through
> a glass, darkly, are evoked by the words adopted by this great nation:
> "Truth alone triumphs,[18] not falsehood. The divine path to liberation has
> been laid with truth, which the seers who have overcome desire tread,
> and wherein also is that supreme treasure to be gained by truth."[19]

The quotation is reverent, but Paul, speaking to his fellow Catholics,
cannot help but state that this occurs only "through a glass, darkly."

Yet on the same day, we find Paul speaking in a quite different context, addressing "the members of the Non-Christian Religions." He again
includes a quote from an Upanishad, this time the ancient *Brhadaranyaka
Upanishad*:

16. Pope Paul VI, *Ecclesiam Suam*, Encyclical Letter, August 6, 1964, par. 107–8.

17. In his *Evangelii Nuntiandi* (1975), Paul speaks positively of the religions in measured terms that in part echo *Nostra Aetate*: "The Church respects and esteems these non-
Christian religions because they are the living expression of the soul of vast groups of people.
They carry within them the echo of thousands of years of searching for God, a quest which
is incomplete but often made with great sincerity and righteousness of heart. They possess an
impressive patrimony of deeply religious texts. They have taught generations of people how
to pray." *Evangelii Nuntiandi* then reverts to an older language: "They are all impregnated
with innumerable 'seeds of the Word' and can constitute a true 'preparation for the Gospel,'
to quote a felicitous term used by the Second Vatican Council and borrowed from Eusebius
of Caesarea" (par. 53). More explicitly than *Nostra Aetate*, he distinguishes the work of the
Gospel from what otherwise can happen in the religions: "In other words, our religion effectively establishes with God an authentic and living relationship which the other religions do
not succeed in doing, even though they have, as it were, their arms stretched out towards
heaven" (par. 53). *Nostra Aetate* neither makes nor denies this kind of claim; it is not about
that kind of measurement but about the learning that can and should take place in the interreligious realm.

18. By 1964, "Truth alone triumphs" had already been adopted as the motto of the government of India.

19. Mundaka Upanishad III.1.5–6.

This visit to India is the fulfilment of a long cherished desire. Yours is a land of ancient culture, the cradle of great religions, the home of a nation that has sought God with a relentless desire, in deep meditation and silence, and in hymns of fervent prayer. Rarely has this longing for God been expressed with words so full of the spirit of Advent as in the words written in your sacred books many centuries before Christ: "From the unreal lead me to the real; from darkness lead me to light; from death lead me to immortality."[20]

Paul's consequent elaboration of the text is very interesting. He says that in a time of historic change, both globally and in India, this is a prayer "which belongs also to our time." It is a prayer that "should rise from every human heart." Given the crises facing all human beings, "we must come closer together, not only through the modern means of communication, through press and radio, through steamships and jet planes—we must come together with our hearts, in mutual understanding, esteem and love. We must meet not merely as tourists, but as pilgrims who set out to find God—not in buildings of stone but in human hearts." That the Upanishad offers a prayer arising from the human heart indicates the way forward, since all of us need to meet heart to heart. There is no language of condescension here or pleading of a Christian distinction but, rather, a simpler plea for all present to hear the Upanishad in their hearts and meet in deep mutual understanding: "Such a union cannot be built on a universal terror or fear of mutual destruction; it must be built on the common love that embraces all and has its roots in God, who is love." This does not change when Paul turns then to reflect in very explicit Christian language on the Eucharist Congress that brought him to India and on the Eucharist as "the commemoration of Jesus Christ and his love for God the Father in heaven, and for all men, a love unto death." Quite directly, he links this love in Christ to the love in every human heart from which arises the prayer of the *Brhadaranyaka Upanishad*: "This love of Jesus is not a matter of the past; it is meant to remain present and to live in every human heart." For Paul, these words of Christian witness are opening up, not closing off, a dialogue grounded in common human needs and in love: "This is the meaning of the Congress: true love must be renewed in our midst and must become the inspiring force of all our efforts. We need peace and stability in our world, we need food, clothing and housing for millions, we need honesty and devotion and untiring work for bettering man's condition, but all these efforts must be animated by true love." Again, these are words uttered and heard in the space of dialogue, where reverence for what is true and holy in

20. Brhadaranyaka Upanishad I.3.28.

Hinduism is not diminished by added observations on natural religion, preparation for the Gospel, or even fullness in Christ.

We can hardly generalize based on just several quotations that in any case are not directly linked to the Council, albeit included in a 1964 speech of the pope. But I suggest that here we see the two sides of what will be the legacy of the Council. The quotation from the *Mundaka Upanishad* is couched in terms that point to fulfillment in Christ. This is in the spirit of the preconciliar documents and *Lumen Gentium* and *Ad Gentes*, with their ample placement of the true and the holy in other religions in the context of the Christian narrative. The *Upanishad* speaks only "through a glass, darkly." By contrast, the *Brhadaranyaka Upanishad* passage, quoted on the same day but in a context of dialogue, bears no "glass darkly" qualification but rather speaks of the origin of such prayers in *every* human heart. This spirit of this manner of speaking will, less than a year later, be formally articulated in *Nostra Aetate* 2.

Among the Council's own documents, *Lumen Gentium*, promulgated already in 1964, is of course key. Paragraph 16 of that document speaks of God's unfailing work for the sake of people in other religions: "Nor does Divine Providence deny the helps necessary for salvation to those who, without blame on their part, have not yet arrived at an explicit knowledge of God and not without divine grace strive to live a good life." This divine activity has an elevating purpose: "Whatever good or truth is found amongst them is looked upon by the Church as a preparation for the Gospel. She knows that it is given by Him who enlightens every person so that he may finally have life." Thus far, very much like *Nostra Aetate*. But the paragraph goes on to say that given the work of the devil in the world, no whole-hearted embrace of these religions is possible; evil is nearby: "But often humans, deceived by the Evil One, have become vain in their reasonings and have exchanged the truth of God for a lie, serving the creature rather than the Creator." Indeed, "some there are who, living and dying in this world without God, are exposed to final despair." Missions are urgently required to counter this evil and despair. The pattern is constant: divine activity has implanted whatever is good and holy in the religions; even if the devil remains at work in other religions, the Church seeks to build on such leads, sifting through the good and the evil in other religions. Such are the judgments on the religions that *Nostra Aetate* chooses not to make.

Even after *Nostra Aetate*, the cautious mix of openness and constraint is evident. Adopted in December 1965,[21] *Ad Gentes* reverts to the more familiar mix of guardedness and openness. In section 1.9, we read of the epiphany

---

21. *Ad Gentes* was promulgated after *Nostra Aetate*, though composed largely before it.

that is missionary activity, God's divine plan working itself out in the world. Indeed, "by the preaching of the word and by the celebration of the sacraments, the center and summit of which is the most holy Eucharist, He brings about the presence of Christ, the author of salvation." There are truth and grace among the pagans, but these riches are still in need of purification: "whatever truth and grace are to be found among the nations, as a sort of secret presence of God, He frees from all taint of evil and restores to Christ its maker, who overthrows the devil's domain and wards off the manifold malice of vice." Due to the Church's work, the good that is present in these religions, in their beliefs and rites, "not only is not lost, but is healed, uplifted, and perfected for the glory of God, the shame of the demon, and the bliss of men."[22] Again, the pattern is clear: *Nostra Aetate*, written and read in the space of dialogue and aiming to open new avenues for learning, simply chooses not to make the negative judgments we find here.

Ad Gentes 1.11 reflects on how valuable it is for non-Christians that Christians should live among them, edifying them and revealing to them the hidden presence of the Word:

> For all Christians, wherever they live, are bound to show forth, by the example of their lives and by the witness of the word, that new man put on at baptism and that power of the Holy Spirit by which they have been strengthened at Confirmation. Thus other men, observing their good works, can glorify the Father and can perceive more fully the real meaning of human life and the universal bond of the community of mankind.

By this loving presence among the pagans, Christians "gladly and reverently lay bare the seeds of the Word which lie hidden among their fellows." This is indeed a positive attitude that by no means dismisses what is good and holy in the non-Christian religions. But as stated, the passage seems to be suggesting that God's presence has little to do with those religions in themselves since their adherents may not even know of the seeds of the Word hidden among in their traditions. *Nostra Aetate* suggests nothing of the sort.

In regard to the citation of scriptural texts, what is not said matters too. As noted earlier, *Nostra Aetate* 2 is carefully understated in its citation of John 14:6. All that is true and holy in the religions can be affirmed by Catholics since those religions "by no means rarely reflect the radiance of that Truth which enlightens all people." Then we hear, not as a counterbalancing gesture toward evangelization but, rather, as justification for this great openness, the reference to John 14:6: "Truly she announces, and ever must announce Christ 'the way, the truth, and the life.'"[23] That is, wher-

22. Vatican Council II, *Ad Gentes: Decree on the Mission Activity of the Church*, par. 9.
23. Author's translation.

ever people are on the way, wherever there is truth, wherever there is life, there Christ is. But there is no such leeway in *Ad Gentes*, where the meaning of John 14:6 is clearly fixed:

> Wherever God opens a door of speech for proclaiming the mystery of Christ, there is announced to all men with confidence and constancy the living God, and He Whom He has sent for the salvation of all, Jesus Christ, in order that non-Christians, when the Holy Spirit opens their heart, may believe and be freely converted to the Lord, that they may cleave sincerely to Him Who, being the "way, the truth, and the life" (John 14:6), fulfills all their spiritual expectations, and even infinitely surpasses them.[24]

This is explicitly a language of fulfillment and supersession, a language that the authors of *Nostra Aetate* seem resolute in avoiding.

In the preceding paragraphs I have sketched how, in its openness and positive attitude, *Nostra Aetate* is part of a longer tradition but is also distinctive and new. Indeed, in many ways it will seem familiar to those who know the long tradition of the Church regarding the accommodation of cultures and philosophies generated outside the Church and to those who have read the more recent documents of Pius XII, Paul VI, and pertinent council documents. Such comparisons locate *Nostra Aetate* 2 where it belongs, in the great tradition of the Church, but also show how it is different from those earlier and proximate documents too.

What is different about *Nostra Aetate* 2 is its lack of a priori judgments and already-settled conclusions about what other religious traditions are to mean. It stands exceptionally on a middle ground, neither conservative nor liberal, free of many of the theological judgments and a priori conditions common to the other documents. Written in the space of dialogue, it stands open and receptive in the presence of the Other, expecting listeners and hence conversations rather than monologues, true learning rather than confirmations of what we already know. It is not that the authors of *Nostra Aetate* were unaware of or unsympathetic to the cautions posed in other documents. To emphasize this, I have stressed its continuity with the Church's great tradition. My point is that *Nostra Aetate* speaks in its own way and leaves unsaid much that was and is said elsewhere. It shifts from talking about to inviting listeners to do something. Again, the simple words bear hearing: "The Church, therefore, exhorts her sons that through conversation and collaboration with the followers of other religions, carried out with prudence and love and in witness to the Christian faith and life, they recognize, preserve and promote the good things, spiritual and moral,

24. *Ad Gentes* 13.

and even the socio-cultural values found among these men." Christian witness is essential; it is possible because Christ is the way, the truth, and the life. It is this witness that indicates respect, preservation, and promotion of all that is true and holy in the world's religious traditions.

I close this section by noting two other views of *Nostra Aetate*. First, Gavin D'Costa, in his *Vatican II: Catholic Doctrines on Jews and Muslims* (2014), reads *Nostra Aetate* in a way that keeps it firmly in the realm of balancing proclamation and dialogue. In his brief consideration of *Nostra Aetate* paragraph 2, he mentions *Nostra Aetate* as "the key elaboration of *Lumen Gentium* 16." It too places "stress on the necessity of mission right in the middle of its positive exposition of other religions."[25] Indeed, *Nostra Aetate* "reiterates *Ad Gentes* 9," even if *Nostra Aetate* "carefully avoids any negative implications regarding other religions." He gives the reason rather candidly: "This is understandable for *Nostra Aetate* was in part composed with representatives of other religions commenting on the document in the press and privately. . . . *Nostra Aetate* purposively sought only to build bridges and that does not happen if comments are negative."[26] In a long footnote, D'Costa criticizes those who stress only the dialogical component of *Nostra Aetate* without highlighting its commitment to mission, which in his view is the point of the citation of John 14:6. He favorably quotes Arthur Kennedy, who wrote that "rightly sets up these two statements (good and holy elements on the one hand and the necessity of mission on the other) as the guiding principles for reading *Nostra Aetate*."[27] D'Costa, I suggest, is making clear what was designedly not clear in *Nostra Aetate* itself. His suggestion that the document refrained from the negative because non-Christians were reading it would hardly have made sense even in the 1960s, when it was already becoming clear that all conciliar documents could and would be read by insiders and outsiders.

By contrast, in a 2006 essay, "*Nostra Aetate* and the Questions It Chose to Leave Open," Daniel Madigan, SJ, has aptly highlighted the openness we find in *Nostra Aetate*.[28] Instead of seeking to detect a theology of religions and of proclamation in *Nostra Aetate*, a different manner of

25. Gavin D'Costa, *Vatican II: Catholic Doctrines on Jews and Muslims* (Oxford: Oxford University Press, 2014), 84.

26. Ibid., 84.

27. Ibid., 85n63; Arthur Kennedy, "The Declaration on the Relationship of the Church to Non-Christian Religions, *Nostra Aetate*," in *Vatican II: Renewal within Tradition*, ed. Matthew Lamb and Matthew Levering, 397–409 (Oxford: Oxford University Press, 2008). For another view supporting D'Costa's interpretation, see Miikka Ruokanen, *The Catholic Doctrine of Non-Christian Religions according to the Second Vatican Council* (Leiden; New York: E. J. Brill, 1992).

28. *Gregorianum* 87, no. 4 (2006): 781–96.

recognition is operative: "Instead of asking 'Is this religion a structure or vehicle or way of salvation?,' should we not rather ask 'Are there elements in this religion that God appears to be using to save people?'" When this becomes the question, there is required a different manner of attentiveness and openness: "Thus, there is no single, a priori answer to the question of how salvific other religions are. We can only make an a posteriori judgement, based on an observation of the fruits of the Spirit and the distinguishing marks of the Kingdom in the followers of that particular religion." Such a posteriori judgments "cannot or need not be made about the whole religion, but rather about the individual elements." Madigan then catches nicely what is different about *Nostra Aetate*, its "tendency to list positive elements while avoiding general assessments, especially in the case of the two traditions that are nearest us." I would add it is also in the case of Hinduism and Buddhism.[29]

I respect the view offered by D'Costa and those he cites, but I find Madigan to be more persuasive and true to the form and message of *Nostra Aetate* 2. No longer is it necessary, *Nostra Aetate* shows us by its example, to curtail every positive statement by a matching negative judgment or caution. Madigan points to the heart of the matter: the power of *Nostra Aetate* lies in its turn to the a posteriori. It asks for study of the other traditions; one must go and find out. This is comparative study that is robustly, deeply theological, *comparative* theology. It is a kind of study that, from a Christian starting point, is particular, intense, open, indebted to the other, yet still inspired and guided by faith.

It is necessary also to admit that *Nostra Aetate* 2 offering a truly new and practical call for open learning from Hinduism and Buddhism was not the official consensus position regarding the paragraph in the decades after the Council.[30] By my reading, *Nostra Aetate* was read back into the mix of the general concerns about balance that we see even in *Lumen Gentium* and *Ad Gentes* and in accord with the explicit judgments passed on religions in those documents. It is certainly legitimate to affirm obligations of the post-

29. Ibid., 787–88. For a reading of the relevant conciliar documents that is largely consonant with Madigan's, see Gerald O'Collins, SJ, *The Second Vatican Council on Other Religions* (Oxford: Oxford University Press, 2013).

30. Space does not allow the necessary detailed consideration of the destiny or fate of *Nostra Aetate* in postconciliar documents such as *Dialogue and Proclamation*, *Dominus Iesus*, and John Paul II's *Redemptoris Missio*. I suggest, however, that a study of those documents will show that in their desire to ensure that dialogue does not diminish the centrality of proclamation, they in effect marginalize the genuine openness to unrestricted learning that is the distinguishing characteristic of *Nostra Aetate* 2. But it would be a mistake to assess *Nostra Aetate* solely in terms of its contribution to doctrinal matters; it is an extremely important nondoctrinal statement.

conciliar Church to both proclamation and dialogue, but *Nostra Aetate* 2 is wrongly interpreted if seen as either opting for a pluralist theology or, on the contrary, conceding nothing in terms of theological openness to the other. It is not less than a doctrinal statement, but it is fundamentally and practically of a different kind. It is about dispositions conducive to openness and true learning. While *Nostra Aetate* should not be read on its own without due attention to Catholic context, reading it simply in keeping with, and merely as analogous to, other documents, is a disservice to all concerned. It is not about the balance of dialogue and proclamation; rather, it is a very Catholic statement written in the space of dialogue, to be read both by Catholics and by people of other faiths. As such, it is a fresh voice that is not merely a reduced or supplementary version of other more doctrinal texts such as would be used to predict in advance what *Nostra Aetate* 2 is permitted to mean.

Nostra Aetate 2 and the Church's Commitment to Learn from Hinduism

The preceding study of *Nostra Aetate* 2 and of its place in relation to other conciliar documents, and documents before and at the Council, was a rather lengthy but necessary contextualization for how I have read the document and how I think it ought to be read. It inculcates a spirit of openness, the virtues of true learning, into the Catholic calculus of engagement with other traditions. It poses a challenge to us—that we engage the traditions and learn in detail what is holy and true in them: seeking the light *within* other traditions. The declaration encourages an openness that is practical, minimalist, and allows for experimentation.

Nostra Aetate 2 supports the serious study of Hindu traditions. As noted earlier, it sketches what is in effect a detailed list of areas for learning of and from them: their "thorough examination of the divine mystery," their "inexhaustible abundance of myths," their "acute efforts of philosophy" and "forms of the ascetical life," their "profound meditation," and "a flight to God with love and trust."[31] It honors Hindu (and Buddhist) "teachings, rules of life, and sacred rites," and all that is "true and holy" in these religions, "the ways of conduct and of life . . . precepts and teachings," and all the "good things, spiritual and moral," as well as "the socio-cultural values" contained therein.[32] Listing these points of attention marks out a field for practical and unprejudiced interreligious learning. Given the matrix, the mandala, of nearly infinite religious possibilities that is Hinduism, *Nostra Aetate* is the document that enables us to engage Hinduism

31. Author's translation.
32. Ibid.

in a respectful and fair manner, with that certain generosity of intellect and imagination by which one can negotiate its myriad possibilities in a way that is productive for Catholic faith and Catholic theology.

Implicitly, too, this spirit of *Nostra Aetate* has shaped my own study over the decades: a comparative theological study that is an ongoing manner of learning yet does not pretend to resolve, in a liberal or conservative manner, the issues debated, often in an a priori manner, by theologians of religions and soteriologists.

This is why, over the years and in keeping with my relative expertise in certain areas of Sanskrit and Tamil Hindu literature, I have designed projects that look into select Hindu traditions in very precise ways. I can only give several examples here. In *Hindu God, Christian God: How Reason Helps Break Down the Boundaries between Religions* (2001), for instance, I opened up a conversation between Christian and Hindu theologies on four key issues: reasons for the existence of God, the true religion, the possibility and meaning of divine incarnation, and revelation. In none of these topics did I come to settled conclusions. Rather, by a method of intensive study of particular texts, I cleared away many misconceptions, particularly about Hindu theologies, and highlighted new areas of possible rapprochement and also good new difficulties that inevitably arise with new learning that is seriously theological. A follow-up, kindred volume, *Divine Mother, Blessed Mother: Hindu Goddesses and the Virgin Mary* (2005), explores three Hindu goddess traditions, and in light of them looked anew, experimentally, at three texts of Marian devotion. By studying primary texts of Hindu goddess traditions, we dispel age-old misconceptions, understand more deeply the Hindu piety and theology of these divine female persons, and gain new insights into the feminine in relation to the divine. Consequently, I suggested, we also become able to see and imagine the Virgin Mary in a new light.

Arising from a different project and set of texts, *The Truth, the Way, the Life: Christian Commentary on the Three Holy Mantras of the Srivaisnava Hindus* (2008) was, as its title suggests, implicitly inspired by John 14:6—and of course by *Nostra Aetate* 2. I studied in context the truths and values inscribed in three traditional mantras regarding the truth, the path, and the fulfillment of the devout life in Srivaisnava Hinduism. At least as a useful literary strategy, these mantras can be seen to stand in creative tension with John 14:6, neither saying the same thing nor saying something merely philosophical or merely incomplete or in error. Again, it was *Nostra Aetate* that enabled me to think of John 14:6 in this fresh venue, alongside truths dear to Hindu tradition.

More recently, and in a way that is demanded by the intense imaginative and poetic traditions of Hinduism, I read together the Song of Songs, guided by the medieval masters, Bernard of Clairvaux, Gilbert of Hoyland, and John of Ford. I read these along with the Hindu mystical classic, the *Holy Word of Mouth* of the mystic poet Nammalvar, along with its medieval master commentators. The fluidity and intensity of poetry were key to the project. The resultant book, *His Hiding Place Is Darkness: A Hindu-Catholic Theopoetics of Divine Absence* (2013), drives an exploratory venture into the passionate site of divine absence and presence in the imagery of love. Here, too, it is of significant importance that I have found in *Nostra Aetate* a deep openness such as allows the Christian scholar—because Christ is the way, the truth, and the life—to find in Hindu poetry something of the immeasurable depths of divine presence.

This search for a Catholic grounding for deep openness has guided my classroom practice too such as can here be exemplified in my teaching the *Bhagavad Gita* as early as fall 1974 and as recently as spring 2015. This teaching has not been a matter of promoting the *Gita* as would its devotees in a temple setting, nor as an apologist aiming to undercut the *Gita* or show how it is superseded by the Gospel, nor even to dissect it with the cool eye of the Indologist who uses the *Gita* as a window on the social and economic conditions and power differentials at work in India during the eras of the redactions of the text. Rather, *Nostra Aetate* early on made it possible for me to read and teach the *Gita* with empathy, as a wisdom into which we are to be drawn, so as to be transformed by it. This transformation is possible simply because learning is possible, a learning in which similarities are noticed even as differences too are more precisely ascertained and taken into account. I have not tried to force the *Gita*'s teachings into a narrow theological frame, for instance, by asking whether Krishna is a historical figure or not, or by enumerating verses in the *Gita* that conflict with Catholic doctrine and verses that harmonize nicely. The learning experience that occurs in the classroom is not restricted to questions such as these. Of course, others will teach differently. Honest learning may proceed in many ways, as long as we find and respect all that is true and holy in the text, and as long as a Catholic reader or teacher or student proceeds with the confidence that *because* Christ is the way and the truth and the life, we can believe that the *Gita* is radiant with meanings we Catholics can receive profitably.

Such learning, and writing and teaching, is not simply a matter of my own work; it is also a matter of how *Nostra Aetate* is instructing the Church on how to learn from other religions. The Church's own understanding of itself in a world of many religions is disciplined to remain open to transformative self-understanding of the kind that follows upon serious study. If we expect to recognize Christ in the world around us, we become a different kind of Catholic community, a Church that is open—opened because there is a plurality of religious truths and holy ways around us and because we affirm all that is good and holy in those traditions.

Another voice can be introduced usefully at this point. In a 1971 essay, "Christ, Abel, and Melchizedek: The Church and the Non-Abrahamic Religions," Raimundo Panikkar highlighted the theological grounding of the openness apparent in *Nostra Aetate*: "The first thing that must be said is that by contrast with the rest of the Council's pronouncements, and particularly with the pronouncements of other councils, this one impresses the reader as the opening bar to a piece of music rather than the closing one."[33] With quiet innovativeness, *Nostra Aetate* 2 points to a new depth of inter-religious exchange: "To use what hitherto has been in effect the professional parlance of canon lawyers, we might say that the text declares the true shape of communication with the other religions is *communicatio in sacris*: that is, cooperation not in secularized, desacralized areas but in the religious sphere—cooperation with them in their capacity as believers."[34] Taking for granted ordinary exchanges among people of different faiths, *Nostra Aetate* is pointing us to "cooperation with believers of other religions as believers—a thing plain enough, after all, since nine religions out of ten would recognize no distinction, much less any divorce, between spiritual and social concerns, between morality and religion."[35] My contribution here is to suggest that this "*communicatio in sacris*" simply marks the possibility of a truly theological and truly Catholic interreligious learning: faith seeking understanding across religious boundaries, in a way that is not entirely different from faith seeking understanding within the biblical and Christian contexts.[36]

33. Raimundo Panikkar, "Christ, Abel, and Melchizedek: The Church and the Non-Abrahamic Religions," *Jeevadhara* (September/October 1971), 391–403, cited at 392.

34. Ibid., 401.

35. Ibid.

36. To clarify what I mean and the obligation incumbent upon us, recall again how a year before *Nostra Aetate*, on December 3, 1964, Paul had exemplified a new attitude by his extraordinary quotation from the *Brhadaranyaka Upanishad*: "From the unreal lead me to the real; from darkness lead me to light; from death lead me to immortality" (I.3.28). The words are cited without criticism or curtailment, but simply as arising from the human heart and human longing, indeed "from every human heart." Paul does not venture further to exegete the text, but his respectful citation of it, without criticism or hesitation, opens the door to further questions and thus further moments of appreciation. Of course, what Paul started, we must continue. As Catholics, we can hardly read *Brhadaranyaka* I.3.28 out of context without noting its place in section I.3 of this very old *Upanishad*. Respectful of text and tradition, we cannot be among those who would blithely ignore the long tradition of exegesis around the verse by scholastic commentators in the various schools of Vedanta. If we do take the traditions seriously, then the Upanishad's words, arising from the heart, also lead us into a respectful consideration of the Vedanta teachings on self, world, and reality that flow from the *Upanishad*.

The announcing and founding deeply of this deliberate and very serious openness is one of Vatican II's most important gifts to the Catholic community, and we find it nowhere as clearly and prominently expressed as in *Nostra Aetate*, a document in continuity with tradition and yet truly new. The Catholic community in the world today, not despite Christ but energized by Christ, stands for a deeply religious openness, for finding God in learning from the other. While theological and dialogical dynamics keep changing, the Church will be a learning Church for a very long time—indeed until the end of time—and able to live in the present, reverent and open to the other, because Christ is the Way, the Truth, and the Life.

For well over a millennium, Hindus and Christians have been in encounter, first in India and in recent times increasingly all across the globe. This relationship has had its ups and downs and dark and light moments, and it continues to take new forms even today. Hindus and Christians have much to be thankful for, and we share many opportunities for future collaboration. Hope is justified, but we also need reconciliation. We dare not forget the difficult moments in our history, as when Christian powers, uninvited, came to rule over large parts of India and imposed Western customs and values on the people of India. We can honestly praise what is good in our past while yet confessing our sins, and on that basis we can do better in the future. In our era, Catholic Christians can no longer imagine that Hindu traditions are merely outside or apart from the mystery and love of God manifest in Jesus Christ. The Catholic vision of the world requires Catholics to recognize with gratitude that God works deeply and continually in the lives, words and actions, and faith and practice of devout Hindus of every tradition. This means that Hindu learning and wisdom invite Catholics to think anew about a wide range of matters of theological importance: the nature of the divine and how the divine is revealed to us; the importance of God's entrance into the world and of sacramental realities; the importance of seeing and affirming God as a person; the possibilities and limits of images and words about the divine reality; the riches and limits of ritual practice; who we ourselves are, as embodied beings subject to birth and death; the delicate balance between affirming the true, the good, and the beautiful and respecting very diverse paths; the promise of liberation for all beings, in the long run. Learning along with our Hindu brothers and sisters is a blessed opportunity for Catholics, even as new insights and attitudes find their way into our Catholic minds and hearts. A fruitful Hindu-Catholic relationship, then, is not merely a matter of necessity or convenience but, rather, a truly spiritual opportunity with firm foundations. God is one; we are all the children of God; God wills the salvation and well-being of all; and God is a mystery, ever greater than our efforts at exact definitions and boundaries.

A Vaishnava Response to Dr. Francis X. Clooney's Essay, "*Nostra Aetate* and the Catholic Way of Openness to Other Religions"

Anuttama Dasa

In our time, when day by day humankind is being drawn ever closer together and the ties between different peoples are being strengthened, the Church examines with greater care her relation to non-Christian religions. In her task of fostering unity and love among individuals, indeed among peoples, she considers above all in this Declaration what human beings have in common and what draws them to live together their destiny.

—*Nostra Aetate* 1, translation by Thomas F. Stransky, CSP

The Catholic vision of the world requires Catholics to recognize with gratitude that God works deeply and continually in the lives, words and actions, and faith and practice of devout Hindus of every tradition.

—Francis X. Clooney, SJ, "*Nostra Aetate* and the Catholic Way of Openness to Other Religions"

We truly live in remarkable times. Many people believe that the most significant aspect of modernity is the ever-changing technology that constantly reconfigures our lives. I disagree. I believe the most significant catalyst in human society over the last fifty-plus years is the extent to which global religious communities are now engaged with and impacting each other.

We live in a world torn by religious strife and conflict. But we also live in a world where religious men, women, leaders, and communities have been obliged by immigration, political remapping, economic pressures, social upheaval, social mobility, communication innovations, and other factors to acknowledge, live with, and respond to other religious ideas and people on a scale never seen before. Having to acknowledge and interact with the religious "Other" is a powerful force of change in the world.

With this conviction, I attended the Catholic University of America conference on *Nostra Aetate* in May 2015 with great interest. The commitment of the Catholic Church, laid out in this document's first paragraph, to examine "with greater care her relation to non-Christian religions"[1] is a

---

1. *Nostra Aetate* 1.

prime example of this new, previously unheard of positive religious inter-action. The conference was a chance to learn first-hand, by hearing from faithful Catholics and scholars both inside and outside the Church, about this historically significant pivot point in the Church's understanding and vision of other religions. It was an inside look at how the world's largest religious institution has grappled with a changing notion of the Other.

In particular, as a practicing Caitanya Vaishnava Hindu,[2] I found the essay presented by Francis X. Clooney, SJ, a scholar of Hinduism and the director of Harvard's Center for the Study of World Religions, to be intriguing. Herein he analyzed *Nostra Aetate* in terms of its impact on the relationship of the Church and Hindu traditions.

In this response, I offer some reflections on Professor Clooney's pres-entation and on *Nostra Aetate* itself. I do so in a mood of respect and grat-itude for the Catholic Church's willingness to wrestle with such serious topics, its creation of a forward-looking document on interfaith relations, its genuine endeavor to apply such precepts, and its openness to a critical view (via the conference) of these evolving ideologies.

Thinking Anew

Clooney addresses the opportunities of "our era" and informs us that "Hindu learning and wisdom invite Catholics to think anew about a wide range of matters of theological importance."[3] I find it refreshing that Clooney writes, teaches, and, as he says, "challenges" his readers from sev-eral perspectives, seemingly at once. His voice is that of a scholar, a teacher, a priest, and a leading thinker in both the secular academic environment and the Church.

I find Clooney most compelling in his role as priest, spiritual guide, and commentator; for here he brings his deepest theological perspectives to bear. Clooney articulates the view that *Nostra Aetate* empowers learning and openness by emphasizing Christ's presence everywhere. It is because of this presence that Catholics can see Christ within, and guiding, even the Hindu heart.

---

2. Within the broad diversity of Hindu culture, belief, and practices, the Vaishnavas, or the devotees of Lord Vishnu or Lord Krishna, are said to be the largest subset. Vaishnavas believe in one Supreme God who appears in different forms and has many names. Vaishnavas reject the claim that ultimate reality is impersonal. The Caitanya Vaishnavas, or Gaudiya Vaishnavas, are followers of Sri Caitanya Mahaprabhu, a sixteenth-century Bengali saint who is worshipped as an avatar (incarnation) of God. I write this article as both a Vaishnava and a member of the broader Hindu community.

3. See Clooney's essay in this volume, p. 58.

For Hindus, and Vaishnavas in particular, a similar vision of open-mindedness toward others is inspired by our faith that God is active in everyone's heart in ways beyond our ability to understand. As stated by Lord Krishna in the *Bhagavad-gita*: "The Supreme Lord is situated in everyone's heart, O Arjuna, and is directing the wanderings of all living beings, who are seated as on a machine, made of material energy. . . ."[4] "All of them, as they surrender to Me, I reward accordingly. Everyone follows my path in all respects. . . ."[5]

Respect for Religious Striving

I am appreciative of the historically innovative and gracious manner by which *Nostra Aetate* describes and values Hindu, or Vedic,[6] thought. In particular as a Vaishnava, a student of bhakti,[7] and one who seeks to awaken love of God as the essential purpose of my life, I am moved and pleased by the poetic description of my faith as "a flight to God with love and trust."[8]

I also find of interest *Nostra Aetate*'s reference that religions seek "answers to the profound enigmas of the human condition . . . What is the meaning, the purpose of life . . . Whence suffering and what purpose does it serve . . . Which is the way to genuine happiness?"[9]

This passage reminds me of Arjuna's call to his Lord in the *Bhagavad-gita*. When distraught with the complexities of trying to live as a pious king while faced with civil war, he proclaimed, "Now I am confused about my duty and have lost all composure because of miserly weakness. In this condition, I am asking you tell me for certain what is best for me. . . . Please instruct me."[10]

Hindu thought repeatedly acknowledges the urge within the human heart to seek answers to life's most profound questions and to link with the Divine. Yoga itself refers to yoking with, or reconnecting with God, the Absolute Truth. This truth is understood by different Hindu traditions as

4. *Bhagavad-gita As It Is*, trans. A. C. Bhaktivedanta Swami Prabhupada, 18.61 (New York: Bhaktivedanta Book Trust, 1972).
5. Ibid., 4.11.
6. The Vedas are the ancient sacred Sanskrit texts of India that form the scriptural basis of a variety of Vedic, or Hindu, traditions, including the Vaishnavas, who consider the *Bhagavata Purana* as well as the more well-known *Bhagavad-gita* to be essential texts.
7. Vaishnavas practice bhakti-yoga, the yoga of devotion. As Krishna advises in *Bhagavad-gita*, "All that you do, all that eat, all that you offer and give away, as well as any austerities you may perform, should be done as an offering unto Me" (*Bhagavad-gita As It Is*, 9.27).
8. *Nostra Aetate* 2.
9. Ibid. 1.
10. *Bhagavad-gita As It Is*, 2.7.

Brahman, the all-pervading energy; or as Paramatma, God within the heart; or as Bhagavan, the Personality of Godhead.[11]

Both Christians and Hindus, therefore, value the religious urge and expression of others. The question, though, is can we be both committed and faithful members of our traditions—yet be open to see the light in another's practice? *Nostra Aetate* takes a step in that direction proclaiming the Church "rejects nothing that is true and holy in these religions" [Hinduism and Buddhism]. However, for the non-Christian, a doubt is raised by the very next sentence, where we are *immediately* reminded that Christ is "the Way, the Truth, and the Life." Repeating this emphatic statement that Christ is *the* way implies that ultimately there is little to be gained from other traditions because Christ alone remains the truth.

Clooney however, reads the import of this statement differently. He argues that *Nostra Aetate* is calling us to see Christ's light at work *within* other religious traditions.

The Role of Christ

Clooney's analysis of the text of *Nostra Aetate* 2—particularly the mention of Jesus Christ as the way, the truth, and the life—is both traditional and expansive. He provides evidence and guides us to this conclusion: *Nostra Aetate* "encourages, even mandates, a deepening of the interreligious learning process because of who Christ is."[12]

Clooney notes that prior Church writings, while appreciative of interreligious discourse, encouraged Catholics to sift "through the good and the evil in other religions." But he stresses, "Such are the judgments on the religions that *Nostra Aetate* chooses not to make."[13]

Nostra Aetate "neither makes nor denies this kind of claim [distinguishing the power of the Gospel from other religions]; it is not about that kind of measurement but about the learning that can and should take place in the interreligious realm."[14]

For Clooney, the reference to John 14:6 quoted in *Nostra Aetate* is not presented as "a counterbalancing gesture toward evangelization but, rather, as a justification for this great openness." When *Nostra Aetate* declares that the Church "announces, and ever must announce Christ 'the way, the truth, and the life,'"[15] Clooney reasons, "That is, wherever people are on

---

11. *Srimad Bhagavatam*, or *Bhagavata Purana*, 1.2.11.
12. See Clooney's essay in this volume, 62.
13. Ibid., 66.
14. Ibid., 64, n17.
15. Clooney's translation.

their way, wherever there is truth, wherever there is life, there Christ is."[16] In sort, Christians are exhorted to learn from the Hindu because it is Christ who is the operative element in the spiritual lives of all. Clooney summarizes: *Nostra Aetate* "poses a challenge to us—that we engage the traditions and learn in detail what is holy and true in them: seeking the light *within* other traditions."[17]

I find this an essential element in the evolution of Catholic thought before, during, and after Vatican II. It gives rise to an openness to Hinduism and other traditions that was previously not present.

Exclusivity and Inclusivity in Hinduism

Balancing exclusive and inclusive statements about one's religion and the other religions may seem like a peculiarly Christian problem, but in fact, it arises in Hinduism as well.

There are many Hindu texts that lend themselves to be interpreted in dogmatic ways. For example, some may find the conclusion of *Bhagavad-gita* to be a closed-ended, exclusive proposal. Krishna's order is simple: "Abandon all varieties of religion (dharma) and surrender unto Me. I shall protect you from all sinful reactions."[18] One could read this and conclude that other religious practices are condemned or simply preliminary.

As a Vaishnava, I can point to many texts that demand single-minded focus on Lord Krishna.[19] In a verse that echoes the emphatic tone of John 4:16, Krishna states, "I am the source of all spiritual and material worlds. Everything emanates from Me. The wise who perfectly know this engage in My devotional service and worship Me with all their hearts."[20]

On the other hand, within Hindu thought, the diversity of spiritual experience, realizations, and paths to truth is a given, not an anomaly. For example, Lord Krishna confirms the validity of diverse religious teachings and expression early in the *Bhagavad-gita*: "Whenever and wherever there is a decline in religious practice, O descendant of Bharata, and a predominant rise of irreligion—at that time I descend Myself. To deliver the pious and to annihilate the miscreants, as well as to reestablish the principles of religion, I Myself appear, millennium after millennium."[21]

---

16. See Clooney's essay in this volume, 67–68.

17. Ibid., 71.

18. *Bhagavad-gita As It Is*, 18.66.

19. Here I refer to the Vaishnava conclusion of exclusive devotion to Lord Krishna or Lord Vishnu. However, one can find similar single-mindedness in other Hindu traditions as well.

20. *Bhagavad-gita As It Is*, 10.8.

21. Ibid., 4.7–8.

A. C. Bhaktivedanta Swami Prabhupada, the founder-acarya[22] of the International Society for Krishna Consciousness (ISKCON) and a respected Vaishnava teacher, writes in his commentary on this verse:

> Therefore each and every avatara, or incarnation of the Lord, has a particular mission, and they are all described in the revealed scriptures. . . . It is not a fact that the Lord appears only on Indian soil. He can manifest Himself anywhere and everywhere, and whenever He desires to appear. In each and every incarnation, He speaks as much about religion as can be understood by the particular people under their particular circumstances. But the mission is the same, to lead people to God consciousness and obedience to the principles of religion. Sometime He descends personally, and sometimes He sends His bona fide representative in the form of His son, or servant, or Himself in some disguised form.[23]

Thus, while *Nostra Aetate* cautiously advises us to reject "nothing that is true and holy in these religions," Krishna is more assertive. He and His followers embrace whatever is true and holy in the different religious traditions and declare that such truths, although differing in style, originate from God via his many incarnations or representatives. As such, these teachers and teachings share the same mission—to lead people to God-consciousness.

Perhaps a parallel to the ambiguity of Christ as the way, the truth, and the life in *Nostra Aetate* 2 is a verse of the Gita that expresses open-mindedness in Krishna's instructions to relish exchanges with devotees, or people of God, even while affirming the centrality of Krishna:

> The thoughts of my pure devotees dwell in me, their lives are full devoted to Me, and they derive great satisfaction and bliss from always enlightening one another and conversing about Me.[24]

One could choose to read this verse in a sectarian way, but I think the spirit of the text is different. We should hear from all spiritually minded souls, or devotees of God, and learn from them what we can about the Lord; to do so is enlightening and brings happiness to the soul. This means we should not only learn from those who self-define as Vaishnavas or Hindus. We can also learn from those who have been inspired by God's messengers "in the form of His son, or servant."

This instruction is similar to *Nostra Aetate* 2 where the Church "exhorts her sons and daughters to recognize, preserve, and foster the good

---

22. *Acarya* means a teacher who teaches by example.
23. *Bhagavad-gita As It Is*, 4.7 Purport (Commentary).
24. Ibid., 10.9.

things, spiritual and moral . . . among the followers of other religions . . . through conversations and collaboration with them, carried out with prudence and love and in witness to the Christian faith and life."

> Overall, for Vaishnavas I believe the message is clear. We are taught to see Krishna, the "all attractive Lord," guiding and accepting the progress of all His children, whether Hindu, Christian, or other: "The Supreme Lord is situated in everyone's heart, O Arjuna, and is directing the wanderings of all living beings. . . ."[25] "All of them, as they surrender to Me, I reward accordingly. Everyone follows my path in all respects. . . ."[26]

Bhaktivinode Thakur, a nineteenth-century Caitanya Vaishnava teacher, offered his insight regarding interactions with other traditions. In particular, he advised against extolling our own teachers, our own names for God, and our own texts above others. Writing perhaps a century or more ahead of his time, he says: "It is not proper to constantly propagate the controversial superiority of the teacher's of one's own country [or religion] over those of another country although one may, nay one should, cherish such a belief in order to acquire steadiness in faith of your own. But, no good can be affected by such quarrels."[27] Thus, we are reminded of the ongoing need to seek balance and clarity in our interpretation of exclusive and inclusive texts. At the same time, we should continue to recognize and honor our traditions' appeals for openheartedness, respect, and inquisitiveness.

A Need for Reconciliation

Ignoring such appeals for openheartedness, clashes of ego, pride, power, and politics carried out under the guise of religiosity have become all too common. After all, the Vedas state that we live in the Age of Kali, the Age of Quarrel and Hypocrisy.

Painfully aware of our shared history, Clooney closes his essay by pointing out the need for reconciliation in the relationship between Hindus and Catholics. Addressing the past, he acknowledges the need for all to "[confess] our sins, and on that basis, we can do better in the future." Significantly, he urges his readers to "dare not forget . . . Christian powers, uninvited, came to rule large parts of India and imposed Western customs and values on the people of India."[28]

---

25. Ibid., 18.61.
26. Ibid., 4.11.
27. *Sri-Caitanya-Siksamritam*, 7.
28. See Clooney essay in this volume, p. 75.

While not his paper's focus, it is important that Clooney recognizes this historical hurdle in Catholic-Hindu relations. There are many voices today within the Hindu diaspora who have difficulty looking beyond the abuses of Christian power. Without acknowledging this dilemma we ignore a trying aspect of our blossoming dialogue. One continuing issue is the perception among many Hindus that Christians use economic and other social advantages as leverage in their conversion schemes. It is a sensitive topic, but one that needs to be explored in light of *Nostra Aetate*'s openness and expressed goal of "fostering unity and love . . . among peoples."[29]

Not to be overlooked, of course, are recent and serious abuses of minority Christian communities in India by Hindus. Hindus, too, need to rectify their "sins." In a country where Hindus hold political and cultural dominance, it remains with the majority to abide by its avowed historical and philosophical respect for religious liberty and the diversity of religious expression.

Forgiveness is a virtue esteemed by both the Catholic and Hindu communities. Yet as Clooney alludes, it is only after remorse is articulated and our errors and offenses are acknowledged (and ideally corrected) that we can best move forward with shared openness and trust.[30]

A Call for Humility

To go forward, as expressed by *Nostra Aetate* in its call for prudence and love, humility is required. Vedic scriptures proclaim that the antidote to the quarrelsome nature of this age—difficult as it may seem for modern men and women—is humility.

Krishna states humility to be the first quality of one in knowledge. Absence of humility is ignorance, and ignorance is an obstacle in understanding God.[31] Furthermore, *japa*, or the chanting of God's names, is an essential religious practice that awakens God consciousness. But to chant God's names without offense, Caitanya taught we must feel ourselves "lower than the blade of grass, more tolerant than a tree and ready to give all respect to others."[32]

29. *Nostra Aetate* 1.
30. I have learned from colleagues specializing in mediation and reconciliation that often we defend our actions, being aware of our good intentions, while minimizing the harmful impact of those actions. Meanwhile, those we have offended seek assurance that we understand the gravity of our mistakes before reconciliation can be achieved. It need not be a catch-22 if we are willing to be honest and self-critical, both good qualities to bring forward in dialogue.
31. *Bhagavad-gita, As It Is*, 13.8.
32. Sri Caitanya Mahaprabhu, *Sri Siksastakam*, 3.

There is a story in this regard in the 10th Canto of the *Bhagavata-Purana*, or *Srimad Bhagavatam*, where Lord Krishna plays upon His flute to call His most devoted followers, the gopis (or cowherd maidens), to dance with Him in the full moon night in the mystical forest of Vrindavana. Vrindavana is Krishna's divine abode, the Kingdom of God.

While much has been written about this dramatic exchange of devotion, one aspect is particularly relevant here. At one point the gopis, who are described as worshipable by great sages because of their single pointed devotion to Lord Krishna, become proud. They begin to think that they are the most fortunate women in the universe because Krishna was with them.

They were, of course, special and fortunate. But their small trace of pride was an impediment to pure heartedness. Consequently, in an instant Lord Krishna mystically disappeared from their midst.

As men and women of faith from the Hindu, Catholic, and other traditions, we are reminded to be humble in the presence of God. Or, like the gopis, He may withdraw His presence. But what if His presence comes in ways we are not accustomed to or comfortable with? *Nostra Aetate* advises that Catholics remain humble and always look for learning, knowing that Christ is present. Bhaktivinode Thakura, the Vaishnava teacher, puts it this way:

> When we have the occasion to be present at the place of worship of other religionists at the time of their worship, we should stay there in a respectful mood, contemplating thus: "Here is being worshipped my adorable highest entity, God in a different form than that of mine. Due to my practice of a different kind, I cannot thoroughly comprehend this system of theirs. But seeing it, I am feeling a greater attachment for my own system. I bow down with prostration before His emblem as I see here and I offer my prayer to my Lord who has adopted this different emblem that he may increase my love towards Him. . . ."[33]

He thus challenges his readers to see Krishna, God, present always. Moreover, he advises us to see how (my) God is present in the worship of others. This is a thought worthy of deeper introspection and dialogue.

Mission and Dialogue

Does this call for humility and reconciliation require the cessation of missionary activity? Clooney states that *Nostra Aetate* does more than bal-

---

33. *Sri-Caitanya-Siksamrita*, Introduction. I find a parallel spirit in the verse from Philippians that Clooney, in his footnote 3, points out was referenced in an earlier draft of *Nostra Aetate*: "Finally, beloved, whatever is true, whatever is honorable, whatever is just, whatever is pure, whatever is pleasing, whatever is commendable, if there is any excellence and if there is anything worthy of praise, think about these things" (Phil 4:8).

ance dialogue and proclamation, and that is true. But to balance these two vibrant religious callings is also an important need. *Nostra Aetate* clarifies the Church's vision of promoting positive relations and dialogue with other faiths, without minimizing or compromising the commitment to teach the message of Christ.

My community, ISKCON, also endeavors to achieve this balance. We have been criticized for our sometimes overzealous attempt to spread the message of Lord Krishna. Despite these shortcomings—which cost us friends, inspired some persecution, and led to public apologies on behalf of our society—we are both a missionary religious community and open to dialogue.[34]

This tension is addressed in the foundational document "ISKCON and Interfaith: ISKCON in Relation to People of Faith in God,"

> Some may feel that for a missionary movement, a dialogue with those who do not share the same spiritual or religious views is a contradiction in purpose. Gaudiya Vaishnava teachings, however, support dialogue and cooperation with other religious traditions as a means of mutual enrichment, through discovery of the unique and the universal virtues of the various theistic and ethical traditions. . . . These relationships can inspire religious people from all traditions to work together to establish theistic conclusions that will lead to a God conscious ethos in our modern world [which are also] important for social harmony.[35]

For Vaishnavas, there is no block to dialogue with others, including those who have a commitment to their own mission. In fact, it is a necessity. In this spirit, I have been honored to convene the annual two-day Vaishnava-Christian Dialogue in Washington, D.C., for nearly twenty years. For many of those years, the United States Conference of Catholic Bishops was cosponsor, and USCCB representatives have attended every dialogue except one.[36]

In January 2015, the first Vaishnava-Christian Dialogue in India was held. During that meeting in the holy Hindu city of Tirupati, ten Vaishnavas and ten Christians (some Catholic and Protestant) spent two and a half days in retreat and dialogue. Our topics were "Love of God" and "Theological Foundations for Dialogue." We were honored to have with us

---

34. Arvind Sharma discusses Hinduism and mission in his book, *Hinduism as a Missionary Religion* (Albany: State University of New York Press, 2011).

35. Saunaka Risi Dasa, "ISKCON and Interfaith: ISKCON in Relation to People of Faith in God," *ISKCON Communications Journal* 7, no. 1 (1999): 5.

36. A special edition of the *Journal of Vaishnava Studies* was dedicated to publish papers from this dialogue. It is available online at iskconcommunications.org/assets/jvs-se.pdf.

Archbishop Felix Machado, Michael Amaladoss, Professor Clooney, and other esteemed Christian and Gaudiya and Sri Vaishnava[37] representatives.

On the second day, as participants grew in friendship and openness with each other, one Christian minister commented, "I am beginning to see that while we Christians have a deep theological understanding of how God loves us, you Vaishnavas are particularly enriched and studied in how to love God."

I was profoundly moved by the comments of this dialogue partner. I believe they exemplify *Nostra Aetate*'s call for learning from each other. Personally, I am inspired by the Christian understanding that "God so loved the world, He gave His only Son." And, like this minister, I believe the Vaishnava teachings of *Rasa* theology, the study of varieties of loving exchanges between God and his devotees, can be of interest and enriching to many in the Christian community.

Parijata Dasi, a thirty-five-year-old Indian woman who heads the ISKCON Communications Office in Mumbai, surprised a few at the Tirupati dialogue when she told her personal story: "I want to thank the Catholics present for my education. I went to a convent school for my entire schooling, and I believe the moral and other training they provided laid the foundation for my commitment as a Vaishnava."

After she finished, two other Vaishnavas spoke: a male priest and a swami, or renunciate. Both leaders in ISKCON, they revealed the same Catholic educational background. Both offered their thanks.

I offer these stories as evidence that our two communities can and do live in mutual respect, service, and support of each other. Much more can be achieved. All that is required is a willingness to learn and grow, coupled with humility.

A Shared Year of Importance

As a final reflection, I note with interest that in 1965, the year *Nostra Aetate* was adopted, another lesser-known event of religious significance occurred. It was in summer 1965 that A. C. Bhaktivedanta Swami Prabhupada left India via passage on the Indian freighter ship, *Jaladuta*. He landed in New York City in September at the age of seventy practically penniless, with several trunks of his translations of the *Srimad Bhagavatam* as his only possessions. After a year of struggle, he began his Hare Krishna movement, ISKCON. Prabhupada, a 1920 graduate of Scottish Churches College in

---

37. Sri Vaishnavas are followers of the eleventh-century Vaishnava teacher Ramanuja and are historically based in South India, whereas the Caitanya, or Gaudiya Vaishnavas, are originally based in what is today West Bengal.

Calcutta,[38] brought with him respect for the teachings of Jesus.[39] He referred to Jesus as both a Vaishnava (devotee of God) and a guru (one who teaches about God). His openness was expressed thus: "We do not advocate any sectarian religion. We are concerned to invoke our dormant love for God. Any method that helps us in reaching such a platform is welcome."[40]

In his commentary on the sixteenth-century text, *Upadeshamrita*, he mirrors the spirit of *Nostra Aetate* in its appreciation of God's presence throughout the world. "In all parts of the world, however downtrodden human society may be, there is some system of religion. . . . When a religious system develops and turns into love of God, it is successful."[41]

Perhaps it was coincidence that Prabhupada landed in New York in 1965. Perhaps it was divine plan. Either way, his arrival in the west and the later founding of ISKCON—which may be the most active global Hindu community in interfaith dialogue—coincided exactly with the adoption of *Nostra Aetate*, that colossal shift in thinking about interfaith relations and Hinduism within the world's most prominent Church.

Unanswered Questions

The celebration of the fiftieth anniversary of *Nostra Aetate* gives reason to hope. The world's largest religious organization, a powerful and influential voice throughout most of the globe, five decades ago called for "fostering of unity and love among individuals, indeed among peoples." The Church also stated its commitment to reject "nothing that is true and holy" in the other great religions traditions of the world. Questions remain, however.

First, beyond the important influence of *Nostra Aetate* on members of the Catholic Church, how much does it matter to others today what the Church—or the rest of us—have to say on such topics? Annually we are told of the increasing numbers of the spiritual but not religious population. Such people find truth in spirituality yet disdain religious organizations and the very official pronouncements we are discussing.

If that is the case, do such treatises make much difference on the larger society? And if we believe they do, how do we share our messages in mean-

---

38. As a follower of Gandhi at the time, student Abhay Charan De, as Bhaktivedanta Swami was known at the time, declined to accept his diploma in response to Gandhi's call for noncooperation with the British.

39. For more on Prabhupada's views on Christ, see Ravi M. Gupta, "'He Is Our Master': Jesus in the Thought of Swami Prabhupada," *Journal of Hindu-Christian Studies* 23 (2010).

40. Prabhupada, *Letter to Rupanuga Das*, June 3, 1968.

41. Sri Rūpagosvāmī, *Upadeshamrita* (*The Nectar of Instruction*), trans. Prabhupada (New York: Bhaktivedanta Book Trust, 1975), 44.

ingful and effective ways with an ever-increasing number of people who do
not care much what we say?

Second, we see in the Middle East and elsewhere that major conflicts
are harming millions and spreading a dangerous mix of religion and politics. What can we do to ensure our messages of mutual respect are not mis-
read as insincere or naive, or simply dwarfed by the politically motivated
misuse of religious identities and themes? Can our positive messages penetrate regions where hate and interreligious violence have become a norm?
Similarly, can the call for respect via *Nostra Aetate* be heard in places like
India, where the rebounding spirit of a nation long exploited is mixed with
calls for *Hindutva*, or Hindu-ness, and a definition of national identity
based on sectarian concepts of what it means to be Indian?

The pressure to pair national identity and religious identity is a global
problem. My community is on the vanguard of spreading Vaishnava
Hindu culture around the world. Like many other religious minorities, we
continue to face discrimination and persecution in some countries, including those where not identifying as a member of the majority faith is
frowned upon and sometimes dangerous.

Third, *Nostra Aetate*'s call for learning opens the door for further
exploration from a theological perspective. For those who believe God is at
work in the world and guides us all, to what extent can we be genuinely
transformed and spiritually uplifted in each other's presence?

As a Vaishnava, can I be with my Christian friends, sit in their worship service, listen to their prayers, and be *transformed* by such experiences?
Can an interfaith experience uplift me and bring me closer to God? If so,
should we not more actively advocate for such shared transformation? Or
is it meant for just a few?

Some in the Hindu and Catholic communities may find the value of
interreligious exchanges to be small; at best, an exercise in friend-raising.
For others, it is clear: such dialogue is God's call to us to learn and be transformed with and by each other.

Conclusion

Clooney ends his essay with a quote from Raimundo Panikkar, who
said of *Nostra Aetate*, "by contrast with the rest of the council's pronouncements, and particularly with the pronouncements of other councils, this
one impresses the reader as the opening bar to a piece of music rather than
the closing one."[42]

42. "Christ, Abel, and Melchizedek: The Church and the Non-Abrahamic Religions,"
Jeevadhara (September/October 1971), 391–403; cited at 392. Quoted by Clooney, this
volume, p. 74, n33.

This spirit of openness Clooney states is "one of Vatican II's most important gifts to the Catholic community."[43] ISKCON and the broader Hindu community, as friends and partners in dialogue with the Catholic Church and Catholic people around the world, are grateful that we, too, share in this gift.

The Vedas advise that the easiest and most sublime method of spiritual progress is to sing together God's names and glories.[44] We may do so in whatever tune, in whatever meter, and whatever language inspires us. Raising our voices in praise with our Catholic friends, we welcome the opening bar of music that was and is *Nostra Aetate*.

43. See Clooney essay in this volume, p. 75.

44. *Brihanaradiya Purana* 38.126. Although this text can be interpreted in a sectarian manner—promoting the chanting of the names of Hari—Vaishnavas teach that God has many names and encourage meditation and prayer involving any of these. Sri Caitanya Mahaprabhu wrote, "O my Lord, Your holy name alone can render all benediction to living beings, and thus You have hundreds and millions of names like Krishna and Govinda. . . . [O]ut of kindness You enable us to easily approach You by Your holy names" (*Sri Siksastakam* 2). Also, Caitanya taught that congregational chanting, or sankirtan, is "the prime benediction for humanity at large" (*Siksastakam* 1). Bhaktivedanta Swami Prabhupada, referring to the chanting of God's names, often called it "the most sublime method" of spiritual advancement.

Part III

Dialogue with Muslims

In the course of centuries there have indeed arisen not a few quarrels and hostilities between Christians and Muslims. But now this Sacred Synod pleads with all to forget the past, to make sincere efforts for mutual understanding, and so to work together for the preservation and fostering of social justice, moral welfare, and peace and freedom for all humankind.

—*Nostra Aetate* 3, trans. Thomas F. Stransky, CSP

The Catholic Church in Dialogue with Islam since the Promulgation of *Nostra Aetate*

JEAN-LOUIS CARDINAL TAURAN

I wish to begin my reflections by expressing my thankfulness to God, our Creator and provident Father, who in His loving wisdom inspired the celebration of *Fifty Years of Catholic Church's Dialogue with Jews and Muslims* at The Catholic University of America for which these remarks were originally prepared. I also wish to express my profound thanks to the entire university family and to the United States Conference of Catholic Bishops (USCCB) for jointly organizing that event and for inviting me to participate in the same.

Celebrating a major dialogue event at a university has its own special significance; it demonstrates the interest on the subject, not only of the administration but also of its staff and students. This augurs well for our present and our future in this multireligious world. One of the important features of a university is that it is a laboratory for knowing each other, respecting each other, and relating with one another in a positive and constructive way. Friendships nurtured during the student years are probably destined to last the whole of a life; we grow from being just classmates to becoming faithful and trustworthy friends.

The theme entrusted to me is "The Catholic Church in Dialogue with Islam since the Promulgation of *Nostra Aetate*." Just before my conference talk, I was in Switzerland from May 13 to 15, participating in a meeting with the representatives of Europe's Episcopal Conferences, who have been entrusted with the responsibility of promoting relations with Muslims. The meeting was aimed at making the participants more familiar with Islam. Islam, we must remember, is one at the same time a religion, a political system, and a civilization. We must also acknowledge that Islam, in today's context, represents a challenge.

Though I am expected to focus on the Catholic Church's dialogue with Islam since the time *Nostra Aetate* was promulgated, I wish to draw your attention to the fact that dialogue between the followers of these two religions existed even before this document was promulgated. It must in fact be said that dialogue between Christians and Muslims is as old as Islam itself. We can find the presence of a tentative dialogue in the Qur'an itself: "and argue not with the People of the Book except by what is best, save such of them as act unjustly. But say we believe in that which has been revealed to us and to you, and our God and your God is One, and to Him we submit."[1]

Nostra Aetate therefore does not really mark the beginning of dialogue between Catholics and Muslims, and for that matter with the people of any other religion. Rather, *Nostra Aetate* must be understood as a statement that gave a new orientation to dialogue, a dialogue built on a more positive attitude toward and constructive relationship with the followers of other religious traditions. Today we speak of interreligious dialogue as a normal religious activity, and we are right. But such was not the case in the past. With *Nostra Aetate*, for the first time since the time of the apostles, the official teaching of the Church recognizes that there are elements of truth in other religions. "The Catholic Church rejects nothing that is true and holy in these religions. She regards with sincere reverence those ways of conduct and of life, those precepts and teachings which, though differing in many aspects from the ones she holds and sets forth, nonetheless often reflect a ray of that Truth which enlightens all men."[2] One can raise an objection to this quoting what Saint Justin originally said in in the second century ("*semina Verbi*"), but it must be kept in mind that he stated it as a private position, and it does not amount to be in any way that of the Catholic Church.

The Pontifical Council for Interreligious Dialogue (PCID) is the organ of the Universal Church for the relations of the Roman pontiff and the competent dicasteries with the people of other religions. Whenever the pope wishes for advice, a text, or an initiative related to interreligious dialogue, it is the PCID that, in general, organizes it in collaboration with other dicasteries of the Roman Curia. For example, the Day of Prayer for Peace in Assisi was a joint organization of the Pontifical Council for Justice and Peace, the Pontifical Council for the Promotion of Christian Unity (PCPCU), and the PCID. The celebration of the fiftieth anniversary of *Nostra Aetate* in Rome from October 26 to 28, 2015, saw the PCID and the PCPCU collaborating again. In some cases, cooperation from the Pontifical Council for Migrants and People on the Move is also sought as many of the immigrants are believers of other religions, especially of Islam.

The establishment of a Commission for the Religious Relations with Muslims (CRRM) by Blessed Pope Paul VI is to be understood in this framework for the need of study, reflection, prayer, and consultation for a fruitful dialogue with Muslims. The fact that CRRM has no other parallel

---

1. Surah Al-Ankabut 29:46.
2. *Nostra Aetate* 2, official Vatican translation.

excepting that of the Commission for Religious Relations with Jews shows the special status Islam enjoys and the importance given to it by the Catholic Church. We must, however, remember that the Declaration of the Vatican Council II about relations between the Church and the non-Christian religions titled *Nostra Aetate* had not been easily adopted by the Council fathers. Those of us who are familiar with the history of the Council know that it was almost cancelled. But it was Pope Saint John XXIII who made sure that the document remained on the agenda of the Council. The first draft of the document dealt only with the responsibility of Christians in the wake of the Holocaust. But some patriarchs and bishops from the Middle East contested that approach, arguing that a document concerning only the Jews would be interpreted by the Arab countries as a step toward the normalization of relations between the State of Israel and the Holy See. After intense discussions it became clear that *Nostra Aetate* had nothing to do with the State of Israel per se. The document was finally adopted after its scope was widened to include other religious groups as well, in particular Muslims. Catholics were invited to know and to understand Muslims better in order to promote together a world where women and men of our times can enjoy social justice, freedom, and peace. *Nostra Aetate* is among the documents of the Vatican Council II that has maintained its relevance all through these decades; the relevance is only becoming more pronounced and greater day by day. The document gives a special responsibility to the Catholics, to be promoters of reconciliation in the present-day international scenario. Pope Saint John Paul II, Pope Benedict XVI, and Pope Francis have all rendered an immense service to the cause of interreligious dialogue through their teachings, initiatives, and apostolic visits.

An additional sign of the particular attention given to Muslims by the PCID is the message for the end of Ramadan that the dicastery has been sending to them since 1967. Two of these messages deserve a special mention: the first one signed by John Paul II during the Gulf War (April 16, 1991); the second one signed by Pope Francis in the very first year of his pontificate (July 10, 2013). The message is sent to the Muslims in all the countries of the world. Besides the good wishes for the feast, there is always, in the message, a theme proposed for reflection with the possibility also for discussion between Muslims and Christians for their own education and for the development of their children.

Another structure of dialogue with Muslims within the PCID is the establishment of permanent committees for dialogue with international Islamic institutions and organizations. The PCID has engaged itself in such an activity since the time the demand for the same was made by its members during one of the plenary assemblies of the dicastery. The PCID thus has ongoing institutionalized dialogues with the World Islamic Call

Society (Tripoli, Libya), the Center for Interreligious Dialogue of the Islamic Culture and Relations Organization (Teheran, Iran), and the International Islamic Forum for Dialogue (Jeddah, Saudi Arabia), and it has formed the Islamic-Catholic Liaison Committee, a Permanent Committee for Dialogue with the Iraqi Endowments. With the signatories of the open letter addressed to Pope Benedict XVI and to other Christian leaders, the PCID established the Christian-Muslim Forum for Dialogue. The Permanent Committee for Dialogue between the PCID and al-Azhar has unfortunately been suspended since 2011, due to a unilateral decision taken by this important Muslim institution as a protest against Pope Benedict XVI's Regensburg address, which it considered an insult to Islam. I have always affirmed, and do so even today, that our doors are always open to dialogue. A permanent dialogue with the Ismailis of the Aga Khan is under study and will hopefully see the light soon. The same could be said of Shiite and Sunni institutions or organizations in Iraq.

These bilateral meetings normally are held once every two years, with the venue of the meeting alternating between Rome and their respective headquarters. At the end of such encounters, either a final declaration is made or a press statement is released, informing about the discussions held or the points agreed upon.

Our dicastery is aware of both the strong and weak points of the meetings just mentioned. These are, no doubt, dialogues of the elites, limited to only a small number of persons, some of whom are, so to speak, "addicted" to dialogue. You may rightly ask: What happens after these meetings? What has really changed since such meetings? The dialogue of the elites is obviously necessary and has proved to be useful too, but I must add that these initiatives have not been sufficient. Through this kind of dialogue, ideas are clarified, information is shared, new methods are explored, misconceptions and misunderstandings are overcome, and mutual trust and friendships are built for the benefit of all. As a comparison, one could speak of a laboratory, where new products see the light and then go to the public. What counts the most in all these exercises is that it must contribute toward the peaceful and fruitful coexistence of believers, especially the Christians and the Muslims who are all members of the human family that also includes those who do not profess any religion.

When we talk about Catholic-Muslim dialogue, we do not forget about the involvement in and the initiatives taken by our brothers and sisters who belong to the Orthodox churches, as well as to the different Christian denominations either independently or in collaboration with the Catholic organizations, most especially with the PCID. The most important illustration of such collaboration with the PCID is that of the Programme on Interreligious Dialogue and Co-operation (IRDC) of the

World Council of Churches (WCC). This office has collaborated with us in publishing documents such as *Interreligious Marriage* (1994–1997), *Interreligious Prayer* (1997–1998), and *African Religiosity* (2000–2004). The last document jointly brought out was *Christian Witness in a Multi-religious World: Recommendations for Conduct* (2006–2011). Besides the WCC-IRDC and the PCID, the World Evangelical Alliance (WEA) was also part of this project. While receiving a delegation of the WEA in Rome on November 6, 2014, Pope Francis, in respect to this document said: "I hope, too, that the document *Christian Witness in a Multi-religious World: Recommendations for Conduct* may become a motive of inspiration for the proclamation of the Gospel in multi-religious contexts."

In Washington, D.C., is the Christian Muslim Summit, founded as a result of the initiative of Bishop Chane, former Episcopalian Bishop of Washington, and ably assisted by Canon Peterson. This biennial summit brings together well-known religious leaders and scholars from both Christianity and Islam and the Sunni and Shi'ia. The first summit took place in Washington, the second one in Beirut, and the third one in Rome. At this point, I wish to make an important remark concerning the role of the local churches in promoting interreligious dialogue. Interreligious dialogue, as a matter of fact, does not take place in the Vatican but, rather, in the local churches, at the grassroots, where the followers of the different religions live either side by side or face to face, sharing the same joys and trials in day-to-day life. As participants in the dialogue know well, there are four modalities of a harmonious dialogue: the dialogue of life, the dialogue of works, the theological dialogue (when possible), and the dialogue of spiritualties. All of these need to be encouraged and promoted at the local levels, in the families, schools, colleges, universities, workplaces, and every circumstance.

Let us now turn our attention to the current situation. The caliphate was abolished in 1924, following the dissolution of the Ottoman Empire and the rise of the Turkish Republic. But in the twenty-first century we have been witnessing the rise and the attempted re-establishment of the caliphate, which, although it is occasionally invoked by the Islamists as a symbol of global Islamic unity, has not found much favor from mainstream Islamist groups such as the Muslim Brotherhood in Egypt. It did, however, figure prominently in the rhetoric of violent extremist groups like al-Qaeda. In June 2014, an insurgent group known as the Islamic State in Iraq and the Levant (ISIL), also known as the Islamic State in Iraq and Syria (ISIS) or, simply, the Islamic State (IS), took control of areas of eastern Syria and western Iraq. This group declared the establishment of a caliphate with the group's leader, Abu Bakr al-Baghdadi, as the caliph. We live today in the midst of and with the results of such violence and aggression.

We at the PCID, along with others, recognize that Muslims are living a difficult period of their history and are facing many challenges. One of these challenges is the necessary and not-so-easy dialogue with modernity. Another challenge is of a legal nature. It is the recognition of human rights, including those of women, the challenge of full citizenship to non-Muslims living in the Muslim majority countries, the real integration of the Muslims in countries where they have emigrated, and the challenge of a sound relation between religion and politics. They have to cope with some of their co-religionists who sometimes use the name of religion to justify violence and violation of the fundamental human rights (I refer to the atrocities committed by the terrorists of the so-called Islamic State). Still a major challenge is that of the fundamental liberties—liberty of conscience, of expression, of religion, of intellectual research; the blasphemy law (if it were even fair that it exists); poverty and underdevelopment in numerous Muslim societies; and confessional tensions and conflicts, in particular between the Sunnis and the Shiites. The list could go on and on.

In this context, I would like to say that as Catholics, we are not and we cannot afford to remain passive to the aforementioned challenges and problems faced by many of our Muslim brothers and sisters. On the contrary, we must remain close to them in mind and prayer; ready to share our experiences with them in finding solutions to these problems, particularly perhaps in the field of human rights and in the attitude toward modernity. Obviously, our attitude should not be one of paternalism or of giving lessons, but that of enhancing brotherhood and friendship.

I must mention here about another important field of dialogue, the Jewish-Christian-Muslim dialogue. Although put in difficulty because of the Israeli-Palestinian conflict, it remains of great significance and importance and a sign of hope for the Middle East and the entire world.

Another sign of hope is that the Muslims are always more enterprising in dialogue, especially with the Christians. This is the case, for example, of the Doha International Centre for Dialogue and of the King Abdullah bin Abdul-Aziz International Centre for Interreligious and Intercultural Dialogue, established in Vienna. It is true that politics is not totally absent from these and similar initiatives, but regardless of that, what is more important is the motive behind the organizing of meetings by these well-known centers: it is one of purification and healing and not one of arriving at solutions to put an end to the problems. A particular initiative of our Muslim friends that merits our appreciation and thanks is the translation of the catechism of the Catholic Church into Farsi by Iranian Muslims.

I am aware of the fact that many more things could be said. Before concluding, all I wish to underline is that it is realistic to foresee that the coming fifty years will be decisive for a more fruitful and honest interreligious dialogue between Muslims and Christians. In the context of the growing radicalization of Islam, there is a great challenge to the Church—ordinary people, scholars, the clergy, and the religious—to know Islam better; there is the need for further theological reflection on Islam by Christians and also—why not—a theological reflection by the Christians and the Muslims together. For Muslims the great challenge will be the encounter with modernity. They will also have to resist the temptation of going back to their countries of origin; they need to be active members in the democratic and pluralistic societies wherever they are.

The Christian and Muslim leaders therefore need to be prepared to meet these challenges. Besides facilitating the formation of their co-religionists in their own respective religions, they also need to prepare specialists not only of their religions but also of each other's religion. In my opinion, Christianity and Islam share two fundamental convictions: (1) the human person has been created by God, and (2) as creatures, we recognize the truth, which is greater than we are. If we are truly convinced of these and are honest in living by these convictions, interreligious dialogue would be more and more the grammar of human conviviality today and tomorrow.

To dialogue is, first of all, to understand our agreements and disagreements and consider what we can do together for the common good of our pluralistic society. We must humbly admit that even after fifty years of Christian-Muslim dialogue inspired by *Nostra Aetate*, we still do not know each other well enough. As a matter of fact, many of the difficulties and problems that we face are due to ignorance. If we have avoided the clash of civilizations, we can also avoid the clash of ignorance.

Response to His Eminence, Cardinal Tauran

SEYYED HOSSEIN NASR

In the Name of God, the Most Merciful, the Most Compassionate

B efore everything else I want to thank God for having afforded this opportunity to me to speak, discuss, and exchange ideas with our Catholic brothers and sisters. I am also grateful to our hosts at The Catholic University of America for accommodating us and for giving me the opportunity to respond to His Eminence, Cardinal Tauran, with whom I have participated in many ecumenical dialogues over the years. Today my task is to respond to his presentation specifically and not to speak of dialogue between us in general.

It is necessary to begin with the significance of *Nostra Aetate* for Muslims and the Islamic religion in its relation to Christianity in general and to Catholicism in particular. Before the declaration of this document, there had been some dialogue between Muslims and Christians going back, as far as formal gatherings are concerned, to the very important conference on Christianity and Islam held in a Benedictine monastery at Tioumliline in Morocco in 1957, which I had the honor to attend. *Nostra Aetate*, however, opened a new chapter in this dialogue. After its declaration, many Muslims, who were interested in serious discourse with the Catholic Church, saw a new opening for thoughtful dialogue, and since then numerous conferences have been held by Muslims for this purpose in countries such as Turkey, Iran, Egypt, Jordan, Pakistan, and Morocco. In fact, the Common Word Initiative grew in an ambience influenced by the *Nostra Aetate* declaration.

Although many issues have been discussed in this ongoing dialogue, I believe that theological issues must remain our central concern because, for us Muslims and Christians, all other issues are linked to our relation to God and the revelations He has sent to us. A person's attitude toward the absolute determines his or her attitude toward the relative. We cannot put theological issues aside, no matter how intractable, and hope to have serious dialogue.

I also believe that although the Catholic-Muslim dialogue is crucial and can be very fruitful if carried out in depth and with sincerity and compassion, it is now time to include, in at least some of our dialogues, not only other branches of Christianity but also other religions. So many of the issues we discuss not only concern other religions such as Judaism, Hinduism, and Buddhism, but the presence of other religions is necessary in the implementation of so many of our proposed joint programs.

From the Islamic point of view it is necessary to have a clear understanding of the position of the Catholic Church concerning the theological issue of the Islamic revelation coming after Christianity and the question of its authenticity for Christians. Similarly, it is necessary for Muslims to re-examine the Islamic doctrine of abrogation (*naskh*) as far as Christianity and other religions are concerned. We cannot have serious dialogue and discourse while shying away from such central issues. Those Muslims who are sincere in carrying out dialogue with Catholics ask if the opening created by *Nostra Aetate* really means acceptance by Catholics of Islam as an authentic revelation by God or if it means accepting it only as a historical reality to be dealt with accordingly.

Cardinal Tauran speaks of the necessity of dialogue with both Sunnism and Shiism with which I agree heartily in the same way that the Islamic side dialogue with Christianity must include not only Catholicism but also different branches of both Protestantism and the various Orthodox churches. Here, it is necessary to point to a fact not mentioned by Cardinal Tauran. Iran is not the only Shiite country. Iraq, Bahrain, Azerbaijan, and Lebanon also have a Shiite majority; Yemen is half Shiite; and Syria, Pakistan, and India have large Shiite minorities. Catholic dialogue with Shiites must include not only Persian Shiism but also Shiism in the Arab world and the Indo-Pakistani subcontinent as well.

Nostra Aetate is in a sense one of the products of the challenges of modernism to religion. Islam can learn a great deal from Catholicism's experiences of confrontation with modernism from the Reformation and the Galileo trial to Teilhardism and even later to the present day. In this domain Muslims can benefit greatly from dialogue with Catholicism, which was the first religion to confront the challenges of modernism. Let us not forget that modernism first arose and gained strength in Europe and only later spread elsewhere. Furthermore, Muslims now face a modernism that has already failed as an ideology. In such a situation Catholicism and Islam can face many of the new challenges in joining forces in numerous domains, from the environmental crisis to the breakdown of the structure of traditional societies such as the family, all caused by modernism and its consequences.

Since we speak of trialogue, I need to mention the Kennedy Trialogue, whose sessions I attended regularly in Washington, D.C.[1] They were held

1. Eugene Fisher, "Kennedy Institute Jewish-Christian-Muslim Trialogue," *Journal of Ecumenical Studies* 19, no. 1 (Winter 1982): 197–200.

in the early 1980s at Georgetown's Kennedy Institute, a program that came to an end with the Israeli invasion of Lebanon in 1982. Fortunately, similar initiatives were undertaken later, such as the Children of Abraham Initiative and The Common Word Initiative, which is an ongoing process. I believe that *Nostra Aetate*'s fiftieth anniversary could be a catalyst in renewing such efforts in which Catholics have usually played a major role along with their Jewish and Muslim brothers and sisters.

Cardinal Tauran mentions the translation of the catechism into Persian. I should add that an excellent translation of the Bible has existed in Persian for a long time, and Persia over the centuries has been one of the Muslim countries in which great interest has been shown in religious dialogue. This interest continues to this day, as can be seen in the numerous dialogues held in Iran since the establishment of the Islamic Republic of Iran in 1979 with not only Catholics but also with Protestant and Orthodox Christians.

Finally, I want to mention that dialogue is not only a challenge to Catholics but also a challenge to Muslims. The question of how to have authentic dialogue and understand the faith of the "other" without diluting one's own faith faces every religious person in whatever faith he or she belongs. Does dialogue mean the transformation of those who dialogue, and if so, what kind of transformation will be or should be brought about? Are we going to come closer to God through dialogue, or will we sacrifice the intensity of our faith as the price to pay for gaining understanding of and empathy for the "other"? These are basic issues that men and women, whether Catholic, Muslim, or of another faith, face together. Let us hope and pray that the next half century in the life of *Nostra Aetate* will be witness to our coming closer to each other spiritually and through this empathy, mutual understanding, and respect for each other, we also come closer to God.

Muslim Dialogue with the Church after *Nostra Aetate*

SEYYED HOSSEIN NASR

On this occasion, marking the fiftieth anniversary of the declaration of *Nostra Aetate*, it is appropriate to review the reaction of Muslims and the Islamic world to this document over the past half century. When the declaration was first announced by the Vatican, it received little attention in Islamic countries, but gradually a number of Muslim scholars who either dialogued with Christians before or were particularly interested in the views of Catholics toward Islam became aware of this document and its possible importance for future Catholic-Muslim relations. Some saw in this initiative a new opening for genuine and positive dialogue, while others were skeptical and saw it as a mere political maneuver. The latter group pointed to the continuation of aggressive Catholic missionary activity in several Islamic countries and attacks by some Catholic writers against Islam. The former group pointed to the necessity of patience for matters to change over time. Both sides were right in a sense. On the one hand, we have witnessed the rise and increase of Islamophobia in which many Catholics have participated and continue to participate. On the other hand, cooperation and genuine dialogue between Catholicism and Islam continue to expand and increase. Moreover, these two opposing views and currents are also to be seen in the Islamic world where opposition to Christians is on the rise, especially among so-called fundamentalists, in such countries as Syria, Iraq, and Egypt, but also where there is ever greater interest in religious dialogue and accord with Christians in many circles, both Sunni and Shiite, as we see in Lebanon, Iran, Pakistan, Indonesia, and elsewhere.

There is another element that needs to be mentioned when we seek to understand the Islamic response to *Nostra Aetate*, and that element is the difference in the two religions in not only the theology of the multiplicity of religions but also the historical experience of religions other than one's own. During its long period of incubation, growth, spread, and finally domination over western Europe, Catholicism knew only one other religion (Judaism being a special case)—Islam—and Western Christianity relegated Islam to the category of a Christian heresy and a false religion. Only after the advent of modernism and weakening of Catholicism in the West did Western Christianity become aware of such religions as Confucianism,

Taoism, Hinduism, and Buddhism. In contrast, even before modern times Islam had had contact with and awareness of many religions from, of course, Judaism and Christianity to Black African religions to Hinduism, Buddhism, North Asian Shamanism, Confucianism, and Taoism, and so the experience of the multiplicity of religion was not combined with modernism, as was the case of Western Christianity.

Nostra Aetate in a sense opened the door for Catholics to other religions. Muslim scholars, however, felt that for them the door had already been opened many centuries before and that awareness of other religions was not something new for them. In fact, the principles of the multiplicity of revelation go back to the Qur'an, which mentions explicitly God having sent prophets to all people. The *Hadīth* also speaks of 124,000 prophets having existed, and many other *ahādīth* refer to other religions and the centrality of the doctrine of unity (*al-tawhīd*) at the heart of all authentic religions, not only Islam. This difference in both theological perspective and historical experience between Western Christianity and Islam must be remembered when Western scholars seek to evaluate the Muslims' response to *Nostra Aetate*.

During the past fifty years, numerous ecumenical meetings have been held involving Catholicism and Islam, many inspired by the *Nostra Aetate* document and some not, but even in the latter case there has been an indirect influence and presence of this declaration. There is no doubt that this document has been of cardinal importance in the process of dialogue between us during the past half century. It transformed the Catholic ambience for dialogue and indirectly the Islamic one as far as dialogue with Christianity was concerned. As I mentioned, even the Common Word Initiative, which was undertaken by Muslims following the Regensburg address by Pope Benedict XVI in which Islam was criticized, was drawn up by people who were fully aware of *Nostra Aetate*.

Over the years since the declaration of the document, many Muslims have wondered why the Catholics have become so much more interested in dialogue than followers of other religions, including Islam, have been. Few Muslims understand the internal existential and theological needs of contemporary Catholicism, which are not the same as those of Islam, but gradually Muslims gained greater understanding of these matters through their dialogues with Christians. Moreover, through this process many Muslim scholars became aware of the necessity of dialogue for Muslims themselves. This awareness led not only to the Common Word Initiative but also to numerous other dialogues with Christians hosted by Muslims in Cairo, Tehran, Amman, Istanbul, Lahore, and other Muslim cities.

On this occasion I want to say a few words about my own experience of dialogue with Christianity during the past fifty years. As I have written before, my experience of dialogue with Christianity began in 1957 before the declaration of *Nostra Aetate*. I was then president of the Harvard Islamic Society and Dom Denis Martin, the abbot of the Tioumliline Monastery in the Atlas Mountains near Fez in Morocco, came to Cambridge and invited me to attend the conference on Islam and Christianity that was to be held there that summer. I accepted and attended that memorable gathering. The conference features such luminaries as the Catholic Islamicists Louis Massignon and Louis Gardet and the American philosopher F. S. C. Northrop. I shall never forget the discourse on that occasion of Massignon, that noble scholar who was such an important bridge between the West and the Islamic world. He said, "It is too late for conferences. What matters now is the prayer of the heart (*la prière du coeur*)."[1] And he ended by reciting in Persian the famous poem of Hāfiz: *hargiz namīrad ānk-i dilash zindishud bi-'ishq thabtast dar jarādiy-i 'ālam dawām-i mā* (He whose heart is enlivened by love shall never die—our subsistence is recorded in the cosmic book). Massignon's discourse did not, however, bring ecumenical conferences to an end; what it did do was set a high bar and the spiritual conditions for any future serious dialogue in the domain of religion, a dialogue that was to become ever more frequent after the declaration of *Nostra Aetate*.

Another highlight in dialogue for me happened in the 1960s when I led an Islamic delegation to the Vatican during the papacy of Paul VI. Cardinal Pignedoli led the Catholic delegation for five days, and we had a most meaningful dialogue. We were even permitted to perform our canonical prayers in the chapel in Assisi where St. Francis had received the stigmata. A special friendship was created between the Cardinal and me that lasted until his death. It was he who talked me into attending the conference in Tripoli in 1973 on Islam and Christianity, attended by many leading Muslims and Christians. The political use that Muammar Gaddafi tried to make of the conference, however, caused strong negative reactions in Europe. Many blamed Cardinal Pignedoli for this matter even though his intentions were very positive and noble. Yet some Catholic friends of mine said the Tripoli Conference resulted in destroying the chances of the cardinal becoming the next pope.

As for the last few years, most of the dialogue carried out with Christians, in which I have participated, has been associated with the Common Word Initiative with which I have been connected since its inception,

1. Also quoted in Seyyed Hossein Nasr, "The Prayer of the Heart in Hesychasm and Sufism," in *Orthodox Christians and Muslims*, ed. N. M. Vaporis (Brookline, Mass.: Holy Cross Orthodox Press, 1986), 203.

being one of its original signatories. I have led several delegations to the Vatican to pursue the goals of this initiative, and I can say that during these many meetings that have been held not only in the Vatican but also in Washington, D.C., New Haven, Amman, and elsewhere, the goals pursued are to a large extent those intended by the Church in *Nostra Aetate*.

* * *

During all these meetings and exchanges, much has been discussed concerning both theological matters and ethical, social, and practical ones. But not all the goals set forth by the two sides have been attained. Many questions remain, and there is still much to do to bring about greater understanding and accord leading to possible cooperation between us. Let us first of all turn to those issues that still pose difficulties for one side or both and then turn to matters wherein we can or have been able to find greater commonalities and even cooperation.

Let us start with what comes first by nature, that is, God. Of course we are both monotheists and the God of Abraham is our God. The Catholic credo *in unum Deum* reflects so closely *lā ilāha illa'Llāh*. The problem for Muslims arises with the doctrine of the Trinity, of which there have been so many different interpretations among Christians themselves. As some Catholic participants in our dialogues and other scholars have pointed out, the traditional Islamic understanding of the Trinity is close to the views of some eastern churches and not to the doctrine of the Trinity as defined by the Nicene Creed. Nevertheless, Muslims cannot accept anything that would compromise *tawhīd*, the oneness of the One, or *al-ahadiyyah*. For Muslims, all relationality in the Divine Order belongs to the level of the Divine Names and Qualities and not to the Divine Essence (*al-Dhāt*). Muslims, in fact, would have no problem with accepting the doctrine of *Gottheit* or *Urgrund* of such Christian mystics as Meister Eckhart, Angelus Silesius, and Jakob Böhme or of relegating the three hypostases to the level of the Divine Names and Qualities.

On the level of formal theological creed, however, there cannot exist total accord between Catholicism and Islam. Nor should either side expect such an accord on the level of theological creeds. On that level we have to agree to disagree respectfully. As Frithjof Schuon once said, "There cannot be accord and harmony between religions in the human atmosphere. There can be accord and harmony only in the Divine Stratosphere."[2] On the human plane, the most we can do is to have Christians understand and

2. Seyyed Hossein Nasr, *The Essential Frithjof Schuon* (Bloomington, Ind.: World Wisdom, 2005), 15.

respect why Muslims insist so much upon the Oneness of God (*al-tawḥīd*), whose assertion as the central reality of religion is the very raison d'être of the Islamic revelation, and to have Muslims understand that according to Christians the Trinity does not negate the unity of God, this being a Christian mystery that cannot be comprehended by logic alone. It is for metaphysicians of both sides to point to "the Divine Stratosphere" wherein is to be found the harmony and accord that do not exist on the human plane. This task has been already performed by certain Muslim metaphysicians.

Closely linked to the doctrine of the Trinity is that of the incarnation. Christianity is based on the manifestation of God in Christ, the son, and so quite rightly the religion brought by him is called Christianity. For a long time in the West, Islam was thought to be similar *mutatis mutandis* and wrongly was called Muhammadanism by even well-known Western scholars of Islam, and this practice continued until a few decades ago. But Islam is based on the One, the Absolute, and not on its manifestation, and so Christianity is Christocentric while Islam is not Muhammado-centric. Furthermore, being based on the Absolute Itself, Islam cannot accept the idea of the Absolute becoming incarnated as the Absolute unless by incarnation (*ḥulūl*) we understand theophany (*tajallī*), and even then it is not the Divine Essence (*al-Dhāt*) but the Divine Names and Qualities that are the sources of all theophanies. This is an intractable issue on the theological (but not metaphysical) level, and therefore on the theological level, the best that we can do is to try to understand each other with empathy.

In a sense matters are made more complicated by the fact that there is not only a Christian Christology but also an Islamic one. Christ and the Virgin Mary play important roles in Islam both at the level of ordinary piety and metaphysically. Mary is the only woman named in the Qur'an, and in fact a chapter of the Islamic Sacred Scripture is titled "Maryam." Christ is considered by Muslims the most important prophet after the Prophet of Islam, and 'Īsā ibn Maryam is seen as "the Prophet of Inwardness" associated with love, forgiveness, and compassion. His miraculous birth from a virgin mother and exceptional life filled with miracles are recorded in the Qur'an. Over the centuries many Christians have spoken disparagingly about the Islamic understanding of Christ, but now it is perhaps time for them to realize that this exceptional being belongs not only to Christianity but also to Islam, where he also plays an important spiritual function.

I have had occasion to point out in some of my earlier writings that there is one crucial event concerning the life of Christ that on the level of accepted fact separates Christians and Muslims. It is not his miraculous birth or words preached to his followers. It is his death. Whereas Christians believe that he was crucified on what has come to be known as Good Friday and resurrected on Easter Sunday and taken alive to Heaven forty days later, Muslims believe that he was not crucified and did not die on the cross but was taken directly to Heaven. For one community the cross became the central symbol of its religion; for the other the event that the cross symbolizes never took place. It seems that God revealed two understandings of this central event to create an isthmus (*barzakh*) to prevent the two oceans of Christianity and Islam from flowing into each other and becoming one. He wanted both religions to survive as distinct realities and paths leading to Him. Doctrinal differences concerning the Trinity, incarnation, and so on, can be understood metaphysically and the differences overcome, but one cannot do so with what would appear as historical fact.

A closely related issue to the nature of Christ is the question of revelation. If there is only one incarnation, there can be only one authentic religion. If God has spoken more than once and to many prophets, then there can be many authentic religions. I understand that it is easier for Muslims, who accept the second view, to recognize other religions as authentic than it is for Christians who accept the first view to do so. And yet this question remains a great challenge for Christian theologians and must be faced with honesty if there is to be serious religious dialogue between us. A solution is not impossible but needs deep spiritual commitment to dialogue. In any case, it has been said that with God all things are possible.

The doctrine of the uniqueness of Christianity, especially Catholicism, leads to the well-known doctrine of *extra ecclesiam nulla salus.* Can sincere Catholics dialogue with Muslims while many more traditional Christians still believe that their partners in dialogue cannot be saved and are condemned to Hell? Of what use would such a dialogue be except to serve the cause of political expediency? It is very important to mention, however, that the Church has announced in recent years that Muslims can also be saved. *Lumen Gentium,* promulgated at the Second Vatican Council, states: "[T]he plan of salvation also includes those who acknowledge the Creator. In the first place among these there are the Muslims, who, professing to hold the faith of Abraham, along with us adore the one and merciful God."[3] Many Catholic thinkers have been grappling with this issue, but while a number of the traditional doctrinal views of the Church have been cast aside during the past half century, this doctrine has not been formally rescinded as far as I know.

Turning to sacred history, it is obvious that Christians and Muslims do have elements in common in that they both accept and honor the chain of Hebrew prophets, but even here there are differences in that, in Christianity, the sun of Christ completely dominates the spiritual sky under

---

3. Vatican Council II, *Lumen Gentium,* November 21, 1964, par. 16.

which the stars symbolizing the older prophets are no longer visible—one might say they do not play a direct role in Christianity, spiritually speaking. As for Islam, not only does the Qur'an refer to some non-Hebrew prophets, but also for Muslims the Prophet is like the moon dominating the night sky, but the other stars are also present and can and do play a spiritual role in that sector of the cosmos dominated by the Quranic revelation. Moreover, there are different understandings between Muslims and Christians of some of the Hebrew prophets starting with Adam himself, who marks the origin of the prophetic chain for Muslims. Those differences can also be seen in how the two religions view David and Solomon.

Moreover, these differences are reflected in how the two religions view the flow of time from a religious point of view. Christians have a linear and historical, albeit sacralized, concept of time that is marked by Adam, Christ, and his Second Coming. For them, through the incarnation the Truth has entered into the stream of historical time. For Muslims the Truth is above time, and historical time is cyclic, marked by cycles of penetrations of the Divine Word into the human order through a long series of revelations. It is not accidental that secularization, which is in a sense the divinization of historical time leading to the idea of progress, arose in the Christian and so-called post-Christian world in the West and not elsewhere. The idea of linear progress that is still prevalent, but now challenged by many Western thinkers themselves, is the result of the secularization of the Christian concept of the march of time, not the Islamic one, although now many modernized Muslims like other non-Westerners have come to accept and even espouse the modern Western view of linear progress.

On the social level there is this difference between us, also pointed out by others, that the concept of law differs in our two religions. Like Moses, the Prophet brought a Divine Law that concerns not only spiritual and religious matters but also laws governing everyday human life; whereas Christ brought laws pertaining primarily to the spiritual world, and later Christianity integrated Roman law and in some cases Germanic and common law into its teachings when it became the religion of a whole civilization. All one has to do is to remember that in Christianity, canon law means the law of the Church, whereas *qānūn* in Arabic (which also comes from the Greek word *canon*) means laws derived from nonreligious sources, while the law that should govern Islamic society is called *al-Sharī'ah*. This difference has had deep implications for the difference in the responses of Christianity and Islam to modernism. This difference in the concept of law between Christianity and Islam cannot be bridged to create a united perspective, but its understanding is essential for each side to gain greater insight into and respect for the responses of the other side to this very important issue.

Finally, in discussing the difficulties in dialogue, it is not possible not to mention missionary activity especially as it intertwines with medicine, technology, and education. On the one hand, both Christianity and Islam are traveling religions, and some form of missionary activity, called *da'wah* in Arabic, exists in both religions. But that is where the symmetry ends. During the last thousand years Islam has spread in sub-Saharan Africa, the Indian subcontinent, south Asia, and elsewhere mostly through Sufi orders and pious merchants, while Christianity has spread mostly through missionary activity by people specifically called missionaries and trained as such. It is only since the nineteenth century that some Muslims, reacting to and also emulating Western missionaries, began to train their own professional missionaries, especially in sub-Saharan Africa and the Indian subcontinent.

There is, therefore, an asymmetry between Christianity and Islam in the domain of missionary activity of the two sides. One side came to identify Christianity with the successes of the modern world and tried to propagate Western Christianity on the back of worldly activities such as modern medicine and hospitals, various forms of modern technology, and modern education. The other—that is, Muslim missionaries—was deprived of such means and had to rely on the truth of Islam itself and not its advantage in getting its converts better jobs or medical care. Interestingly enough, the Orthodox Church has followed a path similar to that of Islam when it comes to missionary activity. To see the asymmetry of Western Christianity and Islam in this domain, it is sufficient to ask the questions: How many children of the social, economic, and political elite of countries such as Pakistan or Egypt go to Western-dominated Christian missionary schools or schools originally founded by the missionaries, and how many children of Christians, or for that matter secularists, go to Islamic schools?

We cannot sweep the missionary question under the carpet and need to devote much more time and effort to it. We cannot be hypocrites. Are we to dialogue with each other for better mutual understanding while trying to convert each other? Or are we to be a religious and spiritual presence for each other and without worldly factors allow each religion to grow in a free atmosphere dominated by mutual respect and trust? That does not mean that there will never be any conversions. Much of the future success of the dialogue between us will depend on how we face such questions with sincerity and honesty. This issue is one of the most important that will face those devoted to the message of *Nostra Aetate* during the decades to come, especially in light of such new developments as the rise of the Islamic population and the increase of Islamic schools in the West, anti-Christian sentiments by many Muslim fundamentalists in the East combined with the rise of Islamophobia in the West, and certain local political factors in many Islamic and some European counties.

* * *

Not all issues are obstacles between us to be overcome. There are many areas of accord and possibilities of cooperation that need to be emphasized. The most obvious are the common beliefs in God, the sacredness of life, the immortality of the soul and its judgment by God, and other beliefs that are obviously foundational to both of our religions and need not be elaborated here. Perhaps less obvious to some is the field of ethics. A number of Christian authors have pointed out that turning the other cheek is unique to Christianity and does not exist in Judaism or Islam. That is true, but first of all this was an ideal set by Christ for the spiritually accomplished and the saintly, and once Christianity became the religion of a whole civilization, it needed to have recourse to a system of justice in which there had to be retribution for crimes and the breaking of laws without which society could not function. And so the end result was not very different from the situation of Islam.

Moreover, this issue is not the whole of ethics. When we look upon the field of ethics as a whole, we see remarkable similarities, concrete ethical actions, in doing good and avoiding evil. Generosity, helping the poor, honesty, justice in one's actions, and numerous other ethical norms are shared by us, as are categories of action that are unethical—from lying and deceit to theft, to adultery, and of course to taking of a human life outside of the question of war and established laws.

In the ethical domain there is, however, one subject wherein there are some differences of view but similarity to a large extent in results, and that is the question of sexuality. In traditional Christianity, sexuality was associated with original sin and the fall and was made religiously possible through the sacrament of marriage. In Islam sexuality is itself positive and sacred but has to be regulated according to the Divine Law, the *Shari'ah*, and so marriage is based on a contract between the two sides; a contract, however, that possesses a religious character and is not secular. Despite this difference, both religions join hands in honoring highly the institution of marriage and opposing sexual promiscuity. The question of monogamy versus polygamy is a separate issue with which I shall not deal here except to say that what is happening in the West now with same-sex marriage, condoned by some Christians, requires a whole review of age-old criticism by Western writers of Islam for permitting the practice of polygamy.

Ethics in our religions has a direct relationship to eschatology because our actions in the world, whether ethical or unethical, have a bearing on our posthumous status. Therefore, it should not be surprising to observe so many similarities in eschatology between our two religions, although there are also some differences. For example, as part of the eschatological events that will mark the end of this world, both Muslims and Christians believe in the coming of the Anti-Christ and the Second Coming of Christ, but Muslims believe that Christ will come again to preach *tawhīd*, or Divine Unity, and will come as a *muslim* in the most universal sense of this term, as one submitted to the one God, a term by which he is also referred in the Qur'an. As for the tripartite division of Hell, Purgatory, and Paradise, it exists in both of our religions. To demonstrate this unity, it is enough to point to the *Divine Comedy* of Dante, the most Christian of poets and arguably the greatest poet in Western civilization. As such Catholic scholars as Miguel Asín Palacios and Enrico Cerulli have shown, the schema and architecture of this Christian poetic masterpiece was taken from Islamic sources, which does not make the work any less Christian. This fact only reveals the deep accord between the two religions concerning many central eschatological issues. There are, of course, some differences in the description of posthumous states as well, and many Christians have criticized the Quranic description of paradise as being too sensual, not understanding the symbolic significance of the Quranic language and the fact that no earthly language is sufficient in its outer form to describe what belongs to higher orders of reality.

Turning to matters of more everyday concern, one of the most dangerous forces that Christianity and Islam face together is the secularism that negates and seeks to eradicate all religions. This challenge is shared by both of our religions, and many of the problems caused by this powerful challenge are the concern of all of us. Although the history and theological understanding of secularism is different in Christianity and Islam to the extent that there is not even a word in classical Arabic or Persian for secularism, today the reality of what is called secularism and its effects in domains as far removed as economics and art is faced by both Christianity and Islam. In this area, as I have had occasion to mention to our Catholic partners in dialogue before, Muslims, who are often naive about this matter, can learn a great deal from the Catholic Church, which was the first religious body to experience secularism in the modern sense. When Catholicism was facing such Renaissance skeptics as Montaigne or the founders of a purely secular science as Galileo, Muslims were not even aware of the existence of such secularist ideas. Their awareness came two or three centuries later, and so they can learn in both a positive and a negative way from the centuries-long experiences of Catholicism with secularism, from both its achievements and what many consider its errors or misjudgments. As an example of the latter category, one can mention Catholicism's handing the whole of the natural order to modern science after the Galileo trial and suddenly finding itself in the twentieth century with the task of finding a Christian solution to the environmental crisis, one of whose basic causes is the triumph of a purely secular and quantitative science and its applications in the form of modern technology placed in the hands of endless human greed.

I am fully aware of this issue because I was one of the first voices to predict the environmental crisis when I gave the Rockefeller Series Lecture at the University of Chicago in 1966, whose text appeared as *Man and Nature*. It was at first severely criticized by many Christian writers who had believed that Christianity made modern science and technology possible, and this was proof of its superiority over other religions. This whole argument of course collapsed with the rise of the environmental crisis. Since then, Catholics have done much work in this field, and Muslims are doing more and more. This crucial issue, which involves the very survival of humanity on earth, is one in which there is much accord, putting aside some Christian theological views concerning the incarnation being the cause of the sacredness of nature, an issue over which Islam and Christianity differ.

When we come to the field of education, despite problems caused by missionary schools that I have mentioned earlier, so much of our educational philosophy is similar. We both believe that teaching of subjects, which involves the training of the mind, must be combined with the training of the soul and ethics. That is why education is called *al-ta'līm wa'l-tarbiyah, ta'līm* in Arabic, referring to the theoretical instruction of various forms of knowledge and *tarbiyah* to the training of the soul. Also, historically the medieval Western university was very similar to and influenced by Islamic models in both the subjects taught and the manner of teaching. The present-day use of the word *chair* in Western universities is witness to this long historical relationship, *chair* in this context being the translation of the Arabic *al-kursī*, literally the chair on which a professor would sit to teach while his students would sit around him. It is not accidental that in modern times, while many Muslim students sent to Christian missionary schools became "de-Islamicized" at least in their minds, if not souls, many also became more devout Muslims. We Muslims and Christians have so much in common in our philosophies and goals of education upon which we could build today, rather than making Western-inspired education, whether it be Christian or secular, a major source of contention between us.

Finally in the list of our commonalities, one must mention that which is the most important: the fact that we both believe in God, the sacred, the entelechy of men and women in states beyond this world, and our responsibilities in this world to God and His creation. The two commandments of Christ, to love God and to love the neighbor, are shared by both of us,

Muslims as well as Christians. These commonly held beliefs become even more significant in a world in which secularism is rampant, and as a result one sees opposition to all religion on the one hand and the rise of exclusive fundamentalism on the other hand, along with the revival of both Islam and Christianity, the latter especially in Russia but unfortunately not in Western Europe. In such a situation, what can be more natural than Islam and Christianity joining forces together to confront a common enemy that is determined to destroy both?

* * *

In light of what has been stated, it is not difficult to identify areas in which Catholics and Muslims can have close cooperation, as has also been pointed out by some of our Catholic partners in dialogue with us. What is needed for success is emphasis on cooperation rather than rivalry. Needless to say, this task is easier to perform in the private sector than in areas controlled by various governments. Nongovernmental organizations, both Christian and Islamic, can cooperate successfully in many projects especially in areas where there are both Christians and Muslims. We can clearly see some examples of this mutual cooperation in such areas as sub-Saharan Africa, Lebanon, and Pakistan. A lot more can be done, however, if the spirit of cooperation increases among well-intentioned men and women on both sides.

The same is true for education, despite the one-sided present state of affairs in which there are numerous Catholic educational organizations in many Islamic countries and very few Muslim ones with a similar situation in the West. How wonderful it would be if in some countries such as Nigeria and Lebanon, where there are large Christian and Muslim populations, schools could be set up jointly by Christians and Muslims with a curriculum based on a perspective that would honor both traditions. This could also be done in countries with a Muslim majority but with a notable Christian presence, such as Egypt, Pakistan, and Indonesia. Graduates of such schools could do wonders to increase harmony, cooperation, and mutual understanding between our two religions, and such efforts would be an antidote for the poison spewed forth from certain quarters on both sides against the other.

The loss of species, global warming, the destruction of forests, the pollution of bodies of water and dry lands on the earth, and the depleting of natural resources are not only Christian or Muslim problems. They concern the whole world. Amid such horrendous tragedies, why cannot Christians and Muslims combine their voices in reclaiming the whole earth as a sacred trust given to humanity and not as a prostitute to be violated over and over to satiate the ever-increasing worldly desire of those men who are blind to the process of suicide for the benefit of ever-greater material prosperity. The recent encyclical of Pope Francis on the environment was a positive step in this direction and is certainly accepted as an important message by Muslim environmentalists. Unfortunately, the encyclical does not deal with the deeper causes of the environmental crisis that originate from the worldview that dominates modern science and technology and is based on the false thesis that the material world is a reality independent of the higher levels of being and God—if many people still believe such realities exist—and that the statement that nature is sacred is scientifically meaningless and at best only a helpful metaphor. There is no end to the possibilities of mutual cooperation between Muslims and Christians when we come to the most critical issue of today, that is, the destruction with our own hands of our home here on earth.

* * *

Finally, there are issues of practical, everyday concern that confront the two religions and if faced jointly could, despite obvious difficulties, bear positive fruit such as the problem of Palestine, local wars and terrorism in parts of Africa, the destruction of historical and religious sites of both Muslims and Christians in Syria and Iraq, and so on. There are also challenges posed to both Christianity and Islam in such matters as abortion, euthanasia, artificial intelligence, and so many other new intrusive technologies. The response of the two religions to this issue does not have to be identical, but most of the deepest moral issues and questions that arise in such matters are nearly the same for Muslims and Christians, as well as followers of other religions, especially Judaism. Cooperation would allow us to learn much from each other and in many cases present a common front that is so rare these days.

In most of the acutest crises and global battles of the day that are going on, nearly everywhere Islam and Christianity are on the same side. Let us hope and pray that during this second half century in the life of *Nostra Aetate*, cooperation will become even greater between us, and contentious problems and confrontations will decrease. We face a common future together. May God help us join hands in honesty, sincerity, and compassion and remember that if the "other" is not ours, he or she is His, and that all who believe in Him and follow an authentic religion are like passengers on a single ship amid an unprecedented storm that dominates the period of history in which we live.

Thoughts on Reading Professor Nasr's "Muslim Dialogue with the Church after *Nostra Aetate*"

SIDNEY H. GRIFFITH

In his succinctly comprehensive review of Muslim-Catholic relations during the fifty years that have elapsed since the promulgation of *Nostra Aetate* on October 28, 1965, Professor Seyyed Hossein Nasr has deftly put his finger on a number of points for conversation. He speaks from a distinctly Islamic point of view, which, as he points out, is somewhat different from the ways in which Western Catholics have traditionally approached other religions, and he accents in particular the historical responses to Islam on the part of Latin Catholic and Greek Orthodox Christians over the centuries, which has for the most part been disparaging of Muhammad, the Qur'an, and Islam.

In this connection, however, it is important for the sake of balance to take into consideration the wider horizon of historical Christian-Muslim relations both geographically and chronologically. Islam as a distinctive religious tradition in its own right arose and came to maturity well within the purview of and in conversation with Christians, especially those of the so-called Oriental Patriarchates, who lived within the world of Islam and whose views were traditionally expressed in Greek, Syriac, Coptic, and eventually Arabic. In due course many of these Christians learned to articulate their faith in terms reflective of the Islamic ambience in which they lived, and along with Jewish scholars in the same milieu they became major contributors to the development of the intellectual life of Muslims in what has come to be called the classical period of Arabic, Islamic culture. While for various reasons, both religious and political, Latin Catholics in the West have historically had little or no exposure to the thought and experience of their Eastern co-religionists living in the world of Islam, from many of whom they have been ecclesiastically estranged, this situation began to change in the twentieth century and well before *Nostra Aetate*. Only now and very slowly have Catholics begun to look for inspiration in their dialogues with Muslims to the experience of their fellow Christians who have lived among them from the beginning of Islam. This openness to the East is itself in many ways a move encouraged by the ecumenical and interreligious concerns of Vatican II. And the Arab Christian heritage provides a point of reference for Latin Christians of the twenty-first century who would want to present their beliefs in a respectful, interreligious dialogue in a theological idiom readily intelligible to Muslims.

But why, especially during the past fifty years, have Catholics been so anxious to enter into interreligious dialogue, even persisting in the effort when their prospective partners in conversation have sometimes been reluctant, unwilling, or even suspicious of the integrity of their motives? *Nostra Aetate* itself provides the first step in answering the question when it declares, "The Catholic Church rejects nothing that is true and holy" in other religions and goes on to say, "The Church therefore exhorts her sons and daughters to recognize, preserve, and foster the good things, spiritual and moral, as well as the socio-cultural values found among the followers of other religions."[1] What is more, as it concerns Muslims in particular, the Council's dogmatic constitution on the church, *Lumen Gentium*, says specifically that "the plan of salvation also includes those who acknowledge the Creator. In the first place amongst these there are the Muslims,"[2] the very ones of whom *Nostra Aetate* says, "The Church also regards with esteem the Muslims."[3] So the Catholic motive for interreligious dialogue with Muslims may be said to be the pursuit of what is "true and holy." It was the goal of many notable Catholics who were already in close conversation with Muslims long before the Council, most notably the French Catholic Islamicist Louis Massignon of whom Professor Nasr speaks so highly.

The pursuit in dialogue of what is true and holy in another's religion necessarily includes carefully highlighting of the challenges in doctrine and practice that characterize the differences and difficulties that separate them. In his carefully expressed reflection on Muslim dialogue with the Church after *Nostra Aetate*, Professor Nasr has done just this as he reflects on the unresolved doctrinal and practical differences between Muslims and Christians. For this respondent, it is important to acknowledge in this connection that the Qur'an itself provides the basis for the doctrinal difficulties he mentions in that when it comes to Christians, the Islamic scripture explicitly criticizes and rejects the truth of what Christians say and believe about Jesus the Messiah and, as a consequence of that, what they say and believe about the one God.[4] In other words, on the doctrinal level, it is not just a matter of theological difference; the Qur'an and Muslim teaching challenge two of the most basic articles of faith in the Christian creed. So

1. *Nostra Aetate* 2, trans. Thomas F. Stransky, CSP.
2. Vatican Council II, *Lumen Gentium*, November 21, 1964, par. 16.
3. *Nostra Aetate*, 3.
4. Qur'an 4:171; 5:72–73, 116.

the question arises: what can one reasonably hope for in interreligious dialogue in the search for what is true and holy on these very points?

From early Islamic times onward, unlike in the West, Arabic-speaking Christians and Muslims have been discussing the Christian doctrines of the Trinity and the Incarnation in terms mutually intelligible to both of them, albeit the mutual intelligibility has not brought them to any doctrinal rapprochement. Rather, the largely apologetic and polemical records of their conversations with one another suggest that they have been talking past one another. Or, seen more positively, one might readily suggest that what one sees in the apologetic and polemical texts written in Arabic by Christians and Muslims in conversation with one another on the Christian doctrines of the Trinity and the Incarnation over the centuries has not been dialogue with a view to rapprochement but a theological exercise in defining one another's monotheism in doctrinal counterpoint, sharpening the notes of difference between them, the better to accent their contrast. In other words, it has been an exercise seemingly leading inevitably to *aporia*, a conceptual impasse; what one affirms the other denies, producing not harmony but clarity of difference. But from the perspective of *Nostra Aetate*'s concept of interreligious dialogue, clarity of difference might be just the point.

The interreligious dialogue espoused and encouraged by the Roman Catholic Church envisions an effort on the part of dialogue partners honestly and forthrightly to set forth in mutually intelligible terms the doctrinal and moral positions their authentic creeds require. Where this process leads to rapprochement, a blessing is received; where it leads to inevitable contradiction, it may also lead to that clarity of difference just mentioned, which on scriptural grounds might prompt Christians and Muslims peaceably to leave the judgment on this matter to God and in the meantime to respect one another's goodwill and integrity. After all, in the matter of Trinity and Incarnation, for Christians the difference with Muslims arises in the course of our deeper explorations into the scriptural terms of our mutual profession of faith in the one God of Abraham, Isaac/Ishmael, and Jacob,[5] a basic truth that both our communities are anxious to proclaim to the world.

Professor Nasr brings up one matter concerning the life of Christ over which Christians and Muslims differ about what actually happened, as a matter of historical fact. Regarding Christ, he says, "Muslims believe that he was not crucified and did not die on the cross but was taken directly to Heaven."[6] This belief is grounded in the traditional interpretation of a

---

5. Exodus 3:6; Matthew 22:31–32; and Qur'an 2:133.
6. See Nasr's essay in this volume, p. 108.

verse in the Qur'an that speaks of those who said, "We have killed the Messiah, Jesus, son of Mary, the Messenger of God." The verse goes on to say, "They did not kill him, nor did they crucify him," and the Qur'an immediately comments, "*walākin shubbiha lahum*,"[7] an Arabic phrase that is often interpreted to mean that it only appeared so to them or even that it seemed to them that someone else had been the substituted victim of the crucifixion. The next verse says of Christ, "Rather, God raised him up to Him."[8] One wonders if there is not room even here for careful dialogue to disclose plausibly that on the face of it the Qur'an bespeaks not so much a contradiction between what Christians and Muslims allege about this particular event in the life of Christ, but the Qur'an is addressing a different matter; it rejects the claim of those who, in its view, were falsely claiming responsibility for Christ's death on the cross. The dialogue then becomes a conversation about the religious issue that lies at the heart of the traditional Muslim interpretation of this passage in the Arabic scripture, a concern about the truth of what can rightly be said about Jesus, the Messiah, the Messenger of God.

Professing the truth about God and God's messengers and commending it to others is of major importance to Christians and Muslims alike. Both Muslims and Christians are called to proclaim their faith; for Catholic Christians interreligious dialogue and the proclamation of faith go together, just as for Muslims the duty to call others to Islam in dialogue is an ever-present duty. And as Professor Nasr notes, the mention of this shared imperative immediately brings up the matter of proselytism and missionary activity as an issue between our communities. The issue is particularly contentious because of the long history of military hostility between Christians and Muslims, lasting more than a millennium, and the succeeding eras of Western colonialism, imperialism, and economic exploitation of many Muslim majority countries. These oppressive developments yielded political conditions of dominance that allowed and protected Christian missionary activity in many of these countries, missionary activity that often proceeded by demeaning Islam and Islamic culture, taking unfair advantage of the concomitant social and political weakness of the unjustly subordinated societies. Here is not the place to elaborate on this point; suffice it to say that one effect of it was the production of a large Christian, anti-Islamic polemic literature, answered by an equally large Muslim, anti-Christian literature, all composed in the local languages. Hostility prompts the demonization of the other. The perception of the

7. Qur'an 4:157.
8. Ibid. 4:158.

fundamental wrongness of this state of affairs from a religious point of view
is the very fact that motivated the members of Vatican Council II to own
Nostra Aetate's statement, "In the course of centuries there have indeed
arisen not a few quarrels and hostilities between Christians and Muslims.
But now this Sacred Synod pleads with all to forget the past, to make sincere efforts for mutual understanding. . . ."[9] One might take this statement
as a confession and an expression of the Catholic Church's act of contrition
for past sins, coupled with a firm purpose of amendment, made concrete
by the call for and encouragement of interreligious dialogue.

   Nostra Aetate's call for dialogue and for the recognition of what is true
and holy in Islam and in other religions did not come about without initial
preparation within the Catholic Church earlier in the twentieth century.
Regarding the dialogue with Islam, one thinks most immediately of
French Catholic Islamicist scholar Massignon (1883–1962) and of the
influential circle of Christian and Muslim believers who in one way or
another circulated within his sphere of influence. One thinks in this connection, too, of Charles de Foucauld (1858–1916), who lived as a Christian
hermit among Muslims in North Africa, in many ways Massignon's spiritual father; Père Georges Anawati, OP (1905–1994), and his Dominican
confreres at the Institut Dominicain d'Études Orientales in Cairo; Louis
Gardet (1904–1986); Fr. Jean Mohamed Ben 'Abd al-Jalīl, OFM (1904–
1979); Mary Kahil in Cairo (1889–1979); Fr. Giulio Basetti Sani, OFM
(1912–2001); Msgr. Paul Ali Mehmet Mulla Zade (1881–1959) in the
Vatican; not to mention Giovanni Battista Montini (1897–1978), named
Pope Paul VI in 1963. All of these and more were in the deep background
of the two paragraphs on Islam in *Nostra Aetate*.

   There remains a question, however, about how to understand the conduct of dialogue, coupled with the proclamation of faith in word and deed,
as the Church encourages us to do, while avoiding even the hint of taking
unfair advantage of one's partners in interreligious conversation. This
question gives rise to another one: are dialogue and proclamation even
compatible with one another? The answer should be yes, when we remember that an essential feature of dialogue is complete openness on the part
of each participant about the beliefs and practices of each one's faith. In
this circumstance, proclamation is the true and accurate statement of that
faith. It inevitably has an element of invitation to acceptance inscribed in
it. But the invitation comes with an awareness of why it cannot be accepted
by the other, due to the matters mutually explored in the dialogue. One's
response to the recognition of the inability to reach complete agreement in

9. *Nostra Aetate* 3.

dialogue and the consequent inability to accept proclamation's invitation to agreement in faith might reasonably be the realization that mutual understanding of seemingly irreconcilable difference is itself a measure of rapprochement. And it is on the basis of this understanding that worshippers of the one God, Creator of all that exists, might "work together for the preservation and fostering of social justice, moral welfare, and peace and freedom for all humankind" as *Nostra Aetate* bids them to do.[10]

The Catholic Church's understanding of the theological dictum, *extra ecclesiam nulla salus* ("outside of the church there is no salvation"), to which Professor Nasr calls attention, does not mean for Catholics that salvation is not a possibility for non-Christians and especially for Muslims. And in this connection Professor Nasr himself calls attention to a passage from Vatican II's Dogmatic Constitution on the Church, *Lumen Gentium,* "The plan of salvation also includes those who acknowledge the Creator, in the first place amongst whom are the Moslems."[11] But Nasr goes on to say, "This doctrine has not been formally rescinded as far as I know."[12] One must point out, however, that a dictum is not a doctrine, and the reason this dictum has not been rescinded, nor is it in the Catholic view rescindable, is that it articulates an important, traditional principle of thought about the nature of the Church in Catholic theology. The authoritative teaching document, the *Catechism of the Catholic Church,*[13] explains how this principle functions in the Catholic understanding of the role of the church in the divine plan of salvation for mankind. But here once again is not the place to explore the matter further. Rather, one might point out that it is precisely the sort of topic about which dialogue might well be expected to bring about mutual comprehension, albeit without agreement or mutual acceptance.

Professor Nasr calls attention to the fact that the Qur'an has a distinctive view of the role of the Hebrew prophets in what Christians call "salvation history," which in turn frames and even determines how Christ "belongs not only to Christianity but also to Islam," as he goes on to say: "There is not only a Christian Christology but also an Islamic one." The Qur'an envisions a chain of messengers and prophets sent by God to the many human communities, calling them back to their hitherto neglected and compromised ancestral faith in the one God. The Qur'an enfolds the Israelite patriarchs and prophets into this chain, including David and

10. Ibid, 108.

11. *Lumen Gentium* 16.

12. See Nasr's essay in this volume, p. 108.

13. *Catechism of the Catholic Church* (Vatican City: Libreria Editrice Vaticana, 1993), 838–39, 849.

Solomon, whom Eastern, Syriac-speaking Christians also consider prophets, culminating in the mission of Jesus to his fellow Israelites. The Qur'an presents Jesus, the Messiah, Mary's son, as the penultimate prophet and messenger of God, who on the Islamic view then foretells the coming of Muhammad, the "seal of the prophets."[14] The Qur'an's accounts of God's prophets and messengers follow a distinctive, narrative pattern that highlights the basic similarity of their divinely inspired careers, and it is this distinctive pattern of prophetic witness that shapes the Qur'an's recollections of the Bible's patriarchs and prophets, up to and including Jesus, the Messiah, and his mother Mary. The Qur'an recalls their stories within the parameters of its own distinctive, narrative pattern, including scenarios familiar to Jews and Christians not only from the Bible but from Jewish and Christian extrabiblical traditions as well. As Professor Nasr points out, this Quranic presentation of the Hebrew prophets, and of Jesus himself, which lies behind and determines Islamic Christology, is different from the traditional Christian reading of the Bible's accounts, which contrariwise discerns the multiple messianic typologies and foretellings of Christ's coming when read from the perspective of the gospels' announcement of the good news of human salvation in Christ. The recognition of this difference requires one to realize that there is not an exact fit between the Christian or Jewish definitions of prophetic witness or assumptions about the role of God's messengers. Failure to recognize the differences has sown confusion in the minds of Jews and Christians in the past and continues to do so even now when they encounter the Qur'an's portrayals of the biblical patriarchs and prophets.

In addition to scriptural, doctrinal, and historical topics that call for dialogue between Christians and Muslims, Professor Nasr calls our attention to the fact that there are also some differences of view in the ethical domain. He speaks in particular of sexual ethics, which in the past have been the subject of mutual recrimination. But there are also issues having to do with social ethics, particularly in the areas of the right governance of peoples and nations, the rights of nonbelievers, and freedom of conscience. It is heartening that Professor Nasr can envision the possibility that sustained Muslim-Christian dialogue might yet "allow each religion to grow in a free atmosphere dominated by mutual respect and trust." And yet in our own times we live in an atmosphere of increased Islamophobia while also seeing increased anti-Christian hostility. The fact is that in many parts of the world where Christians and Muslims live together today, even in the so-called secularized, democratic West, despite fifty years of irenic, inter-

14. Qur'an 33:40.

religious colloquy at the highest levels of society, or centuries of living together in a measure of mutual respect and even harmony, their blood is still flowing at one another's hands, and the processes of intercommunal demonization are in full swing.

As one looks back over the past fifty years and takes note of the numerous moments of Muslim-Christian theological dialogue that have taken place both formally and informally, sometimes under the auspices of religious authority and sometimes not, one cannot help noticing, as Professor Nasr points out, that much remains to be clarified. For example, from a Catholic perspective one notices that it has been precisely the experience of interreligious dialogue before and after *Nostra Aetate* that has brought the need for a deeper Catholic theology of other religions to come to the fore. Given the fact that *Nostra Aetate* says that "the Church rejects nothing that is true and holy in these religions" and goes on to speak of discussion and collaboration, and mutual understanding, the document itself might be seen to suggest that there is something for Catholics to learn about God and religious life from reading and studying other religious texts, such as the Qur'an. But we are still discussing how theologically to assess the true and holy that we find in such a text, not to mention how to answer such questions as whether or not one could correctly think that the Holy Spirit could be speaking to us Catholics in the Qur'an. The Congregation for the Doctrine of the Faith's International Theological Commission has so far provided two pertinent studies, "Christianity and the World Religions" (1997) and "God, the Trinity, and the Unity of Humanity: Christian Monotheism and Its Opposition to Violence" (2014). But for the most part these important studies provide a synthetic *status quaestionis*, along with a clear delineation of the magisterium's current parameters for Catholic theology engaged with the issue, within which the further discussion might take place. They do not break new ground, nor do they provide suggested or plausible answers to concrete questions that arise constantly in the course of interreligious dialogue, especially the dialogue between Christians and Muslims. Massignon long ago identified several critical questions in Christian-Muslim dialogue, topics for which Muslims often ask Catholics for a theological response. They include questions about the truthfulness of the Islamic witness to the one God, recognition of the authenticity of Muhammad as a prophet and messenger of God, the inspiration of the Qur'an, the mission of Islam in the world, and the vocation of Arabic as a language of revelation. The challenge arises: is it possible for there to be a Catholic theology articulated within the purview of Islam that might appreciably respond to such questions?

Fifty years of interreligious dialogue on many levels have done much to begin a fruitful theological conversation between Christians and Muslims, but so far one might suggest that the result has been the identification of areas and topics that require much more in-depth attention than they have yet received on the part of either Muslims or Catholics. Professor Nasr's masterly essay, "Muslim Dialogue with the Church after *Nostra Aetate*," clearly highlights this state of affairs. One wonders if the time has not come for the dialogue partners to try an additional way to reach a deeper measure of mutual understanding, namely the inauguration of long-term Muslim-Christian study circles, convoked under scholarly auspices by Catholic university theology departments, as well as, or along with, ecclesiastical sponsorship. It may well be the case that a longer, more intense method of interreligious colloquy ultimately would be the shorter route to a measure of intellectual accord that could eventually, in tandem with continued dialogues, promote more effectively interreligious harmony as a desideratum among Christians and Muslims generally rather than the continuing, customary recourse to intercommunal war, violence, and foreign invasion.

In addition to continued interreligious dialogue and the development of programs for the deeper study of Christianity and Islam, Professor Nasr makes a number of concrete suggestions for further Muslim-Christian cooperation. One that has a special appeal is his hope that "schools could be set up jointly by Christians and Muslims with a curriculum based on a perspective that would honor both traditions." He envisions such a possibility especially in countries with a Muslim majority and also a sizeable Christian presence. These are the very areas in today's world where interreligious hostilities often reach crisis proportions. The idea that shared education might ameliorate the situation in the long term is a good one. But its satisfactory implementation would require a much deeper interreligious understanding between Christians and Muslims than currently obtained. It is a credit to the wide-ranging influence of *Nostra Aetate* that such a hope for the future could even be entertained.

Why Muslims Celebrate *Nostra Aetate*

Sayyid M. Syeed

Muslims have every reason to welcome and celebrate the *Nostra Aetate* as a major leap toward the reinforcement of religious pluralism. The Qur'an praised Christians as the nearest to Muslims because

> Among the Christians there are people who stand for the right, they deliberate on the signs of God all night and they prostrate themselves in adoration. They believe in God and in the day of Judgement, they enjoin what is right and forbid what is wrong. They hasten in emulation in all good works. They are in the ranks of the righteous. Of the good that they do, nothing will be rejected of them . . . for God knows well those that to right.[1]

The Qur'an celebrated religious pluralism as a divine gift and insisted that no one should be coerced to change one's religion. The Prophet was sternly warned in the Quran[2] not to expect people to follow him against their will. The freedom of religion was declared as a core value of Islam.[3]

To hear that the Second Vatican Council has declared these values as the driving force for Catholicism in the new millennium calls for joint celebration by all.

The critique that the Qur'an addressed to Christians and Jews was for them for not recognizing the spiritual roots of each other and not linking them with their own legacy.[4] *Nostra Aetate* did just that and recognized the Jewish origins of Christianity, the same way as Islam does by projecting itself as a continuity of the historical Abrahamic tradition. The concept of *tasdiq* has been repeatedly mentioned in the Qur'an as a witness to affirm the truth of the earlier revelations, Christian and Jewish.

The history of American Islamic community as an organized and well-coordinated institution builder begins with the establishment of the Muslim Students Association of the U.S. and Canada in 1963. It was soon transformed into a modern-day community organization, Islamic Society of North America. It is a historical coincidence that a couple of years ago

---

1. Qur'an 5:82; 3:113.
2. Ibid. 10:99.
3. Ibid. 2:256.
4. Ibid. 2:113.

we were celebrating the fiftieth anniversary of our growth and development while also celebrating the fiftieth anniversary of the end of segregation and the beginning of a more inclusive America. It is very clear that 1963 meant the beginning of not only a more inclusive America in terms of race and color but also more inclusiveness in terms of religions, adding Islam to the religious diversity of America.

We are celebrating *Nostra Aetate* because our humble beginnings in America were accelerated by another great development besides the civil rights movement. Thousands of Catholic bishops converged in the Vatican, re-evaluating some of the traditions and theological positions of the Church. The experience of the most horrible tragedy that was the Holocaust and the end of colonial occupation of the Muslim world provided an inspiration to usher in a new millennium away from anti-Semitism and the memories of crusades, inquisition, slavery, and colonial occupation. This provided a new vision of mutual respect and dialogue.

We in America were the greatest beneficiaries of these new ideas and new attitudes shaping the Catholic Church's relationship with other faiths. The Catholic Church acted as a big brother and facilitated our community building. Having experienced discrimination and exclusion as a minority, the Church was sympathetic to a new minority in America. It has not been easy for us to keep pace in building mosques and schools for our growing community. In many cases our neighboring churches have come forward and opened their doors for us to host our religious activities.

In the face of the rising Islamophobia, we have received strong support from the Catholics. In 2010, when a lone pastor in Florida was threatening to burn the Qur'an with utmost hate and malice, and when at the same time the hate against Muslims took the form of opposition to the building of the so-called ground zero mosque in New York while Muslim community centers in the Midwest were vandalized and attacked, it was the U.S. Conference of Catholic Bishops that took leadership in rejecting the anti-Muslim rhetoric. They were joined by other major denominations of Christians and Jews in strongly denouncing attacks on Muslims as an attack on all religions in America. Along with other faith partners, they founded a powerful campaign called Shoulder-to-Shoulder: Standing with American Muslims; Upholding American Values.

This campaign is steered and funded by a large number of Christian and Jewish organizations and housed in our office of the Islamic Society of North America on the Capitol Hill.

It is this support from Christians and Jews in America for our community, reinforced by our own Islamic commitment to protect minorities of other faiths living in the Muslim world, that has prompted us to take our outreach to Muslim countries where the minorities are under attack.

American Muslims have created multiple alliances like Muslim Christian Collaboration for the Welfare of Christians in the Arab World and other projects promoting Muslim Christian understanding, conflict resolution, and peace building in countries that are witnessing the destruction of a centuries-old legacy of mutual respect and cooperation between Christians and Muslims. Historically the churches and other places of worship have been protected by Muslims with the same vigor as their own mosques because of the Quranic command to do so.[5]

Nostra Aetate has clearly identified a natural alliance between the Abrahamic faiths and other religious communities. This is the shape of the new millennium of alliance building for common values of mutual respect and recognition. All faiths are striving to promote those divine values enshrined in their sacred texts and interpret their scriptures so that those who exploit them for reinforcing hate, extremism, violence, and instability are identified as the enemies of all faiths.

Thanks to *Nostra Aetate* as a response to our collective prayers over centuries.

5. Ibid. 22:40.

Response to Dr. Sayyid Syeed's Essay, "Why Muslims Celebrate *Nostra Aetate*"

BISHOP DENIS MADDEN

It is a joy and an honor to respond to the essay offered by my dear friend Dr. Sayyid Syeed. We have known each other through the years, and one of the great blessings of this good man is that he makes himself available to all who seek a greater union of heart and mind. A thousand thanks, Sayyid, for moving us to that greater union, one that will indeed bring us closer to each other and closer to God.

The opening paragraph of *Nostra Aetate* describes as its primary feature a consideration of "what men have in common and what draws them to fellowship."[1] This notion of commonality prepares those engaged in this process for friendship, which opens the door for true sharing and true dialogue.

Typically when introduced to a stranger, one tries to find shared interests and common characteristics that allow for conversation to move forward and promote the forging of a relationship. *Nostra Aetate*, this short but most important document of Vatican II, follows this process by recognizing that there are fundamental features that all humankind has in common, among them one source of life and a need to probe the "unsolved riddles of the human condition."[2] We all wonder from time to time about the meaning of life, the path to true happiness, the difference between right and wrong, the purpose of suffering, and the mystery of death and what follows.

Dr. Syeed also follows this same approach by reminding us at the start of his remarks that the Qur'an set the stage for future dialogue by praising and describing Christians as being close to Muslims:

> Among the Christians there are people who stand for the right, they deliberate on the signs of God all night and they prostrate themselves in adoration. They believe in God and the day of Judgement, they enjoin what is right and forbid what is wrong. They hasten in emulation in all good works. They are in the ranks of the righteous. Of the good they do, nothing will be rejected of them ... for God knows well those that do right.[3]

1. *Nostra Aetate* 1, official Vatican translation.
2. Ibid.
3. Qur'an 5:82; 3:113.

Dr. Syeed's words are encouraging for us, especially today living in the shadow of ISIS, which by its tactics bears little to no resemblance to true Islam. He, again quoting from the Quran, states that there is a stern warning issued to all Muslims that no one should be coerced to change religions and that freedom of religion is a core value of Islam so that no one should be forced to follow the Prophet against their will.[4]

Catholics join with Muslims in bringing to the forefront the need to protect the constitutionally guaranteed freedom of religion. Muslims and Catholics stand "shoulder to shoulder" in protecting this right.[5]

Since some of these same values represent a driving force for Catholics and Muslims, Dr. Syeed reminds us that this is a time for joint celebration and a time for further working together. Dr. Syeed makes so very clear the sincerity of his words and his commitment to dialogue by his actions in the community, coupled with his heartfelt enthusiasm, that there is indeed much that unites us; we might even say more than divides us.

The value of "fraternal dialogues" to bearing the fruit of "mutual understanding and respect" is raised in *Nostra Aetate* in the context of Jewish-Christian relations,[6] but this applies to dialogue with Muslims as well; the more we talk to and listen to each, and the more we open ourselves to the possibility of finding common ground in these dialogues, the greater the chances for peace and harmony. This begins with the respect and dignity afforded to all humankind when we recognize each other as children of God who are created by Him, loved by Him, and valued by Him, a status which demands of us to act with the same respect and dignity.

Pope Francis has shown himself to be masterful at calling attention to the common ground that unites humankind. In *Joy of the Gospel*, he devotes an entire section to interreligious dialogue, focusing especially on dialogue with Muslims.[7] Not only does the pope highlight the Islamic teachings that have their roots in Judaism and Christianity, as does Dr. Syeed, but the pope also emphasizes the traditions that unite religions: the importance of daily prayer, the gift of life that is from God and for God, and the importance of showing mercy to those most in need. He writes, "In order to sustain dialogue with Islam, suitable training is essential for all involved, not only so that they can be solidly and joyfully grounded in their own identity, but so that they can also acknowledge the values of others, appreciate the concerns underlying their demands and shed light on shared

---

4. Ibid. 10:99; 2:256.

5. *Nostra Aetate* 4.

6. Ibid.

7. Pope Francis, *Evangelii Gaudium*, 250–54 (Vatican City: Libreria Editrice Vaticana, 2013), http://w2.vatican.va/content/vatican/en.html.

beliefs."[8] In a sense, Pope Francis has expanded on the seeds for dialogue and understanding that were planted with *Nostra Aetate* and challenges us to take responsibility for our own education and to truly live out our understanding of the gospel: to love God by loving others, in part by recognizing the valuable truths that exist in other religions.

Our dear Pope Francis places great emphasis on a culture of dialogue built on the premise that the other has something of value to say and that the other has something that is of import to the listener. And, of course, this attitude of a culture of dialogue is of great importance in our dialogue with Islam.

Nostra Aetate recognizes dialogue and collaboration as key to honoring the value of other faith traditions. It also urges that we put the pains of the past behind us and move forward in a spirit of understanding so that peace can be promoted. This is so important to the Muslim-Christian dialogue. There is much common ground between us. Dr. Syeed in his essay spoke of the concept of *tasdiq* by which Islam projects itself as a continuity in the historical Abrahamic tradition, a concept repeatedly mentioned in the Qur'an. And yet there are those who would perpetuate the misunderstandings and the gruesome legacy of wrongdoings, both recent and, in some cases, centuries old.

Indeed, we find ourselves living in a time when all of these shared values are challenged or seem to even be ignored occasionally, and instead new evils done in the name of our religions require a shared response.

Dr. Syeed's own gracious spirit of gratitude to his dialogue partners is exemplified by stating his appreciation of the Catholic Church in supporting Muslims in the face of a rising Islamophobia. By recalling the action of the United States Conference of Catholic Bishops (USCCB) in rejecting anti-Muslim rhetoric and (along with other Christians and Jews) strongly denouncing attacks on Muslims as their centers were vandalized and attacked, Dr. Syeed generously saw the Catholic Church as acting as "a big brother" in protecting the rights of Muslims. This action by the USCCB, he stated, also helped in facilitating community building and made quite clear the stance of the Church with regard to this abhorrent behavior leveled against our Muslim sisters and brothers.

But the situation is different internationally, where the history of organized Islam is much longer than the fifty years since the Muslim Students Association of the U.S. and Canada was founded, and the Catholic Church has not always been supportive of the Muslim presence. Close to the time of our meeting at The Catholic University in Washington, D.C.,

---

8. Ibid., 253.

bishops and delegates in charge of relations with Muslims in Europe met in Switzerland from May 13 to 15, 2015, to discuss the theme of "The Radicalization of Islam: Experience of Dialogue in Act." This rather strongly worded theme perhaps reflects the feelings of pain and frustration of those committed to dialogue.

In his opening remarks, Cardinal Jean-Pierre Ricard, the archbishop of Bordeaux, asked a number of probing questions about the state of Islam in the contemporary world.

> What is the true face of Islam?
> Can there be a peaceful perception of the presence of Muslims in our European societies?
> Are we perhaps seeing a radicalization of some Muslims?
> How can we analyze the different currents sweeping through Muslim communities today?
> What do you think of those young people who "convert" to Islam and are tempted to join the armed forces of the Islamic State?

These rather pointed questions from this European group dedicated to pursuing dialogue with Muslims resulted from attacks by those who call themselves Muslims in different European countries as well as the experience of Christians being expelled from their homes by the so-called Islamic State.

Cardinal Ricard suggested "analyzing with realism our situation today" and strongly expressing our convictions as a beginning to finding solutions to the issues raised by that series of questions.[9] Cardinal Ricard's suggestion is quite similar to past statements by Cardinal Jean-Louis Tauran, president of the Pontifical Council for Interreligious Dialogue, who time and again has emphasized the need for honesty in dialogue and the need not to ignore the truth of what is happening in our respective communities.

As these actions of ISIS have contributed to an increase in Islamophobic reactions even in Christian countries, the questions are not to accuse but to understand. "Mutual respect can realistically prepare for the future. This is both a challenge for our societies and a call from the Lord," said Cardinal Ricard.[10]

Lacking the hierarchical structure that Catholics have become accustomed to, it is understandably difficult for Muslims to speak with one voice on behalf of the whole Muslim community. As Catholics we should be

---

9. Jean-Louis Cardinal Ricard, "The Radicalization of Islam: Experience of Dialogue in Act: Opening Remarks," quoted in "Card Ricard: Dialogue Necessary to Prepare for Future," May 15, 2015, Vatican radio website, http://en.radiovaticana.va (accessed May 21, 2015).

10. Ibid.

sympathetic to this as even we with our hierarchical structure cannot pretend that Catholics always agree on all matters, especially those that are highly political. The cardinal also noted in his remarks that, understandably, Muslims as a whole take badly being continually challenged to show their loyalty to the laws of European societies. I would imagine the same holds true for Muslims in our country as well.

I believe that those bishops and delegates who met in Switzerland would have benefited greatly had Dr. Syeed spoken at their meeting and had they the blessed opportunity of spending time with him in private dialogue. I also think that some of their rather pointed questions concerning the state of Islam in the contemporary world would have been helpfully answered by the presentation we heard this day from Dr. Syeed. Perhaps he could have explained to them much more about the different currents sweeping through Muslim communities today, where dialogue based in the Quranic teaching that Dr. Syeed cited is occurring at the same time that young people are converting to Islam only to join the oppressive forces of ISIS. It would also be interesting to know how Dr. Syeed's own efforts and those of the Islamic Society of North America to further their vision of dialogue are being acknowledged and accepted in Europe and outside the West.

I can also speak from my own experience while working for the Catholic Near East Welfare Association and the Pontifical Mission in the Middle East and living at Tantur in Jerusalem, a center of learning and dialogue. This unique opportunity was provided to listen to and learn from expert practitioners in dialogue amid a land called holy but one in which so often there was a seeming scarcity of love and dialogue.

Despite intifadas and all kinds of unrest, dialogue can still be present, as I learned, through the dialogue of charity. The Pontifical Mission striving to fulfill the wishes of all the popes since its founding in 1949 has worked on the principle of responding to need not creed. And it was often in those times of unrest that there was the greatest need. This at the same time opened many a door to a better understanding of the other and planted seeds for future dialogue as we are speaking about.

Charity was by no means offered in one direction. Our Muslim brothers and sisters shared with us many of the principles of life that they had come to treasure, such as mercy, hospitality, forgiveness, courage, endurance, faithfulness to God, and care of the stranger.

Listening to Syeed's beautiful words that afternoon in Washington served to not only awaken these memories but to encourage my better practice of these principles. And for this also I am most grateful, and I hope others will be inspired by his essay as well.

A Muslim Reading of *Nostra Aetate*:
Response to Dr. Sayyid Syeed

ARCHBISHOP MICHAEL L. FITZGERALD, MAFR

D r. Syeed is to be congratulated and thanked for the rich reflections that he has offered us. Reflecting on the way *Nostra Aetate* approaches the different religions of the world, he has called attention to the way the Qur'an speaks about religious diversity. It is in fact interesting to note that the Qur'anic message is addressed to different categories of people. At times it is Muslims (usually called "believers") who are addressed: "You who believe, fasting is prescribed for you, as it was prescribed for those before you, so that you may be mindful of God."[1] A distinction is made here between the believing Muslims and those who preceded them while having their own religious practices. In other places the message is addressed to a wider circle (named simply "people"): "People, worship your Lord, who created you and those before you."[2] The mention of "those before you" implies a history of the human race that includes pluralism. Belief in the Creator God, who is also the judge to whom the whole of humankind is to return at the end of each one's human life and also at the end of time, is in the Qur'an a foundation for the common endeavor of all human beings. Yet perhaps it is useful to maintain the distinction between the invitation to all human beings to submit (*islām*) to God in loving obedience and the invitation to Muslims to practice the precepts of Islam as a distinct religion.[3]

The Christian vision of humanity is also commanded by belief in God, the Creator, who has created human beings for Himself. This does not mean that the purpose of creation is merely God's self-interest; rather it is that He created human beings in order to share with them divine life. All human beings, therefore, are united in their origin and in their proposed

---

1. Qur'an 2:183.
2. Ibid. 2:21.
3. Since in Arabic there are no capital letters, it is sometimes difficult to determine the exact meaning of some Qur'anic phrases. For instance, in 3:19, *inna l-dīn 'inda Llāhi l-islām*: does this mean that for God the (true) religion is Islam or that "True Religion, in God's eyes is *islām*: [devotion to Him alone]," as Abdel Haleem translates (cf. M. A. S. Abdel Haleem, *The Qur'an*, Oxford: Oxford University Press, 2010)? Quotations from the Qur'an in the present paper are given according to the translation of Abdel Haleem, unless otherwise stated.
4. *Nostra Aetate* 1, trans. Thomas F. Stransky, CSP.

destiny; nevertheless in the ways that they move toward this destiny they are divided. Hence the insistence of *Nostra Aetate* on the human family: "One also is their final goal, God."[4] Pope John Paul II took up this idea in his allocution at the end of the day of prayer and fasting for world peace held in Assisi on October 27, 1986:

> The very fact that we have come to Assisi from various quarters of the world is in itself a sign of this common path which humanity is called to tread. Either we learn to walk together in peace and harmony, or we drift apart and ruin ourselves and others. We hope that this pilgrimage to Assisi has taught us anew to be aware of the common origin and common destiny of humanity. Let us see in it an anticipation of what God would like the developing history of humanity to be: a fraternal journey in which we accompany one another toward the transcendent goal which he sets for us.[5]

These words are surely still relevant today.

With regard to religious plurality, Dr. Syeed did not quote the well-known text from the Qur'an:

> If God had so willed, he would have made you one community, but He wanted to test you through that which He has given you, so race to do good: you will al return to God and He will make clear to you the matters you differed about.[6]

This would seem to establish religious pluralism as something positively willed by God.

Nor was there a reference to this clear statement:

> Say [Prophet], "Disbelievers (*yā ayyuhā l-kāfirūn*): I do not worship what you worship, you do not worship what I worship, I will never worship what you worship, you will never worship what I worship: you have your religion and I have mine (*la-kum dīnu-kum wa-lī dīni*)."[7]

This *sūra* is addressed to the *kāfirūn*, that is, those who are in *kufr*, the root meaning of which is lack of gratitude to the Creator God—in other words, disbelief. It is said to have been addressed to the Meccans who proposed a

5. Pope John Paul II, "Discourse to Representatives of the Various Religions of the World at the Conclusion of the World Day of Prayer for Peace, Assisi, October 27, 1986," in *Interreligious Dialogue: The Official Teaching of the Catholic Church from the Second Vatican Council to John Paul II (1963-2005)*, ed. Francesco Gioia (Boston: Pauline Books & Media, 2006), 546.

6. Qur'an 5:48.

7. Ibid. 109:1–6.

compromise to Muhammad: he should follow their way of worshipping for a year, and then they would follow his way of worshipping. The offer was refused, but the result was an acceptance of plurality. The Indian translator and commentator of the Qur'an, Yusuf Ali, comments: "In matters of Truth we can make no compromise, but there is no need to persecute or abuse anyone for his faith or belief."[8]

The Qur'an and Christians

Dr. Syeed has reminded us that, among believers in the one God, the Qur'an considers Christians to be the closest to Muslims. It must be recognized, however, that there is a degree of ambiguity in the attitude of the Qur'an toward Christians. As Fr. Sidney Griffith has said: "The Qur'an's posture towards Christians in the Arabian milieu is somewhat guarded"; positive comments being combined with sharp criticisms.[9]

Dr. Syeed makes reference in his paper to two passages in the Qur'an, 5:82 and 3:113, in which there is praise of Christians. Of course the different contexts of these statements are to be taken into consideration in order that they may be understood correctly.[10] In the second of these texts the reference is in fact to "the People of the Book" (*ahl al-kitāb*), among whom Christians are usually counted (although Christians in fact prefer to be recognized as disciples of Jesus rather than followers of a revealed book). It can be noted that the group of people referred to "recite God's revelations during the night." The Arabic text speaks of *āyāt Allāhi*, which means literally "the signs of God," but since the term *āyāt* also covers the verses of the Qur'an, the translation *revelations* can be justified. In this case, however, these People of the Book would appear to be people who have accepted Islam.

The same is true in the following passages:

> You [Prophet] are sure to find the most hostile to the believers are the Jews and those who associate other deities with God; you are sure to find that the closest in affection towards the believers are those who say "We are Christians," for there are among them people who are devoted to learning (*qissīsīn*) and ascetics (*ruhbān*). These people are not given to arrogance, and when they listen to what has been sent down to the Mes-

8. Abdallah Yusuf Ali, *The Holy Qur'an: Text, Translation and Commentary* (Beirut: Dar al Arabia, 1968), 1799.

9. Sidney H. Griffith, "Christians and Christianity," in *Encyclopedia of the Qur'an*, vol. I, ed. Jane D. McAuliffe, 307–16 (Leiden: Brill, 2001–2006), 311.

10. On this question see Jane D. McAuliffe, *Qur'anic Christians: An Analysis of Classical and Modern Exegesis* (Cambridge; New York: Cambridge University Press, 1991).

senger, you will see their eyes overflowing with tears because they recognize the Truth [in it]. They say, "Our Lord, we believe, so count us among the witnesses."[11]

It can be noted that the terms used in verse 82 above, *qissīsīn* and *ruhbān*, are usually translated as *priests* and *monks*. There was certainly respect for monks, even if not for the institution of monasticism, as can be seen from the *sūra* of Light.[12]

The attitude of the Qur'an toward the Jews is generally severe. Muhammad probably expected them to welcome his monotheistic message and was disappointed when this did not happen. The Qur'anic texts give evidence of a general mistrust of the Jews. Christians in Arabia at this time were not as numerous as the Jews so did not constitute a threat. Those to whom verse 83 refers would seem to have accepted the truth of the Qur'an and so wished to be counted "amongst the witnesses"; it can perhaps be understood that they have pronounced the *shahāda*, or the Islamic formula of faith.

There are, of course, other texts on Christians that would be important to consider.

> Today all good things have been made lawful for you. The food of the People of the Book is lawful for you as your food is lawful for them. So are chaste, believing, women as well as chaste women of the people who were given the Scripture before you, as long as you have given them their bride-gifts and married them, not taken them as lovers or secret mistresses.[13]

It still holds true today, according to Islamic law, that although a Muslim woman is not allowed to marry a non-Muslim (for it is understood that the children will follow the religion of the father), a Muslim is allowed to marry a Jewess or a Christian. Sometimes, however, undue pressure is put on the non-Muslim spouse to convert to Islam.

> You who believe, do not take the Jews and Christians as allies: they are allies only to each other. Anyone who does take them as an ally becomes one of them—God does not guide such wrongdoers—yet you [Prophet] will see the perverse at heart rushing to them for protection, saying, "We are afraid fortune may turn against us."[14]

11. Qur'an 5:82–83.
12. Ibid. 24:35–38.
13. Ibid. 5:5.
14. Ibid. 5:51.

Whereas before the "closest in affection" to Muslims were the Christians, here in the above-quoted verse, the distrust of both Jews and Christians is evident.

> When the [four] forbidden months are over, wherever you encounter the idolators (*al-mushrikina*), kill them, seize them, besiege them, wait for them at every lookout post; but if they repent, maintain the prayer, and pay the prescribed alms, let them go their way, for God is most forgiving and merciful.[15]

This is known as the *āyat al-sayf*, the Verse of the Sword. It can be noted that those who accept Islam are to be spared. A scholar comments:

> It is clear, therefore, that the Verse of the Sword was a context-specific verse relating to the purification of Mecca and its environs of all Arab polytheism and idolatry so that the sanctuary in particular, with the Ka'ba at its center, would never again be rendered unclean by the paganism of those locals and pilgrims who had long been worshipping idols (reportedly hundreds of them) there.[16]

Since it is context-specific, this verse, therefore, cannot be held to have a universal application.

What about Christians? They are included in this instruction regarding the People of the Book: "Fight those of the People of the Book who do not [truly] believe in God and the Last Day, who do not forbid what God and His Messenger have forbidden, who do not obey the rule of justice, until they pay the tax promptly and agree to submit."[17] "Truly" has been added by the translator, since he thinks that it is implied. "Who do not obey the rule of justice" might be more accurately rendered: "who do not acknowledge the Religion of Truth" (i.e., Islam). The tax to be paid is the *jizya*, a compensation for being freed of the obligation of military service and of paying *zakāt*. Non-Muslims who accepted to pay this tax became protected persons (*ahl al-dhimma*), willing to live under Muslim rule. The *jizya* is to be paid "promptly" (*'an yad*), literally "from the hand," possibly meaning "willingly" or "from what they possess." Those who accept the payment of this tax "agree to submit," which means literally "making themselves small" or "being submissive." In fact, the *ahl al-dhimma* in Islamic society were inferior citizens and subject to a number of humiliations. As *sūra* 9 is reckoned to be one of the last of the *sūras*, if not

---

15. Ibid. 9:5.

16. Cf. Joel Hayward, "Warfare in the Qur'an," in *War and Peace in Islam*, ed. Prince Ghazi bin Muhammad et al. (Cambridge: The Islamic Texts Society, 2013), 40.

17. Qur'an 9:29.

the last taken chronologically, it does not give a very favorable portrait of the situation of non-Muslims in Islamic society. It must be clear that such a situation is no longer acceptable in modern society where all citizens are to be considered equal.

Abrahamic Religions

Dr. Syeed refers to the Abrahamic religions. This concept is, to my mind, a valid one, though it must be recognized that there is a difference in the way Abraham is understood by Jews, Christians, and Muslims. Briefly one could say that for Jews, Abraham is the one to whom the promise of the land is given. For Christians he is essentially a man of faith; for Muslims he is the champion of monotheism.[18] To speak about the Judeo-Christian origins of Islam would seem, however, to be more difficult. As I have noted elsewhere, the relationship of the Abrahamic religions one to another is asymmetrical:

> Christianity accepts the Hebrew Bible as the first part of its own Scriptures, as a part of revelation. But Judaism naturally does not accept the New Testament. Were Jews to recognize the New Testament as revelation from God they would become Christians. Similarly Islam considers the Torah to have been "sent down" by God to the Jews, and the Gospel to have been "sent down" to Christians, but Jews and Christians do not accept the Qur'an as revelation from God. If they did, they would become Muslims. The difference in attitude is a reflection of separate identities.

> Yet there is a further difference in the way Christians relate to what they term the Old Testament, and the attitude of Muslims to the Scriptures that preceded the Qur'an. For Christians the Old Testament is an integral part of their own Scriptures, and this is shown, for example, by the use of readings from the Old Testament in Christian worship. Texts from the Old Testament or the New Testament would never form part of *salāt*, the Islamic ritual prayer. Here again the validity of the adage *lex orandi, lex credendi* is verified.[19]

18. Giving the Islamic understanding of Abraham, Mahmoud Ayoub, referring to Qur'an 22:78, writes: "He is not simply the father of Muslims but also the founder of Islam. It was to his communal religion (*millah*) that Muhammad is believed to have been sent by God to call the people of Mekkah, all the Arabs, and all of humankind. Abraham is therefore, for Muslims, the father of all the people of faith, and the archetypal founder of true religion." Mahmoud M. Ayoub, "Abraham and His Children: A Muslim Perspective," in *Heirs of Abraham: The Future of Muslim, Jewish and Christian Relations*, ed. Bradford E. Hinze and Irfan A. Omar, 94–111 (New York: Orbis Books, 2005), 94.
19. Cf. Michael L. Fitzgerald, "Relations among the Abrahamic Religions: A Catholic Point of View," in *Heirs of Abraham*, ed. Bradford E. Hinze and Irfan A. Omar, 64–65.

This argument from liturgy may be contested, given the great disparity between Christian and Muslim worship. Nevertheless, according to my understanding, Islam, while drawing upon the Judeo-Christian tradition to support its monotheistic message, is a completely independent religion.

Working for Peace

On the basis of the Qur'an, Dr. Syeed is pleading for a common vision for world peace. This, of course, is what *Nostra Aetate* is strongly recommending. After speaking about Muslims and Islam, the declaration states: "In the course of centuries there have indeed arisen not a few quarrels and hostilities between Christians and Muslims. But now this Sacred Synod pleads with all to forget the past, to make sincere efforts for mutual understanding, and so to work together for the preservation and fostering of social justice, moral welfare, and peace and freedom for all humankind."[20] As I have pointed out elsewhere, the first part of this sentence is a rather euphemistic way of describing both the *futuhāt*, the Islamic wars of conquest, and the Crusades. Behind this phrase lies also the experience of many Christian communities, particularly in the Middle East, surviving under Islamic domination, as well as the colonial period, experienced as a humiliation by the world of Islam. These memories are still very much alive and continue to shape current attitudes. It is perhaps difficult to "forget the past," as the Council exhorts, but it may be possible to redeem the past through a process of re-reading history together and coming to a purification of memories. As Pope Saint John Paul II stated in his Message for the World Day of Peace in 2004:

> *By itself, justice is not enough.* Indeed, it can often betray itself, unless it is open to that deeper power which is love. For this reason I have often reminded Christians and all persons of good will that *forgiveness is needed* for solving the problems of individuals and peoples. *There is no peace without forgiveness!* I say it again here, as my thoughts turn in particular to the continuing crisis in the Palestine and the Middle East; a solution to the grave problems which for too long have caused suffering for the peoples of those regions will not be found until a decision is made to transcend the logic of simple *justice* and to be open also to the logic of *forgiveness.*[21]

The further suggestion of *Nostra Aetate* is to forego confrontation and to refrain from exchanging mutual accusations with regard to the past in

---

20. *Nostra Aetate* 3, trans. Thomas F. Stransky, CSP.

21. John Paul II, "Message for the World Day of Peace 2004," in *Interreligious Dialogue*, ed. Francesco Gioia, 1350, emphasis in the original text.

order to look together toward the needs of humankind at the present. There are many themes that can be addressed in common discussion leading to active cooperation: the defense of life, marriage, and the family; an ethical approach to business and finance; respect for the environment; the banning of nuclear armaments for the sake of true peace. Such questions are, of course, not confined to Christians and Muslims, nor to any followers of religions, but the religious point of view can be a valid contribution to their discussion.[22]

Gaudium et spes, the Pastoral Constitution on the Church in the Modern World, concludes with a similar note on dialogue with all, whether they be Christians or people belonging to other religions or nonbelievers. It says: "Since God the Father is the beginning and the end of all things, we are called to be brothers [and sisters]; we ought to work together without violence and without deceit to build up the world in a spirit of genuine peace."[23] This statement echoes paragraph 5 of *Nostra Aetate* in which the fatherhood of God is seen as the basis for banning all forms of discrimination and fostering universal fraternity. Muslims may object to the name of Father being given to God—it is not included in the Ninety-Nine Most Beautiful Names—since they would consider that it lowers God to human level. They may nevertheless accept the idea of human dignity and universal fraternity being rooted in divine creation.[24] On this basis there is much room for cooperation in promoting peace in the world.

I am sure that Dr. Syeed would agree with me that this dialogue and cooperation is not always easy today, for it is true that in many parts of the world the social climate is not conducive to good relations between Christians and Muslims. The effects of 9/11 are still being felt, producing an attitude of suspicion toward Muslims in general. Conversely, the invasion of Iraq, the war in Afghanistan, and the lack of resolution of the Israeli-Palestinian conflict continue to stoke the fires of resentment of Muslims, particularly in the Arab world, toward the West. Christians, for their part, point to the violence against their fellow believers in Iraq and Syria, the slaughter of Coptic workers in Libya, and the continuous attacks of Boko Haram. Added to these are the killings in Paris, in Copenhagen, and in Brussels, but also the murder of Muslims in Chapel Hill. Such events lead many people to question whether there is any future for Christian-Muslim dialogue. To my mind, this violence only increases the need for dialogue.

22. Cf. Michael L. Fitzgerald, "Revisiting *Nostra Aetate* after Fifty Years," in *Revisiting Vatican II: 50 Years of Renewal*, ed. Shaji George Kochuthara, CMI, 433–34 (Bangalore: Dharmaram Publications, 2014).
23. Vatican Council II, *Gaudium et spes*, December 7, 1965, par. 92.
24. Cf. Fitzgerald, "Revisiting *Nostra Aetate*," 435.

There must be a readiness to start all over again when, for one reason or another, relations have been broken.

Foundational Experiences

I would like, at this juncture, to try to clarify three points as a way encouraging perseverance in dialogue.[25] The first is to call attention to the difference in the foundational experience of Christianity and Islam. Both Jesus and Muhammad were called to give a message to the world, a message of conversion, and both gathered a group of disciples around them. Yet Jesus preached the Kingdom of God, a kingdom that was not of this world. His was an essentially religious message that, although aiming to have an effect on people's behavior in this world, could be lived out within any political setting. Muhammad, for his part, preached a message that was to bring about a renewal in the Arabia of his time. His message, too, was essentially religious, the acknowledgement of the one God as against the prevalent polytheism, but it had a social dimension to it that was to bring about the formation of a new community, a community bound not by blood ties or tribal loyalty but by religion, the *umma*. Opposition in Mecca led Muhammad to persuade his followers to emigrate to Yathrib (which was to be renamed Medina), where agreements were made with the two Arab tribes and the three groups of Jews or Judaized Arabs. In this way the *umma*, perhaps more by accident than design, became at one and the same time a religious and political community, and consequently Muhammad, as the leader of this community, fulfilled the role of both prophet and statesman.[26] This is very different from Jesus, who had no political role, and from the situation of his followers, who likewise had no political ambitions. One could say that Christianity, at least until the time of Constantine, was in the nature of a religious opposition movement. It did not take up arms to fight for survival. So although Christianity was, as it were, taken over and used by political entities, in the first place by the Byzantines, and then afterward by various monarchs and rulers, in essence it remains independent of any political power. Whereas Islam, from its very beginning as a separate community, has been both religious and political, and one would be tempted to say that striving to defend the community, if necessary by force of arms, is a natural component of the religion.

---

25. The following reflections were treated more fully in a talk delivered at The Catholic University of America on March 6, 2015, later reproduced in *Origins* 44, no. 42 (March 26, 2015): 681–90.

26. Cf. W. Montgomery Watt, *Muhammad: Prophet and Statesman* (London: Oxford University Press, 1961). This is an abridged version of Watt's two volumes, *Muhammad at Mecca* (1953) and *Muhammad at Medina* (1956).

There would seem to be within Islamic history a tendency to look back to its first period, that of the Rightly-Guided Caliphs, as the time of glory and true Islam. This has led to a number of revivalist movements within Islam, which often engaged in jihad against fellow Muslims in order to enforce an observance of "pure Islam."[27] Boko Haram could be considered one of these. As has been said: "The dramatic point of no return in the development of Islamic militancy was when militants reintroduced the concept of *takfir* by declaring as infidels those who had previously been considered Muslims."[28] Very often these revivalist movements were of short duration; one would hope that this will apply to Boko Haram. One effort to enforce pure Islam that has had a more lasting effect is the Wahhabi movement. Unlike the jihad movements already mentioned, the Wahhabi movement has survived until today through its association with the Saud family in Arabia. Its influence is widely felt. One could say that the Wahhabi movement has benefited by the phenomenon of globalization, particularly in the realm of communications. This is also true of other militant groups. Today's jihadists are not necessarily limited to particular localities but are internationally interconnected and remain in connection for the scope both of propaganda and recruitment. So we see new groups spring up that claim affiliation to already existing groups, such as al-Qaeda or the so-called Islamic State. This globalization is a factor to be reckoned with.

The Attraction of the Caliphate

The mention of the Islamic State brings me to the second point, namely the attraction of the caliphate. The tendency of Muslims to look back to the golden age of the Rightly-Guided Caliphs has already been mentioned. Although the last of the Abbasid Caliphs was executed by the Mongols at the sack of Baghdad in 1258, a semblance of the caliphate lived on under the Mamluks in Egypt and later under the Ottomans. Consequently "the caliphate retained its symbolic importance as the emblem of a Muslim world order."[29] This may explain why the abolition of the caliphate in 1924 by Mustafa Kemal Atatürk was considered a catastrophe by many Muslims across the world and why, almost immediately, a movement started for the restoration of the caliphate. A conference for this purpose was held in Mecca

27. On these movements, see Fred M. Donner, "Muhammad and the Caliphate," in *The Oxford History of Islam*, ed. John L. Esposito, 49–52 (New York: Oxford University Press, 1999).
    28. Ibid., 497.
    29. Ira M. Lapidus, "Sultanates and Gunpowder Empires," in *The Oxford History of Islam*, 354.

in 1926, and another in Jerusalem in 1931, though without obtaining the desired result. In 1949 the World Muslim Congress was formed in Karachi to continue the search for Islamic unity, and this movement still exists. Yet Abu Bakr al-Baghdadi's pronouncement that he is the caliph of the newly proclaimed Islamic State has been condemned by Muslim authorities. A leading scholar, Yusuf al-Qaradawi, chairman of the International Union of Muslim Scholars, has stated that "the title of Caliph can only be given by the entire Muslim nation." One wonders how this could come about, but one can conclude that a UDC, the Unilateral Declaration of the Caliphate, quite naturally does not rally all Muslims and indeed only serves to bring about a greater fragmentation in the world of Islam.

Understanding Shari'ah

My third point concerns *sharia*, which these Islamic revival movements wish to apply in the areas over which they have established authority. It should be remembered that there are four sources of sharia: the Qur'an, the Sunna (the tradition of the Prophet Muhammad), analogy (*qiyas*), and consensus. While the first two sources could be considered divinely sanctioned, for the Qur'an is for Muslims the word of God and Muhammad has been declared in the Qur'an to be a model to be followed,[30] the other two sources are human activities. The transposition of a ruling from the first century of Islam to the circumstances of the present time is a work of reason, as is the process of coming to agreement on different points of law. As the consensus of the whole Islamic *umma* would be difficult to ascertain, it is thought sufficient that there should be a consensus of the leading legal scholars of the time. Now scholars can, with difficulty, come to an agreement, but they can also agree to differ. Thus it is that four legal schools, the Maliki, the Hanafi, the Shafi'i, and the Hanbali, have developed over time and are recognized as having authority within the Islamic legal system. To these could be added the Ja'fari school, which is that of the Ithna'ashari Shi'a. So when there is a proclamation that, from now on, sharia law is going to be applied, the question naturally arises as to which form of sharia. It may be useful to remember that sharia is not something given once and for all but is a human construct that is always developing.

In my opinion, the Takfiri jihadists who have proclaimed an Islamic State, or who have declared their allegiance to this Islamic State, where the shari'ah is to be observed under the guidance of a self-designated caliph,

---

30. Cf. Qur'an 33:21.

are not upholding Islamic tradition, whatever they may say. Can there be dialogue with such people? I fear not. For these people are convinced that they hold the truth, and therefore they have no need of listening to others. They will not listen to fellow Muslims, many of whom they consider not to be true Muslims, and even less will they speak to non-Muslims except to invite them to embrace Islam. Fortunately the majority of Muslims are not of this bent, and dialogue between Christians and Muslims is certainly possible and in fact is ongoing all the time.

I would have been interested to hear the comments of Dr. Syeed on the points I have just presented: the different foundational experiences of Christianity and Islam, the attraction of the caliphate, and the understanding of sharia, but within the time limits of the conference this was understandably not possible. Let me continue with a reference to something Dr. Syeed has mentioned: his visit to Pakistan together with other Muslims in order to bear witness to the fact that it is quite possible to live fully as a Muslim within a democratic society such as the United States. It would be interesting to know how this message was received. Dr. Syeed is well aware of how much prejudice there still is in the world today against Muslims in the West, but also in the Muslim world against the West. I am reminded of an occasion during the first international meeting between Christians and Muslims that I attended. It took place at Broumana, Lebanon, in 1972. An Indian Muslim read a paper in which he defended the choice made by many Muslims at the time of partition to continue living in a country with a Hindu majority. He succeeded in arousing the opposition of his co-religionists to such an extent that he was reduced to silence for the rest of the meeting.[31] The nonacceptance of reality is a serious drawback in the search for equitable relations around the whole world.

Religious Freedom

Finally, I wish to express my satisfaction that Dr. Sayyid Syeed has brought up the question of religious freedom. This, of course, was an important topic at Vatican II and the subject of much debate. It resulted in the document *Dignitatis Humanae*, the Declaration on Religious Liberty, without which *Nostra Aetate* would never have seen the light. This document defines religious freedom in the following terms: "Freedom of this kind means that all men should be immune from coercion on the part of individuals, social groups and every human power so that, within due

---

31. Cf. Michael L. Fitzgerald, "Lebanon-Broumana: Muslim Christian Consultation (July 1972)," in *Bulletin, Secretariatus pro non Christianis* 21 (1972): 58–62.

limits, nobody is forced to act against his convictions in religious matters in private or in public, alone or in association with others."[32] The final words of this definition are important. As the declaration notes further on: "The freedom of immunity from coercion in religious matters which is the right of individuals must also be accorded to men when they act in community. Religious communities are a requirement of the nature of man and of religion itself."[33] It is not sufficient, therefore, for authorities to say to religious minorities that they have the right as individuals to pray at home. They also have the right to assemble for prayer and worship as communities and, consequently, the right to have their own places of worship. I was present at the inauguration of the main mosque in Rome in 1995. This took place on a Wednesday, and during the audience that takes place on this day each week, Pope John Paul II welcomed this new place of worship to the one God but expressed the wish that all communities be allowed to construct their own places of worship. The president of Italy, Sandro Pertini, who was present at the ceremony of inauguration, was even more forthright. He emphasized that religious liberty is absolutely fundamental for civilization, stating that the treatment of minorities, religious or otherwise, is a test of civility.[34]

It will have been noted that the definition of religious freedom given by *Dignitatis Humanae* includes a limitation, "within due limits." Local authorities have the right to ensure that public order is not disturbed by expressions of religious worship and to take steps against persons who would be inciting to religious intolerance. They should not, however, interfere in the internal affairs of religious communities.

Nostra Aetate, at the end of its paragraph on Islam, exhorts "all," presumably both Christians and Muslims, to work together "for the preservation and fostering of social justice, moral welfare, and peace and freedom for all humankind."[35] I am sure that Dr. Syeed would agree with me that there is much room here for collaboration between Christians and Muslims. Indeed gratitude is due to Dr. Syeed for showing that the declaration *Nostra Aetate*, even fifty years after its publication, can still be an inspiration to both Christians and Muslims.

32. Vatican Council II, *Dignitatis Humanae*, December 7, 1965, par. 2.
33. Ibid., 4.
34. See the report on this event in *Islamochristiana* 21 (1995): 176–78.
35. *Nostra Aetate* 3, trans. Thomas F. Stransky, CSP.

Reflection on *Nostra Aetate*

Sayed Hassan Akhlaq Hussaini

Theology, moral values, mysticism, and canon law, in different degrees of emphasis, are substantial parts of Abrahamic religions, including Islam and Christianity, but we cannot reduce them to just one. The aim of religion seems to transcend each of these aspects; it wants to form the entirety of a human being according to truth throughout living, promoting, and expanding experiences of religious life. Neither Jesus nor Muhammad merely wanted to present a system of theology. Although they greatly contributed in the promotion of both private and public virtues and linked morals to spirituality, they are much more than mere ethical instructors.

Nostra Aetate, the promulgation of which we commemorated in 2015, is a significant move beyond a merely theological discourse to expose the nature of faith. It touches the profound enigma of humanity, "which encompasses our existence," including what a human being is, the purpose of our life, the nature of good and sin, the meaning of genuine happiness, and what death and judgment are.[1]

The spirit of *Nostra Aetate* (*In Our Time*) is more than only updating the relationship of the Catholic faith to other religions; it is about living humans who change and experience time and movement with all their beings. Time here is not only a cosmological and physical time but also an existential time that offers humanity "resurrection" in Islam and "the Risen one" in Christianity. It also addresses existential features of humankind that "day by day . . . is being drawn ever closer together,"[2] the critical qualities of which are integrated with human existence. We as people face the challenge within our own heart and life—particularly during boundary occasions like major events of unexpected joy or sorrow—of the questions of the meaningfulness of life, of sin, of eternity, and of true justice, which is related to Judgment Day, genuine happiness, and the like. Therefore we find that salvation, happiness, eternity, and true justice are more than speculative and theological examinations; they are within the "restlessness of the human heart."[3] It is similar to chapter 13, verse 28 of the Qur'an, which relates the peace of heart to the remembrance of God. It is obvious that

---

1. *Nostra Aetate* 1, trans. Thomas F. Stransky, CSP.
2. Ibid. 1.
3. Ibid. 2.

this remembrance is not a merely intellectual activity that comes from theological speculation, because many scholars of faith are suffering from restlessness, stress, and anxiety like other people. This is an existential remembrance that each single moment of life ties the bottom of the heart to God,
the source of confidence and providence.

The document *Nostra Aetate* apparently celebrates differences and
diversity of ways without falling down into relativism or abandoning unity.
There are "teachings, rules of life, and sacred rites" that link humanity to
God. It thus "rejects nothing that is true and holy in these religions"
because "those ways of acting and of living, those precepts and teachings
. . . often reflect a ray of that truth which enlightens all."[4] It is not relativism, for these multiple ways all are reflections and manifestations of the
same truth and therefore can be in interrelation with other ones and contribute together in enriching humans' life with meaning and inspiration.
Instead of seeking to overcome the others on earth, celebrating its own vic-
tories or defeats, the Church endeavors to support and celebrate the salvation or guidance of humanity "in the Holy City, the city ablaze with the
glory of God, where the peoples will walk in His light."[5] In this way,
polemical relations shift to constructive relations.

Muslim Foundations for a Friendship with Christians

Just as Catholics in *Nostra Aetate* look to their own claims about the
truth—that Jesus is "the Way, the Truth, and the Life"[6]—in order to participate in dialogue, so Muslims must be able look to its sacred revelation
to pursue these constructive relations. In earlier essays in this book, Dr.
Sayyid Syeed and Archbishop Michael Fitzgerald cite key Quranic texts
that speak to how Muslims approach Christians and dialogue with them.
But such an exploration cannot remain merely at the level of individual
texts. Rather, we must examine the texts in light of the overall principles
that we learn from the Quran. Three principles here bear mentioning, and
I will examine the third in detail. These principles are *Jihad*, *Hidayat*, and
Wilayat.

The Qur'an states, "those who struggle in our cause, we will surely
guide them to our ways; and God is with those who do good."[7] This struggle (jihad) is left unconditioned to include struggle with inner temptation,

---

4. Ibid. 2.
5. Ibid. 1.
6. Jn 14:6, cited in *Nostra Aetate* 2.
7. Qur'an 29:69; citations from *The Noble Quran* (Medina: King Fahd Complex, 1420
A.H.).

satanic inspiration, and outer evil.[8] The Arabic term *jihad* is now greatly misused, but it was used primarily in the Mecca time not referring to war but to ethical attempts to reform the faithful's own character. Moreover, the term *those who* also is used to include all strugglers for the truth, benevolence, and good. It is not limited to particular denominations or faiths. Furthermore, this verse is a conclusion to the chapter started with "do men think that they will be left alone on saying, we believe, and not be tried?"[9] It addresses all humanity with various faith and links true faith with examination, which can be passed easily with supporting alliance. Finally, the struggle covers both individual and collective efforts to create better people and community.

But those who take up this struggle have God with them, not just as an observer but as a guide. And hence the second term is *Hidayat*, God's guidance. The position of guidance in Islam is similar to the importance of salvation in Christianity. God in the Qur'an describes himself as "as guide and a helper."[10] All physical things are created and guided in their natural order (20:50); all nations are gifted with a guide (13:7; 34:28); the position of humanity is who is guided but he or she decides to be grateful or ungrateful (76:3). As we will see below, in the first verses of chapter 2, the Qur'an recognizes people of the Book as faithful, alongside Muslims, and continues, "these are guided by their lord; these surely are the prosperous."[11] The point is that the guidance like faith is an analogical fact (47:17) because as much as there are more levels of faith to be accomplished, there is more room to explore God's mercy. Also, this verse clearly states if people ask for guidance, God guides them. The Qur'an tells us that God is guiding human beings who ask into a *Wilayat*, a supporting alliance, and this is the term I will analyze at greatest length.

Wilayat

The elaboration of *Wilayat* is such a crucial issue that it shaped the major split of Islam into two divisions: Sunni and Shia. This term in different forms of speech appears in the Qur'an around one hundred times. It is reflected through various stories that condition the same common meaning: alliance and support. This is the true and common relationship between children and parents (19:4–6), friends (17:111), relatives (29:22),

8. Jar Allah Al-Zamakhshari, *Al-Kashshaf*, ed. Adil Ahmad Abd al-Mawjud and Ali Muhammad Muawwadh (Riyadh: Maktabat al-Abikan, 1998), 4:562.
    9. Qur'an 29:29.
    10. Ibid. 25:31.
    11. Ibid. 2:5; also see 64:11.

lord (6:14), gods (29:41), and gracious friends (3:28). Moreover, the Qur'an characterizes the relationship within faithful using the term *Wilayat*, meaning as follows: "And the faithful, men and women, are supporting alliance one of another; they enjoin the right and forbid the wrong, and they establish worship and they pay the poor-due, and they obey God and his messenger. As for these, God will have mercy on them. Surely God is mighty, wise."[12]

At the first glance it might seem odd to apply the model of *Wilayat* to the people of the Book rather than limiting its use among Muslim faithful.[13] However, the Qur'an describes mainly the people of the Book as faithful rather than infidel (*Kafir*). The fundamental Islamic value ("there is no compulsion in religion")[14] declares it. Most first commentators of the Qur'an, including Ibn Abbas, a cousin and a companion of the Prophet, narrated that this verse was revealed regarding situations in which the Prophet's companions had children who had converted to Judaism and Christianity; the companions were forbidden, on the basis of this verse, from forcing their children to convert to Islam.[15] It means the Qur'an considered Judaism and Christianity in its camp of faith. The first verses of chapter 2 of the Qur'an address the faithful, and most exegetes elaborated that they address people of the Book because they share with Muslims articles of faith; the only difference is about the details.[16] These common articles of faith indeed lay the foundation for calling upon the common word (3:64). Moreover, chapter 5, verse 57 clearly distinguishes between infidels and people of the Book. Finally the Quranic chapter Rome (30) is revealed to the Prophet to tell him and Muslims that they are sharing in the camp of the faithful with the people of the Book and to give them the good tidings that the Christian faithful will overcome the enemies of the people of the Book.[17]

This clarifies what is narrated, that the Prophet was accustomed to act in harmony with the people of the Book when there was no revelation on the matter. Considering people of the Book, thus K-F-R in the Qur'an

---

12. Ibid. 9:71.

13. I intentionally prefer using term *faith* rather than *belief* in translating the Arabic term *Iman*, which means faith and Mumin faithful. The Arabic term for belief, *Itiqad*, comes from A-Q-D, meaning tying and clinging. All Quranic applications of the root A-Q-D refer to that meaning, a fixed and static state, and do not mention faith, which is flexible and dynamic (e.g., see 4:33, 5:89).

14. Qur'an 2:256.

15. Abi al-Fida Ismail Ibn Kathir, *Tafsir al-Quran al-Azim*, ed. Sami bin Muhammad al-Salamah (Riyadh: Dar Rayyiba, 1999), 1:682.

16. Ibid., 1:170–171; also see 2:121, 3:199, 4:159.

17. Jalal ad-Din Al-Suyuti, *Asbab al-Nuzul* (Beirut: Muassisa al-Kutub al-Thaqafiyyah, 2002), 201.

refers to its literal meaning, being ingratitude or covered, which is used in other places of the Qur'an as well.[18] In another words, the Qur'an uses two different terms to articulate the position of faithful to others: *Mu'min* (faithful), which contradicts *Kafir* (infidel), and *Muslim*, in its narrow meaning, which disagrees with Jew and Christian.[19] The basics for faith are acknowledging the origin and the end, God and Judgment Day. Thus, people of the Book are inside the camp of faith, and Muslims should treat them as part of their supporting alliance. This is what the chapter Rome announced and the Prophet used to operate.

Still, there is a controversy because we have several Quranic verses that seem to discourage Muslims from friendly ties with people of the Book. To be clear, these verses all are subject to several conditions in order to inspire Muslims in managing situations carefully. As Muslims are not alike in practicing faith or supporting their friends in faith, so are people of the Book. The Qur'an explicitly differentiates among people of the Book and does not oversimplify by placing them in one category. Oversimplification of faith is among the most dangerous attitudes common today, as the mentality of many people is shaped by mass media into a global climate of oversimplification. Nonbelievers do so with the faithful, extremist Muslims do so with people of the Book, and some people of the Book do so with Islamic faith. The Qur'an in many places distinguishes among faithful people of the Book to suggest insight for audiences on the issue. To cite more of the verse also cited by Dr. Syeed in his essay:

> They are not all alike; of the people of the book there is an upright party; they recite God's communications in the nighttime and they adore (him). They believe in God and the last day, and they enjoin what is right and forbid the wrong and they strive with one another in hastening to good deeds, and those are among the good. And whatever good they do, they shall not be denied it, and God knows those who guard (against evil).[20]

The commonality among Abrahamic religions, which is emphasized repeatedly in the Qur'an, inspires the faithful to learn from each other and support each other in sacred experiences and building a better community.

---

18. The Qur'an applied the term *K-F-R* to people of the Book (3:70, 3:98), but it is necessary to know that K-F-R literally means "covering." It is used in the Qur'an also in its literal meaning (5:12; 14:7). It is used describing being ungrateful as well (2:34, 2:152, 4:155–61, 26:19–20). Another Quranic implication is declaring oneself to be clear of somebody or something (60:4).

19. Islam in a broader sense merely means submission to God, either His religion (sharia) by free will or His creation by nature, so it entails all creatures. See 2:128; 3:20, 3:83, 7:111.

20. Qur'an 3:113–15.

Of course, when constructive and mutual coalition is replaced with a disrespectful and polemical state, the field for supporting alliance is destroyed. This is the situation when the Qur'an warns Muslims to distance themselves from other faithful: "O you who are faithful! do not take for guardians (Wali) those who take your religion for a mockery and a joke, from among those who were given the book before you and the unbelievers; and be careful of (your duty to) God if you are faithful."[21] This verse obviously distinguishes people of the Book from unbelievers by addressing two groups separately. It also gives an account why this friendship is dangerous because, in this case, the mutual respect is lost. The converse, therefore, can also be true; if there is a mutual respect and willingness to learn from each other, there is no prohibition and thus they can contribute together to promote virtue and justice within community. Additional Quranic verses stress this distinction:

> God does not forbid you respecting those who have not made war against you on account of (your) religion, and have not driven you forth from your homes, that you show them kindness and deal with them justly; surely God loves the doers of justice. God only forbids you respecting those who made war upon you on account of (your) religion, and drove you forth from your homes and backed up (others) in your expulsion, that you make friends (Wali) with them, and whoever makes friends with them, these are the unjust.[22]

Thus, the verses referring to not take them as *Wali* highlight several conditions that destroy the common ground necessary for shared work: belittling, fighting against, and preventing the fundamental needs of humanity like freedom of residence.[23] It is worth mentioning that the verse before the warning even states that God might bring friendship between faithful and their previous enemies because He is powerful, forgiving, and merciful.[24] The context, before and after discussion, is about unbelievers (*Kafirs*), not even people of the Book, and so it is a step ahead and broader than the Vatican's call to overcome the centuries of quarrels and hostilities between Christians and Muslims, "to forget the past, to make sincere efforts for mutual understanding, and so to work together for the preser-

---

21. Ibid. 5:57.
22. Ibid. 60:8–9.
23. To learn more about the suggested Quranic model of relationship between Muslims and non-Muslims see my paper: Sayed Hassan Akhlaq Hussaini, "Identity and Immigration: A Quranic Perspective," in *Immigration and Hospitality*, ed. John Hogan, Vensus A. George, and Corazon Toralba, 83–103 (Washington, D.C.: CRVP, 2013).
24. Qur'an 60:7.

vation and fostering of social justice, moral welfare, and peace and freedom for all humankind."[25]

In contrast to these conditional statements warning against a supporting alliance between Muslims and people of the Book, in terms of the Qur'an there are many encouragements to work together that establish among faithful the state of *Wilayat*, a supporting alliance to promote love, knowledge, kindness, and qualified public and private life. The most significant is the calling upon the common word (3:64) consisting of the very foundational principles of both Muslims and people of the Book, love of the one God, and love of neighbor, as detailed in "An Open Letter and Call from Muslim Religious Leaders to His Holiness Pope Benedict XVI."

Wilayat affords us to understand better how to apply calling upon a common word. While this meaning of *Wilayat* is common among several grades of that case, it is also the average of an analogical reality that begins with love and ends with guardianship. It is an analogical and graded entity because the faith has the same quality; faith simultaneously consists of various levels, including controversial, rational, and intuitive levels, from less dedication to high dedication and so on. Many verses of the Qur'an motivate the faithful to attain a higher degree of faith (8:2, 48:4, 3:173, 33:22). There is no place here for thinking that the current state of faith is the final step. The analogical nature of faith and constant inspiration for further steps caused the Qur'an to consider the prophets different in their levels but the same in nature (2:253, 2:285). Also, because Muslims and people of the Book are not considered the same, the differences are highlighted, they cannot reach to the level of guardianship.[26] However, the average meaning of *Wilayat*, alliance and support, provides us with enough means

---

25. *Nostra Aetate* 3, trans. Thomas F. Stransky, CSP.

26. This analysis helps explain a Quranic verse often mentioned nowadays by many politicized and extremist Muslims: "let not the faithful take the unbelievers for guardians [Awliya] rather than faithful" (3:28). This warning is not related to supporting alliance in terms of faith to explore God's mercy and promote justice, benevolence, and love. The context shows it is only about the highest level of *Wilayat*, guardianship. Verse 25 discusses God's total operating authority on Judgment Day; verse 26 His omnipotence, which gives power or weakness; and verse 27 His power over the day and night and the living and dead. This verse, therefore, explains that faithful are not allowed to take unbelievers for their guardians and remain oppressed, because God is their true guardian and protector, and it is against piety to look to another. The two next verses continue with mentioning God's omniscience and His power to do justice on Judgment Day. It is another form of Quranic statement (4:141), which gives confidence to Muslims to operate their rights to govern themselves. One could even say it is another version of Immanuel Kant's call for the Enlightenment, "man's emergence from his self-imposed immaturity," so Muslims and faithful are encouraged to reach their maturity and take responsibility for their government. And finally, it must be mentioned that there is no clear and textual sign to demonstrate that "unbelievers" here refer to people of the Book (see 3:21).

to enrich the faith of the faithful, including Muslims and Christians, as well as to promote faith and related values among humanity in general regardless of their culture, religion, and ideology.

Practical Consequences of *Wilayat*

The concept of *Wilayat* among the faithful highlights many common values among Muslims and Christians, and thus it is totally applicable. Let us take a look at the verse that articulates how to apply *Wilayat* among the faithful. Accordingly, the *Wilayat* features the following characteristics: (a) enjoining the right and forbidding the wrong, (b) establishing worship, (c) paying the poor-due, and (d) obeying God and his messenger. As subsequent, these people meet God's mercy because God is mighty and wise.[27] The faithful operate the desired relationship considering public and private life. Regarding public life, the faithful should reinforce their alliances to serve humanity, particularly the needy. It is a part of their duty rather than an arbitrary thing.

In relation to enjoining each other toward good and inhibiting each other from evil, they can support a true dedication to God and help each other get rid of much stressful technological life. They should help each other see God's power, wisdom, and mercy behind all phenomena, no matter if pleasant or unpleasant. Worshiping God is not merely visiting the worship places and participating in prayers, it is a means of experiencing self-confidence by leaving anything to God, the most merciful and the most compassionate who watches for us and takes care of all: "Surely by God's remembrance are the hearts set at rest."[28]

Obeying God and his messenger suggests experiencing freedom from all idols that capture the modern mind, particularly a consumer mindset enslaved to technology. The true meaning of obedience to God in Islam is liberation from all other authorities that are not established by us, the case of democratic society. Rumi the great Sufi explains the meaning of *Wali* exactly in this way, connecting the essence of the prophethood to the *Wilayat*. He wrote, "Who is the 'protector' [Wali]? He that sets you free and removes the fetters of servitude from your feet. Since prophethood is the guide to freedom, freedom is bestowed on true believers by the prophets. Rejoice, O community of true believers: show yourselves to be 'free' as the cypress and the lily."[29]

---

27. Qur'an 9:71.
28. Ibid. 13:28.
29. Jalal ud-din Rumi, *The Mathnawi of Jalal ud-din Rumi*, trans. and ed. Reynold Alleyne Nicholson (Tehran: Research Center of Booteh Publication Co., 1381/2002), 6: 4540–42.

Thus, talking about *Nostra Aetate* within this Quranic concept heartens us to think to implement a supporting alliance among the faithful in terms of "In Our Time." First of all, it requires spreading the word among both religious leaders and religious ordinary people. Second, it requires understanding how enjoining the right and forbidding the wrong can take place in democratic communities and an individualistic world. How could modern institutions and associations help the faithful work together and criticize materialistic reductionism? How do modern concerns, styles of life, and habits ask for a new subject of focus and a new method of encountering? Although the features of worship and prayers in Islam are more or less restricted insofar as they are limited to obligatory acts of worship, there is much room for other prayers that Muslims and Christians can learn from each other. Many charities by the faithful are active among various nations; the faithful from different backgrounds can join each other and work alongside each other for social justice and elimination of poverty. There are many golden chains in modern times that create modern slavery; the faithful in this context could work together for public awareness and human dignity. Acknowledging each other and working together regarding realities of our time bring the faithful under God's mercy because God is mighty and wise.

Furthermore, reducing ecumenism to socio-intellectual, and in worse cases to politico-economical, aspects means losing the spirit of *Nostra Aetate*. This means reducing humanity to a selective phenomenon; the whole to the particular; living dynamic reality to a stable and static entity. Without ignoring these aspects, I am highlighting the significance of *Nostra Aetate*'s spirit, suggesting the interaction among various aspects around that spirit and then exploring that spirit in the light of the Quranic approach. It goes to a deeper conversion among religions—a mystagogy in which all partners in the dialogue extend their search for understanding God to a deeper aspect of humanity, an awareness of subjectivity that comes after the abandonment of ideologies and of hopes that humankind could save itself.

If Jesus and Muhammad were to gather in a place and meet each other, what would they discuss? Do they want to convince each other to follow the other one? The Qur'an clearly states, "We make no distinction (they say) between one and another of his messengers"[30] and "of these messengers, we have preferred some above others."[31] This is similar to what is said in the Gospel: "Do not think that I have come to abolish the law or the prophets. I have come not to abolish but to fulfill."[32] In both texts, the similarity is associated with a uniqueness—the sameness with differences;

30. Ibid. 2:285.
31. Ibid. 2:253.
32. Mt 5:17.

the Qur'an suggested *preference* and the Gospel *fulfillment*. The competition and conflict among religions occur when, first, the preference and accomplishment is taken separated from all prophetic contexts, and second, when it deforms to a merely theological approach. One can relate to this point both as an outsider and an insider. As a philosopher, an outsider view to faith, there is a distinct difference between a nominalist understanding of reality as composed of single atomic entities opposed to each other and a Platonic vision that understands reality in terms of a unity that is translucent and joyful.[33] The second approach joins the religious vision and considers different religions as diverse manifestations of the same, while the first keeps them separated and far from each other. From an insider perspective, there are several Hadiths in which the Prophet said to not consider him above the prophets like Jonah and Moses.[34] As a result, the sameness and differences come together to help the faithful face the "resurrection,"[35] or "raised one," in order to acquire an existential change from an "ordinary person" to a faithful one who experiences transcendence as immanence. In other words, "favored" and "perfect" are an ideal state which Muslims and Christians are directed toward. This is the duty of the Church and *ulema* (scholars of Islamic religious law) to mediate between the current and ideal states without limiting their mission to theology, ethics, or law. Church and mosque have to provide the field in which the faithful find their authentic share of holy experiences of Jesus and Muhammad in order to open their heart to spiritual worlds. During the age of globalization, there is an unparalleled chance for both faiths to discover other aspects of the beloved figures through, first, recognizing the vision of the other and, second, borrowing the other's glasses. This is the major reason we celebrate *Nostra Aetate* and see it as a miraculous event and liberating phenomenon. It reflects the true nature of spiritual leadership as Rumi interpreted the significant verse of the Prophet. The Prophet called himself *Wali*, friend and protector, which is also called the proper relationship among the faithful in many verses of the Qur'an. Regarding its highest degree, Rumi reads it as a capacity to free people, as discussed earlier.

While traditionally the orthodox perspective in faith has been calling people to abandon their sinful nature, in both theological and moral

33. John P. Hogan and George F. MacLean, eds., *Multiple Paths to God:* Nostra Aetate, *40 Years Later* (Washington, D.C.: The Council for Research in Values and Philosophy, 2005), 7.

34. Imam Abi Abdullah Muhammad Al-Bukhari, *Sahih al-Bukhari* (Beirut and Damascus: Dar Ibn Kathir, 2002), 843, 845.

35. It is Rumi's metaphor for the Prophet. See Jalal ud-din Rumi, *The Mathnawi of Jalal ud-din Rumi*, 6:750–53.

aspects *Nostra Aetate* goes a step further, calling upon people to make their static theology flexible. The essence of faith is more related to movement rather than to firmness; a continuing rebirth in deeper level of faith. This significant quotation of Jesus is recounted in the New Testament and an Islamic source: "No one can see the kingdom of God without being born from above."[36] The majesty and limitlessness of God's kingdom require a dedicated and purified heart like of our common father, Abraham.[37] Interestingly, the witnessing of God's kingdom by Abraham in the Qur'an is conveyed by his move among many faces of faith.[38] The kingdom's splendor and richness is so astonishing and inviting that the enduring faithful explore a new spirit step by step. The path toward acquiring perfection in God's kingdom cannot be finished, so the Muslims are recommended to pray at least ten times a day to "show us the straight path."[39] In Islamic wisdom, this process of accomplishment within continuous rebirth resembles a snake's constant shedding of previous skin and getting a new one.[40] Of course, one great skin is a fixed theology. However, the critical point is that this is not only a call for peaceful coexistence but, one step further, a call for active and cooperative coexistence to explore a higher level of religious life. The peaceful life, mutual respect, and social values are fundamentals for exercising a spiritual life that aims for the realization of the grace or guidance within humanity. The religious call for the faithful from diverse faiths to coexistence and sharing the efforts consists of emphasizing two aspects simultaneously: similarity and distinction. I as a faithful have to first explore the common spirit of all faiths and then realize my special share of faith with my own existential relation and quest to my own faith. I as a Muslim have to first discover the commonality of Jesus and Muhammad and then realize my own share of Muhammad's spiritual quality.

Conclusion

I see *Nostra Aetate* mirroring the true nature of religion, much more than a socio-historical phenomenon. It encourages living faith rather than only imagining it. This life in a global village requires a supporting alliance among the faithful. There is a respect for the uniqueness of each faith and

---

36. Jn 3:4.
37. Qur'an 6:75.
38. Ibid. 6:76–79.
39. Ibid. 1:6.
40. Ibn Sina, *Resaleh al-Tair* (commentated by Umar bin Sahlan Sawi, tran. Ahmad ibn Khadiw (Tehran: Noor-e Muhibbat, 1391), 31–32; Motahheri, Morteza, *Kulliyat-e Uloom-e Islami* (Tehran: Sadra, 1382), 2:104.

plurality of life. I would like to conclude this discussion with three stories of the Qur'an. Once Jews, Christians, and Muslims in Medina each boasted that they had the very best faith. Chapter 4, verses 123–124 were revealed, which said the criterium for salvation is good deeds, not wishes and ambitions.[41] In this context we can also understand the story (in 2:62) that recognizes religious pluralism when Salman al-Farsi, the great companion of the Prophet, asked him about his precious friends in other faiths.[42] It inspires Muslims and Christians to exercise approaching God instead of arguing about Him, to support each other in obtaining more religious experiences and building a qualified community rather than focus on the theological distinctions and speculative explorations. Finally, it is narrated that the Prophet repeated Jesus's prayer (5:118) for Muslims a whole night, asking forgiveness for his people.[43] Muslims explicitly do not believe in the Trinity and the Prophet is not asked to do so by God. So why did Muhammad repeat that verse? What is hidden commonality under apparent difference?

---

41. Suyuti, 2002, 92–93; Abi Ali al-Fadhl Al-Tabarsi, *Majma al-Bayan fi Tafsir al-Quran* (Beirut: Dar al-Murtaza, 2006), 3:164.

42. Suyuti, 2002, 14–15. This verse is repeated with a little change in Qur'an 5:69.

43. Abu Hamid Al-Ghazzali, *Ihya al-Uloom al-Din*, ed. Badawi Tabanah (Indonesia: Kariata Futra, n.d.), 283. See also Ibn Kathir, *Tafsir al-Quran al-Azim*, 3:234–35.

Part IV

Dialogue with Jews

Since the spiritual heritage common to Christians and Jews is thus so rich, this Sacred Synod wishes to foster and commend mutual understanding and esteem. This is the fruit, above all, of biblical and theological studies and of friendly conversations.

—*Nostra Aetate* 4, trans. Thomas F. Stransky, CSP

The International Dialogue between the Catholic Church and the Jews since *Nostra Aetate*

Kurt Cardinal Koch

Highlights on the History of the Development of *Nostra Aetate*[1]

"As the sacred synod searches into the mystery of the Church, it remembers the bond that spiritually ties the people of the New Covenant to Abraham's stock."[2] With these words begins the fourth article of the Second Vatican Council's declaration on the relationship between the Church and the non-Christian religions, *Nostra Aetate*. The declaration was adopted on October 28, 1965, by the Council fathers with 2,221 yes votes against 88 no votes and two abstentions—so virtually with moral unanimity, or more precisely with the impressive majority of 96 percent— and promulgated by Blessed Pope Paul VI. The fourth article is devoted to the relationship between the Church and Judaism, and council consultant Joseph Ratzinger, in his highly esteemed reports at that time during the course of the Council, rightly evaluated that in relations between the Church and Israel "a new page had been turned in the book of their mutual relationship."[3] The president of the Secretariat for Christian Unity at that time, the Jesuit Cardinal Augustin Bea, who was responsible to a large extent for editing the conciliar declaration, perceived its fundamental significance in the fact that it was certainly among the subjects "in which so-called public opinion showed the greatest interest" from which he drew the conclusion that "many will judge the council to be good or bad depending on its approval or disapproval of this document."[4]

These very positive judgements and optimistic assessments of the significance of the conciliar declaration scarcely betray anything of the long

---

1. This essay is based on a lecture given in Washington, D.C., on May 19, 2015.
2. *Nostra Aetate* 4, official Vatican translation.
3. Josef Ratzinger, *Die letzte Sitzungsperiode des Konzils* (Köln: J.P. Bachem, 1966), 68.
4. Relatio of Cardinal Augustin Bea on the "Declaration on the Jews and the Non-Christians" held in the Council Hall on September 25, 1964, in Augustin Cardinal Bea, *Die Kirche und das jüdische Volk*, 148–57 (Freiburg im Breisgau: Herder, 1966), 148. Available in English as *The Church and the Jewish People*, trans. Philip Loretz (New York: Harper and Row, 1966).

and complicated history of the development the declaration had to undergo before arriving at its promulgation and that is appropriate to recall now after fifty years in order to better understand its dynamic force at the time and its undiminished actuality today. This long history began when Saint Pope John XXIII, for whom reconciliation with the Jewish people was a heartfelt concern, on September 18, 1960, entrusted into the hands of Cardinal Augustin Bea, first president of the then Secretariat for the Promotion of Christian Unity, the task of preparing a declaration on the Jewish people.[5] At that time the pope, of course, could scarcely foresee the dimensions this task would subsequently assume and the difficulties that were to accompany the furtherance of this declaration. The problems did not lie so much in the sphere of religion or theology but, rather, in the less-than-auspicious political situation of the time, which demanded the highest degree of nuance and balance.

That explains the extremely complex textual history of this declaration,[6] which as already mentioned was initially conceived as an independent document on relations between the Church and the Jewish people. Because this text dealt only with Judaism and therefore provoked protest from the Arab side, it was decided to integrate the draft into the broader context of the stance of the Church in regard to non-Christian religions in general and to add it to the proposed Decree on Ecumenism as a fourth chapter. That location makes good sense insofar as special and deep-reaching connections exist between the Church as the chosen people of God of the New Covenant and the chosen people of God of the Old Covenant, and these connections are shared by all Christians. The first split in the history of Christianity must be perceived in the schism between synagogue and church, which Catholic theologian Erich Przywara defined as the "primal rift" from which he derived the subsequent progressive loss of wholeness of the Catholica.[7] It was primarily the Council fathers living in the Near East who requested that Islam, too, should be included in the declaration, and other Council fathers suggested dealing with all non-Christian religions in general. On the basis of these objections and because of newly emerging difficulties that made renewed reworking of the text

5. Cf. Dorothee Recker, *Die Wegbereiter der Judenerklärung des Zweiten Vatikanischen Konzils. Johannes XXIII, Kardinal Bea und Prälat Oesterreicher—eine Darstellung ihrer theologischen Entwicklung* (Paderborn: Bonifatius, 2007).

6. Cf. J. Oesterreicher, "Kommentierende Einleitung zur 'Erklärung über das Verhältnis der Kirche zu den nichtchristlichen Religionen,'" in *Lexikon für Theologie und Kirche*, Band 13, 406–78 (Freiburg: Herder, 1967).

7. Erich Przywara, "Römische Katholizität—All-christliche Ökumenizität," in *Gott in Welt. Festgabe für K. Rahner*, ed. Johann Baptist Metz et al., 524–28 (Freiburg: Herder, 1964), 526.

necessary, the Council's declaration on the Jewish people ultimately found a place as the fourth article of the Declaration on Non-Christian Religions that bears the name *Nostra Aetate*.

Thus, the question of the relationship of the Catholic Church to Judaism is considered within the broader context of the presentation of the relationship of the Church to the non-Christian religions in general. To a certain extent that involves a compromise, since Judaism for us Christians is not just one among the many non-Christian religions, and the relationship between Judaism and Christianity must not be reduced to just another variant of interreligious dialogue so that its distinctive uniqueness is no longer brought to bear.[8] For the Church has a unique and distinctive relationship with Judaism that it has with no other religion, and the Church cannot understand itself without reference to Judaism, as Saint Pope John Paul II later expressed on the occasion of his visit to the Roman synagogue in these vivid and impressive words: "The Jewish religion is not 'extrinsic' to us, but in a certain way is 'intrinsic' to our own religion. With Judaism therefore we have a relationship which we do not have with any other religion. You are our dearly beloved brothers and, in a certain way, it could be said that you are our elder brothers."[9] Against this background of the history of the development of the conciliar declaration, we may rightly evaluate the fourth article dedicated to the relationship of the Catholic Church with Judaism as not only the starting point but also the essential heart of the whole declaration *Nostra Aetate*.

The great significance of the conciliar declaration *Nostra Aetate* resides without any doubt in the fact that for the first time in history an ecumenical council had expressed a view in such an explicit and positive manner on the relationship of the Catholic Church to the non-Christian religions in general and to Judaism in particular. Furthermore, the Council did not simply engage with purely practical viewpoints but treated the question of Jewish-Christian relations within a theological horizon and on solid biblical foundations. *Nostra Aetate* is not a political document but a strictly religious and theological one. It also deserves mention that this new perspective of the relationship between Christianity and Judaism is not simply a

---

8. Cf. Josef Cardinal Ratzinger, "Der Dialog der Religionen und das Jüdisch-christliche Verhältnis," in *Die Vielfalt der Religionen und der Eine Bund*, 93–121 (Hagen: Verlag Urfeld, 1998). Available in English as *Many Religions, One Covenant: Israel, the Church, and the World*, trans. Graham Harrison (San Francisco: Ignatius Press, 2000).

9. "Let us thank the Lord for the rediscovered brotherhood and for the profound understanding between the Church and Judaism." John Paul II, "Address in the Synagogue during the Meeting the Jewish Community in Rome on 13 April 1986," in *Insegnamenti di Giovanni Paolo II*, IX, 1, 1024–31 (Città del Vaticano: Libreria editrice vaticana, 1986), 1027.

secondary question but one that touches on the essential identity of the Church itself, which becomes apparent in the fact that it also was accorded a place in important constitutions of the Second Vatican Council. With regard to the reception history of conciliar documents, one can without doubt dare to assert that *Nostra Aetate* is to be reckoned among those conciliar texts that in a convincing manner have been able to influence a fundamental reorientation of the Second Vatican Council.

The Magna Carta of Jewish-Christian Relations

With this brief insight into the reception history, the theological orientation of the fourth article of *Nostra Aetate* has become evident. It begins with a biblically grounded reflection on the mystery and the soteriological mission of the Church and a reminder of the deep and abiding spiritual bond linking the people of the New Covenant with the tribe of Abraham. It explicitly points to the Jewish roots of the Christian faith and affirms in a positive manner the common "spiritual patrimony" of Jews and Christians. It expresses the ardent desire that the reciprocal understanding and the resulting mutual respect of Jews and Christians be fostered. It repudiates and condemns all outbreaks of hatred, persecutions, slanders, and manifestations of force that have been directed against the Jews on the part of so-called Christians. It admonishes that, on the part of Christians, any denigration, belittling, or disdain of Judaism must be avoided and condemns every form of anti-Semitism. The fourth article of *Nostra Aetate* is rightly considered the "foundation document" and the "Magna Carta" of the Jewish-Catholic dialogue,[10] and its fundamental principles are to be further explicated and concretized in the following.

The Unique and Complex Relationship between Christians and Jews

That the fourth article of *Nostra Aetate* marks a fundamental new beginning in the relationship between Christianity and Judaism can be made clear by a brief look back at history. This history proves to be very

---

10. Cf. Hans Herman Henrix, "*Nostra aetate* und die christlich-jüdischen Beziehungen," in *Das Zweite Vatikanische Konzil. Impulse und Perspektiven*, ed. Dirk Ansorge, 228–45 (Münster: Aschendorff-Verlag, 2014); Neville Lamdan and Alberto Melloni, eds., Nostra Aetate: *Origins, Promulgation, Impact on Jewish-Catholic Relations* (Berlin: LIT Verlag, 2007); Jan-Heiner Tück, "Das Konzil und die Juden. *Nostra aetate*—Bruch mit dem Antijudaismus und Durchbruch zur theologischen Würdigung des nachbiblischen Bundesvolkes," in *Freude an Gott. Auf dem Weg zu einem lebendigen Glauben. Festschrift für Kurt Kardinal Koch zum 65 Geburtstag*, Zweiter Teilband, eds. George Augustin and Markus Schulze, 857–93 (Freiburg i. Br.: Herder, 2015), 880.

complex, oscillating between proximity and distance, between familiarity and alienation, between love and hate, and it has been so from the very beginning. On the one hand, Jesus cannot be understood without Israel; the early Christian community quite naturally participated in the Jewish liturgy in the temple; and Paul, too, on his various mission journeys always went to the synagogues first before turning to the Gentiles with his proclamation of the Gospel. On the other hand, following the Jewish War and the destruction of the Jerusalem Temple in 70 A.D., postbiblical rabbinical Judaism arose, which was to a great extent constituted by a dissociation from expanding Christianity. In reaction to that, Christianity for its part sought its own definitive identity in dissociation from Judaism. Although contemporary research tends to accept that the process of estrangement and dissociation between Judaism and Christianity extended over a longer period than previously assumed and surely only gradually took shape during the second century after the destruction of the Second Temple in 70 A.D., there is nevertheless no question that this process was set in place at the very beginning of Jewish-Christian relations, and the relationship between Jews and Christians was marked by conflicts already at an early stage. Cardinal Joseph Ratzinger outlined those conflicts in these words: "The church was regarded by her mother as an unnatural daughter, while the Christians regarded the mother as blind and obstinate."[11] While this image reminds us that the conflicts between Jews and Christians were still like family quarrels, the relationship between Jews and Christians has deteriorated progressively as the awareness of belonging to the same family was gradually lost. In the course of history it therefore has been exposed to great strain and hostility, which unfortunately in many cases has led to anti-Jewish attitudes involving outbreaks of violence and pogroms against the Jews.

Hostility toward the Jews in European history reached its lowest possible nadir in the mass murder of European Jews, planned and executed with industrial perfection by the National Socialists. The *Shoah* must be judged as the most horrific expression of that primitive racist anti-Semitism of the Nazi ideology, which had developed already in the nineteenth century. Of course, this thoroughly racist anti-Semitism is fundamentally alien to Christianity and was repeatedly sharply condemned by Popes Pius XI and Pius XII above all. The *Shoah* can and should not however be attributed to Christianity as such. In fact it was led and undertaken by a godless, anti-Christian and neo-pagan ideology. If the *Shoah* must therefore be judged as the horrific nadir of a pagan worldview that intended to annihilate not only

11. Josef Cardinal Ratzinger, "Das Erbe Abrahams," in *Weggemeinschaft des Glaubens. Kirche als Communio*, 235–38 (Augsburg: Sankt Ulrich, 2002), 237. Available in English as *Pilgrim Fellowship of Faith*, trans. Henry Taylor (San Francisco: Ignatius Press, 2005.

Judaism but also the Jewish heritage in Christianity, one can also understand that Pope Benedict XVI, during his visit to the extermination camp
Auschwitz-Birkenau, wished to give expression to this fatal connection: "By
destroying Israel, by the *Shoah*, they ultimately wanted to tear up the taproot
of the Christian faith and to replace it with a faith of their own invention:
faith in the rule of man, the rule of the powerful."[12]

When we call to mind this tragic history, we Christians must
acknowledge with deep shame that this shared National Socialist hostility
should have aroused among us Christians much more empathetic compassion with the Jews than in fact did come into effect. We Christians therefore have every cause to remember our complicity in the horrific developments and above all to confess that Christian resistance to the boundless
inhuman brutality of ideologically based National Socialist racism did not
display that vigor and clarity that one should have expected by rights. We
Christians therefore must sincerely regret that only the unparalleled crime
of the *Shoah* was able to bring about a genuine rethinking as it found
expression on the one hand in the so-called theology after Auschwitz in its
different variants[13] and on the other hand in the clear repudiation of all
manifestations of anti-Semitism in *Nostra Aetate* "moved not by political
reasons but by the Gospel's spiritual love."[14]

Rediscovery of the Jewish Roots of Christianity

Coming to terms with the catastrophe of the *Shoah* and the battle
against anti-Semitism in the Christian sphere formed an important part of
the driving force for the drafting of *Nostra Aetate*, as well as the turning
point it represents in the relationship of the Catholic Church with
Judaism. In the critical questioning of the complicity of Christians, it has
become increasingly clear that the resistance by Christians against the
National Socialist anti-Semitism may well have also been so inadequate
because a theological Christian anti-Judaism had been in effect for centuries, fostering a widespread anti-Jewish apathy against the Jews. Thus, an
ancient anti-Jewish legacy was embedded in the furrows of the souls of not
a few Christians.[15] Christian anti-Judaism was, while not the cause, an

12. "I had to come"; Benedict XVI, "Auschwitz-Birkenau: The Visit to the Concentration Camp on 28 May 2006," in *Insegnamenti di Benedetto XVI*, vol. II, no. 1, 724–29 (Vatican
City: Libreria editrice vaticana, 2007).

13. Cf. Eugen Kogon and Johann Baptist Metz, eds., *Gott nach Auschwitz. Dimensionen
des Massenmords am jüdischen Volk* (Freiburg i. Br.: Herder, 1979).

14. *Nostra Aetate* 4.

15. Cf. *Judaisme, anti-judaisme et christianisme: Colloque de l'Université de Fribourg*
(Saint-Maurice: Editions SaintAugustin, 2000).

attitudinal prerequisite for the expansion of neo-pagan anti-Semitism and the lack of resistance of most Christians. This has to be cause enough for confronting this historical debt with self-criticism.

The point of departure for this is the historical fact that a new situation arose in the relationship between the Church and Israel after the catastrophe of the destruction of the Second Temple in 70 A.D. On the one hand, the Sadducees, who were bound to the Temple, did not survive the catastrophe; in contrast the Pharisees developed their particular mode of reading and interpreting the Old Testament during the period without the Temple. On the other hand, the Christians read the Old Testament in the light of the New and saw in it the fulfilment of the Old Testament promises. As a consequence, two different ways of reading the Old Testament arose anew after the year 70, namely the Christological exegesis of the Christians and the exegesis developed by rabbinical Judaism. Since the Christian church and postbiblical rabbinical and Talmudic Judaism developed in parallel after the destruction of the temple, the crucial new question arose of precisely how these two modes are related to one another. This new situation led increasingly to a state of conflict between perpetuating the tradition of the Old Testament and contradicting the Jewish interpretation to the extent that the New Testament was no longer seen simply as the fulfilment of the promises given in the Old Testament but also as its replacement. As a result Judaism was ultimately stripped of its status as the people of God's covenant, and that dignity was claimed exclusively by the Church—identifying itself as the new people of the covenant, as the "new Israel."[16]

This replacement view came into effect historically above all in the postbiblical period. In response to the question to whom the testament belongs, the Epistle of Barnabas (around 130 A.D.), for example, gave the unambiguous answer that the Jews have gambled away and lost the testament because of their sins, so now the Christians were the hereditary people. In *Dialogue with Trypho*, Justin Martyr took the next step by setting the new covenant in opposition to the old and declaring Christ to be the new covenant in person so that the old covenant had reached its end and its goal in Christ Jesus. Irenaeus of Lyon authoritatively interpreted the relationship between the old and the new covenant in the sense of promise and fulfilment, and consequently postbiblical rabbinical Judaism was viewed as an obsolete religion.

This so-called replacement theory has been influential within the tradition of the Christian church in the most recent past. In view of the cat-

16. Cf. Knut Backhaus, "Das Bundesmotiv in der frühkirchlichen Schwellenzeit," in *Der ungekündigte Bund: Antworten des Neuen Testaments*, ed. Hubert Frankemölle, 211–31 (Freiburg i. Br.: Herder, 1998).

astrophic ramifications of anti-Semitism in the last century and with the critical questioning of an anti-Judaist burden within the Christian tradition, the Church considered itself duty bound to overcome the replacement view and the inheritance theory and to return to the biblical and above all Pauline view of the relationship between Jews and Christians. With this in mind, Cardinal Augustin Bea formulated as the goal of the Council declaration *Nostra Aetate* "to restore to the consciousness of those who believe in Christ these truths about the Jews that are expounded by the Apostle Paul and contained in the patrimony of the faith."[17]

In order to call to mind that the Church has received the revelation of the Old Testament from that people with whom God concluded the old covenant, *Nostra Aetate* therefore makes explicit reference to the image of the "well-cultivated olive tree onto which have been grafted the wild shoots, the Gentiles."[18] This vividly expressive image in the eleventh chapter of the Epistle to the Romans (Rom 11:16–20) represents for Paul the essential key to thinking of the relationship between Israel and the Church in the light of faith.[19] With this image Paul gives expression to a duality with regard to the unity and the difference between Israel and the Church. On the one hand, the image is to be taken seriously in the sense that the grafted wild branches have not grown out of the root itself or sprung from it but represent a new reality and a new work of salvation by God, so that the Christian church cannot merely be understood as a branch or a fruit of Israel. On the other hand, the image is also to be taken seriously in the sense that the Church is only able to live when it draws nourishment and strength from the root of Israel and that the grafted branches would wither or even die if they were cut off from the root of Israel. Speaking literally rather than metaphorically, this means that Israel and the Church are related to and interdependent on one another, precisely because they exist in a state not only of unity but also of difference. Israel and the Church thus are and remain to that extent bound up with one another, and indeed both unmixed yet undivided.

Theological Reflection on the "Common Spiritual Patrimony"

Unity and difference between Judaism and Christianity come to the fore above all in the question of how the Old and the New Covenants

---

17. Relatio of Cardinal Augustin Bea, "On the Attitude of Catholics toward Non-Christians and Especially toward Jews" in the Council Hall on 19 November 1963, in Augustin Cardinal Bea, *Die Kirche und das jüdische Volk*, 141–47 (Freiburg i. Br.: Herder 1966), 144. Available in English as *The Church and the Jewish People* (London: Chapman, 1966).

18. *Nostra Aetate* 4.

19. Cf. Franz Mussner, *Die Kraft der Wurzel. Judentum-Jesus-Kirche* (Freiburg i. Br.: Herder, 1987).

stand in relation to one another. For the Christian faith it is axiomatic that there can only be one covenant history of God with his humanity. This faith conviction is also found in the Old Testament and is already evident in the fact that the history of God with His people has been realized in a series of covenants, whereby each of these covenants incorporates the previous covenants and interprets them in a new way. That is also true for the new covenant that God sealed in Jesus Christ and is for us Christians the final covenant and therefore the definitive interpretation of what was promised by the prophets of the Old Covenant, or as Paul expresses it, the "Yes" and "Amen" to "all that God has promised."[20] The New Covenant is therefore neither the annulment nor the replacement of the Old Covenant, as Cardinal Walter Kasper has correctly stressed: "The New Covenant for Christians is not the replacement but the fulfilment of the Old Covenant. Both stand with each other in a relationship of promise or anticipation and fulfilment."[21] A clear distinction must be drawn between fulfilment and replacement, and any idea of replacement must be excluded.

This view of the relationship between the Old and the New Covenant also has consequences for unity and difference with regard to the testimonies of divine revelation. Because Israel is the beloved people of his covenant, which has never been revoked or repudiated, Israel's book of the covenant, the Old Testament, is part of the lasting heritage of the Christian church. With the existence of the Old Testament as an integral part of the one Christian Bible, there is a deeply rooted belonging and intrinsic kinship between Judaism and Christianity.

With the existence of the New Testament, the question naturally arose quite soon of how the two testaments are related to one another. There also emerged the dangerous idea that the New Testament had superseded the Old Testament book of promises in the context of salvation history, rendering it obsolete through the glow of the new in the same way that moonlight is not needed once the sun has risen. A similar stark antithesis between the Hebrew and the Christian Bible, which was supported above all by Marcion in the second century, fortunately never become an official doctrine of the Christian church. Marcion's refutation of the Old Testament met with the strong opposition of the postapostolic church, and he was excluded from the Christian congregation in 144 A.D. The significance of this verdict of the early Church against Marcionism can hardly be overestimated in the context of the relationship between the Church and Judaism.

---

20. 2 Cor 1:20.
21. Walter Cardinal Kasper, "Foreword," in *Christ Jesus and the Jewish People Today: New Explorations of Theological Interrelationships*, ed. Philip. A. Cunningham, x–xviii (Grand Rapids, Mich.: William B. Eerdmans, 2011), xiv.

This is, of course, only one side of the relationship between the two testaments. The common patrimony of the Old Testament, however, not only formed the fundamental basis of a spiritual kinship between Jews and Christians but also brought with it an elementary tension in the relationship of the two faith communities. This is demonstrated by the fact that Christians read the Old Testament in the light of the New, in the conviction expressed by Augustine in the indelible formula: "In the Old Testament the New is concealed and in the New the Old is revealed."[22] Pope Gregory the Great also spoke in the same sense when he defined the Old Testament as "the prophecy of the New" and the latter as the "best exposition of the Old."[23]

With that we return to the starting point of this line of thought in which we have established that, after the destruction of the temple, two ways of reading and interpreting Sacred Scriptures developed, and we can in conclusion formulate as a consequence the finding that the Pontifical Biblical Commission expressed in its 2001 document, *The Jewish People and Their Sacred Scriptures in the Christian Bible*, that Christians can and must admit "that the Jewish reading of the Bible is a possible one, in continuity with the Jewish scriptures of the Second Temple period, analogous to the Christian reading which developed in parallel fashion." It then draws the conclusion: "Both readings are bound up with the vision of their respective faiths, of which the readings are the result and expression. Consequently, both are irreducible."[24]

The Good Reception of *Nostra Aetate* after the Council

With this theological reflection on the content of *Nostra Aetate*, we have already opened up the prospect of the reception history of this conciliar declaration. Our attention is directed above all to the way the promising perspectives founded by *Nostra Aetate* have been affirmed and deepened in a variety of ways by the popes after the Second Vatican Council. It must not be forgotten, of course, that at the inception of *Nostra Aetate* stands Saint Pope John XXIII, who already during his diplomatic service as Apostolic Delegate in Turkey (1935–1944) had personal experience of the tragic fate of the Jews during the period of the reign of terror of the Third Reich

---

22. Augustine, *Quaestiones in Heptateuchum* 2.73.
23. Gregory the Great, *Homiliae in Ezechielem I*, VI, 15. Available in English as *The Homilies of Saint Gregory the Great on the Book of the Prophet Ezekiel*, trans. Theodosia Gray (Etna, Calif.: Center for Traditionalist Orthodox Studies, 1990).
24. Pontifical Biblical Commission, *The Jewish People and Their Sacred Scriptures in the Christian Bible*, (2001), par. 22.

and saved the lives of thousands of Jews from extermination in the National Socialist persecution. The actual impetus for the preparation of a specific document on the Jews may well have been a meeting of John XXIII on June 13, 1960, with the Jewish historian Jules Isaac, who presented the pope with a memorandum with urgent requests for a new view of the relationship of the church with Judaism.[25]

The endeavor initiated by John XXIII to establish the relationship of the Catholic Church to Judaism on a new foundation could only be truly taken up and carried on by Blessed Pope Paul VI. His great achievement consists in rigorously implementing the new direction introduced by John XXIII, adding theological depth and providing it with new accents.[26] Even before the promulgation of *Nostra Aetate*, Pope Paul felt that the time was ripe for undertaking a visit to the Holy Land. The actual occasion for this trip in 1964 was in fact a meeting between the pope and the Ecumenical Patriarch Athenagoras of Constantinople. But just as this meeting in Jerusalem became a catalyst for Orthodox-Catholic relations and, in a certain sense, even for Christian ecumenism as a whole,[27] this journey to Israel by Paul VI also led to new and promising developments in the relationship of the Catholic Church to Judaism. This became apparent above all in the meeting with the authorities of the state of Israel, when the pope addressed the Jews with the beautiful term "sons of the people of the Covenant" with the intention of expressing the fact that the Jews of today also belong to this people of the covenant and that God's covenant with this people continues to exist. Furthermore, Paul VI recalled the biblical tribal fathers Abraham, Isaac, and Jacob in order to emphasize the common roots of the faith. One can without doubt assess his visit to the Holy Land as "a milestone on the path towards a changed relationship of the Catholic Church to Judaism"[28] and judge that there is a logical development leading from it to the religious and theological stance that the Council later formulated in *Nostra Aetate*. Beside this and other authoritative statements on Jewish-Catholic dialogue, Paul VI also accorded a significant status to direct encounters with representatives of Judaism, which were always characterized by a warm tone, indicating the great interest and high esteem that Paul VI constantly evinced toward

---

25. Cf. Michael Quisinsky, "Jules Isaac" in *Personenlexikon zum Zweiten Vatikanischen Konzil*, ed. Michael Quisinsky and Peter Walter, 139–40. (Freiburg i. Br.: Herder, 2012).

26. Cf. Jörg Ernesti, *Paul VI. Der vergessene Papst* (Freiburg i. Br.: Herder, 2012), especially "Das Verhältnis zum Judentum," 91–106.

27. Cf. Métropolite Emmanuel and Kurt Cardinal Koch, *L'esprit de Jérusalem. L'orthodoxie et le catholicisme au XXIème siècle* (Paris: Cerf, 2014).

28. Thomas Brechenmacher, *Der Vatikan und die Juden. Geschichte einer unheiligen Beziehung* (München: Verlag C.H. Beck, 2005), 245.

Judaism. It is therefore not surprising that in a Jewish obituary at his death we find the following tribute: "The Jewish people throughout the world will always remember the years of Pope Paul's reign as the commencement of a new age for Catholic–Jewish relations."[29]

Further steps in the reconciliation with Judaism were taken by Saint Pope John Paul II, whose passionate endeavors for Jewish-Christian dialogue surely have their roots initially in his personal biography.[30] He grew up in the small Polish town of Wadowice, which consisted of at least one quarter of Jewish fellow citizens, to the extent that friendships with Jews were taken for granted already in his childhood. During his long pontificate it was important for him to intensify the bonds of friendship with Judaism. He therefore repeatedly received Jewish personalities and groups, and during his numerous pastoral journeys his obligatory program always included an encounter with a local Jewish delegation wherever there was a sizeable Jewish community. For the public his passionate engagement for Jewish-Catholic dialogue was visible above all in grand public gestures, among which the following deserve special mention. Already in the first year of his pontificate on June 7, 1979, he visited the former concentration camp of Auschwitz-Birkenau, where in front of the memorial stone with its Hebrew inscription he recalled the victims of the *Shoah* in a particular manner with moving words: "It is not permissible for anyone to pass by this inscription with indifference."[31] A second abiding memory is the visit by Pope John Paul II to the Roman synagogue on April 13, 1986, which is also accorded special significance because there was a Jewish community in Rome long before the Christian faith was brought to Rome. The historical significance of this event, however, is based above all on the fact that it was the first time in history that the Bishop of Rome visited a synagogue to bear testimony to his respect for Judaism before the whole world. A third indelible memory is the public liturgy on March 12 in the Holy Year 2000, during which the pope prayed for forgiveness of guilt toward the people of Israel in the compelling words: "We are deeply saddened by the behaviour of those who in the course of history have caused these children of yours to suffer, and asking your forgiveness we wish to commit ourselves to genuine

---

29. Quoted in *Freiburger Rundbrief* 28 (1978): 93.

30. Cf. John Paul II–Benedict XVI, *Ebrei, fratelli maggiori. La necessità del dialogo tra cattolicesimo ed ebraismo nei discorsi di Papa Wojtyla e di Papa Ratzinger. A cura di Santino Spartà* (Rome: Newton Compton, 2007); E. J. Fisher and L. Klenicki, eds., *The Saint for Shalom: How Pope John Paul II Transformed Catholic-Jewish Relations: The Complete Texts 1979–2005* (New York: Crossroad, 2011).

31. John Paul II, "Victory of Faith and Love over Hatred. At the Brzezinka Concentration Camp on 7 June 1979," in *Insegnamenti di Giovanni Paolo II*, vol. II (Gennaio-Giugno), 1482–87 (Vatican City: Libreria editrice vaticana, 1979), 1484.

brotherhood with the people of the Covenant."[32] In a slightly altered form, Pope John Paul II inserted this prayer for forgiveness as a written petition between the stones of the Western Wall in Jerusalem during his visit to the Holy Land, during which he also visited the Yad-Vashem Holocaust Memorial, commemorated the victims of the *Shoah*, met with survivors of this incomparable tragedy, and entered into contact for the first time with the Chief Rabbinate of Jerusalem. In retrospect one can reflect with gratitude that John Paul II, with his great commitment for the Catholic-Jewish dialogue during his long pontificate, set the course for the future of this necessary conversation.

The many endeavors of Pope John Paul II were theologically legitimated and supported by the then prefect of the Congregation for the Doctrine of the Faith, Cardinal Joseph Ratzinger, who himself published ground-breaking articles on the specific relationship of Christianity to Judaism within the context of world religions.[33] Against the background of these theological convictions it cannot surprise us that Pope Benedict XVI carried on and advanced the conciliatory work of his predecessor with regard to the Jewish-Catholic conversation. During the almost eight years of his pontificate, he took all those steps that Pope John Paul II took in his twenty-seven-year pontificate: Pope Benedict XVI visited the former concentration camp Auschwitz-Birkenau on May 28, 2006.[34] During his visit to Israel in May 2009 he, too, stood before the Western Wall in Jerusalem and also prayed at Yad-Vashem for the victims of the *Shoah*, where he deliberately referred to the name of this place and meditated on the God-given inalienability of the name of each individual person: "One can weave an insidious web of lies to convince others that certain groups are undeserving of respect. Yet try as one might, one can never take away the name of a fellow human being."[35] On January 17, 2010, Pope Benedict was warmly received by the Jewish community in Rome in their synagogue, where he presented an inimitable spiritual meditation on the Decalogue, which he acknowledged as the "pole star of faith and of the morality of the

32. John Paul II, "Let Us Forgive and Ask Forgiveness! The Day of Pardon on the First Sunday of Lent of the Great Jubilee," in *Insegnamenti di Giovanni Paolo II*, vol. XXIII, no. 1, 351–55 (Vatican City: Libreria editrice vaticana, 2002).

33. Ratzinger, *Die Vielfalt der Religionen und der Eine Bund* [Many Religions, One Covenant].

34. Cf. Jan-Heiner Tück, "Wo war Gott? Der deutsche Papst in Auschwitz—eine theologische Nachbetrachtung," in, *Der Theologenpapst. Eine kritische Würdigung Benedikts XVI*, ed. Jan-Heiner Tück, 122–34 (Freiburg i. Br.: Herder, 2013).

35. Benedict XVI, "Never to Be Denied or Forgotten. The Visit to the Yad Vashem Memorial on 11 May 2009," in *Insegnamenti di Benedetto XVI*, vol. V, no. 1, 787–89 (Vatican City: Libreria editrice vaticana, 2010), 787.

people of God."[36] With his spiritual profundity and through the unique power of his words, Pope Benedict XVI illuminated the multifaceted riches of the common spiritual heritage of Judaism and Christianity and added theological depth to the guidelines set down by the declaration *Nostra Aetate*.

Jewish-Catholic dialogue today continues its positive progress with Pope Francis, who already as Archbishop of Buenos Aires fostered close contacts with the Jewish community and above all with Rabbi Abraham Skorka and continues to do so as pope.[37] As was evident at the inauguration of his pontificate in the presence of prominent Jewish representatives from the United States, Israel, Argentina, and the Jewish community in Rome, it is for Pope Francis an important concern to intensify and deepen the bond of friendship between Jews and Catholics. Again and again he receives Jewish personalities and groups in audience and gives them the firm reassurance that it is impossible to be both a Christian and an anti-Semite. The climax of his endeavors so far is without doubt the visit to the Holy Land in May 2014 and his meeting with the two Chief Rabbis, his prayer at the Western Wall, his embrace of a Jewish and a Muslim friend, and the thought-provoking meditation at Yad-Vashem, where he prayed for the grace "to be ashamed of what we as human beings were capable of."

Open Theological Questions and Mutual Service in the Faith

For the popes following the Second Vatican Council, it has been an important concern that those perspectives laid down in *Nostra Aetate* be received and carried further by the whole Church. Despite all these great achievements, the theological questions raised by the relationship between Christianity and Judaism have by no means all been resolved. That a good deal more effort in theological reflection is required is also affirmed by the project published a few years ago, *Christ Jesus and the Jewish People Today: New Explorations of Theological Interrelationships*, which was produced as an initiative of the Holy See's Commission for Religious Relations with the Jews by an informally convoked international group of Christian theologians, to which individual Jewish experts and friends were invited to

---

36. Benedict XVI, "Un cammino irrevocabile di fraterna collaborazione. Incontro con la Comunità Ebraica nel Tempio Maggiore degli Ebrei di Roma il 17 gennaio 2010," in *Insegnamenti di Benedetto XVI*, vol. VI, no. 1, 86–92 (Vatican City: Libreria editrice vaticana, 2011), 90.

37. Cf. Jorge Bergoglio (Pope Francis) and Abraham Skorka, *On Heaven and Earth: Pope Francis on Faith, Family, and the Church in the Twenty-first Century* (New York: Image, 2013).

participate as critical observers.[38] No matter how worthwhile this Jewish-Christian conversation may have been, Cardinal Walter Kasper states realistically in his preface that even this conversation in no way has arrived at a conclusion: "We are only standing at the threshold of a new beginning. Many exegetical, historical and systematic questions are still open and there will presumably always be such questions."[39]

Many Jewish rabbis today increasingly raise their voices that the time is right in Jewish-Christian dialogue for deepening the theological questions. Dialogue should now focus on a highly complex theological question: how the shared conviction that the covenant that God contracted with Israel has never been revoked but remains valid on the basis of God's unfailing faithfulness to his people can be theologically and conceptually combined with the Christian faith conviction of the novelty of the New Covenant granted to us in Christ. Such a proposal must coherently maintain the intrinsic unity between the Old and the New Testament in such a way that neither Jews nor Christians feel hurt but, rather, see that their faith convictions are taken seriously.[40]

This is, after all, not simply an academic question but always involves the earnest and existential question of the salvation of mankind, so great care is required. On the one hand, the Christian faith stands or falls by the confession that God wants to lead all people to salvation, that he follows this path in Jesus Christ as the universal mediator of salvation, and that there is no "other name under heaven given to the human race by which we are to be saved."[41] On the other hand, this Christian confession in no way permits the conclusion that the Jews are excluded from God's salvation because they do not believe in Jesus Christ as the Messiah of Israel and the Son of God. Such a claim would find no support in the soteriological understanding of Saint Paul. In the Letter to the Romans he gives expression to his conviction that there can be no hiatus in the history of salvation but that salvation comes from the Jews, and he clearly proceeds to state that God from the "time of the Gentiles" had entrusted Israel with a specific individual mission. Paul therefore definitively negates the question he himself has posed, whether God has repudiated his own people, and decidedly states, "For the grace and call that God grants are irrevocable."[42] That

38. Cunningham, ed., *Christ Jesus and the Jewish People Today*.

39. Ibid., xiv.

40. Cf. the nuanced study by Thomas Söding, "Erwählung—Verstockung—Errettung. Zur Dialektik der paulinischen Israeltheologie in Röm 9-11," in *Communio. Internationale katholische Zeitschrift* 39 (2010): 382–417.

41. Acts 4:12.

42. Rom 11:29.

the Jews are participants in God's salvation is theologically unquestionable, but how that can be possible without confessing Christ explicitly is and remains an unfathomable divine mystery. It is therefore no accident that Paul's soteriological reflections in Romans 9–11 on the irrevocable redemption of Israel against the background of the Christ–mystery culminate in a mysterious doxology: "Oh, the depth of the riches and wisdom and knowledge of God! How inscrutable are his judgments and how unsearchable his ways."[43]

This cautious response at the same time reveals the insight that the most elementary difference between Judaism and Christianity is nevertheless evident with regard to the question of the salvation of mankind. The fundamental critique by the Jews of the Christian confession of Christ and of Christianity as a whole insists that the world remains unreconciled and the kingdom of God has not yet arrived in our world. Judaism is and remains precisely there where it remains true to its divine calling, a thorn in the flesh of Christianity, because it incisively calls to mind the unredeemed state of the world, as Franz Rosenzweig has stated: "This existence of the Jews compels upon Christianity at all times the insight that it never reaches its goal, never arrives at the truth but constantly remains on the way."[44] The same thorn was given expression by Schalom Ben-Chorin in these words: "The Jew is profoundly aware of the unredeemed character of the world, and he perceives and recognizes no enclave of redemption in the midst of its unredeemedness."[45] In the same sense Martin Buber has profiled the abiding difference with Christianity in this way: "The church rests on its faith that the Christ has come and that this is the redemption that God has bestowed on mankind. We, Israel, are not able to believe that."[46]

With that remark Buber indeed has named the particularity of Christianity, that on the basis of the Christ event, it is convinced that in Jesus Christ the love of God is nevertheless already present amid the unreconciled and unredeemed world: "The particularity of Christianity consists in the belief in the reconciliation of the otherwise unreconciled world in Jesus Christ and in the presence of his Spirit."[47] Since Christianity in faithfulness to its divine mission witnesses to the presence of the love and recon-

43. Rom 11:33.
44. Franz Rosenzweig, *Der Stern der Erlösung III*, 3rd ed. (Heidelberg: Schneider, 1950), 197.
45. Schalom Ben-Chorin, *Die Antwort des Jona zum Gestaltwandel Israels* (Hamburg: Reich, 1956), 99.
46. Martin Buber, *Der Jude und sein Judentum* (Köln: Lambert Schneider, 1963), 562.
47. Wolfgang Pannenberg, "Das Besondere des Christentums," in Pinchas Lapide and Wolfgang Pannenberg, *Judentum und Christentum Einheit und Unterschied: Ein Gespräch*, 19–31 (München: Kaiser, 1981), 29–30.

ciliation of God in the midst of the suffering, groaning, and unreconciled world and perceives in the cross of Jesus Christ itself the "permanent day of atonement of God,"[48] it is also a thorn in the flesh of Judaism.

If Judaism and Christianity remain faithful to their convictions and in so doing mutually respect and challenge one another, they can mutually do one another this service in faith. In this communal service of faith, Judaism and Christianity and synagogue and church remain indissolubly inter-linked with one another whenever Jews and Christians draw upon that "common spiritual patrimony" that *Nostra Aetate* calls to mind. In that sense, this path-breaking declaration of the Second Vatican Council is and remains the compass of reconciliation between Jews and Christians today and into the future.

48. Josef Cardinal Ratzinger, "Israel, die Kirche und die Welt. Ihre Beziehung und ihr Auftrag nach dem 'Katechismus der Katholischen Kirche' von 1992," in *Die Vielfalt der Religionen und der Eine Bund*, 17–45, cited at 43.

From Enemy to Partner:
Toward the Realization of a Partnership between Judaism and Christianity

RABBI IRVING GREENBERG

Two Covenantal Communities Acknowledge Their Closeness

Judaism and Christianity are uniquely close, and Christianity is rooted in Judaism. Ever since *Nostra Aetate*, the Catholic Church has affirmed this truth with increasing firmness and comfort and with the conviction that this acknowledgment is good for Christianity.

The Jewish community also is moving toward affirmation of this truth as a positive phenomenon. The movement within the Jewish community toward unequivocal acceptance of this truth has proceeded briskly—but more slowly than among Catholics. There is some hesitation due to residual concerns about missionary approaches and possible conversions to Christianity. Among Orthodox official religious leadership, resistance to theological dialogue has translated into that community dragging its feet on revising old theological attitudes. Still, from a historic perspective, the mutual affirmation of closeness and respect has never been better.

Therefore, this essay focuses on another, often overlooked, truth about the interconnection between the two religions. Despite the existence of ongoing differences and important contradictions, in their core teachings the two religions are as one. They share their central theological trope. This world is a creation of God (who sustains it). The telos of human history is that creation, as it is now, is moving toward redemption (God's ideal of creation fully realized). In this final state, called God's kingdom, life will fully triumph over death. This movement will be facilitated by a covenantal partnership of God and humanity. In short: from creation to redemption through covenant. Furthermore, both communities have a common central goal—to be the avant-garde of humanity to bring the kingdom.

Both communities, for understandable reasons, continue to obscure or play down this overlap. Some serious Christians fear that if their faith recognizes the commonality and affirms the validity of Judaism, Christianity would lose its monopoly on God and the way to God. Perhaps in their heart of hearts they are concerned that unqualified affirmation of Judaism would impugn the right of Christianity to have become an independent

178

religion in the first place. For their part Jews fear that if they fully acknowledge the value of Christianity, this could be interpreted as not having a need for Judaism. Since Jews are a minority, some fear that unless boundaries are stressed and barriers built high, it would become the path of least resistance for a minority to dissolve into the majority or be absorbed through assimilation.

I believe that if we move beyond our fears, we can lead our people and the rest of humanity in a more constructive way. It follows that we should give priority to advance the common goal—*tikkun olam*, the repair and perfection of the world—more than we should be concerned to protect our institutions. We should have the courage to base the well-being and success of our faith on the infinity of God's love, which expresses itself in plural communities. The consequence of such a decision would enable us to finally—after almost two millennia—to do the will of our Father in Heaven.

This is to say that we can now see that God sought to continue and upgrade the partnership, or *brit*, with Jewry even as the Lord sought to offer and enter into covenant with the Gentiles and bring them into the task of repairing the world. Therefore, it would give great joy to God to see the elder and younger brothers—if you will, the people of the Old Covenant and the New Covenant—work side by side, contributing their unique strengths, helping each other do better, working as true partners of God and each other. In truth, it will require the help of many other allies to achieve our joint cosmic goal, God's kingdom, that is, God's sovereignty. Reaching that state will require the complete redemption—physical and spiritual—of the earth and all its inhabitants. Still, the inspiration of our model and the impact of the transformation of hearts between us would inspire in itself the hearts of many others and considerably raise the probabilities of our success.

The Common Core and Common Goal

Let me first articulate what we have in common.

Material existence is real. (This is unlike many Eastern religions, which teach that mortal life is illusion.) However the physical, empirical is the surface dimension of a deeper, richer, and transcendent reality. The key to all that exists is the presence of an unseen, eternal, and infinite God, creator and sustainer of the universe. God so loved creation that the creator self-limited to establish a finite universe as a continuing physical system, operating on dependable natural laws. The infinity of the divine dwarfs the universe and makes this planet and the humanity on it a speck of dust in a vast cosmos. Nevertheless, the Lord loves this world and all its inhabitants. God expresses this love in wanting the world to be perfected so that human life and all forms of life will flourish while the enemies of life will be vanquished. Poverty, hunger, oppression (injustice), war, sickness, and death must be overcome so that life will be lived at its fullest, quantitatively and qualitatively.[1] This goes hand in hand with establishing a relationship of acceptance and love with God, with creation, and with all humans as my neighbors. To achieve this goal, the deity reveals God's self and gives instructions for living the good life.

God loves all life. God has a special love for humanity—a form of life that has grown toward its maker, that has become so God-like as to be described in the Torah as "the image of God."[2] God so loves humanity that the Lord self-limited again and entered into partnership with humans to achieve *tikkun olam*, the repair and perfection of this world. The self-limitation means that the deity will not act alone to make everything perfect through decisive interventions or divine fiats. Nor will God force humans to live the good life. Through a loving self-binding (i.e., entry into covenant), God commits to stay with existence and work with humans—at their pace and capacity—until all is achieved.[3]

God is so close and involved that the Lord is tormented by present human suffering and undergoes unlimited agony in their pain. Nevertheless God absorbs the infinite pain rather than cutting it short by unilaterally doing humanity's job of perfecting the world. God offers teaching, sends messengers and messages, and serves as a personal role model to inspire humans to do their work. This unending self-restraint grows out of God's boundless love for humans—a love that is selfless and patient enough to let humans grow into the task and is infinite enough to forgive their sins and misbehaviors along the way.

Humans are called to respond to the divine summons to partnership by committing to God and to the covenant. This entails directing every act of life toward God and toward God's goal, the triumph of life. Human participation in the work of repair means that humans are empowered in the covenant. Their dignity is honored and developed when they play an important role in their own liberation.

As they learn to love God—and to love God's creatures and their neighbors as themselves—they mature and become more responsible. Thus they become individually worthy of eternal, loving life with God even as, collectively, they move the state of the world forward toward the longed for, final (Messianic) perfection.

---

1. See among others the Messianic verses in Isaiah 66:12; 9:8–10; Ezekiel 34:25–29; Isaiah 11:4, 9; Ezekiel 37:24–27; Isaiah 2:3–4; Micah 4:2–4; Isaiah 35:5–6, 25:8, and 65:20.
2. Gn 1:27; 5:1; 9:6.
3. Ibid. 8:21–22; 9:1–17.

To inspire humans to greater efforts to fulfill the universal Noahide covenant—and to lead them without overwhelming them by exercising constant control and interventions—God enters into a particular covenant with one family, that of Abraham and Sarah. This covenant is entered into again with their descendants, the people of Israel. (Human pace setters and models are the best way to evoke willing and uncoerced responses from other human beings.)[4] This people will serve as witnesses to God, as teachers to humanity of the way of life God calls on them to live, and as role models of how to live a covenantal life. In another verse, the Abrahamic calling is described as follows: "I have known [i.e., chosen, singled out] him so that he instruct his children and family after him to observe the way of God, to do righteousness and justice."[5] The outcome of the covenant with Abraham and Sarah is that they and their family will be blessed and all the nations of the earth will be blessed through them and their message/example.[6] The final fulfillment will come when all humans will come to know God's way—when knowledge of the Lord fills the earth as completely as the waters cover the sea.[7] Then they will perfect the world so that "they will do no evil nor harm throughout My holy mountain [i.e., Earth]."[8] This moment of worldwide redemption will be marked by an ultimate triumph of life over death—by a universal resurrection of the dead.[9]

All of the above are primary teachings—the common core—in both Judaism and Christianity. Certainly it was so at the time when rabbinic Judaism and classical Christianity were coming into being. In both communities, there was great interest in and anticipation of the achievement of *tikkun olam*, which they described as the coming of God's kingdom.

Differences, Contradictions, and Community Interpretation

The above statements of common core and goal are not meant to minimize the ongoing differences and even contradictions between the two faiths. The most salient of these antinomies is the ongoing conflict over the nature and role of Jesus.

---

4. See the extended treatment of the role of universal and particular covenants in Irving Greenberg, "Judaism and Christianity: Covenants of Redemption," in *Christianity in Jewish Terms*, ed. Tikva Frymer-Kensky, David Novak, Peter Ochs, David Fox Sandmel, and Michael A. Signer, 141–58 (Boulder, Colo.: Westview Press, 2009), especially 141–49.

5. Gn 18:19.

6. Ibid. 12:2–3.

7. Is 11:9.

8. Ibid.

9. Ibid. 26:19.

Christianity teaches: given the difficulty of repairing the world, given the power of entrenched evil, given human weaknesses, God sends God to inspire and lead human beings in this partnership to accomplish a monumental, almost impossible, task. Judaism teaches: given the difficulty of repairing the world, given the power of entrenched evil, given human weaknesses, God sends Torah (wisdom/instruction) and remarkable, really God-like human models and leaders to inspire and lead human beings in this partnership to accomplish a monumental, almost impossible, task.

This is a fundamental disagreement—out of a shared Jewish covenantal trope—as to how to achieve God's goal and humanity's hope. But how do you interpret this clash? For almost two thousand years, each community interpreted that difference in as pejorative a way as possible against the other side. Each explained this clash as diminishing as possible in terms of the ongoing life of the other community.

Christianity started by saying: God came to us, in person. The Jews, by their own affirmation, say that God did not come to them in person. That proves that Christianity is superior to Judaism. We acknowledge that Judaism represents the covenant that God established with Abraham. However, since God did not appear in the earlier stage of Jewish religion, this means that at best that covenant was a preparation. More likely this proves that it was a lower (more carnal) form.

Next, since God came to be our leader, why would God take this incredible step? The answer must be: this is the final realization of the covenant. The early covenant community is finished, superseded. Judaism is terminated with extreme prejudice. Third, since God uniquely appears in our community, no other religion can offer salvation. No other religion has a true connection to God.

But the Jews did not disappear. They go on living in their original covenant, which we acknowledge was valid and out of which we grew. It is as if God did not come. Therefore, we must sharpen our argument. They had the original covenant, but they degraded religiously. They became spiritually blind. They did not recognize God in their own midst so they forfeited their original gift.

But Jews went on living a vital religious life, even developing it in Rabbinic Judaism. They continue to reject our God. They are arrogant. Their current spiritual arrogance is a pre-existing condition. In their earlier arrogance, they turned vicious. They killed God.

The denial escalated. If Jews are not sustained by God anymore, how come they are still alive? The answer is that it is the devil who now sustains them. They pray in the synagogue of Satan. After a while, if you are sustained by the devil, you become devilish. Thus in medieval Christianity, Jews became well poisoners, bakers of blood in their sacred food, murderers of children.

Thus an incredible religious experience—an experience of an incarnate loving God in the community—was turned by human interpretation into a source of contempt and rejection of the other. A wellspring of encounter with the word of God was channeled into a perpetual fountain of hatred. The policy conclusion was obvious: there is nothing to learn from the other religion. There is no need to have a conversation. There should be no dialogue and mutual learning. Nothing good can be absorbed from such a monstrous community and tradition.

How did the Jews reframe the Christian proclamation of their religious event? The community gave a mirror response, intended to demolish. Christians claim that God in the person of Jesus, dwells in their community and they worship him. Thus they openly divert their religious service from the Creator of Heaven and Earth to another. That means that this religion violates every day the central teaching and prayer of the Jewish people (which Christians purport to uphold): *Shema Yisrael, Adonai Elohaynu Adonai Echad*—O Israel, the Lord our God, the Lord is one.[10] In addition, when you think about it, Christians worship a human being. Then Christianity can be branded with an ultimate image of contempt: it is idolatry, the worship of a human fabrication.

But, if so, this faith without merit should have failed. However, instead of disappearing, Christianity grew enormously and spread throughout the world. How can one impeach such success? The answer: this religion purports to be a gospel of love. In actual fact, it teaches a hatred of us. It claims to teach truth to free humanity, but it bears false witness about our religion and behavior. In God's name, it persecutes and kills us. This is a fraudulent forgery, taking Jewish religious teaching and warping it into an instrument to destroy us. Thus, a religion that taught the Ten Commandments and the ethics of human responsibility throughout the world, that redeemed millions of pagans with the word of God and the call to bring God's kingdom was reframed as a spiritual nullity. Thus, the Jewish religion whose fundamental scriptures assert that God sends prophets and appears to many nations, a faith that teaches "love your neighbor as yourself," developed a tradition of contempt in which Christians worship vanity and void out of a faith that offers no redemption. Again came an obvious policy conclusion: There is nothing to learn from the other religion. There is no need to have a conversation. There should be no dialogue and mutual learning. Nothing good can be absorbed from such a brutal community and tradition.

10. Dt 6:4.

The Price of Enmity and Incomprehension

The Penalty Paid by Christianity

Each religion paid a huge price for the denigrating interpretation of the other. Each community's possessive attitude toward its own covenant and rejectionist understanding of the role of the other community took a terrible spiritual toll out of its own tradition. Christianity tried to assert its superiority by demeaning the Jewish religion as carnal and inferior. Further, to escape the Jewish critique, "How can you talk of Messiah and redemption when the world is still economically, politically and culturally enslaved?" Christianity spiritualized its good news of redemption. This faith is not really about overcoming poverty, injustice, and war. It matters not whether you are a slave or free as long as you are one in Christ. Kings and principals need not fear us because we are about overcoming spiritual evil and sin. The goal is not about life defeating death literally; it is about life winning over death in the spiritual sense.

Yet the glory of our common Torah is that it sees the human being as a self—not as a body and soul separate and at war with each other. Nor is one of them more important than the other (albeit these are such sentiments in both traditions). Like God—and in relation to God—the human being is a unity that needs to be redeemed, body and soul. To spread this prophetic vision was our calling; it is our contribution and revolutionary transformation of humanity's understanding. Yet in pursuing its partisan polemical interpretation of its mission, Christianity moved to belittle, if not repudiate, its message of a holistic redemption.

Secondly, when you one-sidedly spiritualize and dismiss matters of this world, then this bleeds into asceticism. Thereafter a tradition develops that the body (and this world) is not just unimportant; the mortal is antithetical to holiness. The body is denigrated. Self-denial is the superior way of serving God. The consequence is that improving the world is not so important. Affluence is also not important; maybe it is inimical to spiritual well-being. Often this attitude spreads: then beauty is vanity, art is folly, and sex should be kept to a minimum. In no small measure due to this religious stunted approach to the physical dimension of reality, the enormous rise in standards of living that characterize the modern period has carried in its wake a growth of secularism and of hedonism as an end in itself.

Thirdly, demoting Hebrew scriptures to a secondary status, or even relegating it to the dustbin of history, diminishes the voice of the Hebrew prophets. They continuously proclaimed that religion is not about just relating to God but how God expects us to treat our fellow human beings. They keep calling for justice between people and special care for the oppressed, the needy, the powerless. When that voice is heard less, then religion is tempted into giving the realm of Caesar unto Caesar. Religious leadership is tempted to accept the status quo as is and to concentrate on the spiritual task. This is the trap that religion falls into that Karl Marx legitimately criticized as serving as the opium of the masses. Marx was wrong on religion, but this criticism is correct. Instead of inspiring people to correct injustice, to stop the evil doers, to end slavery (as Christianity did from time to time), it too often encouraged people to accept the social system and concentrate on other matters. How often did the religion of total redemption let go of the fight for freedom in return for freedom for it to teach and offer spiritual missions?

The fourth penalty Christianity paid for its degradation of Judaism was (in my judgement) perhaps its greatest. The heart of this religion is a teaching that sought the triumph of love. This religion sought to overcome hatred, to abolish and remove this evil trait from human hearts. What happened instead? A privileged sanctuary of hatred was established within the gospel of love. Hatred is wrong; it is the driving force for evil. But toward Jews, it is not only permitted, it is a good deed. Contempt for Judaism is embedded in sacred scriptures. Thus, hatred could survive inside the Christian immune system. It was like a cancer whereby if one cell can escape the chemotherapy or treatment by radiation, the disease can survive and flourish again. In this case the hatred survived not only in the form of a less successful Christianizing of pagans, it also survived in the form of a culturally embedded anti-Semitism that could be exploited by the Nazis. One should never forget that the Nazi leadership hated Christianity (in part because of its Jewish characteristics), but the Nazis exploited the residue of its teaching about Jews for their evil, destructive purposes.

The Joint Penalty

Another spiritual toll was exacted from both religions equally. There are many important truths shared by both faiths that are dialectical in nature. Take the case of love and justice. These are dialectical truths that need each other to remain true. If an ethic is all love and no justice, that can lead to a real deformation. If an ethic is all justice and no love, it too can lead to a real deformation. Go down the list of common dialectical truths: the universal and the particular. Does one focus on instruction, individual groups, families, national traditions, or does one emphasize one homogeneous tradition for humanity? The Hebrew biblical tradition stressed the communal and the collective; the New Testament and Christian tradition shifted to greater emphasis for the individual and religious self-expression. But while each religion is closer to one pole or the other, each needs the corrective dialectical truth to maximize the effectiveness of its position.

Even though the world is deeply flawed, redemption is already in our midst and growing. This is what Judaism acknowledges when it celebrates a Sabbath and reenacts a sacral Passover annually. But this truth needs the corrective understanding that redemption is not fully realized and much of humanity groans under oppression. This last is the truth that Christianity softly acknowledges when it yearns for a Second Coming of its Messiah. However, each side—untouched by the other—polarized its truth and suppressed or minimized the dialectical reality.

How do you reconcile the spirit of the law and the letter of the law? How does one dynamically interact in this world and the world to come? How does one maintain awareness of the need for God's role in *tikkun olam* while upholding the proper level of human activism and responsibility in the work of redemption? It is noteworthy that despite its focus on God personally intervening in Israel's history, and despite its emphasis on Jesus as the ultimate sacrifice to overcome evil and sin, Christianity did not repudiate the central category of covenant. It remained true to its Jewish roots and presented itself as a new (i.e., renewed) covenant. Despite God's augmented role, Christian faith continued to affirm an essential and honorable role for human agency. Similarly, despite its rejection of the idea that God became flesh in order to lead the battle, Judaism insisted that both partners must continue to work in tandem to achieve redemption. Despite ending up at a different (albeit shifting) point of balance, each religion continued to teach and model a continuing engagement of interaction and influence between God and humanity. In all these cases there is no fixed or final resolution of the dynamic tension. The religion is healthiest and the education is most effective when we go back and forth in the dialectic. It takes a constant oscillation between the poles to set it right. More important, the community's behavior and teaching need to be rebalanced regularly.

The best way to rebalance would have been a dialogue with the other faith community to learn from the one that has focused on love and less on justice or to incorporate insight from the one that has focused on justice and less on love. Instead the spiritual dynamic that each community needed to stay vital and on target was turned into polarization. Each faith took its truth and ran with it. Often each truth was distorted in the absence of the other voice or diminished by not being recalibrated.

There was a particularly toxic side effect in concluding that there is one truth and only one narrow side of that truth and that one possesses it to the exclusion of needing to hear or learn from an alternative community. This gives you the authority not only to suppress another group; it gives you the authority to impose conformity to a narrow band of the truth within your own group. So Catholicism set up an Inquisition to enforce the narrower official definition of the Catholic truth and treated heresy with violence. Christians have killed more Christians than they have killed Jews. So Jews have persecuted more Jews than they have Christians. Once you are convinced that you have the one single truth and the whole of that truth, then you are authorized by your own logic to enforce this on everyone, internal or external. And there is little limit to the evil that you can do for the sake of God.

The Penalty Paid by Judaism

Jews have paid no less a price for the total separation and alienation from Christianity. Over the centuries, there was a staggering amount of suffering and oppression and a huge demographic loss to persecution, expulsion, and conversion. Furthermore, having been marginalized by the triumph of Christianity and its dismissal of Judaism spiritually, Jews resorted to the same tactic: to spiritualize Judaism. Thus, the tradition turned to writing off politics and armies, to denigrating the work of this world. Those realms in which Jews are marginal are inconsequential in the eyes of God. We can turn to Kabbalah and mysticism. In that realm we are convinced by our teachings that Jews are still the center of the spiritual world. According to Lurianic Kabbalah, Jewish ritual actions are decisive in helping God's unification and are essential to empower the repairs needed for the cosmos' spiritual *tikkun olam*.

Thus, Judaism's religious dynamic turned away from the human covenantal role in repairing the world. In the nineteenth century, modern Zionism started its movement to revive national life and return to the ancient homeland, as prayed for over the millennia. But Judaism had so spiritualized in its self-understanding that the majority of devout Jews would not participate. They insisted that true faith meant that you had to wait for God to send a heavenly redeemer for Jewry. They proclaimed that it was impious—a rejection of God's sovereignty—for humans to take covenantal responsibility and act to reclaim the holy land. The fact that the return to Zion was a central call in the Hebrew Bible was nullified. The majority of the devout failed to help in redeeming the land. Tragically they remained fixed in Europe, where they fell victim to the archfiend Hitler's cruel Final Solution.

The Jews paid another price: Judaism turned inward, understandably. They were, after all, trying to make meaning of being a persecuted minority. But by turning inward, they forgot (or sidelined) Isaiah's report of their divine call to serve as a "light unto the nations." They ignored that Abraham was chosen to be a blessing, that it was not enough to be blessed but you had to serve as a blessing for the other nations. They played down that the Messianic vision of *tikkun olam* stipulated that the whole earth would be turned into God's kingdom by overcoming evil, poverty, oppression, and sickness for all.

In all these areas the absence of dialogue to reflect on the other faith and to balance one's own understanding led to one-sided conceptions of dialectical truths. In Judaism, too, there was the development of a tradition of contempt for the other. Jews were relatively powerless, so they could not expel or persecute Christians. Still, the dismissal and denigration of the other won out. The internal cost was a weakening of ethical responsibility. There was a real diminution of the spiritual vision and of the breadth of the meaning of life.

The Shoah *and the Bankruptcy of the Past Policies*

The climax of these distortions came in the *Shoah*. The Holocaust uncovered the bankruptcy of the two thousand years' policies, and not just for our two faiths. The so-called Final Solution showed the bankruptcy of modernity operating without controls; it showed the death-dealing consequences of human power wielded without covenantal limits or accountability to God. The catastrophe illuminated the enervating, disastrous fallout of our policies and attitudes toward each other. Jews had so focused on spiritual force that they were powerless in the world. In an age of technology, totalitarian control and unlimited power for evil, the powerless Jews could not resist or stop the aggressor. Furthermore, the Jews who were spiritually isolated received no help and were totally decimated. For example: in the devout sections of Europe, Jews were totally ringed with hatred and isolated from their neighbors. Ninety percent of the Jews of Poland died; ninety-five percent of Lithuanian Jews perished. Although there are more individual Poles listed in Yad VaShem's register of righteous Gentiles who risked their lives to save Jews than anyone from other countries, the plain truth is that the indifference or active collaboration of the Jews' neighbors accounted for the high percentage of Nazi success in killing them. Paradoxically, the assimilated Jews of Denmark, who had close personal ties with the Danish people (and whose churches rallied to help Jews) were almost all saved. The critical step was the Danish people and government's stand not to let the Germans separate the Jews from the rest of the nation. Where the people and the national representatives took an active part in condemning the Nazis' intentions and stood in solidarity, indeed actively rescued Jews, more than ninety-five percent survived.

Of course, this is not meant as a plea for assimilation as a life-saving force for Jewry. The need to motivate religious Christians to stand in solidarity with the persecuted—including with Jews who are utterly different and separated from them—is a driving force behind Christianity's rearticulation of its teachings in the twentieth and twenty-first centuries. Rather, I seek to underline that the excessive turning inward and withdrawal of Judaism from the world had a terrible fallout. One part of the ledger is the spiritual loss: shrinkage in the scope of the redemptive goal, less ethical responsibility to others, and less credibility and attraction in the tradition for Jews who were engaged in the world. No less destructive was the side effect leading to demographic loss and the result that a major portion of religious Jewry turned to a catastrophic political strategy (spiritual isolation and political powerlessness). The truth is that had secular and modernized Jews followed this strategy, the Jewish people would not have survived in the global political situation of our time.

Nostra Aetate as a Covenantal Inflection Point

The Courage to Turn

The bankruptcy of the almost two thousand years of Christian negative interpretation of the meaning of the two faiths' existence has now been acknowledged by the Catholic Church and affirmed by such great popes as Saint John XXIII and Saint John Paul II. This recognition was the driving force behind the articulation of *Nostra Aetate*. Article 4 was somewhat halting and even looked back in certain passages. Yet by a remarkable act of repentance, it turned Christianity (really, both traditions) from rejection and fratricide into a joint covenantal journey toward redemption.

I am filled with awe and wonder at the courage of Christianity in its ability to take responsibility for demonizing the Jews. Think of the profound spiritual strength it takes for an institution that understands itself as divinely inspired and as representing the body of Christ in the world to acknowledge such a failure and past misdeeds. Yet without such depth of insight, a true turning could never take place. I know of no comparable heroic repentance in the history of world religions.

I think that this is what the Talmud meant when it said that in certain situations a repentant person reaches spiritual heights that no *tzaddik* (always-righteous) person can attain.[11] The level of growth in honesty that overrides rationalizations and self-deceptions, the level of trust in God that enables one to accept being labeled wicked or a fool in human eyes in order to be integral and whole-hearted with the Lord, the passion to free up for love by admitting hatred and renouncing it—these reflect spiritual great-

---

11. Talmud Berachot 34B.

ness and nurture it further. Frankly, up to now, my own community or its leadership has not shown the capacity or the willingness to comparably acknowledge or take responsibility for sins of even lesser magnitude.

I credit *Nostra Aetate* with being the first decisive turn away from the past path of denial and hostility toward a future of affirmation and partnership for life. The Church should have been the first—given that it had more to be responsible for. Still, that does not take away from the moral grandeur of its action. Pope John XXIII's genuine regret paved the way for a clear-eyed honesty that saw the shallowness of the Christianization of the pagans. If such behaviors in the Holocaust could go on in Europe, after two thousand years of Christianity, then Christian education had to analyze how its teachings were leading to wrong moral conclusions and shirking of ethical responsibilities. This opened the door for a revisioning of Judaism. *Nostra Aetate* rejected the charge of deicide, repudiated anti-Semitism, and promised to stop the denigration. As its signposts guided the Church over the decades, we understand that it opened up Christianity to the validity of Judaism and to the pluralism of God's love and God's covenant. In this matter, too, Jewry has responded less and more slowly. Still, Jews have entered the dialogue, which I believe will not end without a full revisioning of our understanding of Christianity and its role in God's plan and in bringing God's kingdom.

The Courage in Nostra Aetate

Both Catholics and Jews have to understand that *Nostra Aetate* is not just about passing a council declaration or a papal encyclical that Jews should be treated nicely and respected. The declaration grows out of a much deeper decision—one that grows out of the nature of covenant, the mechanism that we both insist is the divine method of *tikkun olam*. Given the divine respect for humans expressed in joining covenant with them rather than coercing them, given the resistance of human nature to drastic change, given the entrenched nature of evil, the goal of world repair cannot and will not be achieved in one generation. Therefore, the bearers of the covenant must teach it to their children, biological or spiritual. The covenantal leadership must enlist the young to take up the unfinished mission. Each generation is bound to move the world as far as it can, then it must pass on to the next generation the task of completion. In the words of Rabbi Tarfon, "it is not required of you to complete the work [of *tikkun*]; but you are not released [by this recognition] to sit idly by, doing nothing."[12]

12. Talmud, Chapters of the Fathers, ch. 2, m. 21.

There is a further implication. The living generation has responsibility for the covenant in its time. It matters not that the founders had a more sacred status or that our predecessors had greater stature and authority. The living generation cannot ignore its obligation to correct authentic teachings that, in the present context, are having an evil impact. Similarly, when inherited practices have gone out of control or are having side effects that undermine their sanctity, the guardians of the covenant must act. One might say that the founders of our faith counted on later generations to make the adjustments that would enable the covenant to go on functioning in future yet unborn societies or to prevent their going astray in new cultures. A nineteenth-century rabbi, Israel Salanter, once wrote that this is the true meaning of the verse in Deuteronomy 30:12 that "It [the Torah] is not in the heavens." By sending the Word of God to humanity, God has given over responsibility to humans for its understanding and application. There is tremendous love in this gesture—for God is aware that humanity may warp or wrongly apply the instruction. Still, God gives this treasure over and accepts the risk in order that it be a source of blessing to humanity.[13] The divine trust is that people will step forward to guard and correct the teaching. God needs and depends on humans to preserve and apply the tradition so that the word "not come back unfulfilled but achieves what . . . [God] has sent it to do."[14]

Catholics and Orthodox Jews have a particularly close understanding that the tradition has real power and authority. It is binding. We also understand that you bring the whole tradition with you. Throughout history, once a law or a ritual has achieved sacred status, once it has been a channel of connection between God and humans, it never forfeits that status. Yet sometimes it is no longer practiced, say, as sacrifices are no longer in the Jewish tradition. Nevertheless, says the Talmud: *drosh v'kabel s'char*—Explore and understand the meaning and be rewarded [with contemporary insight].[15] Thus, the laws of slavery are no longer practiced in Judaism. But the method underlying them—gradual abolition by ever-increasing restrictions rather than overnight abolition that led to civil war in the United States—is a lesson that can be applied in many areas.

Still, both Catholics and Orthodox Jews understand that the divinity of scriptures and the sacredness of *Mesorah* (tradition) and magisterium does not mean that there is never a revision or a new understanding or a

---

13. Rabbi Israel Salanter, *Ohr Yisrael* [The Light of Israel] (Vilna, Romania, 1900), 90. Available in English as *Ohr Yisrael: The Classic Writings of Rav Yisrael Salanter and His Disciple Rav Yitzchak Blazer*, trans. Eli Linas (Southfield, Mich.: Targum, 2004).

14. Is 55:10–11.

15. Talmud Sanhedrin 71A.

new conceptualization. This is what *Nostra Aetate* represents: the exercise of responsibility by the living generation to reconceptualize the tradition to bring it fully to the side of life and love.

In order to issue *Nostra Aetate*, Vatican Council II had the courage and responsibility to override Church Fathers, spiritual leaders of huge stature and standing in Christianity. Their powerful tradition of teaching of contempt was distanced. Because we bring the whole tradition with us, they cannot be censored; but as faithful devout Christians, the Council members did not dismiss the Church fathers. They continued to honor and draw upon their insights in many areas. But they understood that to do the will of God and to increase life and love in the world, they must listen again and understand anew the word of God. They brought other elements in the tradition to the fore. In fashioning *Nostra Aetate*, the assembled bishops had the courage to revise the interpretation of the New Testament itself and of the application of scripture. As faithful upholders of the divinity of Revelation, the Council, if you will, appealed from Matthew—with his portrayal of Jews invoking God's curse on them and their children and of the veil of the Temple being rent and Judaism being finished. It sought out the corrective word of God, conveyed in Paul, that the original Israel is still precious for the gifts it has brought from God. If you will, the Council moved from Paul's opinion that the only reason the Jews still exist is a temporary situation designed to arouse the jealousy (and positive response) of the Gentiles to Paul's recognition that God does not repent of God's promises.[16] By so doing, this act of faith and courage was a healing for the Church. The Jews are the direct beneficiaries of this act of spiritual heroism.

For the sake of our own healing, the Jews must learn from this Catholic example. This is not a matter of quid pro quo. For the sake of our own ethical and religious growth, Jews must find the inspiration and inner strength for a turning of the heart worthy of this historic declaration. Only then can Judaism regain its full force and persuasive power in this culture—not to mention to develop the credibility and inner capacity to deal with its own spiritual failures and ethical challenges.

Courage Leads to New Insights

Another insight emerges here, which Catholic Church and Orthodox Judaism in particular can help each other grasp. Both communities receive the word of God and revere its distinctive authority. Yet both understand that to begin with, Revelation is shaped and filtered by God to be compre-

---

16. Rom 11:29.

hensive and assimilable by humans. Thus, a tradition legitimately mediates and interprets Revelation to the community, so the word is covenantal by the time it is incorporated into life. There is not a simple binary here. The word is made concrete by the human *traditores'* understanding. Similarly the tradition must regularly allow itself to be remolded or rejuvenated by immersion in the unmediated word of God. When, at a different stage of covenantal history, the community goes back to hear Revelation anew, it will hear instructions, nuances, and values that were always inherent in the divine wisdom but that were not "heard" (or were heard too loudly or too softly) due to a host of historical factors, personal or communal contexts, and cultural filters of that time. Thus, the community hears instruction of yore from God that it could not grasp (or properly acknowledge to itself) until now.

In this light, what is revealed by our newfound ability to acknowledge the common core and goals? I propose that the profound commonality of our two religions bespeaks the original will of our Father in Heaven. God willed that Judaism go on and enter into its rabbinic phase where there is a heightened human role in articulating the covenant and in its realization. In this phase, the message comes less from heavenly revelation and more from human interpretation of heavenly revelation. In this phase, God becomes more hidden—less likely to intervene by force majeure. Since the divine operates more subtly and is less prone to shape events by overturning the outcome of the balance of natural forces, then human policies and behaviors are more responsible for the realization process of the covenant. This new phase is made possible by the acculturation and internalization of Jewry in its covenant. This also made possible a significant expansion of *halachah* and God awareness in every area of life in Jewry. (The process is worth studying by Christians.)

At the same time, it was the will of God to lovingly offer the assurances of divine love and the gift of divine presence to all the nations. The Lord sought to enlist all of humanity into a more active role in the covenant of redemption. Through Christianity, God reached out to the world. As is appropriate in such an opening—and as was done in the original Sinai Covenant—the connection involves more visible divine manifestations, more transcendent mode of instruction, a more directive style of interaction. Thus, the divine, in love, sought to widen the channels of connection and increase the flow of blessings to all.

From a Jewish perspective, Christianity is not to be seen anymore as a historical happenstance or the outcome of a doctrinal error by Jews over-enthusiastically proclaiming the advent of God's kingdom. Rather, it is a divinely willed outcome and a gift to all humans. From the Christian point of view, it is important to recognize that the separation was desirable in the eyes of God. In this way, the child would not swallow up the mother that gave it life by staying inside and taking over the system. The separation also assured that the nascent faith would not stay inside and be attacked by the mother faith's immune system due to its doctrinal departures and shift in ritual structures. Both communities must acknowledge that God was broadening the channels of redemption—not closing one and opening another. The separation of the communities despite their common message was the will of God, who hoped that the two would work together to inspire and light up the world. As partners, operating side by side, the two communities could reach farther and with richer models. These plural models could have avoided the dangers of presenting polarized dialectical truths. As partners, aware of their own limitations, they more likely could have avoided the domineering and coercive tactics to which human monopolists are prone to resort.

It is time to acknowledge that our Father in Heaven viewed with joy the possibility of a full partnership between two sibling communities. The separation was the will of God. The negative, demeaning interpretations of the break was what God did not want. The degradation of the other community, the wasted energy and distorted religious passion expressed in rejection and abuse of others, has been a source of grief for our Father in Heaven for centuries. It is long past time to acknowledge the truth. We need each other as partners and the alliance of many others. Neither of us alone—not even 1.9 billion Christians—is capable of achieving *tikkun olam*.

Drawing the Implications of Partnership

Partnership and Pluralism: Christianity

What are the policy consequences our two religions should draw from the belated recognition that we are called to work as partners in the work of *tikkun olam*? What are some implications for our inner life as faith communities once we acknowledge that we are both blessed to be inducted into the covenant of redemption and joint bearers of its message for the world? For the Catholic Church: I think that it means going the next step to an unambivalent (or, if you will, open) acknowledgment of the pluralism of God's appearance in our different communities. It takes nothing away from the infinity of God's blessing in our midst to acknowledge that the infinity of God's love has not been exhausted or even captured by its operation in our midst. I have watched the steady unfolding of *Nostra Aetate*'s kernel of recognition of Judaism's ongoing efficacy with appreciation and baited breath. I understood the power of Saint John Paul II's proclamation of "the covenant never revoked" and what it left unsaid.[17] I even understood Pope Benedict's recoil. The latter pope held a widely shared feeling in the United States that manifested itself in the negative reaction to the working document "Reflections on Covenant and Mission" because of its open declaration that the Church should no longer seek out Jews for conversion.

There is a protective instinct that asserts itself in the heart of any serious bearer of an eternal covenant, lest a new understanding undermine an established principle that has been spiritually efficacious along the covenantal way in the past. The American bishops expressed their inner anxiety in the document "A Note on Ambiguities Contained in *Reflections on Covenant and Mission*," when they stated that "the fulfillment of the covenant, indeed, of all God's promises to Israel is found only in Jesus Christ."[18] There is a fear that openly acknowledging that Judaism is salvific will undermine the Church's claim of ultimate authority. At the same time, there was a clear recognition that interpreting Jesus's appearance in the Christian community as closing down the Jewish covenant had led to unjust behavior, hatred, and repression—and not only toward the Jews. Yet there was a nagging concern that the authority of the word of God would be weakened by an acknowledgment that its narrowest passages no longer guided a maximum faithfulness to the covenant.

When in doubt, understandably one falls back on the tried and true rhetoric of the past. But this comfort is an illusion. It betrays a wrong governing paradigm. The task of the Catholic Church is not to preserve a tradition but to teach a gospel of love and carry forth a covenant of redemption. Then falling back into the comfort zone is not adequate. The Church leadership must be faithful enough to follow God, who is calling all of us into the unfolding paradigm of partnership. Is that not what Jesus's early followers did? They followed an unfolding new paradigm. They understood it would intensify their service and connection to God even though it would make some of their most familiar affirmations appear as no longer able to guide them adequately. Let me add that in my community also, there is widespread trepidation that a needed change (such as affirmation of Christianity's covenantal role) may occur too swiftly and unintentionally weaken the compelling authority of the tradition and/or the commitment of the masses.

I would argue that the word of God and the hearts of the believers are not that fragile. They can sustain the shock that our Father in Heaven

17. John Paul II, "Address to the Jewish Community in Mainz, West Germany," November 17, 1980.

18. United States Conference of Catholic Bishops, par. 10, http://www.usccb.org/about/doctrine/publications/.

expressed a divinely willed pluralism of presence in the first century and then elected to sustain both our faith communities in history. Catholics should reassure themselves that this dialectical affirmation does not undercut the universality of Jesus as God's offer of salvation. The Vatican's Commission for Religious Relations with the Jews (led by Kurt Cardinal Koch) has suggested that Catholics can live with the contradiction of Jesus's universality and Jews finding salvation "without confessing Christ explicitly" as "an unfathomable divine mystery."[19] Pope Benedict XVI, in his book *Jesus of Nazareth: Holy Week*, suggested a different way for Christians to live in the tension. The divine plan was to offer salvation to the Gentiles through Christ and allow the Jewish covenant to go on operating as is until "the full number of Gentiles" would come to the faith.[20] Only then—at the end of days presumably—would the Jews come to Christianity. Until then, the call of Christians is to carry the faith to the Gentiles, not to the Jews.

Since I have argued previously that the Jewish covenant did not merely carry on as is but matured into a new, more humanly active phase, let me suggest a variation on the divine plan. As Pope Benedict suggested, the Christian thrust for universal evangelization was not built so much on the claim that every human being had to know Christ in order to be saved.[21] Rather, it was based on the idea that the gospel had to be proclaimed to all the nations all over the world in order to bring humanity to God. I submit that the universality of Jesus has never been built on the rock of the claim that only those who believe in Christ can be saved. The demand for conversion as the ticket to salvation meets the self-concerned needs of Christians that they are (exclusively) right. The recognition by others of the offer of Jesus has come primarily from the impact of the witness of the lives of Christians (and their relating that they are sustained and moved by Christ). The testimony that has led people to Christianity has been of the effects of Church religious teachings and behaviors on their lives.

I daresay that in our times the claim of exclusivity in salvation distances people from any tradition making that claim. People live in a world where the presence and weight of all traditions are heard all the time. The exclusivity claim is interpreted by most people, if only unconsciously, as

---

19. Commission for Religious Relations with the Jews, "The Gifts and the Calling of God Are Irrevocable: A Reflection on Theological Questions Pertaining to Catholic-Jewish Relations on the Occasion of the 50th Anniversary of *Nostra Aetate*," December 10, 2015, http://www.vatican.va.

20. Pope Benedict XVI, *Jesus of Nazareth: Holy Week: From the Entrance into Jerusalem to the Resurrection* (San Francisco, Calif.: Ignatius Press, 2011), 43, citing Rom 11:25–26.

21. Ibid., 44.

stamping this particular faith as intended for a narrow band of people—
that is, those who are primarily motivated by the desire to be right at the
expense of others being wrong. Mostly (only?) those who offer Jesus
unconditionally, with a living witness that reveals the power of God in
their lives, impact others. Those who take Christianity as a serious proffer
of Christ to everyone are mostly drawn from the ranks of those who experience a selfless, noncontrolling offer of God's love. In short, by claiming
less of a monopoly, Christians are betraying nothing. You are, in fact,
widening the offer of Jesus to the level of universality.

Partnership and Pluralism: Judaism

For the Jewish community also, recognition of partnership with
Christianity will require going beyond the comfort zone of inherited views
and standard theological boxes. Among devout Jews, the dismissive cate-
gorizing of Christianity as idolatry—inherited from the antagonistic,
polemical rulings of medieval days—remains entrenched. This dismissive
approach has gotten relatively stronger in this generation as orthodoxy slid
to the right—that is, to the more traditional side. This is compared to the
affirmative rabbinic views of Christianity that grew considerably in modern
times, even before *Nostra Aetate*. The ruling of Rabbi Isaac Herzog, the
first chief rabbi of the state of Israel, upholding Christians' freedom of religion in the Jewish state was based on his affirmation that it was a valuable
religion and not idolatry.[22] Instead of becoming the dominant view—all
the more so now that the post–*Nostra Aetate* Church has repudiated hatred
and war on Judaism—Herzog's ruling remains a mountain peak of enlight-
ened *halachah* towering over a relatively unchanged landscape.

A major factor sustaining the old status quo is the lack of dialogue that
would enable Orthodox Jews to experience the vitality and moral power of
Christianity directly. This type of encounter is needed to enable people to
break out of inherited theological boxes and see for themselves the new
creation unfolding between us. From there to embracing partnership is
even more of a journey. Still this must be done if religious Jewry is to
respond anew to its maker's call to heal the world.

22. Rabbi Yitzhak Isaac HaLevi Herzog, *Techukah leYisrael al pi HaTorah* [Legislation
for Israel{Jewry} according to the Torah], volume 1: Sidrei Shilton U'mishpat ba'Medinah
HaYehudit [Processes of Governance and Law in the Jewish State], ed. Itamar Warhaftig,
12–21 (Jerusalem: Mossad Harav Kook, 1989), especially 16–18 [Hebrew]. See also Eliav
Schochetman, "Rabbi Isaac Herzog's Theory of Torah and State," in *Jewish Law Association
Studies V: The Halakhic Thought of R. Isaac Herzog*, ed. Bernard S. Jackson and Chaim Herzo,
113–25 (Atlanta, Ga.: Scholar's Press, 1991).

Again I stress that such steps are not advocated as a favor to Christians or as a quid pro quo. The main driver is the internal need to renew Judaism and strengthen its moral contribution to the world. Nothing less than pluralism will enable Judaism to speak credibly to modern Jews and be a constructive force in the emerging global community.

Among liberal religious and secular Jews who have decisively put behind them the old polemical dismissals of Christianity, there is still a way to go before they grasp the full potential of partnership. There is the danger of stopping the journey at the way station of "no fear of persecution" or even a generalized state of friendship. Such a halt would lead to a failure to grow in love and mutual esteem. It would restrict or divert the priceless opportunity to learn from each other. It would deprive both communities of rich possibilities inherent in partnership, including to advance mutual goals or even to disagree but carry out different policies that may operate pluralistically for a better total outcome.

Dialogue, Mutual Learning, Making Room for the Other

Increasing Dialogue and Learning

To grow into a genuine partnership will require a higher level of dialogue than ever before. Only the love that grows out of deep encounter—out of knowing the value, equality, and uniqueness of the other as an image of God nurtured by their religious system—can overcome entrenched barriers to understanding. Only sufficient encounter with the vitality and holiness of the other's religious life can give us the courage to build a future that incorporates the other's contribution to the world and to my own renewal. The Jewish-Christian dialogue—although it involves numerically fewer people—needs to be intensified. Given the absence of Jewish communities in many parts of Asia and Africa, this expansion probably will have to take place disproportionately in the United States, although Europe and Israel also can be important locations for this work.

I would stress in particular an increase in learning together (as called for in *Nostra Aetate*). There is a lot of enriching wisdom that each tradition has accumulated since we separated and lost contact with the ongoing development of the other. Then, too, in jointly exploring the biblical texts which we share, Christians can gain a deeper insight into the Jewishness of Jesus and can draw forth water out of the wells of wisdom and virtue from which he drank. Both Jews and Christians will gain deeper understanding of the polyphonic culture that nurtured him and the Jesus movement to their own benefit in understanding what they hold most dear.

Above all, I stress the importance of dialogue and mutual learning in rounding out the dialectical truths that we hold in common even as we operate at different points of equilibrium: God's role and human role in *tikkun olam*, scriptures and tradition, collective and individual dimensions of salvation, the universal and the particular, grace and good works, repentance and atonement, the balance and interaction of ritual and ethical in the service of God, redemption present and redemption not yet, sacred and secular, the balance of denial and expression in holiness. The list is endless. Let me underscore that we shall not arrive at a common point in most of these areas. Each faith has carved out distinctive channels and practices in pursuit of its mission. However, in all these cases (and others), the differences between us can help us increase our capacity to hold a broader spectrum of the two poles in dynamic tension inside our own tradition. This will increase each one's vitality. No less important, the richness level of contemporary culture is so high that the wider our range of performance, the more we can influence others. Christianity will be strengthened as it moves to reclaim the material dimension of redemption. Exposure to positive Jewish models will help this process. Judaism has much to gain as it wrestles with the postmodern meaning of Revelation and the role of tradition. Exposure to more developed and sophisticated positive Christian models will accelerate this process. In both cases, we can learn from the errors that the other necessarily made in working through the issues. We might even be able to avoid some of the errors by empathetically grasping the other's experience and process.

I should add that each community will have to increase its investment in this area to raise dialogue to the level necessary to meet the need. Consider that the full-time staff position for Catholic-Jewish affairs at the United States Conference of Catholic Bishops has gone unfilled since the retirement of Gene Fisher (who made such an important contribution to the field). The Jewish community also has reduced its staffing and investment in dialogue from the heady days of the writing of *Nostra Aetate* and the birth of a new relationship between us. In both communities, major protagonists are aging and a new generation has not yet been recruited to continue their sacred work.

Part of this process involves going to the people in the pews. At the popular level, there is still the power of the inherited ways the gospels have been read in the past. These "first naïveté" readings of the gospels too easily translate into a pejorative take on the Jews. On the Jewish side, the folk cultural memories of Christian persecution and conversionist design still circulate to reinforce negative stereotypes or to generate suspicion rather than openness and cooperation.

Self-restraint and Self-obligation for the Sake of the Other

Part of this process will demand a self-restraint that grows out of the desire to make room for the other. In doing this, we imitate our maker who, according to both traditions, self-limited in order to become accessible to humans and to summon them to take up an expanded role in redemption. Thus, the Catholic Church would make extra efforts not to slip into a language that negatively stereotypes Jews (in Eastertime prayers as "perfidious Jews"), or use Pharisee as a synonym for hypocrisy and legalism, or offends them (e.g., targeting them for conversion because they have no access for salvation). There is a particular challenge for the Church in that many Eastern rite churches and Arab Christian churches (affected by the politics of Israel and Arabs in the Middle East) are still unreconciled to *Nostra Aetate*'s demarche toward the Jews.

The Jewish counterpart of this self-correction is to overcome the residue of "anti-*Goyim*" assumptions, values, and attitudes still found in rabbinic sources and lay circles. Similarly, Jewish leadership must train itself not to react to disappointments or to respond to a particular unwanted Catholic action by resorting to use of old characterizations. Angry generalizations about past behaviors should not be wielded as clubs, as if there has not been a major transformation in the interim. There is an ethically sensitive law in Jewish tradition that in speaking to a convert, one is prohibited from throwing up at them a behavior from their past life. Such an act belittles the integrity of their spiritual rebirth and may discourage them into believing they will never be accepted fully as they deserve to be. Jews must understand that they owe a similar respect and sensitivity to a Church that has been so remarkably born again in its understanding of Judaism and its treatment of Jewry.

Such restraint or taking on extra responsibilities for the sake of the other can be expressed negatively—as in not indulging one's own preference out of awareness of the pain the other has suffered from the one who I wish to honor. There are traditional Catholics who wish to honor Pope Pius XII for understandable reasons, that is, for his important contributions to Catholicism in the twentieth century. In their view, Jewish attitudes—or however his actions (or nonactions) may have harmed the Jews—should be irrelevant to the assessment of what makes a Catholic saint. Nevertheless, I think that it was an act of wisdom and of proleptic partnership that the process was not expedited, in part out of consideration for Jews' reactions. We need the Vatican archives to be fully opened and a comprehensive assessment made of Pope Pius's actions and policies so that a fair picture of his total record can be established before any final decision is made. Still, there is a deeper point. If a potential saint or *tzaddik* met the internal criteria of our faith community but fell short in a major way in treatment and concern for members of another faith, this should be considered a serious obstacle to a positive judgement on sainthood or *tzaddik* status. Precisely because Christianity is a universal religion and is in the spotlight of an emerging global community, the behavior toward and impact on another community cannot be ignored in judging the ultimate stature of a person.

An important positive statement of the principle (that I should incorporate the other as my spiritual concern) would be for both communities to step up to protect the religious freedom of the other. There are places around the world where religious extremism—or secularist arrogance—is taking away the right to practice one's religion without interference. We need to stand together against legal restrictions and behavioral discrimination against non-Muslim faiths in Turkey, parts of Nigeria, and the Middle East. In the West, we need to alert democracies not to go over the line of invading private religious actions in the name of enforcing human rights. Admittedly, there is a fluid, blurred boundary between upholding rights and respecting religious differences through accommodation. Still, partners should look out for each other and work to prevent overreach. Even well-intentioned authorities seeking to achieve justice are capable of trampling the rights and needs of religious individuals who may differ with the national consensus. Similarly, although it is not usually embedded in legislation and law, unthinking anti-Catholicism on the left often demeans and pushes back unfairly on Catholic positions in the public square. Even if Jews are not directly in the line of fire in such matters, we owe it to our partners to stand in solidarity with them against coercion, legal or cultural.

Currently the most urgent and immediate action on behalf of the vulnerable is needed to condemn the wave of anti-Semitism in Europe. Together we need to pressure European governments to more aggressively check organized hatred of Jews, including those groups and forces that pose as anti-Zionism in order to disguise their anti-Semitism. Even more urgent is the need to speak out and recruit help for the embattled religious minorities—mostly Christian—that are being violently assaulted and killed in many lands, especially in Africa, the Middle East, and Asia. This attack has sunk to shocking depths. The very existence of these communities is endangered as they face murder, rape, and destruction of holy sites. This demands a much more intense response from both partners, now.

Joint Witness to the World and Islam

As partners we need to offer joint witness to the world that past traditions of rejection and hatred, nurtured by religion, can be rolled back and even replaced by constructive relationships. This kind of transformation is particularly needed at the present time when extremists are employing violence against nonbelievers or practitioners of religions other than theirs—in the name of religion. The Talmud says that to fulfill the commandment "you shall love the Lord your God," you must behave so kindly and ethically to others that they will love a God who inspires such behavior in the followers. There is a danger that religion is becoming so identified with the right to conquer and/or abuse others that a massive withdrawal of respect for religion and God has already begun.

It is particularly important, therefore, that as partners, we approach Muslims everywhere. We must give joint testimony not only in self-defense but also for the sake of Islam itself. Although Muslims are not the only source of religious violence today, the intense struggle for the soul of Islam is on full display to the world in the daily news of death and destruction. Muslims who seek to renew it with greater emphasis on its ability to make room for democracy and for pluralism need to know that we are in solidarity with them. Only they can recover Islam's traditions that make room for others, that allow for recognition of past errors as well as the right to apply the tradition in new ways. Muslims need to hear how Jews and Christians deeply committed to the authority of the past tradition nevertheless were able to hear the word of God in a new way, more respectful of the other.

Both Jews and Christians in the Middle East are tempted to choose political expediency—for Israel in the case of Jews, against it in the case of Christians in countries dominated by those who would destroy Israel. But despite the pressures these communities face, in the long term the best strategy is rather a moral alliance with Muslims aiming to confront Islam's pathological elements from within. Christians in particular can give particularly telling witness to Muslims. They, too, were led by powerful traditions to policies vis-à-vis Jews that they now regret. They now realize that sacred teachings were diminished morally because of elements of hatred in how they were interpreted and applied. They can testify firsthand that the repentance and confession, which they feared would undermine the authority of their faith, actually liberated love and increased the influence of Christianity as well as respect for it in the world.

Jews, meanwhile, cannot witness to the need for solidarity with the other until they speak up—as a community and jointly with Christian partners—against the widespread destruction of religious minorities in the Middle East. Jews outside of Israel must pressure their national governments to make the decline of Middle Eastern Christian populations an important point in foreign relations. Even in Israel, where the Christian population has surged in the past half century, government policies can further improve the atmospherics as well as the functioning of Christian communities. Diaspora Jews can remind Israelis of their experience that greater sensitivity on the part of the majority population to the difficulties of being a minority can improve the quality of life of outsider groups. I would add a personal concern of mine: that private, nonofficial intervention is needed to restrain some of the ultra-Orthodox pressure on Christian institutions and worship in Israel, such as haredi demonstrations and semi-official harassments. Violence in response to past or purported Christian missionary abuses does not further the further of mutual witness to a forgiving and reconciling God.

Joint Witnesses and Joint Workers for *Tikkun Olam*

As common bearers of the message of a covenant of redemption, we have to give a joint witness to the culture leaders of modernity in which the public sphere is dominated by secularity. Here a joint witness would grow out of the strength we give each other as countercultural partners. We should seek to offer a prophetic voice, one that is fully in the world and committed to the task of social development but is independent enough to identify and check the excesses in the very movements and societies of which we are a part, recovering an awareness of our independence from dominant groups that was lacking when Christianity was coopted into Western imperialism or colonialism or when traditional Judaism sought twentieth-century alliances with right wing, culturally reactionary, pro-business, anti-labor parties in Eastern Europe, out of common fear of modernization.

But a revival of an independent stance from the dominant culture should not mean an inability to recognize the ways that modernization and the expansion of human power have advanced the cause of *tikkun olam*. Instead, we should critique our own past failures to welcome positive advances in economics, politics, and culture that accompanied modernization. Often scientific and medical advances were challenged as threatening religious authority, divine prerogatives, or nature itself. We would do well to confess the extent to which the creation of the neutral, national democratic state has checked our excesses and weaned us from asserting power at the expense of nonestablished religious groups. We should acknowledge the extent to which the secularist critique of religion—often one-sided and unfair—nevertheless helped us weed out harsh, even cruel, past behaviors. These acknowledgments will make clear that our joint witness is not driven by desire to reassert our political power and to seek reestablishment or even to regain control of the cultural consensus.

Nevertheless, we must critique the growing self-referential—and self-reverential—secularism that proclaims that humans are the masters and measures of all things. Humanity desperately needs our joint reassertion of covenantal limits, without which the constructive forces turn lethal. Indus-trial productivity, uncontrolled by a sense that "the Earth is the Lord's," has morphed into global warming, pollution, habitat, and species destruc-tion. Where humans see themselves as masters of creation and lose a sense that "the Earth is the Lord's," this is what happens. Despite the countless miracles of modern medical science, when researchers lose the sense that these are miracles—that is, scientists employing God-given talents to unlock and utilize God-given laws of nature to assure the victory of life over death—then the power overextends. The outcome is a tendency to treat the patient as an object of research or to employ medical science to hasten death or to select gender and sex in discriminatory fashion. Indeed, in all frontiers of advance, the loss of covenantal limits turns beneficial development into pathological outcome. Then pluralism is falsely general-ized into relativism; self-interest is unleashed to become unchecked and exploitative; a greater sense of human dignity becomes an idolatry that ironically can lead to totalitarianism (because the ruler is the highest judge) and the triumph of death over life.

In particular, our partnership should free us up to participate in and judge both capitalism and socialism. The capitalist market system is cur-rently in a dominant phase partly due to globalization, technological inno-vation, and the failures of a socialist system in the second half of the twen-tieth century. The credibility of this system has grown out of its success in generating more affluence and higher standards of living than the socialist alternatives. Also in the past few decades, a half a billion people have been brought out of poverty—an extraordinary accomplishment despite the human and environmental costs along the way. Nevertheless, poverty and social dysfunction, discriminatory practices, and unequal legal processes still are widely present in the better-off countries; they are prevalent in a third of the globe. And another result of affluence is a growth in material-ism and selfish philosophies that further penalize (or neglect) the poor.

Our joint task is to identify with our Lord who dwells with the humble and "seeks to revive the heart of the depressed"[23] to imitate God "who ren-ders justice to the oppressed and feeds those who are hungry, who sets the captives free, opens the eyes of the blind, raises up those who are bowed down."[24] The "father of orphans and champion of widows"[25] calls on us: "How long will you judge unjustly? . . . do justice to the poor and fatherless, deal righteously with the afflicted and the destitute. . . ."[26]

23. Is 57:5.
24. Ps 146:7–8.
25. Ibid. 68:6.
26. Ibid. 82:2–4.

But we must also not forget that the same Torah that demanded special help for the poor and warned us "not to favor the rich and the powerful"[27] also warned us against subverting justice in the form of "favoring the poor."[28] When one sets up a system that acts unfairly in the name of the poor,[29] it ends up mistreating all, including the needy, as the experiences under communism showed. One welcomes that Christian liberation theology rose up to plead the cause of the deprived and neglected. But to the extent that it excessively incorporated Marxist analysis, it ended up justifying a different set of abuses or swallowing elements of the radical dismissal of religion. Jews were quicker to spot this danger because various strands of liberation theology revived anti-Judaic typologies and anti-Semitic allegations to pillory the elites whom they identified as Pharisees. Jews have learned too often from past experience that drawing false moral equivalences between the imperfect and the rotten—or perverting justice for the sake of the needs of the poor—corrupts the very foundations of justice and of the economy to the detriment of all. We need to help each other be independent enough to work hard for the poor without yielding our integrity in standards of right and wrong. We need to continue to foster service corps and other works that genuinely serve the poor and respect their dignity. We need the help of God, and we need the ability to identify with the eternal enough to not compromise our ability to correct and guide those with whom we identify strongly because they lack so much.

In conclusion, we need to be partners in this joint testimony because we must recognize that we are a minority. We need each other and the help of others to have an effect. We are in the process of becoming a counterculture upholding the sacredness of life and the untrammeled presence of a hidden God who continually reaches out to humanity. We each testify from our traditions that the covenantal way—combining visions of perfection with gradualist mechanisms, incorporating boundaries and limits—is an enduring tree of life. We need to speak against the thrust for amnesia, which erases the foundations of faith on which the democracy and science of our time were built. We must speak up and challenge the myopia that excessively focuses on the present moment. Such short sightedness blocks out the transcending vision of the Messianic future and closes our ears to the calls to human creation and reverence for life that emanates from the Eternal One. We will need to strengthen each other and to partner with many other groups in society through the opportunity to speak provided us by democracy if we are to reverse the drift along the dominant current. We

27. Lv 19:15.
28. Ibid.
29. Ex 23:6.

will need each other's support—and the help of God—to carry on without tiring or despairing.

Together we must show that the best way to serve God—the best way to find the presence of God in life—is to heal and nurture the image of God everywhere. We need to be able to do this selflessly and not for the sake of bringing them to God in our institutions and community. In general, we need to grow in partnership to do the will of our Father in Heaven to repair the world while giving up the selfish need to be deemed God's exclusive agents. The sight of two former enemies now partnering in love to do God's will in itself will inspire our people (and give joy to God). It will give hope to all that even as we can get around our own embedded selfish conflicted past, so we can overcome the entrenched enemies of life and the twisted elements in human character. Together with all who will join us, we can make major strides to bring closer God's kingdom on earth.

Nostra Aetate and the
Church's Dialogue with Jews:
Fifty Years and Forward in the United States

TIMOTHY CARDINAL DOLAN

"What's the big deal?" sincerely asked a young priest when I told him how much I was looking forward to the golden jubilee of *Nostra Aetate*.

He inquired about the significance of the day not sarcastically or cynically, but genuinely. Simply put, he so took Catholic-Jewish amity for granted that he wondered why it was necessary to celebrate this half-century-old document.

For this fine young priest, that anyone would have ever considered the Jews guilty of deicide, thus meriting scorn, harassment, isolation, or tragically worse was utterly illogical and stupid. He had been raised in a Catholic grade and high school where textbooks treated Jews with dignity and respect and the full horror of the *Shoah* had been carefully examined. He had grown up in a parish where Catholics and Jews alternated years coming together in prayer on the eve of Thanksgiving, one year in the synagogue, the next in the parish church. As a seminarian, he had taken a course in Judaism taught by a rabbi. Now, as a parish priest, he is in a weekly scripture study with an interfaith group of local clergy that includes a rabbi.

He had no idea that it was not always so, which is only another argument for the case we make today: that the implementation of *Nostra Aetate*, especially here in the United States, has been remarkably successful, that the invitation to respect and dialogue offered by the Council fathers has been enthusiastically accepted and has borne much fruit.

His "ho-hum" reaction about the *Nostra Aetate* celebration, though, is not only a cause for gratitude in that Jewish-Catholic friendship is now so taken for granted but is also a cause for some concern since, well, Jewish-Catholic friendship is now so taken for granted! For, as my grandpa used to say, "What you take for granted can easily be ungranted!"

To be with cardinals, bishops, priests, scholars, rabbis, and leaders in interfaith dialogue is an honor. To work on behalf of my brother bishops as co-chair with Rabbi David Strauss of the official dialogue with the National Council of Synagogues, following the towering achievements of

Cardinal William Keeler and a generation of devoted Catholic and Jewish leaders, is a privilege.

Veterans in this sacred task will note that Jewish-Catholic friendship and cooperation has never been stronger, and I would concur.

The recent passing of the former chief-rabbi of the Eternal City, Elio Toaff, reminds us of his deep companionship with Pope Saint John Paul II, as we realize that the late pontiff expressed explicit gratitude to only two people in his last testament: his loyal priest secretary and spiritual son, Stanislaus Dziwicz, and Rabbi Toaff.[1]

Here in the United States we note the perseverance of the official Jewish-Catholic dialogue in the previously mentioned meetings between bishops and the representatives of Reform, Conservative, and Reconstructionist Judaism in the National Council of Synagogues, in our consultations with the Rabbinic Council of America, and with the Orthodox Union.

Nor can we forget the nearly four dozen centers of joint study between Christians and Jews, such as the Council of Centers on Jewish-Christian Relations, or the thousands of local and neighborhood partnerships between parishes and synagogues in prayer, theological discourse, and community service.

Catholic clergy and people regularly benefit from ongoing education sponsored by the American Jewish Committee (AJC), the Anti-Defamation League, the Hartman Institute, the Jan Karski Institute, and *Yahad-in-Unum* in Paris.

I could go on and on, but I think those of us involved in the dialogue are all in concert observing that the brave fathers of the Council, aided by Jewish *periti*, could never have foreseen such progress.

Besides the organizational and educational progress referred to above, two other areas this last half century deserve special mention.

One is the fruitfulness of mutual theological study. It was Pope John Paul II's dream that Christians and Jews could return to the theological conversations between one another so rudely interrupted 1,945 years ago when the Roman army leveled Jerusalem. Beliefs cherished by each of us—creation, election, covenant, promise, redemption, the law, grace, and revelation, to name a few—were kitchen table talk, or arguments, between Jews and Christians in the decades right after Jesus but faded in 70 A.D. when another priority—survival!—took over. Thanks to the green light of *Nostra Aetate*, such topics are back on the agenda. Alleluia!

---

1. Pope John Paul II, *Testament of the Holy Father*, published on April 7, 2005, in an addition dated March 17, 2000, no. 5. See http://www.vatican.va/gpII/documents/testamento-jp-ii_20050407_en.html and http://zenit.org/articles/john-paul-ii-s-last-will-and-testament/.

The second area of progress has been the candor with which we have confronted the testy controversies that have arisen. Raised voices over such issues as the Good Friday prayer, the cross and convent at Auschwitz, the visit of Kurt Waldheim to Pope John Paul, the lifting of the excommunication of a schismatic bishop without taking note that he was a Holocaust denier, the neuralgia over *Dominus Jesus*, the role of the Holy See during World War II, the reputation of Pius XII, necessary revision in the Oberammergau Passion Play, diplomatic exchanges between Israel and the Vatican, and even last week's nod to Palestine by Pope Francis—just to name a few—have caused spats and arguments. That we have not dodged them and have actually persevered through them is a test of our mettle!

I remember my first meeting as a bishop-member of the Jewish-Catholic dialogues, being amazed at the blunt bickering over Mel Gibson's movie, *The Passion of the Christ*. "I could have stayed home and had dinner with my family if I wanted this kind of arguing," I whispered to an older bishop during the break. "But that's the point," he came back. "We <u>are</u> family, so we argue because we get scared and mad when something threatens to tear us apart."

As we look back over the last five decades of progress since *Nostra Aetate*, I wonder what our successors will observe in May 2065 when they gather to savor—please God—the advances made since today.

I do see five areas where we have indeed begun to "cast out to the deep," challenges that could bring us into an even more durable and beneficial alliance.

One is an intensification of the most obvious imperative for any enterprise by any group of believers: to reclaim the primacy of God in a world that prefers not to take Him seriously, to ignore Him, or even to deny Him. Here we face together the impact of that loaded word: *secularism.*

This is a point I spent a whole lecture on two weeks before the Catholic University symposium at the Jewish Theological Seminary back home in New York, proposing that this effort at the core of both Jewish and Catholic belief was the essence of Pope Saint John Paul II's post–*Nostra Aetate* agenda.[2] I was glad that the respondents, Rabbi Burton Visotzky and Chancellor Arnold Eisen, agreed.

Simply put, I pointed out that John Paul II was convinced that the most insidious toxin infecting humanity was the denial of God's sovereignty, even existence, and that the Church's most natural ally in restoring faith in a world gone skeptical was the Jews. Humanity's fateful preference, lurking since the Enlightenment, lurching now, was—to paraphrase Rabbi

---

2. Timothy Cardinal Dolan, "50 Years of Nostra Aetate," http://learn.jtsa.edu/content/video/public-event/timothy-cardinal-dolan-50-years-nostra-aetate.

Jonathan Sacks's definition of secularism—"to get along just fine without God." The pope was convinced that the Jewish community would share his urgency that such a cultural sidelining of faith must be reversed. He died, while not without hope, certainly with an impatience that neither Jews nor Catholics seemed to be making much progress in inviting the world to believe that, in the words of the psalmist, "Only in God is my soul at rest."[3]

I recounted the story of John Paul's heroic and tumultuous 1979 return to Poland in what historians now call "nine days that changed the world" and how, inspired by his presence and words, a two-million-strong throng in Warsaw on his last day chanted at the top of their voices, to the grimaces of the KGB and Polish communist officials, "We want God!"[4]

"We want God!" The primitive cry of faith, humanity's innate longing for the Divine, a thirst denied, ignored, ridiculed, outlawed, and rationalized away for too long by the oppression of a regime that had vainly sought purpose in systems that forgot God! It was as if the Polish Pope had put on the lips of his people the pining of the Hebrew psalmist, "As the deer longs for streams of water, so my soul longs for you, O God."[5] And it was his aspiration that what most naturally bound Jews and Catholics together would be the common effort to help humanity articulate once again the desire too long suppressed: "We want God!"

Both Jews and Christians look out their windows daily to behold, in the prescient observation of Blessed John Henry Newman a century and a half ago, "a world" that is "simply irreligious."[6]

Two, the friendship inspired by *Nostra Aetate* coaxes us to explore together the *pastoral issues* that befuddle both of us.

Not long after my arrival in New York, Rabbi Peter Rubenstein kindly invited me to meet a group of his congregants at Central Synagogue. They thoughtfully spoke to me about their concerns, not surprisingly concentrating on those familiar two categories that have characterized postdialogue; namely, *theological issues* such as covenant, election, Israel, and *neuralgic points* such as the hoped-for opening of the Vatican archives, and their apprehension at the time that the Church's commitment to *Nostra Aetate* was slackening.

Then they kindly asked me what I thought should concern us Catholics and Jews. I stayed away from the theological and neuralgic and went for the *pastoral*.

---

3. Ps 62:2.
4. George Weigel, *Witness to Hope* (New York: Harper, 2001), 2.
5. Ps 42:1.
6. John Henry Newman, *Catholic Sermons of Cardinal Newman* (London: Burns & Oates, 1957), 123.

"I have a hunch," I began, "that you committed Jews at this synagogue have the same concerns that my parishioners at Saint Patrick's have: how to pass on the faith to our kids and grandkids who are growing up in a culture that hardly has room for religion, how the reality of intermarriage affects us, how to preserve the Sabbath in a society where soccer and shopping reign, how to make sure our kids have some tether to the faith when they leave for college, how to entice back the crowds of our spiritual kin who have drifted away."

It was a light bulb moment, as my new Jewish neighbors sat up and exclaimed, "Oh, my, you Catholics worry about all that, too?" You bet we do! And putting our shoulders and yarmulkes together to talk about them could be one of the more rewarding results of our celebrated *Nostra Aetate* friendship: comparing notes on common *pastoral challenges*.

A couple months ago, I was invited to preach a Sabbath service at a local synagogue. During the prayer, a young boy celebrated his Bar Mitzvah. After the ceremony I commented to the rabbi how powerful such a ritual was. He looked at me and commented, "Odds are, we won't see that young man again for thirty years, until he brings his son here for Bar Mitzvah! "Oh," I replied, "We Catholics call that the Sacrament of Confirmation!" That's what I mean by common pastoral challenges!

And point *three* is a common front on the most pressing pastoral burr in the saddle of all: the unavoidable fact that what sociologists call "inherited religions"—read: Jews and Catholics—are losing their members.

Both Jews and Catholics now approach the findings that Pew Research Center publishes regularly as we do the obituary page, but we can hardly ignore their challenge. Yes, both can rejoice in the data that the majority of Catholics and Jews remain steadfast in their allegiance; yes, there's a bit of evidence that the rate of defection may be leveling off . . . but it's alarm-clock time for both of us because the statistics present unavoidable conclusions: *belief* may be high, *belonging* is not, and no longer can we presume that being born Jewish or Catholic is a guarantee that one will freely choose to live and die in that faith.

As Pope John Paul soberly commented, no longer can we count on birth, family tradition, or culture to automatically pass on the faith.

We Jews and Catholics—and, lest we forget, Islam (which brings up yet another challenge!)—believe we are born into the faith, we inherit it. We did not choose our faith; God chose us! We have no more business choosing our supernatural family than we do our natural family. We're stuck with it. Rabbi Joshua Heschel titled his masterpiece not *Man's Search for God* but *God's Search for Man*!

When the teenage girl asked the "Whisky Priest" fleeing Mexican troops persecuting the Church in Graham Greene's classic, *The Power and the Glory*, why he didn't just renounce his faith and save his life, he replied, "It's impossible. There's no way. I'm a priest. It's out of my power." And the girl understood, explaining, it's "like a birthmark."[7]

In Jewish and Catholic belief, our belonging, our religious identity, is like a birthmark. But that is no more for a growing swath of our people. And therein is the most towering pastoral problem we face together: to recover the sense of *belonging* we believe essential to our relationship with God.

We Jews and Catholics face two obstacles in our mutual insistence on *belonging*: The first is the sociological phenomenon noted above, that people today prefer belief over belonging: they want God as their Father as long as they're the only child; they want the Lord as their shepherd as long as the flock consists of one lamb—themselves; they want God as their general as long as it's an army of one. None of this sits well with Jews who believe God chose a people, or Catholics who believe we are only a part of a body with many members.

The second obstacle we face is America itself, which stresses *personal choice* in everything from coffee to religion. In fact, our highly Puritan, Calvinist religious climate puts the premium on my personal choice of God, not His choice of me. Cardinal Francis George used to worry that Catholics in America were becoming "Calvinists with incense." His fear was well grounded.

So what's happening is that religion is now listed under "hobby" or "personal interests," if at all, instead of "family background and history"—and that, my friends, is a juicy challenge for both of us. For us to tackle it together could be a good time!

Four, the gruesome reality of religious persecution is yet another worry that unites us. Somewhere right this moment a Jew or a Catholic is in the crosshairs of the rifle scope of an extremist. All believers—Jews, Christians, and, yes, genuine moderate Muslims, which means most of them—are at risk in vast regions of the world. Christians fear ISIS and Boko Haram in the Middle East and Africa, and Islamic and Hindu extremists in the Far East, while Jews fear Islamic terrorists in Israel and anti-Semitic thugs in Europe.

Our God, we both believe, can bring good out of evil, leading to what Pope Benedict, Cardinal Koch, and Pope Francis have called an "Ecumenism of Martyrdom" as Jews and Christians huddle more closely together to protect, advocate for, and care for each other as mobs with torches and swords threaten our churches and synagogues in other parts of the globe.

---

7. Graham Greene, *The Power and the Glory* (New York: Penguin, 1990), 41.

Five, and finally, *Nostra Aetate* has given us an infrastructure of friendship these past fifty years, allowing us to reclaim and preach again the biblical reality that popular soothing spirituality would rather us forget: *sin and redemption*.

Why in the world we Jews and Catholics have lost our voice in preaching sin and redemption is beyond me. If our people believe they are without sin, that they need no salvation, why would they sense a need for church, synagogue, religion, belonging? Affirmation and fellowship they can find much easier over a latte at Starbucks or working out at the gym—and they are!

Here I will defer to an eloquent author, David Brooks, whose new best seller, *The Road to Character*, should be gift wrapped for every graduate these days. Recently I interviewed him on the radio and got red with embarrassment when he asked why the Church and the Synagogue had stopped preaching *sin* and *redemption*, without which culture is doomed to pledge continued allegiance to the central fallacy of modern life, that "The Big Me"—the culture of achievement, our total focus on what he terms *resumé virtues* as opposed to *eulogy virtues*—can lead to true fulfillment.

No, Brooks insisted, we must preach that I am flawed, I am imperfect, I have a dark side, I am incomplete, I am a sinner, I need redemption, and I can't give it to myself! That's our forte, folks! That's the Jewish and Christian vocabulary. That's what the prophets and saints claimed.

Earlier I suggested that we Jews and Catholics are losing our people. Where are they going? I can only answer for Catholics: most go to no other religion but become a "none." But those who do join another church sure aren't registering with the Unitarians. They are more than likely signing up at a Bible-waving mega-church that bellows *sin* and *salvation* in the name of the God of Abraham, Isaac, Jacob, and Jesus, because all they are hearing at Sunday Mass is a version of the discredited "I'm OK, you're OK" therapy of thirty years ago.

It is time to reclaim our specialty as Jews and Christians: *sin*, grace, mercy, *redemption*.

By now it's obvious that I am far from a theologian and still a rookie in Jewish-Catholic dialogue compared with distinguished veterans at the conference. I was only fifteen when *Nostra Aetate* was promulgated by Blessed Paul VI.

But I am a pastor and, as such, both rejoice in the progress that has been made and relish the goals we realistically admit loom before us.

And, for the record, I told that young priest, "Listen, buddy, this is a *big deal!*"

From Regret to Acclaim:
A Jewish Reaction to *Nostra Aetate*

RABBI NOAM E. MARANS

Barukh shehecheyanu vekiyimanu vehigianu lazman hazeh. Blessed are you, God, for granting us life, for sustaining us, and for bringing us to this moment. That is the Jewish *b'rakhah*—blessing—for celebrating auspicious occasions. The fiftieth anniversary of *Nostra Aetate* is certainly a milestone worthy of that *b'rakhah*. The document transformed not only Catholic-Jewish relations and wider Christian-Jewish relations but even the course of Jewish history, and all for the better. *Nostra Aetate*'s power is not limited to the past. It is ongoing, influencing the present and the future.

If for nearly two millennia Christian anti-Jewish sentiment provided the grounds for contempt, violence, and murder directed at Jews, then we must acknowledge *Nostra Aetate* as a life-saving document. The potential to save Jewish lives is what motivated Rabbi Abraham Joshua Heschel when he agreed to engage the Vatican and Cardinal Augustine Bea while the document was composed. His role as a Jewish advisor in the fashioning of *Nostra Aetate* was both complex and controversial. But for Heschel one thing was clear. He viewed his encounters with the Vatican, Pope Paul VI, and Cardinal Augustin Bea in the early 1960s as an unprecedented opportunity to save Jewish lives.[1]

Over the last six months, we at American Jewish Committee (AJC) have been preparing for a uniquely Jewish commemoration and celebration of *Nostra Aetate*'s fiftieth anniversary. Perhaps the greatest revelation in our research was the mixed reviews that *Nostra Aetate* received from AJC and others when the final version was first announced, a historical truth we dutifully documented in a brief history of *Nostra Aetate*'s fifty years that AJC recently published.[2] In fact, after the October 15, 1965, landslide vote approving the Second Vatican Council's "Declaration on the Relation of the Church to Non-Christian Religions," AJC's public statement was notably restrained. The official reaction opened as follows: "The Vatican Council

---

1. Edward Kaplan, *Spiritual Radical: Abraham Joshua Heschel in America, 1940-1972* (New Haven: Yale University Press, 2009), 239.
2. *In Our Time: AJC and* Nostra Aetate: *A Reflection after 50 Years* (New York: American Jewish Committee, 2015).

Declaration on the Jews has been awaited with hope by men of goodwill everywhere. We regret keenly some of the assertions in the Declaration, especially those that might give rise to misunderstandings." "Keen regret"! And only then some very carefully worded, modest but guarded applause: "Nevertheless, we view the adoption of the Declaration, especially its repudiation of the invidious charge of the collective guilt of Jews for the death of Jesus and its rejection of anti-Semitism, as an act of justice long overdue. We trust the Declaration will afford new opportunities for improved interreligious understanding and cooperation throughout the world." And lastly, "Much will depend on the manner and vigor with which the affirmative principles embodied in this Declaration will be carried out."[3]

Any sense of unbridled Jewish enthusiasm would have to wait for the moment two weeks later, when AJC reacted to the official *Nostra Aetate* promulgation on October 28, 1965, a date chosen by Pope Paul VI to honor his predecessor, Pope John XXIII, the inspiration behind *Nostra Aetate*, who had been elected pope on that date seven years earlier. This AJC statement began much more generously:

> The American Jewish Committee welcomes the promulgation by Pope Paul VI and the Vatican Council of the Declaration on Non-Christians, as a turning point in 1900 years of Jewish-Christian history and the climax to a historic effort to bring about a new era in relations between Catholics and Jews. A rejection of the charge of Jewish collective guilt for the Crucifixion and repudiation of anti-Semitism are significant clarifications of Church teachings that we hope will help purify the climate of relations between Christians and Jews throughout the world.[4]

No "keen regret" this time. One wonders what was going on at AJC between October 15 and October 28, 1965, that caused a change in tune. AJC's organizational angst regarding *Nostra Aetate* was not unique among American Jewish agencies. The *Nostra Aetate* ambivalence played out elsewhere in the Jewish world and foreshadowed a key element of how American Jews would engage in Catholic-Jewish relations after *Nostra Aetate*.[5] I will elaborate further on that theme later in this essay.

Sometimes first reactions are the most candid and authentic, and "keen regret" was indeed the first AJC response. Why? It may have been disappointment that the word "deicide" was dropped from the final version

---

3. American Jewish Committee, located in Press Release Collection, Box #13, July–December 1965, October 15, 1965. Print.

4. Ibid., October 28, 1965. Print.

5. Judith Hershcopf, "The Church and the Jews: The Struggle at Vatican Council II," *American Jewish Year Book* 67 (1966): 71–75.

or that anti-Semitism was only "decried" in the final text instead of "condemned," as in an earlier draft.[6]

It is also possible that AJC leaders were nervous that they had invested so much time, resources, and energy without getting everything they had hoped for in the document. AJC had been working on Catholic-Jewish relations since soon after its founding in 1906, and ever more assiduously after World War II. And yet there was no mention in *Nostra Aetate* of the Holocaust or of Christian culpability in violence committed against Jews over millennia, and certainly no apology. The State of Israel, already in its seventeenth year and central to Jewish identity around the world, is not mentioned. Maybe Jewish leaders were hedging their bets on the prospects of this brief document.

It is similarly conceivable that AJC leaders were rattled by the proverbial "Who speaks for the Jews?" The answer, I always tell my dear Catholic friends, is no one. With the run-up to *Nostra Aetate*, some of the Jewish communal fault lines were surfacing, not only the usual interorganizational jockeying and politics but also heated debates on religious, theological, and doctrinal matters related to Catholic-Jewish dialogue. It is not coincidental that Rabbi Joseph Soloveitchik, the leader of modern Orthodoxy, set very severe restrictions on interreligious dialogue in 1964, at the peak moment of conversations between Jewish organizations and the Vatican.[7] These restrictions are still applied by much of modern Orthodox leadership today. These debates may have influenced AJC's initial cautionary reaction to *Nostra Aetate*, since no unified Jewish communal response emerged regarding the process or the end result.

So how did we get from "keen regret" to full-blown Jewish acclaim today, fifty years later? The simple answer is that although *Nostra Aetate* is a revolutionary transformative document, its greatness depended on its implementation. It is only now, from the perspective of fifty years, that we can see how dramatic the impact would be on Catholic-Jewish relations and wider Christian-Jewish relations. If *Nostra Aetate* had become like so many other documents—just one herculean effort at one moment in time—we would not have gathered at Catholic University in 2015 to sing its praises.

Nostra Aetate did not just gather dust on the shelf. As a result of remarkable Catholic leadership in following up with "Guidelines,"[8]

<hr />

6. Ibid., 59.

7. Joseph B. Soloveitchik, "Confrontation," *Tradition: A Journal of Orthodox Thought* 6, no. 2 (1964): 5–29.

8. Johannes Cardinal Willebrands, "Guidelines and Suggestions for Implementing the Conciliar Declaration *Nostra Aetate*," December 1, 1974, http://www.vatican.va/.

"Notes,"[9] *We Remember: A Reflection on the* Shoah,[10] and a vast array of educational materials, *Nostra Aetate* was brought to life. The U.S. Conference of Catholic Bishops (USCCB) played a singular role in making that happen.[11] It was ably supported by the explosion of academic interest in Catholic-Jewish studies, with dozens of institutions affiliated today with the Council of Centers on Jewish-Christian Relations.[12] That is how *Nostra Aetate* would become the gold standard by which all other Christian denominational documents on Judaism would be measured.

Without getting involved in the controversial subject of American exceptionalism, it is fair to say that significant leadership in implementing *Nostra Aetate* came from America because that was the place where Jews and Catholics could live out the practical implications of *Nostra Aetate*. It was where Christians and Jews already lived side by side with genuine respect in unprecedented ways. America is home to the largest and most successful Jewish diaspora community in history. With the destruction of European Jewry, it was in America that the success of *Nostra Aetate* would be measured.

I offer an analogy from Jewish tradition. Jews call *Tanakh*, their Bible, the "written Torah," *Torah shebichtav*. The interpretation and application of that written Torah throughout the ages is known as the oral or unwritten Torah, *Torah sheb'al peh*, because until about eighteen hundred years ago there was a Jewish reluctance to write down that oral Torah. Today Judaism is not the written Torah alone. It is the written Torah as understood through the oral Torah. And the same could be said regarding *Nostra Aetate*. There is no *Nostra Aetate* today without its explication, amplification, and implementation.

The most important element of the *Nostra Aetate* oral Torah has been the visuals created by the dramatic gestures of successive popes. Pope John

9. Johannes Cardinal Willebrands, "Notes on the Correct Way to Present the Jews and Judaism in Preaching and Catechesis in the Roman Catholic Church," March 6, 1982, http://www.vatican.va/.

10. Cardinal Edward Idris Cassidy and Pope John Paul II, *We Remember: A Reflection on the* Shoah, March 16, 1998, http://www.vatican.va/.

11. See Bishops' Committee for Ecumenical and Interreligious Affairs, National Conference of Catholic Bishops, *Guidelines for Catholic-Jewish Relations* (Washington, D.C.: National Conference of Catholic Bishops, 1967); Secretariat for Catholic-Jewish Relations, Bishops' Committee for Ecumenical and Interreligious Affairs, National Conference of Catholic Bishops, *Guidelines for Catholic-Jewish Relations: 1985 Revisions* (Washington, D.C.: United States Catholic Conference, 1985); Secretariat for Ecumenical and Interreligious Affairs, National Conference of Catholic Bishops, *Catholic Teaching on the Shoah: Implementing the Holy See's* We Remember (Washington, D.C.: United States Catholic Conference, 2001). All available on U.S. Conference of Catholic Bishops website, http://www.usccb.org.

12. Council of Centers of Jewish-Christian Relations, http://www.ccjr.us/.

Paul II did this with the first papal visit to a synagogue since Peter, pil-
grimages to Holocaust sites, and most dramatically his state visit to Israel
in 2000, after the 1993 establishment of diplomatic relations with Israel.
Pope Benedict repeated all of these actions as a clear statement and confirmation that this is what popes do. Pope Francis, who had been the bene-
ficiary of post–*Nostra Aetate* ordination, did all of these things in a most
natural way as he rose through the Church in Argentina. He continues in
that path as the leader of all Catholics.

Although they are not official Church documents, these visuals have
had an indelible impact that cannot be overemphasized: not only on
Catholics and Jews and not only on Christians, but on all who take note of
the respect paid to the Jewish people and Judaism by the most influential
religious leader in the world, the pope.

The *Nostra Aetate* oral Torah was not just about what Catholics were
doing but also about how Jews were responding. Jewish leadership showed
courage in responding to the Catholic outreach. A positive response was not
inevitable. Jews could easily have rejected the Catholic turnaround, dismiss-
ing it, as one rabbi did, as "too little and too late"[13] or as not going far enough
to balance the atrocities of the centuries.[14] Nevertheless, allowing for some
significant exceptions, the overwhelming majority of the Jewish community,
particularly among its religious leaders, has been receptive to Catholic outreach. In barely one or two generations we moved from Jewish fear of, and
derisiveness toward, Catholicism to varying levels of mutual respect.

Let us go back, then, to the question of why AJC first issued a guarded
statement regarding *Nostra Aetate* in October 1965 and then, two weeks
later, released a more optimistic one. This pattern was in fact emblematic
and symptomatic of the Jewish approach to the entire *Nostra Aetate* process
before, during, and after the main event. The Catholic-Jewish relationship
has been moving on an upward, positive, advancing trajectory. But there
have been many challenging moments or hiccups along the way. On
numerous occasions—some of them huge contretemps, others in the
minutiae of insider theology, liturgy, and the like—the Jewish community
has shared its concerns regarding the general and particular direction of the
evolving Catholic-Jewish relationship, but always in a style that would
allow the relationship to live for another day. Repeatedly, Jewish leadership
has criticized, sometimes quite strongly, various Catholic actions or statements that disturbed the Jewish community, but responsible Jewish leadership always stopped short of allowing the particular challenging moment

    13. Rabbi Harry Essrig quoted in Judith Hershcopf, "The Church and the Jews: The
Struggle at Vatican Council II," *American Jewish Year Book* 66 (1965): 127.
    14. Hershcopf, 1966, 68–71.

to undermine the course of our new history together. Controversies notwithstanding, there was enough trust to persevere in a new relationship despite the heavy burden of history.

Between October 15 and October 28, 1965, no doubt there were some very interesting conversations held in the offices of AJC. I suspect the leaders were asking themselves whether their initial reaction was too critical and could endanger future progress. They ultimately listened to the Talmudic dictum, "*Tafasta merubeh, lo tafasta*,"[15] literally, if you grab too much, you'll get nothing. Or in a parallel English idiom, they did not let the perfect be the enemy of the good. *Nostra Aetate* is not perfect, but it certainly is good, and there must have been sufficient trust that the good could become better.

I offer one revealing example when Catholics and Jews allowed the relationship to live for another day even after a crisis, this one from 1987, the twenty-second year of *Nostra Aetate*, nine years into the pontificate of Pope John Paul II, beloved by Catholics and Jews. It was during summer 1987 when John Paul welcomed to the Vatican, in a state visit, the disgraced former secretary general of the United Nations and elected president of Austria, Kurt Waldheim, whose Nazi connections and wartime actions against Jews had come to light during the Austrian presidential campaign.

Lately, I have been thinking a lot about that crisis in Catholic-Jewish relations because I frequently attend services at Temple Israel in Great Neck, New York, where Rabbi Mordecai Waxman, of blessed memory, served for more than fifty years. Waxman was a leader in Catholic-Jewish relations and played a crucial role in navigating the Waldheim episode.

A previously scheduled meeting was to be held on September 11, 1987, between Pope John Paul and hundreds of American Jews in Miami, a city with a large and religiously aware Jewish community. Some Jewish groups had already announced boycotts of the Miami encounter. Rabbi Waxman was serving as chair of the International Jewish Committee on Interreligious Consultations (IJCIC), the official world Jewish dialogue partner with the Vatican. Many of the Jewish organizations who were represented at the symposium at Catholic University are part of IJCIC—AJC, Anti-Defamation League, World Jewish Congress, B'nai Brith, the rabbinic and synagogue arms of the three major Jewish denominations, and the Israel Jewish Council on Interreligious Relations (IJCIR), an Israeli interreligious relations organization. An IJCIC delegation went to the Vatican to discuss how to solve the crisis and met with John Paul at the

15. B. *Yoma* 80a; B. *Rosh Hashanah* 4b; B. *Chagigah* 17a.

papal retreat in Castel Gandolfo. And as has happened many times during
the past fifty years, a crisis was turned into an opportunity.[16]

As a result of the conversations in Italy, Pope John Paul II announced
in Miami two very important milestones in Catholic-Jewish relations: (1)
a commitment to producing a Catholic document on the *Shoah* and anti-
Semitism, which was issued ten years later as *We Remember: A Reflection on
the Shoah*[17] and (2) a public reaffirmation of the Jewish people's right to a
homeland, laying to rest lingering suspicions that the Church had theological objections to the existence of a sovereign Jewish state in the Holy
Land, and setting the stage for the 1993 Vatican recognition of the State
of Israel through the establishment of diplomatic relations between Israel
and the Holy See.[18]

It is hardly a coincidence that the greatest stress points in Catholic-
Jewish relations often revolve around issues related to the *Shoah* and the
State of Israel. These are the two defining events of modern Jewish history,
they shape the contours of Jewish identity today, and it is likely that they
will be the areas of potential Catholic-Jewish controversy in the future.
Regarding Israel, this was most recently demonstrated by the strong critical
reaction both from Israel and from much of the leadership of world Jewry
to the Vatican's new, or not so new, public recognition of the State of Palestine in May 2015, just a week before the symposium at Catholic University.

And regarding the *Shoah*, one of the few remaining major unresolved
chapters in the history of the Holocaust is the role of the Catholic Church
and the leadership of Pope Pius XII. Inevitably, there will be disagreements between Catholics and Jews about the procedure for opening the
Vatican wartime archives, how to interpret what is found there, and the
currently ongoing beatification process of Pope Pius.

As is appropriate among true friends, there will be necessary airings of
disagreement on both Israel and the Church's role in the *Shoah*. But the
two communities have too much at stake to allow even these major matters
of interpretation, in the case of the *Shoah*, or policy, in the case of Israel, to
undermine the progress that has been achieved between us. Navigating
these rough roads will not happen by accident. It will require careful con-

16. Mordecai Waxman, introduction to Zvia Ginor, *Yakar Le'Mordecai: Jubilee Volume
in Honor of Rabbi Mordecai Waxman* (Great Neck, N.Y.: KTAV Publishing House, Inc.,
1998), 36.

17. Commission for Religious Relations with the Jews, "We Remember: A Reflection
on the Shoah," March 16, 1998, http://www.vatican.va/roman_curia/pontifical_councils/
chrstuni/index.htm (accessed January 22, 2016).

18. Joseph Berger, "The Papal Visit: Pope Defends Vatican's Response to Holocaust in
Talks with Jews," *New York Times*, September 12, 1987.

versation and negotiation between leading Catholics and Jews. We will need to continue to trust one another and make our way together as critical friends with mutual respect.

In a memoir, Rabbi Waxman, who addressed Pope John Paul II in Miami on behalf of the Jewish people, wrote that a positive and important result of the Waldheim crisis was the establishment of the USCCB dialogue with the Synagogue Council of America, which Waxman built together with his partner and friend, Bishop (now Cardinal) William Keeler.[19] That dialogue continues to this day on two tracks, one with the National Council of Synagogues and one with the Orthodox Union.

Finally, we cannot gather on the fiftieth anniversary of *Nostra Aetate* without acknowledging that in the last several years our two communities have experienced the kind of tragedy and horror that we thought were part of the past but are, sadly, very real today: the resurgence of anti-Semitism in Europe and elsewhere and the persecution, ethnic cleansing, and murder of Christians in the Middle East and Africa. This is a time that calls out for collaboration and mutual support between Christians and Jews. And in that context we acknowledge that although *Nostra Aetate*'s impact was felt most dramatically in the Christian-Jewish relationship, the document opened the door to that which is "true and holy" in other religions, extending a hand to Hinduism, Buddhism, and Islam—as well as to Judaism.[20]

We have come a long way in fifty years, or perhaps we should say two thousand years. If there was any keen regret, it has surely dissipated by now, and there is genuine cause for celebration on this fiftieth anniversary of *Nostra Aetate*.

I opened with a Jewish blessing. Let me conclude with a Catholic one, a favorite of mine. These are the words of John Paul II: "As Christians and Jews . . . we are called to be a blessing to the world. . . . It is therefore necessary for us, Christians and Jews, to be first a blessing to one another."[21]

If we are not already there, we are certainly on our way.

19. Waxman, introduction, 37.

20. Pope Paul VI, *Nostra Aetate* (Declaration on the Relation of the Church to Non-Christian Religions), promulgated by Pope Paul VI together with the Fathers of the Second Vatican Council, October 28, 1965, 2–3.

21. Pope John Paul II, "Message of His Holiness John Paul II on the 50th Anniversary of the Warsaw Ghetto Uprising," April 6, 1993, http://www.vatican.va/.

Part V

Local Reception in the United States and the Academy

We cannot truly call upon God, the Father of all, if we refuse to behave as sisters and brothers with anyone, created as all are in the image of God. The relation of man and woman to God, the Father, and their relation to their fellow human beings are linked to such a degree that Holy Scripture says, "Whoever does not love does not know God" (1 Jn 4:8).

—*Nostra Aetate* 5, trans. Thomas F. Stransky, CSP

The Narrative Dimensions of Interreligious Dialogue

LARRY GOLEMON

H istorically, my organization—the Washington Theological Consortium—was founded in the wake of renewed energy for ecumenism after Vatican II, by Roman Catholic, Protestant, and Historically Black theological schools in the Washington, D.C., metro region. The Council's decree on ecumenism, *Unitatis Redintegratio*, provided a framework for a new kind of theological education of pastors, priests, and laity that combined a formation into specific Christian traditions with an intentional ecumenical formation. This first goal of the founders—to renew and deepen Christian unity among future religious leaders—became the raison d'être of the consortium. In more recent decades, the consortium has added newer evangelical schools toward that end. In addition, the consortium has added associate and affiliate members in spirituality, Islamic studies, and Christian-Jewish studies in pursuit of a second major goal: to foster interreligious dialogue and understanding. We are discovering once again that Vatican II, this time through *Nostra Aetate*, provides a framework and rationale for this work.

My observations on interreligious dialogue come from this context of a consortium of theological education, emphasizing the complementarity between ecumenical pedagogies and interreligious dialogue. I will place a number of lessons we in the consortium have learned within an interpretive framework, which I call "The Narrative Dimensions of Interreligious Dialogue." This framework draws on narrative theory and methods from psychology, education, leadership studies, and theology.[1] Regarding interreligious dialogue, the narrative dimensions we have employed include

---

1. Diana Butler Bass, *Christianity for the Rest of Us: How the Neighborhood Church Is Transforming Faith* (San Francisco: HarperSan Francisco, 2006), 11; Jerome Bruner, *The Culture of Education* (Cambridge, Mass.: Harvard University Press, 1996) and *Making Stories: Law, Literature, Life* (Cambridge, Mass.: Harvard University Press, 2003); Stephen Denning, *The Leader's Guide to Storytelling: Mastering the Art and Discipline of Business Narrative* (San Francisco: Jossey-Bass, 2005); Howard Gardner, *Changing Minds: The Art and Science of Changing Our Own and Other People's Minds* (Boston: Harvard Business School Press, 2006); Dan P. McAdams, *The Redemptive Self: Stories Americans Live By* (New York: Oxford University Press, 2006), 42; Anne Streaty Wimberly, *Soul Stories: African American Christian Education*, rev. ed. (Nashville: Abingdon, 2005).

Appreciative Narratives, Diverging Narratives, Reframing Narratives, and Healing Narratives.

Appreciative Narratives

The best entrée into interreligious dialogue for many people is through a process of personal storytelling accompanied by deep listening. We have all experienced the wide-eyed, eager novice to interreligious encounters, especially among the young or idealistic, which often describes many of our theological students. By drawing on distinct methods from Appreciative Inquiry and a pastoral care method called Active Listening,[2] we have shaped classroom dialogues that lead participants to share religious narratives with increasingly deep levels of disclosure—all in the spirit of openness and respect. Appreciative Narrative is especially effective in areas of building interfaith friendships and allowing for what some, like Fr. Tom Ryan of the Paulists, call "interreligious gift exchange" of different forms of prayer, meditation, or study.[3]

Unlike some interreligious dialogues, however, we have found that Appreciative Narratives, which stress the particularity of religious belief and practice as much as their similarity, do not yield a "one God, many paths" view of human spirituality but instead yield *surprising and perplexing* points of connection. For example, in a Muslim-Christian dialogue course on Views of Prophecy, co-taught by Dr. Richard Jones, chair of the consortium Al-Alwani, and Salih Sayilgan of The Catholic University of America, some Christian students share their surprise that Islam depicts Jesus as a true prophet, complete with a virgin birth and a second coming. Other students from sacramental traditions are more focused on Mary, and they are surprised to learn that she is considered one of the holiest of women in the Qur'an and even considered a prophetess by some Muslims. Muslim students share their deep appreciation of Islam and Mary and their place in the Qur'an, and the professors model appreciative dialogue in the class as they explain the traditions. Through such classes, a Baptist might gain a new appreciation of the place of the miracles and prophecy of Jesus in his own theology, and a future Episcopal priest can reclaim the

2. David Cooperrider and Diane Whitney, *The Appreciative Inquiry Handbook: For Leaders of Change*, 2nd ed. (San Francisco: Berrett-Koehler Publishers, 2008); David Hoppe, *Active Listening: Improve Your Ability to Listen and Lead* (Greensboro, N.C.: Center for Creative Leadership, 2008).

3. Fr. Thomas Ryan, CSP, used this phrase in a workshop for the consortium's "Emerging Trends in Interreligious Dialogue" in 2014. For implications, see Ryan, *Interreligious Prayer: A Christian Guide* (Mahwah, N.J.: Paulist Press, 2008).

Magnificat as a prophetic proclamation and see Mary as a model for her future ministry.

Even as Christian students appreciate the new connections with Islam in these courses, they can leave with perplexing thoughts: the Baptist is puzzled why Jesus did not really die on the cross in the Qur'an, the Episcopalian wonders why Islam has women prophets but no women imams, and a Catholic student asks himself why Mary's exalted holiness is not backed by a clear teaching about her own pure and miraculous conception. When done well, Appreciative Narratives lead to the second dimension: narratives about difference.

Diverging Narratives

Diverging Narratives emphasize the differences among religious faiths. They usually arise only over time and in a context of earned trust. This attention to difference requires just as much openness and respect as the Appreciative phase, but even more courage to articulate and listen for beliefs or practice that do not at first make much sense to the other. This stage of dialogue invites students to investigate the hard truths of another faith and, by reflection, those of their own.

This dimension is not easy, a fact illustrated for us in a recent Jewish-Christian immersion course for rabbinical students and Christian seminarians done in partnership with the Institute for Christian and Jewish Studies (ICJS) in Baltimore. The joint faculty of Jewish, Catholic, and Protestant scholars chose to "bracket" the question of "Jesus" in the first part of the week, trying instead to illustrate the difference between the Jewish and Christian traditions through distinct methods of reading and varying schools of biblical interpretation. Rabbi Ilyse Kramer of the ICJS and Dr. Brooks Schramm of Gettysburg Seminary led students one year in readings of the Hebrew Bible from both rabbinic and early Christian approaches, and another year Dr. Judy Fentress-Williams of Virginia Theological Seminary helped open the Hebrew Bible to multiple voices with a dialogical hermeneutic that could model interreligious readings.[4] Students deeply appreciated these different ways of reading scripture. The bracketing of Jesus, however, gave an implicit norm to some Christian students during sessions of sharing devotions from their own tradition, as they revised certain Christian prayers to de-emphasize or erase Jesus language, out of respect for their Jewish counterparts.

---

4. Judy Fentress-Williams, *Abingdon Old Testament Commentaries: Ruth* (Nashville: Abingdon Press, 2012).

In the most recent course, students from both traditions began to raise questions by midweek in their fishbowl sessions about why we did not discuss Jesus or understandings of the Messiah more directly. Some Jews asked Christian partners, "What does Jesus mean to you" or "How does his death save anyone?" Some evangelical and Catholic students asked questions like "Why do the Jews not accept Jesus as Messiah?" The exchange was lively and productive, and afterward the faculty opened up about Jesus talk in planned sessions that discussed the Jewishness of Jesus and the New Testament. Some students came to understand how important this question about Jesus was to Jewish-Christian dialogue, but others did not: one Christian student wrote of the fishbowl experiences, "I was mortified at the profusion of Jesus questions," while one of the Jewish students wrote, "I enjoyed asking the others how they understood Jesus—there were so many different answers!" Far from being an embarrassment, the difficult question of Jesus yielded an embarrassment of riches through deeper dialogue.

Reframing Narratives

Reframing Narratives between different religious traditions has become central to our pedagogies of interreligious and ecumenical dialogue in the consortium. As mentioned earlier, drawing on Jewish readings of the New Testament causes Christian students and faculty to see their tradition anew, and exploring nonsupersessionist theologies of Christianity helps Christians and Jews open up to a new appreciation of the entire biblical canon and to explore the possibility of a shared destiny or purpose. We believe that studying these approaches is crucial if we are to continue to move forward, even if it means reframing some of our own faith's doctrines from the past. I understand this reframing according to George Lindbeck's paradigm of honoring the original grammar of a doctrine but seeking new articulations of it.[5]

For example, when Muslim students are part of our consortium courses, they inevitably ask, "Why do you Christians see Jesus as the Son of God and not primarily as a prophet? This seems to lead to a dualistic or tri-theistic view of God." One professor in the consortium, Dr. Ian Markham of Virginia Theological Seminary, often explains the divine nature of Jesus, and by implication the Trinity, in a way that is distinct from the comparative religions tradition of comparing Jesus to the Prophet

---

5. George Lindbeck, *The Nature of Doctrine: Religion and Theology in a Postliberal Age* (Louisville, Ky.: Westminster/John Knox, 2009).

Muhammad. "I prefer to compare Jesus to the Qur'an." He goes on to explain how for Christians, Jesus *is* the Word of God, with all the holiness and completeness of a final revelation of God, similar to what Islam teaches of the Qur'an. "So at the center of your faith," he says, "is a divine book and the prophet who received it, and at the center of our faith is a divine person, and the book that witnesses to him." He sums up, "Because we, too, believe that God is a personal God, and because Jesus is a divine person, we see them in each other: one as Son of the Father." This, of course, does not settle the question for the Muslims, but it does cause them to pause and reflect, because this reframing of the Christian teaching about Jesus's divinity offers them a totally new way of thinking about this core Christian doctrine.

The most difficult Reframing Narratives deal with living memories of abuse and violence between the Abrahamic faiths. These historical and interpretive questions are often harder, in our experience, than theological ones. ICJS scholars helped us face histories of conflict in our traditions, including Dr. Heather Miller Rubens's examination of religion and domestic violence and Dr. Chris Leighton's examination of the close ties between the horrors of the *Shoah* with the centuries of Christian theology's anti-Judaism. Consortium scholars, Dr. Katherine Grieb of Virginia Theological Seminary and Brooks Schramm, helped us reclaim Paul's Letter to the Romans, chapters 9 through 11, as a new paradigm for seeing God's covenant with Israel continuing side by side with that of the Church.[6] And another year, Dr. Kendall Soulen of Wesley Theological Seminary helped us explore a canonical theology that was nonsupersessionist.[7] I explained to one colleague how this work helps with the healing of memories in interreligious dialogue akin to that important phrase in Christian ecumenism, and he asked thoughtfully, "Do you think all memories can be healed?" This leads to our final dimension and challenge.

Healing Narratives

Those of you active in ecumenical dialogues know the importance of the healing of memories in recent times. Pope John Paul II emphasized this work with the Eastern Orthodox in *Orientale Lumen*, and many bilateral dialogues—including Lutheran-Mennonite, Catholic-Mennonite, Catholic-Reformed—have developed a process for the healing of memo-

---

6. A. Katherine Grieb, *The Story of Romans: A Narrative Defense of God's Righteousness* (Chicago: University of Chicago Press, 2004).

7. R. Kendall Soulen, *The God of Israel in Christian Theology* (Minneapolis: Fortress Press, 1996).

ries.[8] This includes fresh narrations of the history of Reformation conflicts written by representatives from each tradition, then studied by the other group, followed by a rewriting of one's own history that acknowledges misunderstandings, missteps, and even grievous sins by one's own religious tradition. The phrase "healing of memories" has been picked up in international conflict and peace studies—by Religions for Peace, schools for conflict resolution, and even diplomats as a key to international conflict resolution and peacebuilding, especially where religious difference is involved.

In the consortium, we occasionally glimpse Healing Narratives in classrooms, as noted above in the Jewish-Christian course, but we have learned more about them from our public dialogues and lectures, which include an annual event on interreligious dynamics of peacebuilding and another in Muslim-Christian dialogue. Here are a few accounts.

One scholar from Eastern Mennonite University, Dr. Lisa Schirch, specializing in Conflict Resolution and Peacebuilding, narrates a history of persecution against her Mennonite ancestors, but less as a judgment against other Christian communities and more as a crucible within which the Mennonite commitment to peace and pacifism was purified and sealed. When she shares this narrative on the ground in her peacebuilding in Afghanistan or Iraq, she builds bridges with various Muslim and Eastern Christian communities that have living memories of persecution, and she opens a new kind of dialogue about religious diversity as a resource for peacemaking.[9]

One Jewish scholar from George Mason University's School of Conflict Analysis and Resolution, Dr. Marc Gopin, tells a story of the importance of self-examination and change of heart, whereby he shares with Palestinians and Jews in the Middle East how his own blind defense of Israeli leaders changed over time to one of challenging them to ongoing peace dialogues toward a two-state solution. This has opened Jewish and Palestinian hearts to re-examine their own "stuck" narratives about the land and each other, thereby moving from narratives of enmity toward ones of coexistence.[10]

8. Pope John Paul II, *Orientale Lumen* (Vatican City: Libreria Editrice Vaticana, May 2, 1995); International Dialogue between the Catholic Church and the Mennonite World Conference, *Called Together to be Peacemakers* (Kitchener, Canada: Pandora Press, 2005); The Lutheran-Mennonite International Study Commission, *Healing Memories: Reconciling in Christ* (Geneva, Switzerland: Lutheran World Federation; Strasbourg, France: Mennonite World Conference, 2010).

9. See, e.g., Lisa Schirch, *Ritual and Symbol in Peacebuilding* (Bloomfield, Conn.: Kumarian Press, 2005), 5–7.

10. See, e.g., Marc Gopin, *Bridges across an Impossible Divide: The Inner Lives of Arab and Jewish Peacemakers* (New York: Oxford University Press, 2012).

Another pair of scholars addressed "Violence in the Name of Religion" this spring—Dr. Amr Abdalla from Addis Ababa University Center for Peace and Ambassador Anthony Quainton from the School of International Service at American University. Each of them lifted up the importance of taking accountability for wrongdoings between Muslim and Christian traditions. The Christian scholar, Dr. Quainton, reminded everyone of the living memory of the Crusades among Muslims and Eastern Orthodox and the call for true and penitential accounting by his faith community. The Muslim scholar, Dr. Abdalla, reminded everyone of the dominant role of sharī'ah law in Muslim-dominated societies and called on Muslims scholars to reframe sharī'ah to acknowledge religious plurality and democracy of modern societies. They also called on each other's traditions for an accounting: one called on Christians to take account of the neocolonial exploits of the nineteenth century, and the other called on Muslims to continue challenging the abuses of their tradition by radical jihadists. This call to accountability is a mixture of historical reframing, testimony, and confession—all of which creates a new dynamic of healing of memories over time.[11]

These are our discoveries so far through our classroom and community work in interreligious and ecumenical dialogue: that an approach through Appreciation, Difference, Reframing, and Healing Narratives can deepen and move this dialogue forward in the future.

---

11. To review a video of this address, visit "WTC Al Alwani Lectures 2015," https://www.youtube.com/watch?v=CrHpuKp_lsg&index=2&list=PLAVUi2N7KxM7sP5oIs5hCp UiX0c7FB8LK.

Official Jewish-Catholic Conversations in the United States: Origins, Content, and Future

John W. Crossin, OSFS

As earlier essays in this volume point out, *Nostra Aetate* began as a document focused on the Church's relationship with the Jews. The Church throughout the world, but particularly in the United States, has taken special care in following its teaching with regard to Catholic-Jewish dialogue.[1] As indicated in the essays by Cardinal Dolan and by Rabbi Noam Marans, the document's fiftieth anniversary is being celebrated not only by the symposium but by Catholics and Jews throughout the country. Two members of our consultations in the United States—Rabbi David Sandmel and Rabbi Gilbert S. Rosenthal—have also authored or edited major works for the anniversary.[2]

There are many forms of official Catholic-Jewish interactions in the United States. Numerous Catholic archdioceses have regular and most cordial conversations and collaborations with local Jewish organizations. More than twenty Catholic colleges and universities sponsor centers for Jewish studies. These form, with other similar institutions, the group of Centers for Christian Jewish Relations that sponsors both a yearly conference and ongoing communication and collaboration.

This essay focuses on the formal relationships with the Jewish community sponsored by the Bishops Committee on Ecumenical and Interreligious Affairs (BCEIA) of the United States Conference of Catholic

---

1. A concise overview of Jewish-Catholic relations since Vatican II can be found in the annual Catholic Almanac: Matthew E. Bunson, *Our Sunday Visitor's Catholic Almanac 2015*, 605–11 (Huntington, Ind.: Our Sunday Visitor, 2014).

2. Rabbi Sandmel presented "Our Spiritual Patrimony: A Jewish perspective on the Transformation of Jewish-Catholic Relations" as the twentieth annual Joseph Cardinal Bernardin Jerusalem Lecture given on March 9, 2015, in Chicago. Published as David Sandmel, "20th Annual Joseph Cardinal Bernardin Jerusalem Lecture," August 10, 2015, http://www.archchicago.org/departments/ecumenical/Lecture2015.htm (accessed January 22, 2016).

Rabbi Rosenthal edited an outstanding book of essays with contributions from many of the leading scholars and practitioners involved in Jewish-Catholic dialogue today: Gilbert S. Rosenthal, *A Jubilee for All Time: The Copernican Revolution in Jewish-Christian Relations* (Eugene, Ore.: Pickwick Publications, 2014).

Bishops (USCCB). The bishop chairman of the BCEIA, currently Bishop Mitchell Rozanski of Springfield, Massachusetts, is the de facto chief ecumenical/interreligious representative of the USCCB. He was a noted participant at the May 2015 *Nostra Aetate* conference at The Catholic University of America, introducing speakers and attending both the formal sessions and the informal meetings.

The official report on the BCEIA Meeting of April 24, 1996, will help set the stage for my reflections.[3] Under "Relations with National Council of Synagogues (NCS)," the report says,

> This is a new group that has emerged out of the demise of the old Synagogue Council of America, with which we have had a BCEIA consultation since 1987. The NCS is composed of four "founding members," the rabbinical and congregational associations of Reform and Conservative Judaism. It will carry forward discussions with us not only on Social/communal agenda items, but also theological and pastoral. Both Cardinals [John] O'Connor and [William] Keeler were present for the meeting on October 20 held at the Union of American Hebrew Congregations in New York.[4]

The report goes on to mention "Relations with Orthodox Judaism" and says, "Representatives of the *Rabbinical Council of America* (RCA) and the *Union of Orthodox Jewish Congregations* (OU) will meet with Cardinal O'Connor and BCEIA staff for an exploratory session on Mary 17, 1996 at the NY Pastoral Center."[5] This discussion led to the current conversation of the BCEIA with Orthodox Jews held once or twice a year for a day, usually in New York.

The report concludes by saying, "The theme of the National Workshop on Christian-Jewish Relations is 'Seeking God: The Challenge of Being Religious in America,' Oct. 27–30 at the Stamford, CT, Sheraton." These national workshops began in 1973 as a Catholic-Jewish event but quickly expanded to become a national Christian-Jewish workshop that continued for many years.[6]

---

3. This report can be found using the committee name and date in the Archives of the Secretariat for Ecumenical and Interreligious Affairs of the USCCB, Washington, D.C.

4. Ibid., 2.

5. Ibid.

6. See "National Workshop on Christian-Jewish Relations," http://www.jcrelations.net/Background.2599.0.html?L=3 (accessed August 10, 2015).

Consultation with the National Council of Synagogues

The twice-yearly meetings between the representatives of the Council of Synagogues and the representatives of the Bishops Committee usually have taken place in New York City or in Baltimore. The agendas of the one-day meeting are set jointly by the co-chairs of the consultation, with appointed experts from each group organizing the topics and invited speakers who have expertise in the topic.

The Jewish participants have been and are distinguished rabbis and Jewish scholars. The Catholic participants have been (arch)bishops, priests, and lay Catholic leaders and scholars. Sometimes distinguished Jewish or Catholic observers or seminary students are also included.

The BCEIA makes three concise reports on these meetings each year to the Administrative Committee of the USCCB. While the rich conversations over almost three decades would be difficult to summarize, I would note several key factors that give the flavor of this relationship:

1. The consultation depends in many ways on **the relationships of the participants**. Thus, the meetings often take time for people to share about their lives and work. There is always a meal where conversations can be shared among smaller groups of participants. There has been a consistency over time with the members on the dialogue, and thus the members have gotten to know one another more deeply. This enables the members to be quite honest with one another. Sometimes the conversation partners seek mutual understanding with the help of speakers drawn from the group or from outside. At other times they will inform each other of what is going on in their communities. As the occasion demands, they address thorny issues.

2. In reading the reports on the meetings, I find it interesting to note **the international influence on the work**. Documents on Jewish-Christian relations that appear from the Vatican, such as *We Remember: Reflections on the* Shoah, are examined thoroughly.[7] This document produced quite a discussion both in the dialogue and well beyond. Subsequently the USCCB published *Catholics Remember the Holocaust*, which brought together a host of reflections on *We Remember* by bishops conferences in different parts of the world, as well as the key explanatory address given by Cardinal Cassidy, president of the Pontifical Council for Promoting Christian Unity.

---

7. See *We Remember: Reflections on the* Shoah, March 16, 1998, http://www.vatican.va/roman_curia/pontifical_councils/chrstuni/documents/rc_pc_chrstuni_doc_16031998_shoah_en.html (accessed August 10, 2015).

Besides the discussion of documents just mentioned, papal journeys, reports on the meetings of the International Jewish Committee on Interreligious Consultations, summaries of what is happening in Israel such as the rise of the "Price-tag" attacks on Palestinians, and negotiations between Israel and the Vatican over their concordat are mentioned regularly and often discussed at the consultations.

3. Of course, many theological topics have been addressed over the years such as importance of the land of Israel, the death penalty, mixed marriages, and the sources of authority, to name but a few. One important recent discussion topic was the *Jewish Annotated New Testament*.[8] In the report on the May 22, 2012, meeting, the authors noted,

> In his response, Father Professor John Donahue of Loyola University in Baltimore described the volume as "an outstanding book" containing splendid commentaries of the books of the New Testament as well as fine essays at the end of the volume on a variety of vital subjects. Professor Donahue recommended that it become a primary or accompanying text in every seminary, along with the *Jewish Study Bible*, which he extolled.[9]

4. The conversation has issued a number of joint statements. These include the following:

- "A Lesson of Value"—Moral Education in the Public Schools (1990)
- On Pornography (1993)
- On Dealing with Holocaust Revisionism (1994)
- To End the Death Penalty (1999)
- Reconciliation and Hope: A Reflection on the Occasion of Pope John Paul II's Historic Pilgrimage to Israel (2000)
- Condemning Acts of Religious Hatred (2000)[10]

There are also a few statements from one of the partners, such as Cardinal Keeler's condemnation of attacks on three synagogues in California on behalf of the USCCB in 1998 and "A Statement of Concern Regarding Anti-Christian Acts," issued by NCS in 2015.

---

8. Amy-Jill Levine and Marc Zvi Brettler, eds., *Jewish Annotated New Testament* (New York: Oxford University Press, 2010).

9. NCS-BCEIA (USCCB) Consultation, "Study and Critique of the New Volume *The Jewish Annotated New Testament*, and Other Topics," May 22, 2012, http://nationalcouncilofsynagogues.org/presentations-prior-dialogue-programs (accessed February 22, 2015).

10. See the website of the Council of Synagogues, "Presentations from Prior Dialogue Programs," http://nationalcouncilofsynagogues.org/presentations-prior-dialogue-programs (accessed August 10, 2015).

5. There have also been a series of discussions of controversial matters. For example, for many Jews, Mel Gibson's *The Passion of the Christ* recalled past passion plays that triggered violence against Jews. The consultation issued a joint communiqué on May 19, 2004, responding to the movie.[11]

A more recent controversy centered on a document from the consultation itself, *Reflections on Covenant and Mission*, issued on August 12, 2002. The reaction to certain claims of this document by some Catholics and other Christians led to a statement titled "A Note on Ambiguities Contained in Reflections on Covenant and Mission" issued by the BCEIA and the USCCB Committee on Doctrine on June 18, 2009. The note of clarification provoked considerable comment and discussion within the dialogue, and as a result this "Note" was revised by the USCCB, and on October 2, 2009, a "Statement of Principles for Catholic-Jewish Dialogue" was issued.[12]

Archbishop Wilton Gregory, in his report regarding the March 23–24 meeting of the Administrative Committee, noted:

> The Bishops also issued a Statement of Principles for Catholic-Jewish Dialogue (October 2009) which said that dialogue "has never been used by the Catholic Church as a means of proselytism—nor is it intended as a disguised invitation to baptism. In dialogue, Catholics expect to meet Jews who are faithful to their traditions just as we expect Catholic participants to be faithful to the teachings of the Church."[13]

Consultation with the Orthodox Union and the Rabbinical Council of America

The consultation initiated in the mid-nineties between the BCEIA and the OU/RCA continues to take place at least once, if not twice, a year. There are many similarities between this conversation and the conversation

---

11. "National Catholic-Jewish Dialogue Warns against Antisemitic Uses of Gibson's *Passion*," http://www.bc.edu/content/dam/files/research_sites/cjl/texts/cjrelations/news/News_May2004.htm (accessed August 10, 2015).

12. These documents can be found under "Documents and Reports," http://www.usccb.org/beliefs-and-teachings/ecumenical-and-interreligious/jewish/catholic-jewish-documents-and-news-releases.cfm#CP_JUMP_106982 (accessed August 10, 2015). See Sandmel, "Our Spiritual Patrimony."

13. Page 53 of official report for the March 23–24 meeting of the Administrative Committee of the USCCB, Archives of the Secretariat for Ecumenical and Interreligious Affairs of the USCCB, Washington, D.C.

with the NCS discussed previously. A distinctive element of this consultation is that it is practical in nature and not theological per se. This is due to
the distinctive authoritative teaching and the practical orientation of Orthodox Judaism. At the May 2013 meeting of the consultation, Dr. Berger
offered "a presentation and reflection on Rabbi Joseph B. Soloveitchik's
landmark work 'Confrontation,' originally published in *Tradition: A Journal
of Orthodox Thought* in 1964. This article explored the nature and limits of
interreligious theological dialogue and offered guidelines for Orthodox
Judaism in dialogue with Christians." A sustained discussion of the implications of the Rabbi Soloveitchik's thesis followed the presentation.[14]

Orthodox Jews and Catholics share certain common interests. Both
communities sponsor religious schools and seek further support in the
states. These concerns are reviewed regularly. While the consultation rarely
issues a common statement, it approved a "Joint Statement on School
Choice" on October 25, 2006.[15]

Catholics and the Orthodox Jewish community often share similar
concerns about the changing stances on moral issues in the wider American culture. Thus, there are discussions of the value of life, the definition
of marriage, and other questions of public concern. The consultation
issued the statement "Created in the Divine Image: Orthodox Jewish-
Catholic Statement on Marriage" on September 2, 2008.[16]

Looking to the Future

The preceding summary highlights some important elements of
Catholic-Jewish consultations in the United States over the last three
decades. There are two rich conversations going on in the United States
under the sponsorship of the Bishops Committee on Ecumenical and
Interreligious Affairs.

What might the future hold? Each of the essays in the Catholic-
Jewish section of this book point to the future. To cite just one, Cardinal
Dolan, in his keynote, lists five important areas for future collaboration.
These include four pastoral areas where he discovers that we have a great

---

14. USCCB Information Report, September 2013, Archives of the Secretariat for Ecumenical and Interreligious Affairs of the USCCB, Washington, D.C.

15. This can be found at "Joint Statement on School Choice," http://www.usccb.
org/beliefs-and-teachings/ecumenical-and-interreligious/jewish/upload/Joint-Statement-
on-School-Choice-2006.pdf (accessed August 10, 2015).

16. "Created in the Divine Image: Orthodox Jewish-Catholic Statement on Marriage,"
http://www.usccb.org/beliefs-and-teachings/ecumenical-and-interreligious/jewish/upload/
Created-in-the-Divine-Image-Orthodox-Jewish-Catholic-Statement-on-Marriage-2008.
pdf (accessed August 10, 2015).

deal in common and where we can fruitfully collaborate—dealing with the effects of secularization, the decline in church and synagogue membership, the increase in religious persecution, and the turn away from belief in sin and redemption.

Rabbi Sandmel, in discussing work that remains to be done, identifies Israel, the *Shoah*, and, above all, covenant and mission as important issues. I think he has identified central questions for ongoing personal and communal reflection and sharing.[17]

These are major questions, and they each deserve extensive thought and conversation; we should not expect immediate definitive conclusions. To me, the discussion over covenant and mission led to the practical and honest modus operandi articulated by Archbishop Gregory. But I think that for Catholics, the underlying theological questions have not been completely resolved—and maybe never will be. I believe that the fifty years since *Nostra Aetate* are a rather short period of time to discuss such important questions.[18] It may take another fifty years or more to develop further in-depth thinking. This long-term view fits in with items I discussed more in detail in my own Bernardin Lecture.[19]

We need to develop a **new narrative**, including both pastoral and theological elements, for a new era of Catholic-Jewish relations. We need to look at the impact of the Enlightenment, the influence of the economy, and the importance of interdependence, to mention just three items, in developing this new narrative.

We also need to search for a **common history** that would attend to both the light and the darkness of our past. We need to work for an **in-depth understanding of one another's theological frameworks** so as to dialogue more deeply and effectively.

What I am suggesting is that a new and coherent mode of Catholic-Jewish self-understanding and acting can emerge in this postmodern period. We might be developing a common—or perhaps better, an overlapping—frame of reference (or even worldview) for studying our common texts, sharing our religious concerns, and aiding those in need.

Catholic-Jewish conversations have come far in these fifty years. There are many challenges and possibilities up ahead.

17. See Sandmel, "Our Spiritual Patrimony."

18. I should note in passing that there was a fortieth-anniversary celebration of *Nostra Aetate* at The Catholic University of America, the John Paul II Cultural Center, and the USCCB. One featured speaker was Cardinal Walter Kasper, then president of the Pontifical Council for Promoting Christian Unity.

19. John Crossin, "19th Annual Joseph Cardinal Bernardin Jerusalem Lecture," March 31, 2014, http://www.archchicago.org/departments/ecumenical/Lecture2014.htm (accessed August 11, 2015).

Continuing on the Path of *Nostra Aetate*: A Summary of Recent Developments and Future Possibilities for the Interreligious Dialogues of the U.S. Conference of Catholic Bishops

ANTHONY CIRELLI

Introduction

In this essay, I will review the accomplishments of the United States Conference of Catholic Bishops' (USCCB) Secretariat of Ecumenical and Interreligious Affairs (SEIA) and its dialogue partners, as well as some of the challenges faced and the future prospects within these dialogues. My goal is not simply to document concrete "products" such as agreed statements and other publications but, rather, to demonstrate the positive and particular virtues of each dialogue that have, in the spirit of *Nostra Aetate*, contributed to the overall success of our work together. Before discussing each of the dialogues in turn, I will open briefly with the importance of *Nostra Aetate* for the post–Vatican II mission of the Church, commenting on the singular role of the popes and the need for a developed faith, as well as the importance of the long study of other traditions. I then will proceed to examine the role of the USCCB in regard to interreligious dialogue over the past fifty years.

The Watershed of Nostra Aetate

With the promulgation of *Nostra Aetate* at the close of the Second Vatican Council in 1965, an intentional ecclesial commitment to interreligious dialogue commenced a new era of engagement with the world's religions. The singular importance of this document, which can rightly be called the Magna Carta or foundation document of interreligious dialogue for the Catholic Church, is obvious to those familiar with Church history, as it marks the first time that dialogue with—rather than (as a primary motive) conversion of—the adherents of other faith traditions would be incorporated into the mission of the Church in the world. And this mandate, which is central to the mission of the Church in the modern world, is an irrevocable dimension of ecclesial life, as Pope John Paul II made plain when, on the eve of the catastrophe of 9/11, he voiced his opinion that world peace required intentional dialogue between cultures and religions and that the Church, in fidelity to the teachings of the Second Vatican Council, shall be committed to this endeavor in the new millennium.[1] Pope John Paul II was singularly prescient in his understanding of the necessity for interreligious dialogue, as captured in his remarks on the Day of Prayer for Peace in Assisi in 1986: "either we learn to walk together in peace and harmony, or we drift apart and ruin ourselves and others."[2]

With respect to the implementation of *Nostra Aetate*, two offices are of crucial importance. First, there is the Secretariat for Non-Christians, which was established in 1964 and in 1988 was renamed the Pontifical Council for Interreligious Dialogue (PCID). Second, there is the establishment of parallel offices for interreligious dialogues that emerged within national episcopal conferences following Vatican II, while in the United States, the National Conference of Catholic Bishops, which was renamed the United States Conference of Catholic Bishops, introduced an interreligious mandate to complement its work in ecumenical relations.[3] With the establishment of these international (PCID) and national (SEIA) offices, the mandate of *Nostra Aetate* for the Church to engage "followers of other religions" in "conversations and collaboration" with "prudence and love" was set in motion.[4] This historical phenomenon in the life of the church (i.e., *Nostra Aetate* and the subsequent establishment of the PCID and SEIA) is truly a miracle when one considers that only a few decades prior to its promulgation, the encyclical *Mortalium Animos*, a strident rejection of intentional dialogue with other Christians that was *not* aimed at "return" or, in the case of other religions, conversion, was written by Pope Pius XI in 1928—less than forty years prior to the promulgation of *Nostra Aetate*! Reading this papal case *against* dialogue, it is striking how the Church utterly changed direction with respect to dialogue in such a relatively short span of time. This encyclical, considered a part of the ordinary magisterium, was nothing novel at the time; it merely captured centuries of intentional nonengagement with other religious groups in official, sanctioned dialogues (the "crisis of modernity," from at least the papacy of Gre-

---

1. Pope John Paul II, *Novo Millennio Ineunte*, Apostolic Letter, January 6, 2001, par. 55. (This and all subsequent references from popes are taken from official translations of the Vatican, which can be found on the Vatican website, http://w2.vatican.va.)

2. "Address of John Paul II to the Representatives of the Christian Churches and Ecclesial Communities and of the World Religions," October 27, 1986, par. 5.

3. The USCCB first established the Commission of Ecumenical Affairs in 1964, which subsequently was renamed the Secretariat for Ecumenical and Interreligious Affairs in 1966. However, interreligious work did not fully emerge at the SEIA until 1987, when staff were added precisely for this purpose.

4. *Nostra Aetate* 2, trans. Thomas F. Stransky, CSP.

gory XVI to Pius XII, only amplified suspicion of such efforts at dialogue from within the Church). In short, *Nostra Aetate* was a watershed in the history of the Church as it set a new and irrevocable course to engage in dialogue with non-Christians—and the results of this new direction have been overwhelmingly positive; not least because, since the promulgation of *Nostra Aetate*, the Church and her non-Christian dialogue partners' commitment to authentic dialogue has, arguably, done more to promote greater understanding, stability, and goodwill among religions than any other single endeavor.

Papal Leadership on Interreligious Dialogue

The subsequent success of the PCID and the SEIA in establishing vital and enduring dialogues did not emerge without assistance; on the contrary, it must be understood that the decades of tangible gains made in dialogue with the world's religions are directly linked, from the perspective of the Church, to the unswerving commitment and leadership of the post–Vatican II popes. For example, Pope Paul VI boldly announced to the world a new era of dialogue in 1964: "The Church must enter into dialogue with the world in which it lives. It has something to say, a message to give, a communication to make."[5] And as we have seen, Pope John Paul II throughout his papacy affirmed the work of dialogue not just in words but in actions as he perseveringly and unprecedentedly reached out to non-Christians in his many travels around the globe. To the leaders and communities of non-Catholics, this pope—the first in history to enter both a synagogue and a mosque—won the respect and friendship of millions, which in turn helped build a foundation of trust and collaboration for the PCID and the SEIA. Pope Benedict XVI and now Pope Francis have continued unabatedly this commitment of their predecessors to dialogue.

On the one hand, despite the difficulties caused by his well-known 2006 Regensburg Lecture, Pope Benedict nevertheless deepened the conversation with other religions by his continual emphasis on an understanding of dialogue as a commitment to the pursuit of truth— that is, the truth about God, man, and the world—truth that is pursued with love and respect for the other. This is a point he made plain in his address to the participants in the tenth plenary assembly of the PCID in 2008 when he declared, "It is the love of Christ which impels the Church to reach out to every human being without distinction, beyond the borders of the visible Church ... it is love that urges every believer to listen to the other and to

---

5. Pope Paul VI, *Ecclesiam Suam*, Encyclical, August 6, 1964, par. 65.

seek areas of collaboration."[6] In order to manifest this priority of love for
the other as a key component of interreligious dialogue, Pope Benedict
promoted the idea of interreligious dialogue as collaboration in practical
ministries that express "the highest ideals of each religious tradition . . .
helping the sick, bringing relief to the victims of natural disasters or violence, caring for the aged and the poor.... I encourage all those who are
inspired by the teaching of their religions to help the suffering members
of society."[7]

On the other hand, Pope Francis has continued this emphasis on collaborative acts of practical concern, especially in the alleviation of suffering,
as a central and defining characteristic of interreligious dialogue. In doing
so, not least through his own example, he has nurtured the seeds planted
by Benedict XVI and, perhaps definitively, has turned the Church's orientation toward an understanding of interreligious dialogue as an opportunity
to join with non-Christians in alleviating the suffering of other humans,
especially the most vulnerable. With all the post–Vatican II popes, therefore, it is not an exaggeration to suggest that a powerful and consistent
thread of support for interreligious dialogue is evident, even though the
particular emphasis of each pope has been different.

The Persistence of Memory

Perhaps the main lesson learned since the exciting journey began fifty
years ago is the relative impossibility of simply forgetting centuries of violence and conflict and moving on to brighter shores of interreligious harmony and goodwill, as *Nostra Aetate* somewhat jejunely invited the world's
religious followers to do.[8] John Paul II developed this originating goal
without losing the thread: to him, forgetting is not something we can do,
but forgiving in the midst of our pain both historical and present is something possible, indeed necessary, as he made clear in his 2002 message for
the World Day of Peace when he said there can be "[n]o peace without justice, no justice without forgiveness: this is what in this message I wish to
say to believers and unbelievers alike, to all men and women of good will
who are concerned for the good of the human family and for its future."[9]

---

6. Benedict XVI, "Address of His Holiness Benedict XVI to Participants in the Tenth
Assembly of the Pontifical Council for Interreligious Dialogue," *Pro Dialogo* 129, no. 3
(2008): 153.
    7. Ibid.
    8. *Nostra Aetate* 3.
    9. John Paul II, "Message of His Holiness Pope John Paul II for the World Day of
Peace," published in *Origins* 31, no. 28 (December 20, 2001): 466.

With Pope Francis, we see the importance of forgiveness accompanied with mercy. And yet one might argue that forgiveness and mercy require something prior—namely, a willingness to make oneself vulnerable to the grace of God that alone enables us to cultivate a *disposition* that is forgiving, merciful, kind, patient, generous, and, perhaps above all, welcoming.

To move beyond the sad and often violent history between religions, the hard work of dialogue must also occupy itself with intensive, careful study of other religions. This study includes the sober task of understanding our mutual narrative histories, which, in the context of academic dialogue, are given priority as participants strive to explain themselves (i.e., their historical and cultural self-understanding) to one another. Over years of patient and attentive listening, this approach has led inextricably to a gradual shedding of past grievances in favor of collaborative interests grounded in trust and friendship. Despite the claims of some that this slow process has been fruitless, intentional and effective dialogue has contributed to the gradual understanding of and moving beyond the negative complexities of historical relations between religions. Intentional dialogue, in short, facilitates the emergence of spaces of encounter that make possible greater understanding and collaboration and thus leads to mutual esteem and friendship. Technical, academic dialogue, therefore, must continue alongside the more increasingly popular praxis-oriented, collaborative model.

Having provided a brief opening on the importance of *Nostra Aetate* for the post–Vatican II mission of the Church, with commentary on the singular role of the popes and the need for a developed faith—so as to allow God's grace to establish the capacity for a welcoming disposition (something critical for sustaining a successful dialogue)—and long study of other traditions (i.e., their languages, history, culture, etc.), I shall now provide a brief summary of the more particular role of the USCCB's SEIA in carrying out the vision and mandate of *Nostra Aetate* in the United States. I will document the accomplishments of the USCCB and our partners in interreligious dialogue since 2005 since a summary of the SEIA's interreligious dialogues was written by John Borelli in 2004.

Our Recent Dialogues with Muslims

Nostra Aetate began the conversation on Islam by saying something quite the opposite of the long-historical narrative (re-emerging after 9/11) that has understood Muslims as "the enemy," declaring: "The Church also regards with esteem the Muslims."[10] This regard, it goes on to say, origi-

---

10. *Nostra Aetate* 3, trans. Thomas F. Stransky, CSP.

nates with a common belief in monotheism, the "One God," which is made even more explicit in *Lumen Gentium* 16. These passages continually have been affirmed, most explicitly by John Paul II, with the implication that the common thread that connects Christians to Muslims (and Jews) is a shared belief in the God of Abraham. This shared status as worshippers is the first fruit of our decades-long encounter with Muslims. However, Muslims will need to continue to deepen their own study and reflection on this question of belief in a common god, which is made difficult by their reading of Christian Trinitarian thought as a polytheistic perversion of divine revelation. Second, as Archbishop Michael Fitzgerald has pointed out, the main frustration of the Muslim community regarding *Nostra Aetate* has been the lack of any reference to Muhammad.[11] Nevertheless, John Paul II opened the door for a Christian regard for their founding prophet when, as Fitzgerald notes, he asserted in his General Audience of September 9, 1998,

> It must be kept in mind that every quest of the human spirit for truth and goodness, and in the last analysis for God, is inspired by the Holy Spirit. The various religions arose primarily from this primordial openness to God. At their origins we often find founders who, with the help of God's Spirit, achieved a deeper religious experience.[12]

And so, these two basic observations are significant, if rudimentary, and demonstrate that progress has been achieved in a remarkably short period of time despite the backdrop of long centuries of conflict.

Regional Accomplishments

Until very recently (May 2015), the U.S. dialogue with Muslims has been conducted on a regional basis. As John Borelli noted more than ten years ago, points of consensus in major areas of our respective traditions have been discerned through dialogue.[13] For example, the West Coast group produced an important statement of consensus in 2003 that demonstrates how in matters of extreme importance—in this case, peace and jus-

---

11. Michael L. Fitzgerald, "Interreligious Relations Today: The Remarkable Relevance of *Nostra Aetate*," *Pro Dialogo* 119, no. 2 (2005): 191.

12. Ibid. For a comprehensive presentation of the teachings on interreligious dialogue of recent popes see Francesco Gioia, ed., *Interreligious Dialogue: The Official Teaching of the Catholic Church from the Second Vatican Council to John Paul II (1963-2005)* (Boston: Pauline Books and Media, 2006).

13. See http://www.usccb.org/beliefs-and-teachings/ecumenical-and-interreligious/interreligious/islam/christian-muslim-dialogue.cfm.

tice and forgiveness—dialogue can be an effective means of coming to some understanding that, in turn, can be used as a resource in our formation programs, et cetera. This statement reads:

1. We, Catholics and Muslims, believe that God is the source of peace and justice, and thus we fundamentally agree on the nature of peace and justice and the essential need of all to work for peace and justice.
2. Our rich teachings and traditions of peace and justice serve as a resource and inspiration for all; however, our immediate and present actions to work together are often wanting. The need to work together for peace and justice is a pressing demand in these troubled times.
3. We believe that it is God who forgives and that as Catholics and Muslims we are called by God to offer forgiveness. Forgiveness is an important step to moving beyond our past history if we are to preserve human dignity, to effect justice, and to work for peace.
4. We may disagree on certain points of doctrine, even as we respect the others' rights to believe in the fundamental integrity of their teachings and affirm all their human and religious rights. With love and in the pursuit of truth, we will offer our criticisms of one another when we believe there is a violation of integrity of faith in God. We must avoid demonizing one another and misrepresenting one another's teachings and traditions.
5. When we meet in dialogue and discuss matters of peace, justice, and forgiveness, while being faithful to our traditions, we have experienced a profound and moving connection on the deepest level of our faith, which must take effect in our lives.[14]

In addition, the areas of difficulty Borelli identified remain as well: mutually false perceptions that often result in stereotyping one another and the confusion and misunderstanding that arise with different approaches to structure, language, and culture. All of these broad topics of difference are deeply embedded but can be overcome through education, which requires effective dialogue in which Muslims and Christians encounter one another in an environment of mutual respect.

It so happens that each of the three regional dialogues was founded in the five years before September 11, 2001. The Midwest dialogue, founded in 1996, is jointly sponsored by the USCCB and the Islamic Society of North America. The mid-Atlantic dialogue, founded in 1998, is jointly sponsored by the USCCB and the Islamic Circle of North America. The West Coast dialogue is jointly sponsored by the USCCB and both the Islamic Society of Orange County, which represents the Sunni community, and the Islamic Educational Center of Orange County, which is run by the Shia community.

14. Ibid.

The dialogues have varied in terms of the composition of their membership, the consistency of their participants, and their public visibility. All of the groups include scholars, clerics (priests and imams), and diocesan officers for interreligious affairs. The Midwest in particular has been blessed with a group of participants (some of whom have been organizing joint Catholic and Muslim local dialogues for decades) and shown how the wide experiences of professional theologians and praxis-oriented grassroots organizers enrich the conversation by bringing to bear the pressing questions of Muslims and Catholics alike, producing a rich horizon of understanding and mutual esteem. The West Coast has also had the benefit of the strong presence of Shia Muslims, as well as female leaders, in contrast with the challenges in recruiting such participants in the other regions. This West Coast group has grown from closely knit friendships that predated the formal dialogue, which has led to high consistency in participation but relatively low public visibility, showcasing the challenge in reaching from a like-minded small group to the wider community. The Midwest has struggled with consistency, in part due to the fallout of economic crisis of 2008 and the following years, which has particularly affected the Muslim side of the dialogue. Meanwhile, though somewhat lacking in diversity, the mid-Atlantic dialogue has gained a wider profile through press attention and relationships with local government officials. This approach has been cultivated by adding a public banquet to the agenda that included community leaders and local press coverage.

Each of the dialogues has focused on different topics, with many successful examples of creating joint documents. These include a seminal document on revelation (Midwest), a statement on marriage from Sunni and Catholic perspectives (mid-Atlantic), a multiyear study of Catholics and Muslims together in the public square (Midwest), a 2012 study of prophetic traditions and qualities of believers (West Coast), a joint history of Islam and Catholicism composed by two Catholic and two Muslim scholars (Midwest), a 2013 study of the afterlife (West Coast), a 2014 discussion of Catholic Just War Theory and Islamic Jihad (West Coast), and a joint document on education for the use of Catholic and Muslim secondary-level religious educators (mid-Atlantic).[15] The education project aimed to produce a resource giving a more balanced and positive presentation of the rudiments of one another's faith traditions for young learners and beginners. The process of Catholic participants authoring an introduction to Islam for Catholic students—and Muslim participants writing an introduction to

---

15. See http://www.usccb.org/beliefs-and-teachings/ecumenical-and-interreligious/
interreligious/islam/index.cfm.

Catholicism for Muslim students—produced years of friendly but often mutually frustrating disagreements and confusion. What the group learned was just how difficult it is, even for scholars, to appreciate *how* the other interprets his or her own history/cultural narrative, as well as how the expectations of each group in a bilateral dialogue can, and often do, run counter to what ends up to be the final product of a multiyear project. Ultimately, it was a pointed lesson in how kindness, patience, and the other virtues mentioned previously must be cultivated for dialogue to succeed.

Future Prospects

In May 2015, at the second national plenary session of the regional Catholic-Muslim dialogues in the United States, all the regional co-chairs and a representative body of the participants agreed to establish a national dialogue. The shared hope of all parties is that a national approach could bring greater public attention to the work of dialogue between the Church and the Muslim community in the United States. From the Catholic side, this approach matches the national profile of our other ecumenical and interreligious dialogues. For the Muslims, it was discerned that the time was ripe for the regional organizations to begin working together in a concerted way; one essential benefit they noted in particular was that such collaboration could help craft a positive, more accurate narrative of Islam in the public square.

This experiment emerged in deliberations at the first national plenary of regional dialogues that took place at the Catholic Theological Union (Chicago). Over the course of three days, the regional members gathered for keynote addresses from scholars, roundtable discussions on best practices, shared meals and conversation, joint sessions of regional reports, and so on. The positive response to this plenary began the creative process of what a national dialogue might look like and what fruits it might produce that would serve the goals of all our groups. Eventually, the co-chairs determined that a proposal prepared by the USCCB's SEIA would be presented to the next plenary session. This session fittingly was held concurrently with the *Nostra Aetate* symposium, whose proceedings formed the basis for this book. In the final discussions, the main concern raised was the need to preserve the regional level of dialogue. Some participants argued passionately against the dissolution of the regional dialogues given their success and the lasting friendships they have produced. It was determined, therefore, that the national dialogue would remain actively tied to the regions. First, each region would be equally represented in membership, and all regional co-chairs would, along with the support of the SEIA staff, direct the national meetings. Each region would send two representatives (identified as regional liaisons or "bridges") to the national dialogue, and these representatives would be local/grassroots leaders rather than academic theologians, thus bridging the work of the national dialogue and the regions. As part of the annual agenda for each region, the bridges would be responsible for preparing reports on the work of the national dialogue, and they would also receive feedback and direction from the regional membership on the work at the national level. As the national dialogue looks to address each topic of concern to both Muslims and Catholics, it will follow a bottom-up approach in which the local and regional members suggest topics for discussion, provide feedback to the national group on how they might better prepare their final report, and at the same time retain their independent status by deciding how best to engage their particular communities.

Hindus, Sikhs, Buddhists, Jains

The USCCB has maintained official dialogues with each of the main South Asian religious traditions present in the United States. Given the difference between these groups, it is necessary to treat them separately, although a common theme is budgetary constraints at the USCCB and recent, tentative steps to renew collaboration at the invitation and encouragement of the PCID and Cardinal Jean-Louis Tauran.

Hindus

In 1998 an official dialogue was established between the USCCB and the International Society for Krishna Consciousness (ISKCON), which is a monotheistic tradition within Hinduism. For many years, the dialogue was cosponsored by the SEIA and ISKCON, but due to the USCCB's budgetary cutbacks in 2006, ISKCON has taken full responsibility for funding and hosting the dialogue, which is now called the Annual Christian-Vaishnava Dialogue, and the SEIA sends a representative. The dialogue, which takes place annually in a retreat setting, met continuously in Potomac, Maryland, until 2014, when it moved to Rockville, Maryland, near the local ISKCON temple. This particular dialogue is composed primarily of Christian (mostly Catholic) and Hindu scholars who have been making the retreat consistently since its inception. The topics have been theological in scope and, given the evident mutual respect and esteem between the participants, have contributed greatly to deepening ties between the communities. The recent years have featured for discussion mystical theology and the sacred feminine. In spring 2012 the editors of *The Journal of Vaishnava-Christian Studies* commemorated the twentieth anniversary of the dialogue by publishing a representative collection of important papers that were presented at the annual meetings.[16]

A future relationship with the wider Hindu community seems to be on the horizon as the SEIA coordinated the first-ever Catholic-Hindu dialogue in Fairfax, Virginia, at the Durga Temple (more than 250 in attendance). The topic for this meeting was "Hindu and Christian Traditions Together." This meeting was requested by the PCID, and Cardinal Jean-Louis Tauran was present to deliver the keynote address: "Hindu and Catholic Traditions: Theological Reasons for Mutual Respect and Reverence." As of July 2015, the SEIA is moving forward in talks with the Hindus, who are part of the Executive Mandir Council, a national organization of leaders from Hindu temples. For budgetary reasons, it is likely that the relationship will be local to the Washington, D.C., region at least for the short term, and it will address issues of mutual social concern and so plant seeds for future collaboration.

Sikhs

Since 2006—when Sikh and Catholic leaders convened for a special meeting with Archbishop Felix Machado (then undersecretary of the PCID) in attendance as special guest and advisor—the USCCB's SEIA has conducted a biannual retreat with the World Sikh Council–America Region.[17] This relatively new dialogue with another monotheist tradition—Sikhism originated in the fifteenth century in the Punjab region and professes belief in one supreme eternal reality (God)—has taken place in both Washington, D.C., and Columbus, Ohio. Since there is no official mandate determining the structure of this retreat, the participants have included several different bishops from each region, as well as scholars, students, and lay representatives from the local community. The agenda always includes time for presentations on topics of mutual concern, group discussion, visits to places of worship (churches and *gurdwaras*), and shared meals. A unique feature of this dialogue is that it is led by scholars and by students and young adults. Both groups deliver papers on a chosen topic, as well as lead discussions. This arrangement is intended to build understanding between generations and to promote interest in the youth to participate in interreligious dialogue. Recent retreats have featured conversation on the following broad topics: the nature of God, the spiritual teachings and practices of both communities,

16. See *Journal of Vaishnava Studies* 20, no. 2 (Spring 2012).
17. Recently the WSC-AR was renamed the American Sikh Council.

and the nature of interreligious dialogue. These topics have educated the groups in the rudiments of each tradition. Moving forward, the planners for the biannual retreat hope to incorporate a public dimension, most likely a social service event involving the participation of related groups; for example, for Catholics, a lay movement such as Focolare (whose members began attending in 2014), which maintains a strong commitment to interreligious dialogue and collaboration.

Buddhists

From 2003 until 2009, the USCCB conducted an annual West Coast dialogue with Buddhists from various communities, including the San Francisco Zen Center, Dharma Realm Buddhist Association, and the Berkeley Buddhist Monastery. The meetings focused on presentations of papers, usually exegesis of sacred texts, formal discussions on particular topics of mutual interest, presence at one another's prayer services, shared meals, and so on. From 2003 to 2007, the group conducted its first planned quadrennium of dialogues, and the topics included "Walking the Bodhisattva Path/Walking the Christ Path," "Transformation of Hearts and Minds: Chan/Zen-Catholic Approaches to Precepts," "Practice: Means towards Transformation," and "Meeting on the Path." The second quadrennium, which included the topic "Abiding in Christ, Taking Refuge in Buddha" (2007 and 2008), as well as "The Dialogues of Religious Experience and Life" (2009), was concluded in 2010. The dialogue was not renewed because of budgetary constraints. However, in 2015, at the request of the PCID, the USCCB convened a dialogue of Buddhist and Catholic leaders from the archdiocesan regions of San Francisco, Los Angeles, Chicago, New York, and Washington, D.C. This meeting featured dozens of presentations by scholars and community leaders, as well as a keynote address by Cardinal Tauran. It took up the topic of "Suffering, Liberation, and Fraternity" in an attempt to establish a dialogue that implements the vision of Pope Francis for a dialogue of fraternity between religions. The meeting was hosted by the PCID and Focolare community at Centro Mariapoli on the grounds of Castel Gandolfo and included a visit to the Vatican and a personal meeting with Pope Francis. This meeting, supported by several groups, including the archdioceses, the Focolare community, and Monastic Interreligious Dialogue, provided a new path for the USCCB's SEIA to engage in dialogue even in the continuing presence of budgetary constraints that prevent the SEIA from fully funding it. Moving forward, the assembled participants committed to meeting in their particular regions and invited the SEIA director to attend as an observer and potential presenter and resource.

Jains

In May 2015, the USCCB's SEIA organized its first encounter with the U.S. association of Jain temples (JAINA). This meeting took place at the Jain Society of Metropolitan Washington, which is the founding location for Jain temples in the United States. The meeting included talks by noted scholars, an address by Cardinal Tauran, and a community meal attended by more than one hundred Jain and Catholic members of the community. Moving forward, the SEIA is planning to nurture its relationship with JAINA and is currently discerning next steps for a mutually profitable dialogue.

Conclusion

In its 2014 publication, *Dialogue in Truth and Charity: Pastoral Orientations for Interreligious Dialogue*, the PCID identified six areas of special importance for future work: (1) defending human dignity and promoting human rights, (2) establishing bonds of trust and friendship among religious leaders, (3) educating the youth for interreligious cooperation, (4) interreligious cooperation in health care services, (5) ministry to persons in interreligious marriages, and (6) prayer and symbolic gestures.[18] In concrete ways, the USCCB's SEIA and interreligious partners in dialogue have been working at these areas for more than twenty years. In this and other ways, we have provided the international community with clear examples and a template for how to conduct successful dialogues.

There are many ideas percolating on how the dialogues will unfold moving forward, but it seems likely that the direct involvement of the USCCB in the traditional national model of dialogue—that is, the kind of dialogue that engages in theological exchange and the building of a network of collaboration between Catholic and interreligious leaders at the national level—will continue. However, it has become almost a given in recent years that the most effective change, in terms of greater understanding and collaboration between religions, will require nurturing grassroots, local initiatives. For the time being, the best way to support this latter approach would be for the SEIA to send representatives to local meetings to serve alongside what I termed earlier as Catholic and Muslim liaisons or bridges, that is, two representatives at both the national and local levels

---

18. Pontifical Council for Interreligious Dialogue, *Dialogue in Truth and Charity: Pastoral Orientations for Interreligious Dialogue*, 38–54 (Vatican City: Libreria Editrice Vaticana, 2014).

who can help keep the regional and national levels together in common cause. In short, I believe it would be acceptable to say that the coming future of successful interreligious dialogue will see more effort given to pastoral collaboration, which in turn can be fed by the theological exchange that will take place at the national level primarily among scholars who then will go about their work with due consideration of what is happening at the grassroots level. Cooperation *within* the Church (and between the mosques, temples, synagogues, etc.) will thus be an integral part of the work. The alternative—where the regional and national operate independently of one another—can only serve to minimize the overall effectiveness that is possible when collaboration and a common purpose are pursued *within* and between the religious groups. The welcome proliferation of new initiatives requires great care on many fronts, but the United States remains a privileged place to provide the world with a new model of carrying out the mission begun by *Nostra Aetate*.

The Academic Reception of *Nostra Aetate*

PIM VALKENBERG

While the previous contributions to this festive commemoration of the document *Nostra Aetate* have largely concentrated on its ecclesial reception, this contribution will focus on its academic reception. I propose to sketch the history of this reception in three phases. The first phase starts some twenty years after the Second Vatican Council with the development of the debate concerning the pluralist approach in the Catholic theology of religions around 1985. The second phase starts some fifteen years later with the development of several reactions to the prominent models in the theology of religions, most prominently comparative theology and scriptural reasoning. The third and last phase began a few years ago with the burgeoning field of interreligious studies. I should add that my perspective on the academic reception of *Nostra Aetate* is very much a Western perspective; in other parts of the world, for instance Asia, the encounter with other religions has certainly been longer and more intense.

Before I elaborate on these three phases, I should make clear how I use the phrase "reception of *Nostra Aetate*." I use it to refer to processes of theological education and research that understand themselves as promoting certain aspects of the relation between the Catholic Church and other religions as addressed in the document *Nostra Aetate*. In my earlier essay in this book I argued that there are in fact two different foci in the document, and therefore it is possible to distinguish two different histories of its reception. The narrower focus relates specifically to the document that originated as *De Iudaeis* and ended up as the fourth section of *Nostra Aetate*. The history of its reception is specifically related to the academic study of Judaism, the Jewish roots of Christianity, and the history of Christian-Jewish relations, and it includes a sizeable number of study centers for Christian-Jewish or Catholic-Jewish dialogue, even though some of them recently have come to include Islam as the third Abrahamic religion. The larger focus relates more generally to the study of the relationships between the Catholic Church and other religions, more specifically Hinduism, Buddhism, and Islam (mentioned in sections two and three of *Nostra Aetate*). In this article I will concentrate more on this larger focus than on the specific focus of Catholic-Jewish relations.

Basis in the Document

Three places can be distinguished in the document *Nostra Aetate* where the Church exhorts its members—academics included—to engage in specific behavior in order to implement the new relationship between the Church and these religions. With reference to the world religions in general, and to Hinduism and Buddhism in particular, the second section of *Nostra Aetate* concludes: "The Church therefore exhorts her sons and daughters to recognize, preserve, and foster the good things, spiritual and moral, as well as the socio-cultural values found among the followers of other religions. This is done through conversations and collaboration with them, carried out with prudence and love and in witness to the Christian faith and life."[1] Similarly, at the end of the third section that deals with the relationship with Muslims, "this Sacred Synod pleads with all to forget the past, to make sincere efforts for mutual understanding, and so to work together for the preservation and fostering of social justice, moral welfare, and peace and freedom for all humankind."[2] Finally, in the middle of the fourth section, we hear the following: "Since the spiritual heritage common to Christians and Jews is thus so rich, this Sacred Synod wishes to foster and commend mutual understanding and esteem. This is the fruit, above all, of biblical and theological studies and of friendly conversations."[3]

Conversations and forms of collaboration are the most important ways of implementing the text of *Nostra Aetate*, and so the question about its reception might be stated as follows: how have developments in the academic world, more specifically in the field of theology and cognate fields, helped us develop such conversations and forms of collaboration? Theology as such (together with biblical studies) is mentioned only in the section devoted to the relations with Jews, and the fourth section of this book has certainly made clear that the theological conversation has been most developed in dialogues between Catholics and Jews. Yet the theological conversation is not the only form of conversation or collaboration; the document *Dialogue and Mission* (1984) by the Secretariat for Non-Christians (renamed Pontifical Council for Interreligious Dialogue in 1988) famously mentions four forms of dialogue—derived from five forms of mission in the same document—that can be summarized as dialogue of living together, dialogue of common purpose, dialogue of experts, and dialogue of religious

---

1. *Nostra Aetate* 2, trans. Thomas F. Stransky, CSP.
2. Ibid. 3.
3. Ibid. 4.

experience.[4] While the academic reception of course concentrates on the dialogue of experts, it contains elements of the dialogue of common purpose and the dialogue of religious experience as well, as I will show in the following survey. One can even say that the new field of interreligious and interfaith studies is meant to include the most basic form of dialogue, the dialogue of living together. Finally, the goal of these dialogues is also given in *Dialogue and Mission*: mutual understanding and esteem.[5]

It might seem strange that my survey of the academic reception of *Nostra Aetate* starts in 1985 and to a certain extent is determined by the perspective of someone who studied theology in the 1970s in Europe. I do not remember that the Second Vatican Council, and more specifically *Nostra Aetate*, was an important issue at that time; the theological agenda was determined by liberation theology, political theology, and feminist theology. Even though I had studied both science of religions and theology, I did not think of interreligious dialogue as an important focus that could bridge these two fields of study, until the dean of the Department of Theology at the Catholic University of Nijmegen asked me to help in implementing a new program of studies focused on dialogue between religions.[6] We built a program that used the famous "unsolved enigmas of the human condition," according to the first section of *Nostra Aetate*, as introductions to the most relevant topics in interreligious studies: "What is the human being? What is the meaning, the purpose of our life? What is moral good, and what is sin? Whence suffering and what purpose does it serve? Which is the way to genuine happiness? What are death, judgment, and retribution after death? What, finally, is that ultimate inexpressible mystery which encompasses our existence: whence do we come, and where are we going?"[7] Around the same time, in 1991, the periodical

4. See Secretariat for Non-Christians, *The Attitude of the Church toward Followers of Other Religions: Reflections and Orientations on Dialogue and Mission*, 28–35 (1984); English translation in Francesco Gioia, ed., *Interreligious Dialogue: The Official Teaching of the Catholic Church from the Second Vatican Council to John Paul II (1963-2005)*, 1116–29 (Mahwah, N.J.: Paulist Publications, 2006). The five forms of mission in no. 13 of the same document: presence, commitment to service, liturgical life, dialogue, and announcement and catechesis.

5. This is further specified in *Dialogue and Mission* as mutual enrichment and fruitful cooperation (nos. 35, 44), as mutual proclamation (no. 40), and even as mutual transformation (no. 43).

6. At that time, the dean was the German theologian Hermann Häring, who had been an assistant to Hans Küng in Tübingen. Küng had already published, with others, a primer on the encounter between Christianity and world religions: Hans Küng, *Christentum und Weltreligionen* (München: Piper, 1984); available in English as *Christianity and World Religions: Paths of Dialogue with Islam, Hinduism, and Buddhism*, trans. Peter Heinegg (Maryknoll, N.Y.: Orbis Books, 1986).

7. *Nostra Aetate* 1, trans. Thomas F. Stransky, CSP.

Studies in Interreligious Dialogue was founded by one of my colleagues, Prof. Arnulf Camps, OFM, together with Prof. Henk Vroom from the Free University in Amsterdam. So at least in my context, interreligious dialogue became a new focus in the early 1990s, and it has remained important since then.

First Wave: Pluralism and Analyzing Forms of Dialogue

It would be incorrect to state that the interest in theology of religions started around 1985 with a number of famous publications by Leonard Swidler, Paul Knitter, and John Hick since it has always been an important part of the theological curriculum for missionary orders and congregations. Moreover, Catholic theologians Karl Rahner and Jean Daniélou, among others, developed inclusivist models in the theology of religions already around the time of the Second Vatican Council. Yet the famous book series *Faith Meets Faiths*, published by the missionary congregation of Maryknoll, marked a new beginning—at least in the United States.[8] I should add once again that what was new for us in Western Europe and the United States was a long-lived reality for many Christians in Asia, Africa, and the Middle East.

It can be expected that the academic reception of *Nostra Aetate* mainly consists in the academic study of the different forms of dialogue as distinguished in the document *Dialogue and Mission*: the dialogue of living together, of common purpose, of experts, and of religious experience.[9] The academic study of dialogue is probably least equipped to deal with the dialogue of living together, and yet a method has been developed to analyze the contents of such grassroots dialogues in the form of analysis of storytelling as a method.[10] The method of Interfaith Youth Core, as developed by Muslim education activist Eboo Patel and others, is a good example of working with

---

8. Among the first books were Paul Knitter, *No Other Name? A Critical Survey of Christian Attitudes toward the World Religions* (Maryknoll, N.Y.: Orbis Books, 1985); Leonard Swidler, ed., *Towards a Universal Theology of Religions* (Maryknoll, N.Y.: Orbis Books, 1987); John Hick and Paul Knitter, eds., *The Myth of Christian Uniqueness: Toward a Pluralistic Theology of Religions* (Maryknoll, N.Y.: Orbis Books, 1987).

9. The survey of the academic reception of *Nostra Aetate* in these pages owes much to the discussions with my graduate students in courses devoted to interreligious dialogue, first at the Catholic University of Nijmegen in the Netherlands, and later at The Catholic University of America in Washington, D.C.

10. See, for instance, Jennifer Howe Peace, Or N. Rose, and Gregory Mobley, eds., *My Neighbor's Faith: Stories of Interreligious Encounter, Growth, and Transformation* (Maryknoll, N.Y.: Orbis, 2012); Rebecca Kratz Mays, *Interfaith Dialogue at the Grass Roots* (Philadelphia: Ecumenical Press, 2008).

such narratives at the grassroots level.[11] Interfaith Youth Core is now present as a student-led interfaith action movement on many campuses.

The second form of dialogue, the dialogue of common purpose, has given rise to a good number of institutions involved in dialogue and peace making. Some of these institutions work at local level, but many extend their initiatives to countries plagued by interreligious conflicts. The literature in this field is growing fast, so I will need to limit myself to a few local authors who nevertheless represent a huge variety of peace initiatives.[12] Some of them have worked together with the Washington Theological Consortium in the last several years.[13] A very important bridge between this form of dialogue and the dialogue of religious experience is the World Day of Prayer for Peace that Pope John Paul II initiated in Assisi.[14] This event has been repeated several times, also by Pope Benedict XVI in a somewhat modified form in 2011.[15] Meanwhile, the monastic traditions in the Church have stimulated the dialogue of religious experience in different manners, such as the so-called Gethsemani Encounters in the United States.[16] In addition, the Monastic Interreligious Dialogue now has a website and a journal of its own.[17]

Since the field of dialogue between experts (including both scholars and religious leaders) lends itself best to documentation, most of the aca-

---

11. See Eboo Patel and Patrice Brodeur, eds., *Building the Interfaith Youth Movement: Beyond Dialogue to Action* (Lanham, Md.: Rowman & Littlefield, 2006); Eboo Patel, *Acts of Faith* (Boston: Beacon Press, 2007).

12. See, among others, David Smock, ed., *Interfaith Dialogue and Peacebuilding* (Washington, D.C.: United States Institute of Peace Press, 2002); Mohammed Abu-Nimer, *Nonviolence and Peace-building in Islam: Theory and Practice* (Gainesville: University Press of Florida, 2003); Marc Gopin, *Between Eden and Armageddon: The Future of World Religions, Violence, and Peacemaking* (Oxford and New York: Oxford University Press, 2000); and Susan Brooks Thistlethwaite, *Interfaith Just Peacemaking: Jewish, Christian, and Muslim Perspectives on the New Paradigm of Peace and War* (New York: Palgrave Macmillan, 2011).

13. See Larry Golemon's contribution to this book.

14. A very thorough analysis of the World Day of Prayer for Peace and the different reactions is available in Gerda Riedl, *Modell Assisi: christliches Gebet und interreligiöser Dialog in heilsgeschichtlichem Kontext* (Berlin: De Gruyter, 1998).

15. See Michael Amaladoss, SJ, "Inter-religious Worship," in *The Wiley-Blackwell Companion to Inter-religious Dialogue*, ed. Catherine Cornille, 87–98 (Chichester: Wiley-Blackwell, 2013).

16. See Donald W. Mitchell and James Wiseman, OSB, eds., *The Gethsemani Encounter* (New York: Continuum, 1997).

17. The journal *Dilatato Corde* can be found on the website of Monastic Interreligious Dialogue / Dialogue Interreligieux Monastique: http://www.dimmid.org. For a good summary of recent developments, see Pierre-François de Béthune, OSB, "Monastic Inter-religious Dialogue," in *The Wiley-Blackwell Companion to Inter-religious Dialogue*, ed. Catherine Cornille, 34–50 (Chichester: Wiley-Blackwell, 2013).

demic reception of *Nostra Aetate* has concentrated on the study of this form of dialogue. Before I discuss the newest developments in the academic world, I want to mention the Building Bridges initiative of the Archbishop of Canterbury for Christian-Muslim dialogue that since 2002 has brought together academics and religious leaders. The yearly meetings of the Building Bridges seminar have been documented in carefully edited volumes, first edited by the Anglican Church offices, but now by Georgetown University Press. The Berkley Center for Religion, Peace & World Affairs' website gives a good survey of the contents of these Building Bridges seminars.[18]

Second Wave: Particularism and Comparative Theology

After the development of the pluralist approach in the theology of religions from about 1985 onward, the focus gradually shifted toward models that tried to combine the new awareness of religious pluralism with fidelity to the Catholic tradition of inclusivist approaches. The most famous synthesis was developed in 1997 by Belgian Jesuit Jacques Dupuis, but the document *Dominus Iesus*, published in 2000 by the Congregation for the Doctrine of the Faith, showed that some questions remain about the feasibility of such a middle way between inclusivism and pluralism.[19] Meanwhile, in his book *Introducing Theologies of Religions*, Paul Knitter added a fourth paradigm to the well-known (and somewhat worn-out) triad of exclusivism, inclusivism, and pluralism, namely particularism—an approach in the Christian theology of religions that wants to take religious particularities more seriously.[20] This implies that less attention is paid to theoretical approaches to other religions, while the focus is directed at specific and concrete dialogues and other forms of encounter with members of other religions.[21]

Comparative theology is usually mentioned as one of the "particularist" approaches in the theology of religions, but in the meantime it has developed as a new theological field of its own. Comparative theology has its roots in older developments, partly by Jesuit missionaries, partly by con-

18. http://berkleycenter.georgetown.edu/projects/the-building-bridges-seminar (accessed August 4, 2015).

19. Jacques Dupuis, SJ, *Toward a Christian Theology of Religious Pluralism* (Maryknoll, N.Y.: Orbis Books, 1997). The questions are formulated in Karl Becker and Ilaria Morali, eds., *Catholic Engagement with World Religions: A Comprehensive Study* (Maryknoll, N.Y.: Orbis Books, 2010).

20. Paul Knitter, *Introducing Theologies of Religions*, 173–237 (Maryknoll, N.Y.: Orbis Books, 2002).

21. See Gavin D'Costa, *Christianity and World Religions: Disputed Questions in the Theology of Religions*, 34–54 (Chichester: Wiley-Blackwell, 2009).

fessional scientists of religion, but in its present form it originated at two Jesuit institutions: Boston College and Loyola Marymount University (Los Angeles). Francis X. Clooney, SJ, and James Fredericks are the two founding fathers of this form of comparative theology that originated out of discontent with the theology of religions mainly in its pluralist form.[22] Comparative theology is wary of grand theories and likes to limit itself to studying texts or rituals from one particular religion—in the case of Clooney, that religion is Hinduism; in the case of Fredericks, it is Buddhism—but David Burrell shows that comparative theology with Abrahamic religions is possible as well.[23] Thanks in part to generous grants from the Luce Foundation, comparative theology has developed into a strong new field both in the Catholic Theological Society of America and in the American Academy of Religion. Clooney is usually seen as the most important theologian in this field, and he argues that comparative theology *can be* related to interreligious dialogue but does not *need to be*.[24] Other theologians, such as Fredericks, seem to argue in favor of a closer relationship in which interreligious friendship becomes an important development.[25] A recent issue of *Studies in Interreligious Dialogue* gives some insight not only into the influence of comparative theology outside of the United States but also into its status as a form of Catholic theology.[26]

While comparative theology in its present-day form has mainly been developed by Catholic theologians, another form of particularism started as Textual Reasoning in an endeavor to bring together Jewish philosophers and scripture scholars.[27] When Christian theologians started to attend the Textual Reasoning sessions at the American Academy of Religion, the movement developed into Scriptural Reasoning with important centers in the United Kingdom (Cambridge) and the United States (Princeton and Charlottesville). In recent times, Muslim scholars have joined Scriptural Reasoning as well, so that the basic idea of studying the scriptures together,

22. This discontent is most clearly visible in James Fredericks, *Faith among Faiths: Christian Theology and Non-Christian Religions* (Mahwah, N.J.: Paulist Press, 1999).

23. Burrell's most recent book is David Burrell, *Towards a Jewish-Christian-Muslim Theology* (Chichester: Wiley-Blackwell, 2011).

24. A short introduction to his position: Francis X. Clooney, *Comparative Theology. Deep Learning across Religious Borders* (Chichester: Wiley-Blackwell, 2010). For his position on interreligious dialogue, see Clooney, "Comparative Theology and Inter-religious Dialogue," in Cornille, ed., *The Wiley-Blackwell Companion to Inter-religious Dialogue*, 51–63.

25. See James L. Fredericks and Tracy Sayuki Tiemeier, eds., *Interreligious Friendship after Nostra Aetate* (New York: Palgrave Macmillan, 2015).

26. See *Studies in Interreligious Dialogue* 24 (2014): 5–118.

27. See Peter Ochs and Nancy Levene, eds., *Textual Reasonings* (London: SCM Press, 2002).

founded on the Jewish concept of *chavruta*, is now extended to the study of the Qur'an.[28] Scriptural Reasoning has developed mainly as a practice of dialogue among academics, but it can be called an ecclesial practice as well, and there are even some grassroots dialogues connected to Scriptural Reasoning.[29] A recent issue of *Modern Theology* on "Interreligious Reading after Vatican II" looks at the connections between Scriptural Reasoning, Comparative Theology, and Receptive Ecumenism.[30]

Third Wave: From Interreligious Dialogue to Interreligious Studies

While the developments that can be shared under Paul Knitter's umbrella term *particularism* are theologically oriented and quite strongly tradition-specific—there are clear connections with postliberal theology associated with George Lindbeck—the latest development seems to head in a less tradition-specific direction: the new field of interfaith and interreligious studies. One of the main publication channels of this field is the *Journal of Interreligious Dialogue*, which was first published on the Internet in 2009 and changed its name to *Journal of Interreligious Studies* in 2014.[31] At the same time, a new Interreligious and Interfaith Study group was founded at the American Academy of Religion in 2013. The majority of scholars associated with this journal and this group tend to conceive interreligious relations on a noninstitutional basis. Other authors writing along these lines are often connected to the European Society for Intercultural Theology and Interreligious Studies (ESITIS) that has adopted *Studies in Interreligious Dialogue* as its periodical next to its website.[32] Members of this society have published a number of important works on interreligious relations; for instance, the volumes *Interreligious Hermeneutics in Pluralistic Europe* and *Understanding Interreligious Relations*.[33] A final publication that

---

28. See David Ford and Chad C. Pecknold, eds., *The Promise of Scriptural Reasoning* (Malden, Mass.: Blackwell, 2006); Marianne Moyaert, "Scriptural Reasoning as Inter-religious Dialogue," in *The Wiley-Blackwell Companion to Inter-religious Dialogue*, ed. Cornille, 64–86.

29. For instance, the St. Ethelburga's Centre for reconciliation and Peace in London; information accessible through the website of *Journal of Scriptural Reasoning* Forum, http://jsrforum.lib.virginia.edu//index.html.

30. David F. Ford and Frances Clemson, eds., *Interreligious Reading after Vatican II: Scriptural Reasoning, Comparative Theology and Receptive Ecumenism* (Chichester: Wiley-Blackwell, 2013); *Modern Theology* 29, no. 4 (2013).

31. See the editorial in *The Journal of Interreligious Studies* 13 (Winter 2014).

32. http://www.esitis.org (accessed August 5, 2015).

33. David Cheetham, Ulrich Winkler, Oddbjørn Leirvik, and Judith Gruber, eds., *Interreligious Hermeneutics in Pluralistic Europe: Between Texts and People* (Amsterdam; New York: Rodopi, 2011); David Cheetham, Douglas Pratt, and David Thomas, eds., *Understanding Interreligious Relations* (Oxford: Oxford University Press, 2013).

deserves to be mentioned is *Interreligious Studies: A Relational Approach to Religious Activism and the Study of Religion* by Norwegian theologian Odd-bjørn Leirvik.[34] The titles of these books betray the tendency to move away from the terminology of *interreligious dialogue* because these authors see it as limiting their work. The European members of ESITIS seem to agree on this with the participants in the events organized by the Interreligious and Interfaith Studies group at the American Academy of Religion. They are more interested in hybrid identity, multiple religious belonging, and other fluid forms of religious identity, and they think that interreligious dialogue is too static a category to catch their approach. They tend to focus more on *interfaith relations* as a broader and more personal, less institutional term. Most of them tend to work along the lines of the pluralist approach in the theology of religions as developed by Paul Knitter, Leonard Swidler, and Diana Eck.[35] Their orientation is toward the dialogue of common purpose.

One person who has contributed to the study of multiple religious belonging is Flemish theologian Catherine Cornille, who is now professor of comparative theology and chairperson of the Theology Department at Boston College.[36] In the last seven years she has published a sizeable amount of studies that bring the term *dialogue* center stage and in that sense contribute most visibly to the academic reception of *Nostra Aetate*. After a book with reflections on the conditions for interreligious dialogue titled *The Im-possibility of Interreligious Dialogue*, she organized a series of five symposia on aspects of interreligious dialogue that resulted in five edited books, and finally she edited the formidable *Wiley-Blackwell Companion to Inter-religious Dialogue*, published in 2013.[37] Yet Cornille is not the only theologian who works along the lines indicated by *Nostra Aetate*; the Institute for Advanced Catholic Studies at the University of Southern California in Los Angeles directed by James Heft, SM, works along similar

---

34. Oddbjørn Leirvik, *Interreligious Studies: A Relational Approach to Religious Activism and the Study of Religion* (London: Bloomsbury, 2014).

35. Diana Eck and Paul Knitter are among the steering committee members of the Interreligious and Interfaith Studies Group at the American Academy of Religion; Leonard Swidler is one of its main advisers.

36. Catherine Cornille, ed., *Many Mansions: Multiple Religious Belonging and Christian Identity* (Maryknoll, N.Y.: Orbis Books, 2002).

37. Cornille, *The Im-possibility of Interreligious Dialogue* (New York: Crossroad/Herder & Herder, 2008); the five edited volumes are *Criteria of Discernment in Interreligious Dialogue*; *Interreligious Hermeneutics*; *The World Market and Interreligious Dialogue*; *Interreligious Dialogue and Cultural Change*; and *Women and Interreligious Dialogue*, all published by Wipf and Stock (Eugene, Ore.) from 2009 to 2013. The *Wiley-Blackwell Companion to Inter-religious Dialogue* is cited above.

lines and has organized lectures on the Catholic Church and interreligious dialogue.[38] British theologian Gavin D'Costa published a similar book but without the responses by representatives of other world religions that characterize Heft's dialogical approach.[39]

Conclusion

In a certain sense, Scriptural Reasoning seems to be the academic method that come closest to *Nostra Aetate*'s commendation of "conversation and collaboration with [the followers of other religions], carried out with prudence and love and in witness to the Christian faith and life."[40] However, Scriptural Reasoning is first of all a practice—it is part of the Building Bridges seminars, for instance—and only secondarily a theory about this practice. Even though the pivotal function of reading scripture together cannot be overemphasized in interreligious dialogue, it tends to leave aside the theological tradition that is important for the Catholic Church. We have heard from several cardinals and from their Jewish and Muslim respondents that it is important to keep theological themes such as salvation and the Trinity on the agenda of dialogues with Jews and Christians. While the interreligious dialogues sketched in other contributions to this book seem to become more and more community oriented and focused on dialogue for the common good, theological questions are less likely to find a place on the agenda of these dialogues. Catholic theologians might be a bit wary to start all over again with classical themes such as Christology and Trinitarian theology that are not likely to lead to any common understanding, even though some theologians try to find new ways to start such initiatives.[41] In the dialogue with Islam, where such a reflection on central theological topics seems most needed, it might be a sign of what Catholics would interpret as the work of the Spirit that Muslim theologians now seem to explore these topics, not only in the Common Word process since 2007, but also in new approaches to Jesus

38. James L. Heft, SM, ed., *Catholicism and Interreligious Dialogue* (Oxford: Oxford University Press, 2012).

39. Gavin D'Costa, ed., *The Catholic Church and the World Religions: A Theological and Phenomenological Account* (London: T&T Clark, 2011). D'Costa also has published two books on the Second Vatican Council and other religions that I have mentioned in my earlier contribution to this book.

40. *Nostra Aetate* 2, trans. Thomas F. Stransky, CSP.

41. In the context of Washington, D.C., two of my colleagues have been active in thinking about such forms of theology in conversation with Islam: Daniel Madigan, SJ (Georgetown University), and Sidney Griffith, ST (emeritus, The Catholic University of America).

and his meaning for Christians and Muslims.[42] *Nostra Aetate* has stimulated a lot of dialogue and collaboration with followers of other faiths in the past fifty years, and it will certainly continue to do so in sometimes unexpected ways in the next fifty years.

---

42. For the Common Word process, see the website http://www.acommonword.com and Miroslav Volf, Ghazi bin Muhammad, and Melissa Yarrington, eds., *A Common Word: Muslims and Christians on Loving God and Neighbor* (Grand Rapids, Mich.: William B. Eerdmans, 2010); for the new approaches to Jesus, see Mona Siddiqui, *Christians, Muslims & Jesus* (New Haven and London: Yale University Press, 2013), and Zeki Saroitoprak, *Islam's Jesus* (Gainesville: University Press of Florida, 2014).

Engaging in Dialogue:
CADEIO and the Diocesan Ecumenical and Interreligious Officer

JUDI LONGDIN

The fiftieth anniversary of *Nostra Aetate*, the seminal Vatican II document on the relationship of the Catholic Church to non-Christians, gave Catholics and our many partners in dialogue just cause for celebration. Many of the theological and practical barriers separating people of faith have been broken down, and we appear to be slowly transitioning from a period of recognition and repentance to a new stage of dialogue where all partners have equal voice.

Academic conferences that focus on *Nostra Aetate*, such as the one held at The Catholic University of America (CUA), have brought together some of our finest scholars and Church leaders to speak to both the progress in relationships and the challenges and opportunities for future dialogue. Less attention has been paid to celebrations on the local level, born out of years of dialogue and relationship building, facilitated in large part by clergy and laity trained in the work of ecumenical and interreligious dialogue by the Catholic Association of Diocesan Ecumenical and Interreligious Officers (CADEIO). CADEIO was pleased to be among the sponsors of the CUA *Nostra Aetate* event and of Dr. Ann Garrido's talk in particular. CADEIO also structured its regularly scheduled Interreligious Institute so that emerging ecumenical and interreligious leaders from dioceses around the country could be full participants in the *Nostra Aetate* conference.

The following reflections offer a brief overview of the history of CADEIO, its contribution to and learnings from the CUA symposium, and its changing profile as religious pluralism and lay participation in the life of the Church continue to alter our religious landscape and approach to interreligious work.

History

CADEIO was originally NADEO, the National Association of Diocesan Ecumenical Officers, formed in 1970 as a direct response to the Second Vatican Council's mandate for each diocese to establish a means to promote ecumenism on the local level, ideally an ecumenical officer able to answer ecumenical questions and animate the work of a diocesan ecumenical commission.[1] In practice, the ecumenical officer was often a member of the clergy who wore many hats. In large part, NADEO was formed as a voluntary association of appointed ecumenical officers to respond to their need for professional development.[2] Although *ecumenism* means "unity among Christians," the third of NADEO'S three purposes mentions the interreligious context:

> 1) to stimulate an exchange of ideas, experiences and evaluations among diocesan ecumenical officers; 2) to promote programs that further the work of Christian unity and cooperation; 3) to cooperate with the Bishops Committee on Ecumenical and Interreligious Affairs of the National Conference of Catholic Bishops and with other ecumenical and interreligious agencies.[3]

Since its inception, CADEIO has worked closely with the Bishops Committee on Ecumenical and Interreligious Affairs (BCEIA, established in 1964), often serving in an advisory capacity as ecumenical and interreligious needs shifted. In the early years, the focus of both NADEO and the BCEIA was primarily on ecumenical relations. But even early on, many ecumenical officers and dioceses were also involved in relations with the Jewish community. The strong focus of *Nostra Aetate* on Jews and Judaism and the particular status of our relationship with the Jews provided a solid foundation and rationale for beginning to build relationships on the local level. NADEO responded to the need for training and resourcing in this area by establishing the Catholic Jewish Relations Standing Committee.[4] The relationship between the Catholic Jewish Relations Committee and the BCEIA has always been one of mutual cooperation and support. This pattern of collaboration continues to be a cornerstone of the relationships between CADEIO and its committees with the BCEIA.

In 1985, NADEO added a standing committee called Faiths in the World (FITW). The work of this committee focused on relations with other traditions besides Judaism, notably Islam and the religions of the East. Organized in 1982, the committee has met every fall over three days to plan programs, to develop resources, and to respond to the concerns of

---

1. *Directory for the Application of Principles and Norms on Ecumenism* (1993), 41.

2. NADEO grew out of the National Workshop for Christian Unity, first held in 1964 in Baltimore, Maryland, and continuing annually. Since 1971, it has been sponsored by the National Ecumenical Officers Association (originally the Association of Denominational Ecumenical Officers). WAB: National Workshop on Christian Unity Records, Box 5, Folder 8, The Burke Library Archives, Columbia University Libraries at Union Theological Seminary, New York.

3. NADEO history, CADEIO.org.

4. Ibid.

CADEIO membership dealing with or contemplating interreligious relationships. The first meeting in 1982 took place at St. Paul's College in
Washington, D.C.[5] The committee brings together ecumenical and interreligious officers and scholars and works in concert with the BCEIA. The
most recent meeting of FITW took place in Salt Lake City, Utah, following the Parliament of World Religions.

The FITW committee spent a full year organizing and planning for
the parliament, collaborating with Catholic Theological Union, the Diocese of Salt Lake City, and many others to ensure that there would be an
authentic Catholic voice at the parliament. In addition to offering sessions
on the theology and practice of interreligious relations, FITW also hosted
hospitality sessions and an exhibit booth and provided CADEIO bags and
buttons to more than four hundred Catholic participants. The presence of
FITW at the parliament and the response received were profound examples of an evangelization based in authentic Catholic belief that respects
the religious identity of the other.

The path from St. Paul's College in 1982 to Salt Lake City has not
always been smooth. In 1997, NADEO, in cooperation with the National
Conference of Catholic Bishops, introduced the first ten-day Interreligious
Institute, facilitated by Dr. John Borelli and Archbishop Michael Fitzgerald.
Since its inception, the institute has been offered every third summer, rotat-
ing with the Introduction to Ecumenism and Advanced Ecumenism Institutes that were established already. In 2002, NADEO, in cooperation with
the United States Council of Catholic Bishops' Secretariat for Ecumenical
and Interreligious Affairs and responding to the crisis of September 11,
2001, offered an Advanced Institute of Islam designed to equip ecumenical
and interreligious officers with a deep understanding of Islam that would
help them develop relationships with Muslims and offer clear responses to
the questions and concerns being raised in local communities about Islam.

Among its tasks, FITW proposed workshops to be offered within the
NADEO track at the National Workshop for Christian Unity. The goal
was to offer one workshop each year, focused either on Jews and Judaism or
our relationships with the larger interreligious community. While the sessions were welcomed by many, there was also resistance from some ecumenical officers who felt that the National Workshop for Christian Unity
and NADEO should focus exclusively on ecumenical relationships. A pro-
longed conversation among the membership resulted in a vote taken at the

    5. Attendees were Rev. John McDonnell (NADEO vice president), Rev. Msgr. Royale
Vadakin, Rev. Msgr. Joseph Gremillion, Prof. John Grim, Prof. William Cenkner, Prof. John
Borelli, and the Rev. John F. Hotchkin, executive secretary, BCEIA; FITW History,
CADEIO.org.

NADEO General Assembly in 2005 to change the name of the organization from the National Association of Diocesan Ecumenical Officers to the
Catholic Association of Diocesan Ecumenical and Interreligious Officers.

CADEIO and The Catholic University of America

The most recent Interreligious Institute was offered in conjunction
with the CUA symposium on *Nostra Aetate* precisely so that participants
could hear and learn from Church leaders, scholars, and other experts in
the field and, more importantly, interact with them on a more informal
basis. The latter was facilitated by the many opportunities to eat together
and the willingness of people to seek out the companionship of someone
they did not know.

Informal dialogue with speakers has been a lynchpin of the CADEIO
institutes. It is in the informal gatherings, which generally happen every
evening over the course of seven to ten days, that local experience tends to
be discussed and shared at deeper levels. In this way, the institute participants begin to build community, a cohort to whom they can turn, while at
the same time drawing out new perspectives on local implications from the
speakers as well as challenging speakers to consider what questions, issues,
and concerns need to be clarified or addressed in academic settings and by
formal dialogues on the national and international level. How are local
communities receiving the results of the dialogues, and how might the
local conversations inform further discussion by scholars and church leaders? In fact, the usual amount of collective conversation was limited by the
structure of the *Nostra Aetate* symposium at CUA, although participants
did note a discussion with Fr. Tom Stransky as a particular highlight.

On the other hand, the benefit of hearing from Cardinals Tauran,
Koch, and Dolan; Archbishop Fitzgerald; and their Jewish and Muslim
partners was for all of those involved in the institute an experience that will
be remembered and processed for a long time to come. In many cases the
style and manner of presentation were as informative as the content. The
history, practical content, and challenges for the future articulated at the
conference are of great significance to ecumenical and interreligious officers; however, much of the question of implementation remains. Ecumenical and interreligious officers serve many roles in which they could apply
new knowledge, including resourcing and perhaps writing for their bishops, teaching in seminaries and congregations, initiating and shepherding
dialogues, and training commission members. The role for academia in
preparing local ecumenists for these duties remains an unsettled question.

CADEIO's invited speaker, Dr. Ann Garrido, associate professor of
homiletics at Aquinas Institute of Theology, opened a small window into

this question. By focusing her remarks on the relational aspects of dialogue that lead to both uncovering conflict and addressing it in healthy ways that avoid doing violence to the relationship, Dr. Garrido's presentation suggests that there might be a greater interdisciplinary role for academics to play in the formation of ecumenical and interreligious leaders at the local level. How do we provide the rationale, content, and skills needed to engage in dialogue at the local level, especially for an ecumenical and interreligious officer playing the multiple roles? The skillset needed to teach and to write about ecumenical and interreligious concerns is informed by, but different from, the skillset needed to establish and maintain dialogue in the four areas of dialogue presented in church documents: life, theology, spirituality, and action. Nor can we approach these areas as independent of one another or as belonging to a specific domain.

Much attention has been paid recently to Pope Francis's focus on the Dialogue of Fraternity, which encourages local faith communities to work together to heal the wounds of the communities in which they live. Such work requires reflection on a common set of values, the ability to assess the actual conditions of the neighborhoods and communities where healing is needed, the ability to listen to and be guided by the voice of the community, and a means for evaluating progress in both the health of the community and the health of the dialogue. Social sciences, communication, and organizational skills play a significant role in developing and maintaining this fraternal relationship. Collaboration with social service agencies and others is critical. There is fertile ground for scholars working in concert with local ecumenical and interreligious leaders to consider how collaboration with other disciplines can enhance and empower relationships at the local level. For example, the issue of how social sciences inform our understanding of dialogue has been considered in the Midwest Muslim-Catholic Dialogue, whose members include local interreligious partners and scholars.

New Frontiers

CADEIO has done and continues to do important work in forming ecumenical and interfaith officers; however, to this day the membership of CADEIO remains largely clergy. It also remains the case that many ecumenical and interreligious officers wear multiple hats. Unlike other ministries of the Church, ecumenical and interreligious work is often on the periphery of Church attention, and formal education tends to focus on history and theology, formal dialogues, and institutional structures. Very few dioceses send individuals on to higher education to become ecumenical officers. Much of what it means to be an ecumenical and interreligious officer is learned in the field, through interaction with others doing the same work and through CADEIO's institutes, workshops at the National Workshop for Christian Unity, and resources developed by its standing committees. There are very few women or laity serving as ecumenical and interreligious officers, due in large part to lack of funding or encouragement to pursue careers as ecumenists on the local level. More work needs to be done to encourage local dioceses to equip lay women and men to serve in a role which continues to be dominated by clergy.

The changing nature of our religious landscape demands that greater attention be paid to interreligious relations at the local level. This will require revisiting traditional modes of dialogue that may not fit our interreligious situation. Already in our local ecumenical dialogues we realize that we need to move beyond the reception of documents and discover ways to be in communion with one another, new models of engagement that focus more on what we hope to accomplish together than on naming commonalities or differences. Here again interdisciplinary studies can help create the foundation for developing holistic ways of working together for the common good.

Conclusion

CADEIO has and continues to embody the message of *Nostra Aetate* and subsequent documents through its work to equip ecumenical and interreligious officers for work in local communities. This work is enhanced by collaboration with scholars and the BCEIA.

Participation in CUA's *Nostra Aetate* symposium provided local ecumenical and interreligious officers with the opportunity to hear firsthand the status of interreligious dialogues and to be in conversation with Church leadership, raising questions regarding the importance of informal dialogue, the contribution of local dialogues to national and international dialogues, the need for mutual collaboration between scholars and ecumenical and interreligious leaders, and the need for increased interdisciplinary work.

As the religious profile of our communities continues to change, Church leaders will need to take ecumenical and interreligious formation more seriously. In particular, in a field dominated by male clergy, efforts should be made to engage more women and laity in ecumenical and interreligious leadership. The position of an ecumenical and interreligious officer should be seen as a legitimate career option, and support should be offered to pursue the educational opportunities offered by CADEIO. Finally, the contributions of CADEIO and its members to the academic and theological conversations should be affirmed and ongoing collaboration encouraged.

Pursuing Truth in Dialogue

ANN M. GARRIDO

Triad Consulting Group, the company I consult for, was founded by two members of the Harvard Negotiation Project, one of the world's most elite groups of negotiators. Our founders have trained hostage negotiation specialists in the Middle East. They have worked with the Ethiopian Parliament and helped mediate the Cyprus conflict between Greece and Turkey. They have worked with big banks and big business. Yet when one of our founders gets up to speak, she often begins by saying, "I was once locked in a room with six theologians for thirteen hours debating the nature of truth."

She says this with a certain degree of pride, as if she wants to communicate, "Look what I survived." Or maybe it is an attempt at solidarity: "See, whatever you've been through, I understand." But whatever the reason, whenever she does this, it makes me roll my eyes and sigh. Because I was one of those six theologians.

Even though, less than a decade ago, I was embroiled in such a tense theological conversation that it required calling in the Harvard Negotiation Project, I want to reassure anyone newer to the world of dialogue about matters of faith that lawyers are not usually required. And for the sake of clarity, the dialogue I was involved in was not interreligious dialogue; it was intrareligious dialogue, taking place within my own academic community.

The primary work of interreligious dialogue, as I understand it, is about looking for similarities or places of overlap between religious traditions. It is about seeking common experiences of the transcendent, not differences. It aims to explore the potential for collaboration, not conflict. If the relationships that you enter into with persons of other faiths begin with a focus on what differs and where you disagree, I imagine that would be a very bad sign. It would be a relationship that would not seem to hold much promise.

But at the same time, if the relationships that are formed in the context of interreligious dialogue are never able to broach difficult topics like the nature of truth—if differences and disagreements are repeatedly avoided and shied away from—I suspect that would also be problematic. If we do not find a way to dialogue also about those things that mean a great deal to us, but upon which we hold radically different points of view, I suspect we will have interesting conversations, but not particularly transformative ones. And if we do not find a way of acknowledging where we are uncomfortable with one another's thinking and behavior—both at a professional and personal level—we will never taste the depths of relationship, understanding, and knowledge for which we truly hunger as human beings.

Therefore, although the story I want to explore comes from an intrareligious dialogue instead of an interreligious one, and although it is about an area of painful difference rather than similarity, I think it is quite instructive for the practice of interreligious dialogue as well. While conflict is certainly not the aim of dialogue, we would be naïve to think that it is not an inevitable part of any sort of dialogue of depth that involves real, living human beings—whether of different faiths, cultures, personalities, or generations.

I came to be locked in a room for thirteen hours with five other theologians and a Harvard mediator because we were also colleagues in the same theologate, and the health and well-being of the school depended on it. Four of the six of us were faculty members. Whenever there was a difference of opinion at a faculty meeting—be it over a theological stance, the choice of opening song for commencement, the advising of a challenging student, the question of who would preside at prayer—you can bet two or more of the four of us were somehow mixed up in it. We thought that we kept it pretty well hidden from our students, but apparently it was not so. As one of my own advisees said to me, "We can tell there is a lot of tension among you. That you disagree about everything and don't seem to like working with one another." Well, as people of any faith, that is hardly the sort of witness you want to be sending out into the world, much less your own student body.

So being of the theological academic sort, we did the thing that theological academics do whenever they encounter an intractable issue they want to understand better: we applied to an arm of the Lilly Foundation for grant assistance. Over the course of a two-year period, we joined the general goodwill of us religious-sorts-of-people with the expertise of the Harvard Negotiation Project to see if we could make progress on the way we dialogued about differences among ourselves. In particular, the four-of-us-who-argued-the-most committed to talking among ourselves about our most neuralgic topic and then modeling, alongside two of our upper-level students, what a good, healthy conversation on this topic would look like. And we would do it in front of the whole school body in a symposium.

The topic that we chose to talk about with one another was *truth*. Perhaps that sounds peculiarly esoteric, but I promise you it is the most practical and pressing topic there is. Whenever you are struggling to talk with another about something that means a great deal to you, isn't the question of truth somehow always what is involved? What is "really real" here? How do we know? Who has the right to claim it and on what grounds? What difference do we think it makes if someone gets "what's really real" wrong? Is it okay to agree to disagree on something if your belief about what is true has real life consequences for me? Can we honestly say that "it doesn't matter what you believe; we can still be friends," or are there times we can't anymore? When is it acceptable to have a diversity of perspectives all claiming to be true on a topic and when is it not? I challenge you to think of any conversation you have had recently with someone who looks at the world differently than you do—be it on a religious belief, a political position, a community issue, a family decision—and consider: does it not have to do ultimately with one of those questions?

One of my mentors in theology is keen on saying to me, "A difference that doesn't make a difference isn't really a difference." The differences-that-don't-really-make-a-difference are easy, intriguing, even fun to talk about. (I offer purgatory as an example here. I believe in it wholeheartedly, but I am not bothered that you have a different intuition about the afterlife and I am curious to hear about it.) Most of us are pretty comfortable with the fact that people think differently than we do on any variety of topics. It gets tough, though, when another's belief in something and their acting on that belief impacts our life or the lives of those we care about in a negative way. (To give another example: whether all children should have to be vaccinated before going to school, especially if your own child has a compromised immune system.) Those kinds of differences-that-do-make-a-difference are rarely easy or fun to discuss with someone who holds a much different opinion.

The nature of truth was not merely a matter of intellectual curiosity for those of us involved in this dialogue. Our varied answers to the questions posed above were impacting our ability to work with each other in daily life. Differences-that-make-a-difference can make all of our professional academic training for objectivity and emotional distance evaporate.
Preparing for the symposium required a four-month process of talking and making decisions with one another. The day of the infamous thirteen-hour practice conversation with the Harvard mediator, we were scheduled to meet for only seven hours, but we got so deeply engaged in discussion that we neglected to take even a bathroom break and finally emerged from the room after sunset to discover that the pizza delivered hours earlier had been burnt to a crisp.

And here is the thing I found most distressing at the end of that marathon day: after thirteen hours of talking, I felt like we had gotten nowhere. Even with the Harvard negotiator present, our positions—and our relationships to one another—seemed frozen in place. As the clock inched toward 10 p.m., I disagreed with one member of the group, who I will call "Dan," more vehemently than when the day began. I had really tried to listen to him, and his reasoning still made no sense to me. When I had spoken, I felt attacked by Dan. It felt to me as if he were dissecting everything I said, parsing words in a way I found to be tedious. It was exhausting and made me not want to say any more at all.

And then the strangest thing happened. I don't quite know how to describe it, because I'm not sure when it started exactly, but perhaps the best way to say it is that the glacier began to move. In the weeks following our fruitless thirteen-hour conversation, I began to see that, although Dan's reasoning did not make sense to me, I could understand why Dan's reasoning made sense to *him*. Why it made sense given how his brain was wired, given the voices he considered most authoritative, given the education he had received and the social circles he ran in, given the family that had formed him and the culture in which he was rooted, given his understanding of history and how revelation works. And while I still did not agree with him, I had more compassion for him, and I could see how things would look from his shoes. I became ever so slightly gentler with him and more understanding of his behavior.

Indeed, all of us were becoming gentler with one another. Nothing big, but a smile in the communion line instead of a steely glare. A nod across the table at the committee meeting. An email response sent in a more timely fashion than accustomed. A gesture of personal concern asking about a sick parent. Each of these slight "meltings" formed a river of ice moving at the speed of about six inches per year. We did not actually understand each other's stances, but we understood better how each person ticked to their own metronome.

It has been six years now since the semester of the Truth Symposium, yet I continue to think about that dialogue and feel its influence in my life. I want to share three practices that I took away from the experience that I consider to undergird a healthy approach to deep dialogue about the things that matter, whether intrareligious or interreligious or even areligious.

Seek Truth

From a Catholic worldview, there is such a thing as reality and truth being in a state of alignment with reality. The classical definition of the term, aptly articulated by Thomas Aquinas and still mirrored in *Webster's Dictionary* today, defines truth as "being in accordance with the actual state of affairs; the body of real things, events, and facts." In Aquinas's own words: *"Veritas est adaequatio rei et intellectus."*[1] It is not a body of knowl-

---

1. Thomas Aquinas, *Summa Theologiae* I.16.1.

edge that one possesses but, rather, a state of knowing that is in the right relationship with reality—in a similar way as justice not being something one "has" but a state of being in the right relationship with others.

From the perspective of this tradition, reality exists whether we believe in it or not. I might not agree that there is such a thing as gravity, but if I step out of a third-story window, I am just as likely as the next person to plummet to the ground. I may not believe in God, but whether God exists does not depend on my belief. In that sense, what is true is never endangered by humans; reality is what it is. Humans, however, stand in peril without truth. We may not believe that there is such a thing as global warming, but if it exists, we are going to be impacted regardless of our belief. It is in our best interest as humans that our beliefs align with reality. Our flourishing, indeed our very existence, is at stake. The kinds of conversations we engage in as religious people are not just quaint, casual, and of no import, as the wider world would sometimes make them out to be. There are differences that do make a difference. It is extremely important that we know what is real. The big, scary question is not whether reality exists but, rather, can we know it?

On the one hand, we humans must trust our capacity to know reality lest we not be able to dive into daily business. Could our ancestors have planted crops if they did not trust the patterns of the sun? Could they have navigated between islands if they could not count on the predictable movement of the stars in the night sky? At some level we must trust our ability to know what is real lest we be paralyzed in our planning, unable to make any decisions. To use an example favored by the philosopher Wittgenstein, what would it be like if every morning when we woke up we had to wonder, "Do I really have two hands or is that just a figment of my imagination?" We are able to get on with life only because there are some things we take as certain.[2]

On the other hand, we acknowledge that the horizon of knowable reality has always extended beyond what any one civilization, much less person, could master. The farther we sail from the shore toward that horizon, the wider the view of the ocean of potential knowledge before us. And the more we learn, the more we realize we do not know. Indeed, we often discover that what we thought we knew is—to use Aquinas's vocabulary— not "adequate" to the reality we encounter. We will think we have understood something such as gravity or the Divine or the earth's climate, and

---

2. Ludwig Wittgenstein, *On Certainty*, trans. G. E. M. Anscombe and G. H. von Wright (New York: Harper, 1972), 245. Quoted in Scott Steinkerchner, *Beyond Agreement: Interreligious Dialogue amid Persistent Differences* (New York: Rowman & Littlefield, 2010), 42.

then realize we have barely skimmed the surface. Over and over again, we confront the realization that our minds are too small to grasp fully the expansiveness, diversity, and surprise of the universe, never mind what lies beyond its farthest edges.

When we make assertions about knowing the truth, we remember that while there is reality and we can know it (indeed we stake our daily existence on being able to know it), what we know of it is always partial and even potentially less reflective of the totality of what is true than it is reflective. For example, when I claim "God is good," my understanding of what "good" means is miniscule in comparison to God's actual goodness. So, while it is true to say that God is good, it is also true that what I have in mind when I say "God is good" is less reflective of the totality of God's goodness than it is reflective of that totality. Humility is of the essence.

Such awareness raises other questions: If we as humans are never going to really be able to grasp the whole picture, should we even bother trying to have conversations about these things? Is it worth it to invest so much of our time and energy on an unmasterable quest? I answer yes.

Though we will never know all that is to be known, and though time may prove that what we think we know is riddled with inadequacies, we do not pursue truth with the assumption that someday we will possess truth but, rather, the hope that someday truth will possess us.[3] Every time that we humbly open ourselves to finding out more—be it about gravity or another's faith or even the source of another's disagreement with us—it is a gesture toward letting truth (that is, God) more and more into our lives. The puzzle pieces of our experience often do not seem to all fit together and indeed appear to contradict what we previously thought was real. Sometimes the best we can do is hold on to new insights like we hold on to unlabeled keys when we are not sure which door they open. We trust that someday it will become clear where everything goes, but for the time being, we must become comfortable with a degree of messiness. In the words of novelist Zora Neale Hurston, "There are years that ask questions and years that answer them."[4] *Years*, she stresses, not hours. Pursuing truth is a life work, not meant for the faint of heart.

The fourteen-hundred-year-old Benedictine community has a remarkable way of expressing this commitment to always remain open to the

---

3. This concept has a long history within Christianity and could be attributed to a number of sources, most recently including Benedict XVI, Christmas Address 2012, as cited in James L. Fredericks, "Francis's Interreligious Friendships: Soccer and Lunch, Followed by Dialogue," *Commonweal* 141, no. 13 (August 15, 2014): 13–16.

4. Zora Neale Hurston, *Their Eyes Were Watching God* (Champaign: University of Illinois Press, 1991), 27.

ambiguous unknown. While the monks take vows of obedience and stability, each monk also takes a vow of "*conversatio morum*," or "conversion of life." Each monk thus makes a lifelong promise to keep changing and learning and growing, believing that ultimately the question marks that trouble our minds are not problems to be dismissed with a shrug nor threats to be feared but, rather, the crooked finger of God beckoning us to draw nearer.

An important insight of the Benedictine tradition is that *conversatio*, or conversion, as implied by the Latin root, most frequently happens through conversation. Critical insights into reality and especially ourselves most often arrive in the form of dialogue with others. The twentieth-century Trappist monk and spiritual writer Thomas Merton was so intrigued by this idea, he titled one compilation of his personal journals *A Vow of Conversation*. He knew that he needed the wisdom and the rub of dialogue partners who did not think like him in order to become ever more aligned with what is real. Truth is not a solitary pursuit.

Speak Truthfully

It seems only natural that if we are going to speak about a "vow of conversation," we need to say something about speaking, and if that conversation is about a quest for truth, the conversations need to be spoken truthfully. Perhaps at no other time in the world's history has it been as clear as it is now that there must be a profound consonance between the content of our communication and our method of communicating it.[5] For example, we know there is an internal contradiction when a teacher instills quiet in a classroom by yelling, "Be quiet!" Or when a rally for peace involves the destruction of property and the condemnation of particular people. There is a mismatch between message and medium.

Our commitment to pursue truth has certain implications for the very tenor of our speech. Often the first thing that comes to mind when we think about speaking truthfully is speaking honestly, not hiding things or holding them back. It is a very important marker of truthful speech, but there is more. The fact that truth is always bigger than what we can see means that our speech must always be marked by curiosity. We must always be asking, "What am I missing?" The fact that truth is always bigger than what we can grasp means that our speech must never be cocky. It is possible others have angles on reality that we have yet to see. And the fact that truth is ultimately another name for God poses many additional implications.

---

5. Pope Paul VI, *Evangelii Nuntiandi*, December 8, 1975, par. 41: "Modern man listens more willingly to witnesses than to teachers, and if he does listen to teachers, it is because they are witnesses."

In the Christian scriptures, St. John says God is love.[6] We have to think about what such a claim means. Love, by its very nature, is not coercive. It cannot be forced. It always allows the other to freely respond. No one wants to be "loved" by someone who is being paid to do so. Hence, speaking truthfully implies absence of coercion or pressure. It leaves people space to explain themselves and change their mind. And it should open us to changing our minds if we are persuaded to do so. It even implies vulnerability—being open to the fact that the other is not in our control and might not respond as hoped.

I feel so strongly about this principle of consonance between message and method that, at this point in time, I keep the Bible and the book *Difficult Conversations: How to Discuss What Matters Most* right next to each other on my bookshelf.[7] One tells me what I believe; the other gives me a way to communicate it curiously, humbly, lovingly—in essence, in a way that is most deeply compatible with what I believe.

Be True

There is one last practice that I see as important for having conversations about things that really matter. Also, perhaps this will appear less obvious than the other two practices, but I suspect it is the most central of them all: if truth is ultimately not an object that one possesses, but a subject to whom one relates, it makes sense that commitment to relationship is going to play a critical role in the quest for what is "really real." Already in the fifth century, Augustine of Hippo postulated, "*Nemo nisi per amicitiam cognoscitur*" (No one learns except by friendship).[8] Whether we are talking about astronomy or calculus, the intricacies of Arabic grammar, the writing of Maimonides, or the woman in the office next door, we will never grasp what that subject has to reveal unless approached with the disposition with which one would approach a friend. If we wish to see a deer in the woods, the last thing we should do is loudly go tromping down the path, demanding it show itself.[9] Subjects only reveal themselves fully when met with patient kindness.

To be serious about pursuing truth requires fidelity to relationships. It requires hanging in there with people, even after they have stopped being interesting. It means still being there even after their jokes seem stale and their laugh just a bit grating. It means still showing up, even when you can

---

6. 1 Jn 4:8.

7. Douglas Stone et al., *Difficult Conversations: How to Discuss What Matters Most* (New York: Viking Press, 1999).

8. Augustine of Hippo, *De Diversis* 83.71.5.

9. This allusion is borrowed from Parker Palmer, *A Hidden Wholeness* (San Francisco: Jossey-Bass, 2004), 58–59.

guess the next word to come out of their mouth and the story they are about to tell, and all of their issues are spectacularly clear to everyone except themselves. And you know they say the same thing about you.

From ancient times, friendship has been regarded as a school of virtue—a place where we can become better people precisely because it is a place where we can feel safe enough to test out our ideas, get feedback on them, make mistakes, and still know ourselves as cared for. Because we are accepted exactly as we are, we can, ironically, actually become different persons. In essence, *conversatio morum* requires the capacity to be true.

Not all of your dialogue relationships need to be this way; indeed, that would be exhausting. But I am saying at least some of your dialogue relationships need to be this way. If you are going to be serious about lifelong discovery and transformation, you must find—as the Benedictines figured out so long ago—some real stability of conversation partners to whom you bind your own journey.

Which is why, months after the actual symposium at the school took place, the six of us found ourselves again sitting around the dinner table engaged in the same kind of back-and-forth debating that had gotten us into this project in the first place. And it was only then that the glacier calved. For the longest time I had experienced Dan's persistence and intensity in conversation as disrespectful and degrading. But it was only when I had come to know him as a person that I suddenly saw him in another light:

"You," I pointed at Dan across the table from me. "You have been disagreeing with me from the day you arrived. There is not one idea I've had that you've not opposed or quibbled about. But you aren't doing this because you find me your intellectual inferior, but because you see me as your intellectual equal. You find it mentally fun to debate." He shrugged like, "Of course, what did you think?"

I had been reading Dan wrong. Because his behavior had impacted me badly, I had assumed that he meant to be difficult; that he meant to hurt me. But for Dan, debating someone was a sign of honor. It meant he found them a worthy conversation partner. Dan's ideas did not change one iota during our remaining time as colleagues, but his behavior simply stopped irritating me after that night. When I could see his intent more clearly, his behavior stopped impacting me the same way.

Conclusion

So you see, the "thirteen-hour" anecdote beloved by my colleague the Harvard negotiator is just the beginning of the story. Although it would not sound good in a grant report—"After having spent twenty thousand of your dollars, we still don't agree on anything, but I am happy to report that *one* of my colleagues no longer continually infuriates me"—this rapprochement should not be underestimated when compared to our current political climate of endless cycles of anger, offense, and revenge fueled by often deliberate misunderstandings. What distinguishes "differences-that-don't-make-a-difference" from those that do, is that "differences-that-don't-make-a-difference" do not tax relationships. It is easy to still laugh and joke, give and take, and do all those things that we have been trained to do as people committed to dialogue. But when we are personally impacted negatively by another's stance, those capacities rapidly disappear.

In those situations—to paraphrase the thought of Roger Fisher, founder of the Harvard Negotiation Project—we often think we have only two options: we can take a "hard" (read: strong, principled) stance on the issue and hence be "hard" (read: demanding, aggressive) on the relationship, or we can be "soft" (read: nice, accommodating, flexible) on the relationship and hence "soft" (read: wishy-washy, relativistic) on the issue. It is possible, though, Fisher thought, to be hard on the issue and soft on the relationship. It is possible to be a person of firm values and convictions and at the same time utterly committed to the well-being of the others and gentle with their person.[10] Or to use the image of the glacier again: it is possible to be both solid and rooted and moving at the exact same time. To the casual observer, it will look like nothing is happening. It will look as if our conversations are going nowhere. But these drips are nevertheless carving mountains and sustaining rivers and changing the landscape with a might beyond our wildest imagination.

And so this summer, at the height of a busy schedule, I will take time out to gather at a cabin in the woods with some of the same people who locked themselves with me in that room for thirteen hours. Long after our initial grant funding has ceased, a couple of us continue to practice the "vow of conversation" with each other. We don't work with each other anymore, having moved on to different positions, in different fields. We even live in different cities. But we still have a commitment to go away with each other two weekends each year, to continue to seek truth, speak truthfully, and be true to one another. We bring the hardest questions we are wrestling with in our current lives to get honest, loving feedback from one another. And we still talk until the pizza burns. Sometimes we even call our Harvard mediator and tell her how we are going at it again. And on the other end of the phone, I can almost feel her roll her eyes and hear her sigh back at us.

10. The language of "hard" and "soft" versus "principled" bargaining is used in Roger Fisher and William Ury, with Bruce Patton, *Getting to Yes: Negotiating Agreement Without Giving In*, 2nd ed. (New York: Penguin, 1991), see especially chapter 1.

Conclusion:
The Church and World Religions

VERY REV. MARK M. MOROZOWICH

The twenty-first century presents new challenges and opportunities for creating a better future. As we evaluate the current state of affairs, many issues bring pause for thought. Religious identity and affiliations seem to be waning in a post-Christian West while fundamentalism and ethnic battles continue to batter the Middle East. In addition, a persistent xenophobia increases in the United States. These issues are just a few of the obstacles to peace throughout the world and specifically in the United States. They affect all religions and have a profound impact on the Catholic Church. Dealing with the other, especially with the other of another religion, provokes many concerns. In response to the differing religions of our neighbors at a time of large-scale migrations, the Catholic Church offers a prophetic stance to other religions as exemplified by the Second Vatican Council's *Nostra Aetate*.

In particular, *Nostra Aetate* 2 compels us to understand others in a more profound manner: "The Church therefore exhorts her sons and daughters to recognize, preserve, and foster the good things, spiritual and moral, as well as the socio-cultural values found among the followers of other religions. This is done through conversations and collaboration with them, carried out with prudence and love and in witness to the Christian faith and life."[1] This exhortation develops a central message of Christianity—to love your neighbor as yourself—however, it confounds many as it clearly calls each of us to deeper responsibility toward all people, especially those who profess other religions. While slow progress moves us ever forward on our aim of making our world a better, more hospitable place, we must not become complacent with the status quo or allow cynicism to corrupt our lofty goals and ideas.

This book of essays, the product of the interreligious community gathered to commemorate the fiftieth anniversary of the Second Vatican Council's decree *Nostra Aetate* in a symposium sponsored by The Catholic University of America and the United States Conference of Catholic Bishops (USCCB) in May 2015, demonstrates the success of this fifty-year-old

---

1. Translation by Thomas F. Stransky, CSP.

document. Buddhists, Hindus, Jews, Muslims, Sikhs—just to name a few—gathered, discussed, debated, and shared one another's company. This type of gathering was certainly not commonplace before the Second Vatican Council, but it became possible because of *Nostra Aetate*. The commitment of the Catholic Church to engage diverse religions throughout the world continues to remain strong as witnessed by the presentations of two cardinals of the Roman Curia, Cardinal Koch and Cardinal Tauran, as well as Cardinal Dolan of New York. In addition, the existence of entire offices of the Roman Curia, as well as the USCCB, dedicated to furthering interreligious dialogue testify to the value placed on such endeavors by the Catholic Church. The cordial and frank interaction at the conference provides prophetic witness in the United States that everyone should engage in such relationships. Likewise, it witnesses to other countries and cultures that it is possible for various religions to gather in peace and to exchange ideas, hopes, and aspirations. I hope that this collection of essays provides a lasting memorial to the conviviality experienced there while providing stimulus for future scholarly and interreligious endeavors. These efforts hopefully will assist in developing lasting peace on our planet.

The essays not only mark the past but also set the stage for the next decades as we build on successes and learn from missteps. Each of us must confront the challenges of extremism of every sort that provoke xenophobia and tend toward simplistic religious understandings. The co-opting of religion for political gain clearly distorts the true nature of our quest for God and demonstrates the need for a deeper and more comprehensive approach in an effort to live together and follow similar paths to God in peace. As Catholics, we have a unique responsibility to fulfill the vision set forth in the Second Vatican Council. *Nostra Aetate* 1 remains so very important today:

> In our time, when day by day humankind is being drawn ever closer together and the ties between different peoples are being strengthened, the Church examines with greater care her relation to non-Christian religions. In her task of fostering unity and love among individuals, indeed among peoples, she considers above all in this Declaration what human beings have in common and what draws them to live together their destiny.[2]

The unique character of dialogue and discussion characteristic of religious leaders and institutions in the United States might serve as an example for other countries. The Secretariat of Ecumenical and Interreligious Affairs of the USCCB focuses the efforts of the Catholic Church in the

2. Ibid. 1.

United States on these types of dialogue. I refer to two essays by staff members of this secretariat that help provide a summation. Dr. Anthony Cirelli provides a comprehensive overview of interreligious dialogue history among the Muslim and other religions apart from Judaism. Fr. John W. Crossin illustrates the well-developed Jewish-Catholic dialogue that has accomplished so much since the publication of *Nostra Aetate*. No other dialogue comes close to matching its efficacy.

I mention these two essays in particular as bookmarks that help summarize and accentuate the importance of dialogue. One of the greatest lessons from the various interreligious dialogues in the United States is that we need to be ever mindful of the need for grassroots efforts. This focus does not diminish the highest levels of academic exchanges. Rather, it recognizes the importance of academic life as an exercise of dialogue in the mainstream. The academy provides the expertise and depth of tradition to provide new perspective and horizons for the wider discussions.

The continual challenges of relationships across religious boundaries should come as little to no surprise. If we examine relationships within faith communities, strife and disagreement often mar the communion that is meant to characterize the fellowship. All too often, these misunderstandings have led to the splintering of communities into smaller groups, destabilizing the original unity. One need only focus on recent events and even the not-too-distant past to see the ravages of such discord, from the infamous Protestant and Catholic strife in Ireland to the Sunni and Shia conflicts played out in the Middle East. Popular American pundits tend to blame religion for violence: this naïve supposition ignores political and ethnic realities that often utilize religious differences to justify their political aims.

Future hopes for peace will depend on a great mutual understanding and mutual trust. While progress over the last fifty years has provided many positive examples of collaboration and interreligious dialogue, we still need to do much more work. I think that the 2014 publication *Dialogue in Truth and Charity: Pastoral Orientations for Interreligious Dialogue*, from the Pontifical Council for Interreligious Dialogue, provides much needed direction by identifying six areas for future work: "1. defending human dignity and promoting human rights; 2. establishing bonds of trust and friendship among religious leaders; 3. educating the youth for interreligious cooperation; 4. interreligious cooperation in healthcare services; 5. ministry to persons in interreligious marriages; 6. prayer and symbolic gestures."[3] An honest appraisal of our world and the still-fractured relation-

---

3. Pontifical Council for Interreligious Dialogue, *Dialogue in Truth and Charity: Pastoral Orientations for Interreligious Dialogue* (Vatican City: Libreria Editrice Vaticana, 2014): 38–54.

ships among people of different faiths reveals how much they are bound by mutual suspicion and fear. Each of these goals builds on top of each other. Perhaps the commitment to human rights and dignity seems obvious, yet it evades the everyday life of so many people, even here in the United States. The other five points flow from this fundamental position. Certainly, religious leaders share the burden of providing the lived examples by developing relationships of trust and exchange as they must initiate it and set the example. Perhaps the most important aspect is the last, prayer and symbolic gestures. As a priest of the Ukrainian Catholic Church, I am often surprised at the lack of interaction and knowledge of the Latin Rite faithful regarding their Eastern Catholic sisters and brothers. If the challenges facing people of the same faith and ecclesial communion are so large, then one easily comprehends the formidable challenge of acquainting people of different religions.

I hope that the closing paragraph of *Nostra Aetate*, paragraph 5, provides some much-needed perspective:

> We cannot truly call upon God, the Father of all, if we refuse to behave as sisters and brothers with anyone, created as all are in the image of God. The relation of man and woman to God, the Father, and their relation to their fellow human beings are linked to such a degree that Holy Scripture says, "Whoever does not love does not know God" (1 Jn 4:8).
>
> No foundation therefore remains for any theory or practice that leads to discrimination between person and person and between people and people insofar as their human dignity and the rights flowing from it are concerned.
>
> The Church reproves, as foreign to the mind of Christ, any discrimination or harassment against men or women because of their race or color, condition in life or religion. On the contrary, following the footsteps of the Holy Apostles Peter and Paul, this Sacred Synod ardently implores the Christian faithful to "maintain good conduct among the peoples" (1 Pt 2:12), and, if possible, to live for their part in peace with all, so that they may truly be sons and daughters of the Father who is in heaven.

This ardent appeal does not call for syncretism among religions; rather, it calls for mutual respect. I trust that these essays both edified and enriched you. Now remains the call to action, to reach out to our own communities and help them grow while being open to people of diverse religions. I hope that the conviviality experienced in May 2015 may take root throughout our communities.

Bibliography

DOCUMENTS OF THE SECOND VATICAN COUNCIL

Each can be found at
http://www.vatican.va/archive/hist_councils/ii_vatican_council/index.htm

Vatican Council II, *Ad Gentes: Decree on the Mission Activity of the Church*. December 7, 1965.
————, *Dignitatis Humanae*, December 7, 1965.
————, *Gaudium et Spes*, December 7, 1965.
————, *Lumen Gentium*, November 21, 1964.
————, *Nostra Aetate*, October 28, 1965.
————, *Unitatis Redintegratio*, November 21, 1964.

ADDITIONAL DOCUMENTS OF THE CATHOLIC CHURCH AND
OTHER RELIGIOUS BODIES

(Unless another publisher is indicated, documents appear at w2.vatican.va)

American Jewish Committee. *In Our Time: AJC and* Nostra Aetate: *A Reflection after 50 Years*. New York: American Jewish Committee, 2015.
Benedict XVI, "Address of His Holiness Benedict XVI to Participants in the Tenth Assembly of the Pontifical Council for Interreligious Dialogue," *Pro Dialogo* 129, no. 3 (2008).
————. "Auschwitz-Birkenau: The Visit to the Concentration Camp on 28 May 2006." In *Insegnamenti di Benedetto XVI*. Vol. II, no. 1, 724–29. Vatican City: Libreria Editrice Vaticana, 2007.
————. *Caritas in Veritate*, Encyclical Letter. June 29, 2009.
————. "Never to Be Denied or Forgotten. The Visit to the Yad Vashem Memorial on 11 May 2009." In *Insegnamenti di Benedetto XVI*. vol. V, no. 1, 787–89. Vatican City: Libreria Editrice Vaticana, 2010.
————. "Un cammino irrevocabile di fraterna collaborazione. Incontro con la Comunità Ebraica nel Tempio Maggiore degli Ebrei di Roma il 17 gennaio 2010." In *Insegnamenti di Benedetto XVI*. Vol. VI, no. 1, 86–92. Vatican City: Libreria Editrice Vaticana, 2011.
Bishops' Committee for Ecumenical and Interreligious Affairs, National Conference of Catholic Bishops, *Guidelines for Catholic-Jewish Relations*. Washington, D.C.: National Conference of Catholic Bishops, 1967.
Commission for Religious Relations with the Jews. "The Gifts and the Calling of God Are Irrevocable: A Reflection on Theological Questions Pertaining to Catholic-Jewish Relations on the Occasion of the 50th Anniversary of *Nostra Aetate*." December 10, 2015.

Commission for Religious Relations with the Jews. "Guidelines and Suggestions for Implementing the Conciliar Declaration *Nostra Aetate*." December 1, 1974.

Commission for Religious Relations with the Jews. "Notes on the Correct Way to Present the Jews and Judaism in Preaching and Catechesis in the Roman Catholic Church." March 6, 1982.

Commission for Religious Relations with the Jews. *We Remember: A Reflection on the Shoah*. March 16, 1998.

Pope Francis. "Message of His Holiness Francis for the Celebration of the World Day of Peace." January 1, 2014.

——, *Evangelii Gaudium*, Apostolic Exhortation. November 24, 2013.

International Dialogue between the Catholic Church and the Mennonite World Conference. *Called Together to be Peacemakers*. Kitchener, Canada: Pandora Press, 2005.

John Paul II-Benedict XVI. *Ebrei, fratelli maggiori. La necessità del dialogo tra cattolicesimo ed ebraismo nei discorsi di Papa Wojtyla e di Papa Ratzinger. A cura di Santino Spartà*. Rome: Newton Compton, 2007.

Pope John Paul II, "Address of John Paul II to the Representatives of the Christian Churches and Ecclesial Communities and of the World Religions," World Day of Prayer for Peace, Assisi, October 27, 1986.

——, "Address to the Jewish Community in Mainz, West Germany," November 17, 1980.

——, "Address in the Synagogue during the Meeting with the Jewish Community in Rome on 13 April 1986," in *Insegnamenti di Giovanni Paolo II*, IX, 1, 1024–31. Città del Vaticano: Libreria Editrice Vaticana, 1986.

——, "Allocution in the Great Roman Synagogue." April 13, 1986. http://www.sacredheart.edu/faithservice/centerforchristianandjewishunderstanding/documentsandstatements/

——, *Centesimus Annus*, Encyclical Letter. May 1, 1991.

——, "Discourse to Representatives of the Various Religions of the World at the Conclusion of the World Day of Prayer for Peace, Assisi, October 27, 1986," in *Interreligious Dialogue: The Official Teaching of the Catholic Church from the Second Vatican Council to John Paul II (1963-2005)*, edited by Francesco Gioia. Boston: Pauline Books & Media, 2006.

——. "Let Us Forgive and Ask Forgiveness! The Day of Pardon on the First Sunday of Lent of the Great Jubilee." in *Insegnamenti di Giovanni Paolo II*. Vol. XXIII, no. 1, 351–55. Vatican City: Libreria Editrice Vaticana, 2002.

——, "Message of His Holiness John Paul II on the 50th Anniversary of the Warsaw Ghetto Uprising," April 6, 1993.

——, *Novo Millennio Ineunte*, Apostolic Letter. January 6, 2001.

——, *Orientale Lumen*, Apostolic Letter. Vatican City: Libreria Editrice Vaticana, May 2, 1995.

——, "Message for the World Day of Peace 2004," in *Interreligious Dialogue: The Official Teaching of the Catholic Church from the Second Vatican Council to John Paul II (1963–2005)*, edited by Francesco Gioia. Boston: Pauline Books & Media, 2006.

————, "Message of His Holiness Pope John Paul II for the World Day of Peace," *Origins* 31, no. 28 (December 20, 2001).

————, *Sollicitudo Rei Socialis*, Encyclical Letter. December 30,1987.

————, Ut unum sint: *On Commitment to Ecumenism.* Vatican City: Libreria Editrice Vaticana, 1995.

————. "Victory of Faith and Love over Hatred. At the Brzezinka Concentration Camp on 7 June 1979." In *Insegnamenti di Giovanni Paolo II*, Vol. II (Gennaio-Giugno), 1482–1487. Vatican City: Libreria Editrice Vaticana, 1979.

The Lutheran-Mennonite International Study Commission, *Healing Memories: Reconciling in Christ.* Geneva, Switzerland: Lutheran World Federation; Strasbourg, France: Mennonite World Conference, 2010.

Pope Paul VI. "Address at the Opening of the Second Session of the Council." September 29, 1963. (*Acta Apostolicae Sedis* 55 [1963]).

————. *Ecclesiam Suam*, Encyclical Letter.August 6, 1964.

————. *Evangelii Nuntiandi*, Apostolic Exhortation. December 8, 1975.

Pope Pius XII, *Evangelii Praecones*, Encyclical Letter. June 2, 1951.

————. *Mystici Corporis*, Encyclical Letter. June 29, 1943.

Pontifical Biblical Commission, *The Jewish People and Their Sacred Scriptures in the Christian Bible.* May 24,2001.

Pontifical Council for Interreligious Dialogue. *Dialogue in Truth and Charity: Pastoral Orientations for Interreligious Dialogue.* Vatican City: Libreria Editrice Vaticana, 2014.

Secretariat for Catholic-Jewish Relations, Bishops' Committee for Ecumenical and Interreligious Affairs, National Conference of Catholic Bishops. *Guidelines for Catholic-Jewish Relations: 1985 Revisions* (Washington, D.C.: United States Catholic Conference, 1985)

Secretariat for Ecumenical and Interreligious Affairs, National Conference of Catholic Bishops. *Catholic Teaching on the Shoah: Implementing the Holy See's We Remember.*Washington, D.C.: United States Catholic Conference, 2001.

Secretariat for Non-Christians. *The Attitude of the Church toward Followers of Other Religions: Reflections and Orientations on Dialogue and Mission.* May 10, 1984. http://www.cimer.org.au/documents/DialogueandMission1984.pdf

World Buddhist Sangha Council, "The Basic Points Unifying the Theravada and the Mahayana." 1967. http://www.buddhisma2z.com/content.php?id=432

World Council of Churches. "Baar Statement: Theological Perspectives on Plurality." January 15, 1990. https//www.oikoumene.org

OTHER RELEVANT LITERATURE

Abbott, SJ, Walter and Joseph Gallagher. *Documents of Vatican II.* New York: Herder and Herder Association Press, 1966.

Abu-Nimer, Mohammed. *Nonviolence and Peace-Building in Islam: Theory and Practice.* Gainesville: University Press of Florida, 2003.

Ali, Abdallah Yusuf. *The Holy Qur'an: Text, Translation and Commentary*. Beirut: Dar al Arabia, 1968.

Amaladoss, SJ, Michael. "Inter-religious Worship." In *The Wiley-Blackwell Companion to Inter-religious Dialogue* edited by Catherine Cornille, 87–98. Chichester: Wiley-Blackwell, 2013.

Anawati, Georges. "Exkurs zum Konzilstext über die Muslim." In *Lexikon für Theologie und Kirche (zweite Auflage)*. Vol. XIII, 485–87. Freiburg i. Br.: Herder, 1967.

Augustin Cardinal Bea. "Declaration on the Jews and the Non-Christians" In *Die Kirche und das jüdische Volk*. 148–57. Freiburg im Breisgau: Herder, 1966. [Available in English as *The Church and the Jewish People*, translated by Philip Loretz. New York: Harper and Row, 1966.]

———. "On the Attitude of Catholics toward Non-Christians and Especially toward Jews" In *Die Kirche und das jüdische Volk*. 141–47. Freiburg i. Br.: Herder 1966. [Available in English as *The Church and the Jewish People*. London: Chapman, 1966.]

Ayoub, Mahmoud M. "Abraham and His Children: A Muslim Perspective." In *Heirs of Abraham: The Future of Muslim, Jewish and Christian Relations*, edited by Bradford E. Hinze and Irfan A. Omar, 94–111. New York: Orbis Books, 2005.

Backhaus, Knut. "Das Bundesmotiv in der frühkirchlichen Schwellenzeit." In *Der ungekündigte Bund: Antworten des Neuen Testaments*, edited by Hubert Frankemölle, 211–31. Freiburg i. Br.: Herder, 1998.

Bass, Diana Butler. *Christianity for the Rest of Us: How the Neighborhood Church Is Transforming Faith*. San Francisco: Harper, 2006.

Becker, Karl and Ilaria Morali, eds. *Catholic Engagement with World Religions: A Comprehensive Study*. Maryknoll, N.Y.: Orbis Books, 2010.

Ben-Chorin, Schalom. *Die Antwort des Jona zum Gestaltwandel Israels*. Hamburg: Reich, 1956.

Pope Benedict XVI. *Jesus of Nazareth: Holy Week: From the Entrance into Jerusalem to the Resurrection*. San Francisco, Calif.: Ignatius Press, 2011.

Berger, Joseph. "The Papal Visit: Pope Defends Vatican's Response to Holocaust in Talks With Jews." *New York Times*, September 12, 1987.

Bergoglio, Jorge Mario and Abraham Skorka. *On Heaven and Earth: Pope Francis on Faith, Family, and the Church in the Twenty-first Century*. New York: Image, 2013.

de Béthune, OSB, Pierre-François. "Monastic Inter-religious Dialogue." In *The Wiley-Blackwell Companion to Inter-religious Dialogue*, edited by Catherine Cornille, 34–50. Chichester: Wiley-Blackwell, 2013.

Borelli, John. "*Unitatis Redintegratio* and *Nostra Aetate*: Reception at the Fifty Year Mark in the New Era of Pope Francis." *Ecumenical Trends* 42, no. 8 (2013): 113–21.

Brechenmacher, Thomas. *Der Vatikan und die Juden. Geschichte einer unheiligen Beziehung*. München: Verlag C.H. Beck, 2005.

Bruner, Jerome, *The Culture of Education*. Cambridge, Mass.: Harvard University Press, 1996.

————. *Making Stories: Law, Literature, Life*. Cambridge, Mass.: Harvard University Press, 2003.

Buber, Martin. *Der Jude und sein Judentum*. Köln: Lambert Schneider, 1963.

Buddhadāsa Bhikkhu. *Dhammic Socialism*, translated and edited by Donald K. Swearer. Bangkok: Thai Interreligious Commission for Development, 1986.

Al-Bukhari, Muhammad b. Isma'il, *Sahih al-Bukhari*. Beirut and Damascus: Dar Ibn Kathir, 2002.

Bunson, Matthew E. *Our Sunday Visitor's Catholic Almanac 2015*. Huntington, Ind.: Our Sunday Visitor, 2014.

Burford. Grace G. "Asymmetry, Essentialism, and Covert Cultural Imperialism: Should Buddhists and Christians Do Theoretical Work Together?" *Buddhist-Christian Studies* 31 (2011): 147–57.

Burrell, David. *Towards a Jewish-Christian-Muslim Theology*. Chichester: Wiley-Blackwell, 2011.

Cassidy, Edward Idris *Ecumenism and Interreligious Dialogue*: Unitatis Redintegratio, Nostra Aetate. Mahwah, N.J.: Paulist Press, 2005.

Cheetham, David, Ulrich Winkler, Oddbjørn Leirvik, and Judith Gruber, eds. *Interreligious Hermeneutics in Pluralistic Europe: Between Texts and People*. Amsterdam; New York: Rodopi, 2011.

Cheetham, David, Douglas Pratt, and David Thomas, eds. *Understanding Interreligious Relations*. Oxford: Oxford University Press, 2013.

Clooney, Francis X. "Comparative Theology and Inter-religious Dialogue." In *The Wiley-Blackwell Companion to Inter-religious Dialogue*, edited by Catherine Cornille, 51–63. Chichester: Wiley-Blackwell, 2013.

————. *Comparative Theology. Deep Learning across Religious Borders*. Chichester: Wiley-Blackwell, 2010.

————. "The Study of Non-Christian Religions in the Post-Vatican II Roman Catholic Church." *Journal of Ecumenical Studies* 28, no. 3 (1991): 482–94.

Congar, OP, Yves. *Mon journal du Concile*. Paris: 2002. [available in English as *My Journal of the Council*. Collegeville, Minn.: Liturgical Press, 2012.]

Connelly, John. *From Enemy to Brother: The Revolution in Catholic Teaching on the Jews 1933-1965*. Cambridge, Mass., and London: Harvard University Press, 2011.

Cooperrider, David and Diane Whitney. *The Appreciative Inquiry Handbook: For Leaders of Change*. 2nd ed. San Francisco: Berrett-Koehler Publishers, 2008.

Cornille, Catherine, ed. *Criteria of Discernment in Interreligious Dialogue*. Eugene, Oregon: Wipf and Stock, 2009.

————. *The Im-possibility of Interreligious Dialogue*. New York: Crossroad/Herder & Herder, 2008.

————, ed. *Interreligious Dialogue and Cultural Change*. Eugene, Oregon: Wipf and Stock, 2012.

————, ed. *Interreligious Hermeneutics*. Eugene, Oregon: Wipf and Stock, 2010.

————, ed. *Many Mansions: Multiple Religious Belonging and Christian Identity*. Maryknoll, N.Y.: Orbis Books, 2002.

————, ed. *Women and Interreligious Dialogue*. Eugene, Oregon: Wipf and Stock, 2013.

———, ed. *The World Market and Interreligious Dialogue*. Eugene, Oregon: Wipf and Stock, 2011.

Dasa, Saunaka Risi. "ISKCON and Interfaith: ISKCON in Relation to People of Faith in God." *ISKCON Communications Journal* 7, no. 1 (1999).

D'Costa, Gavin, ed. *The Catholic Church and the World Religions: A Theological and Phenomenological Account*. London: T&T Clark, 2011.

———. *Christianity and World Religions: Disputed Questions in the Theology of Religions*. Chichester: Wiley-Blackwell, 2009.

———. "Continuity and Reform in Vatican II's Teaching on Islam." *New Blackfriars* 94, no. 1050 (March 2013): 208–22.

———. *Vatican II: Catholic Doctrines on Jews and Muslims*. Oxford: Oxford University Press, 2014.

———. "Vatican II on Muslims and Jews: The Council's Teachings on Other Religions." In *The Second Vatican Council: Celebrating Its Achievements and the Future*. edited by Gavin D'Costa and Emma Jane Harris, 105–20. London: Bloomsbury T&T Clark, 2013.

Declerck, Leo. *Les agendes conciliaires de Mgr. J. Willebrands, secrétaire du secretariat pour l'unité des Chrétiens*. traduction française annotée. Leuven: Peeters, 2009.

Denning, Stephen. *The Leader's Guide to Storytelling: Mastering the Art and Discipline of Business Narrative*. San Francisco: Jossey-Bass, 2005.

Donner, Fred M. "Muhammad and the Caliphate." In *The Oxford History of Islam*. edited by John L. Esposito, 49–52. New York: Oxford University Press, 1999.

Dupuis, Jacques. *Toward a Christian Theology of Religious Pluralism*. Maryknoll, N.Y.: Orbis Books, 1997.

Emmanuel, Métropolite and Kurt Cardinal Koch. *L'esprit de Jérusalem. L'orthodoxie et le catholicisme au XXIeme siècle*. Paris: Cerf, 2014.

Ernesti, Jörg. *Paul VI. Der vergessene Papst*. Freiburg i. Br.: Herder, 2012.

Fentress-Williams, Judy. *Abingdon Old Testament Commentaries: Ruth*. Nashville: Abingdon Press, 2012.

Fisher, E. J. and L. Klenicki, eds. *The Saint for Shalom: How Pope John Paul II Transformed Catholic-Jewish Relations: The Complete Texts 1979-2005*. New York: Crossroad, 2011.

Fisher, Eugene. "Kennedy Institute Jewish-Christian-Muslim Trialogue." *Journal of Ecumenical Studies* 19, no. 1 (Winter 1982): 197–200.

Fisher, Roger and William Ury with Bruce Patton. *Getting to Yes: Negotiating Agreement Without Giving In*. 2nd ed. New York: Penguin, 1991.

Fitzgerald, Michael L. "Interreligious Relations Today: The Remarkable Relevance of *Nostra Aetate*." *Pro Dialogo* 119, no. 2 (2005).

———. "Lebanon-Broumana: Muslim Christian Consultation (July 1972)." In *Bulletin, Secretariatus pro non Christianis* 21 (1972): 58–62.

———. "Relations among the Abrahamic Religions: A Catholic Point of View." In *Heirs of Abraham*, edited by Bradford E. Hinze and Irfan A. Omar, 55–78. Maryknoll, N.Y.: Orbis Books, 2005.

———. "Revisiting *Nostra Aetate* after Fifty Years." In *Revisiting Vatican II: 50 Years of Renewal*, edited by Shaji George Kochuthara, CMI, 55–78. Bangalore: Dharmaram Publications, 2014.

———. "A Theological Reflection on Interreligious Dialogue." In *Catholic Engagement with World Religions: A Comprehensive Study*, edited by Karl Josef Becker and Ilaria Morali, 383–94. Maryknoll, N.Y.: Orbis Books, 2010.

Flannery, OP, Austin. *The Conciliar and Post Conciliar Documents.* Northport, N.Y.: Costello Publishing Co., 1975.

Ford, David F. and Frances Clemson, eds. *Interreligious Reading after Vatican II: Scriptural Reasoning, Comparative Theology and Receptive Ecumenism.* Chichester: Wiley-Blackwell, 2013.

Ford, David and Chad C. Pecknold, eds. *The Promise of Scriptural Reasoning.* Malden, Mass.: Blackwell, 2006.

Fredericks, James L. *Buddhists and Christians: Through Comparative Theology to a New Solidarity.* New York: Orbis Books, 2004.

———. *Faith among Faiths: Christian Theology and Non-Christian Religion.* Mahwah, N.J.: Paulist Press, 1999.

———. "Francis's Interreligious Friendships: Soccer and Lunch, Followed by Dialogue." *Commonweal* 141, no. 13 (August 15, 2014): 13-16.

Fredericks, James L. and Tracy Sayuki Tiemeier, eds. *Interreligious Friendship after Nostra Aetate.* New York: Palgrave Macmillan, 2015.

Gaillardetz, Richard. *The Church in the Making.* Mahwah, N.J.: Paulist Press, 2006.

———. "A Culture of Encounter: Francis Wishes to Release Vatican II's Bold Vision from Captivity." In *National Catholic Reporter* 50, no. 1 (October 2013): 11–24.

Gardner, Howard. *Changing Minds: The Art and Science of Changing Our Own and Other People's Minds.* Boston: Harvard Business School Press, 2006.

Al-Ghazali, Abu Hamid, *Ihya' 'Ulum al-Din*, edited by Badawi Tabanah. Indonesia: Kariata Futra, n.d.

Gioia, Francesco, ed. *Interreligious Dialogue: The Official Teaching of the Catholic Church from the Second Vatican Council to John Paul II (1963-2005).* Mahwah, N.J.: Paulist Publications, 2006.

Gopin, Marc. *Between Eden and Armageddon: The Future of World Religions, Violence, and Peacemaking.* Oxford and New York: Oxford University Press, 2000.

———. *Bridges across an Impossible Divide: The Inner Lives of Arab and Jewish Peacemakers.* New York: Oxford University Press, 2012.

Greenberg, Irving. "Judaism and Christianity: Covenants of Redemption." In *Christianity in Jewish Terms*, edited by Tikva Frymer-Kensky, David Novak, Peter Ochs, David Fox Sandmel, and Michael A. Signer, 141–58. Boulder, Colo.: Westview Press, 2009.

Greene, Graham. *The Power and the Glory.* New York: Penguin, 1990.

Gregory the Great. *Homiliae in Ezechielem I*, VI, 15. [Available in English as *The Homilies of Saint Gregory the Great on the Book of the Prophet Ezekiel*, translated by Theodosia Gray. Etna, Calif.: Center for Traditionalist Orthodox Studies, 1990.]

Grieb, A. Katherine. *The Story of Romans: A Narrative Defense of God's Righteous-ness*. Chicago: University of Chicago Press, 2004.

Griffith, Sidney H. "Christians and Christianity." In *Encyclopedia of the Qur'an*, vol. I, edited by Jane D. McAuliffe, 307–16. Leiden: Brill, 2001–2006.

———. "Sharing the Faith of Abraham: The 'Credo' of Louis Massignon." *Islam and Christian-Muslim Relations* 8, no. 2 (1997): 193–210.

Gupta, Ravi M. "'He Is Our Master': Jesus in the Thought of Swami Prabhupada." *Journal of Hindu-Christian Studies* 23 (2010).

Habito, Ruben. *Zen and the Spiritual Exercises*. New York: Orbis Books, 2013.

Hayward, Joel "Warfare in the Qur'an." In *War and Peace in Islam*, edited by Prince Ghazi bin Muhammad et al. Cambridge: The Islamic Texts Society, 2013.

Heft, SM, James L., ed. *Catholicism and Interreligious Dialogue*. Oxford: Oxford University Press, 2012.

Henrix, Hans Herman. "*Nostra aetate* und die christlich-jüdischen Beziehungen." In *Das Zweite Vatikanische Konzil. Impulse und Perspektiven*. hrsg. Dirk Ansorge, 228–45. Münster: Aschendorff-Verlag, 2014.

Hershcopf, Judith. "The Church and the Jews: The Struggle at Vatican Council II." *American Jewish Year Book* 66 (1965).

Hick, John and Paul Knitter, eds. *The Myth of Christian Uniqueness: Toward a Pluralistic Theology of Religions*. Maryknoll, N.Y.: Orbis Books, 1987.

Hogan, John P. and George F. MacLean, eds. *Multiple Paths to God: Nostra Aetate, 40 Years Later*. Washington, D.C.: The Council for Research in Values and Philosophy, 2005.

Hoppe, David. *Active Listening: Improve Your Ability to Listen and Lead*. Greensboro, N.C.: Center for Creative Leadership, 2008.

Hurston, Zora Neale. *Their Eyes Were Watching God*. Champaign: University of Illinois Press, 1991.

Hussaini, Sayed Hassan Akhlaq. "Identity and Immigration: A Quranic Perspective." In *Immigration and Hospitality*, edited by John Hogan, Vensus A. George, and Corazon Toralba, 83–103. Washington, D.C.: CRVP, 2013.

Ibn Kathir, Isma'il b. 'Umar. *Tafsir al-Quran al-Azim*, edited by Sami bin Muhammad al-Salamah. Riyadh: Dar Rayyiba, 1999.

Jackson, Roger and John Makransky, eds. *Buddhist Theologies: Critical Reflections by Contemporary Buddhist Scholars*. London: Routledge, 2013.

Kadowaki, J. K. *Zen and the Bible*. Maryknoll, N.Y.: Orbis Books, 2014.

Kang, In-gun. *Buddhist-Christian Dialogue and Action in the Theravada Countries of Modern Asia: A Comparative Analysis of the Radical Orthopraxis of Bhikkhu Buddhadāsa and Aloysius Pieris*. London: Heythrop College, Doctoral Dissertation, 2012.

Kaplan, Edward. *Spiritual Radical: Abraham Joshua Heschel in America, 1940-1972*. New Haven: Yale University Press, 2009.

Kasper, Walter Cardinal. "Foreword." In *Christ Jesus and the Jewish People Today: New Explorations of Theological Interrelationships*, edited by Philip. A. Cunningham, x–xviii. Grand Rapids, Mich.: William B. Eerdmans, 2011.

Kennedy, Arthur. "The Declaration on the Relationship of the Church to Non-Christian Religions, *Nostra Aetate.*" In *Vatican II: Renewal within Tradition,* edited by Matthew Lamb and Matthew Levering, 397–409. Oxford: Oxford University Press, 2008.

Kennedy, SJ, Robert. *Zen Gifts to Christians.* New York: Continuum Publishing, 2004.

Keown, Damien, Charles S. Prebish, and Wayne R. Husted, eds. *Buddhism and Human Rights.* Surrey, UK: Curzon Press, 1998.

King, Sallie B. "From Is to Ought: Natural Law in Buddhadāsa Bhikku and Phra Prayudh Payyuto." In *Journal of Religious Ethics,* 3, no. 2 (2002): 275–93.

Knitter, Paul. *Introducing Theologies of Religions.* Maryknoll, N.Y.: Orbis Books, 2002.

———. *No Other Name? A Critical Survey of Christian Attitudes toward the World Religions.* Maryknoll, N.Y.: Orbis Books, 1985.

Kogon, Eugen and Johann Baptist Metz, eds. *Gott nach Auschwitz. Dimensionen des Massenmords am jüdischen Volk.* Freiburg i. Br.: Herder, 1979.

Küng, Hans. *Christentum und Weltreligionen.* München: Piper, 1984. [Available in English as *Christianity and World Religions: Paths of Dialogue with Islam, Hinduism, and Buddhism,* translated by Peter Heinegg. Maryknoll, N.Y.: Orbis Books, 1986.]

Kuschel, Karl-Josef. *Juden—Christen—Muslime: Herkunft und Zukunft,* Düsseldorf: Patmos, 2007.

Lamdan, Neville and Alberto Melloni, eds. Nostra Aetate: *Origins, Promulgation, Impact on Jewish-Catholic Relations.* Berlin: LIT Verlag, 2007.

Lapidus, Ira M. "Sultanates and Gunpowder Empires." In *The Oxford History of Islam.* Oxford: Oxford University Press, 1999.

Lefebure. Leo. *Life Transformed: Meditations on the Christian Scriptures in Light of Buddhist Perspectives.* Chicago: Acta Publications, 1997.

Leirvik, Oddbjørn. *Interreligious Studies: A Relational Approach to Religious Activism and the Study of Religion.* London: Bloomsbury, 2014.

Levine, Amy-Jill and Marc Zvi Brettler, eds. *Jewish Annotated New Testament.* New York: Oxford University Press, 2010.

Lindbeck, George. *The Nature of Doctrine: Religion and Theology in a Postliberal Age.* Louisville, Ky.: Westminster/John Knox, 2009.

Marshall, Bruce D. "The Disunity of the Church and the Credibility of the Gospel." *Theology Today* 50, no. 1 (1993): 78–89.

Martin, Ralph. *Will Many Be Saved? What Vatican II Actually Teaches and Its Implications for the New Evangelization.* Grand Rapids, Mich.; Cambridge: William B. Eerdmans, 2012.

Mays, Rebecca Kratz. *Interfaith Dialogue at the Grass Roots.* Philadelphia: Ecumenical Press, 2008.

McAdams, Dan P. *The Redemptive Self: Stories Americans Live By.* New York: Oxford University Press, 2006.

McAuliffe, Jane D. *Qur'anic Christians: An Analysis of Classical and Modern Exegesis.* Cambridge, Mass.; New York: Cambridge University Press, 1991.

Mitchell, Donald. *Spirituality and Emptiness: The Dynamics of Spiritual Life in Buddhism and Christianity*. Mahwah, N.J.: Paulist Press, 1991.

Mitchell, Donald W. and James Wiseman, OSB, eds. *The Gethsemani Encounter*. New York: Continuum, 1997.

Morali, Ilaria. "Salvation, Religions, and Dialogue in the Roman Magisterium: From Pius IX to Vatican II and Postconciliar Popes." In *Catholic Engagement with World Religions*, edited by Karl J. Becker and Ilaria Morali, 122–42. Maryknoll, N.Y.: Orbis Books, 2010.

Moyaert, Marianne. "Scriptural Reasoning as Inter-religious Dialogue." In *The Wiley-Blackwell Companion to Inter-religious Dialogue*, edited by Catherine Cornille, 64–86. Chichester: Wiley-Blackwell, 2013.

Mussner, Franz. *Die Kraft der Wurzel. Judentum—Jesus—Kirche*. Freiburg i. Br.: Herder, 1987.

Nasr, Seyyed Hossein. *The Essential Frithjof Schuon*. Bloomington, Ind.: World Wisdom, 2005.

———. "The Prayer of the Heart in Hesychasm and Sufism." In *Orthodox Christians and Muslims*, edited by N. M. Vaporis. Brookline, Mass.: Holy Cross Orthodox Press, 1986.

Newman, John Henry. *Catholic Sermons of Cardinal Newman*. London: Burns & Oates, 1957.

Ochs, Peter and Nancy Levene, eds. *Textual Reasonings*. London: SCM Press, 2002.

O'Collins, SJ, Gerald. *The Second Vatican Council on Other Religions*. Oxford: Oxford University Press, 2013.

Oesterreicher, J. "Kommentierende Einleitung zur 'Erklärung über das Verhältnis der Kirche zu den nichtchristlichen Religionen.'" In *Lexikon für Theologie und Kirche*, Band 13, 406–78. Freiburg: Herder, 1967.

Palmer, Parker. *A Hidden Wholeness*. San Francisco: Jossey-Bass, 2004.

Panikkar, Raimundo. "Christ, Abel, and Melchizedek: The Church and the Non-Abrahamic Religions." *Jeevadhara* (September/October 1971): 391–403.

Pannenberg, Wolfgang. "Das Besondere des Christentums." In *Judentum und Christentum Einheit und Unterschied: Ein Gespräch*, edited by Pinchas Lapide and Wolfgang Pannenberg, 19–31. München: Kaiser, 1981.

Patel, Eboo. *Acts of Faith*. Boston: Beacon Press, 2007.

Patel, Eboo and Patrice Brodeur, eds. *Building the Interfaith Youth Movement: Beyond Dialogue to Action*. Lanham, Md.: Rowman & Littlefield, 2006.

Peace, Jennifer Howe, Or N. Rose, and Gregory Mobley, eds. *My Neighbor's Faith: Stories of Interreligious Encounter, Growth, and Transformation*. Maryknoll, N.Y.: Orbis, 2012.

Prabhupada, A. C. Bhaktivedanta Swami, trans. *Bhagavad-gita As It Is*. New York: Bhaktivedanta Book Trust, 1972.

Przywara, Erich. "Römische Katholizität—All-christliche Ökumenizität." In *Gott in Welt. Festgabe für K. Rahner*, edited by Johann Baptist Metz et al., 524–28. Freiburg: Herder, 1964.

Puntarigyivat, Tavivat. "Dhammic Socialism: Political Thought of Buddhadāsa Bhikkhu." In *The Chulalongkorn Journal of Buddhist Studies* 2, no. 2 (2003): 189–207.

Queen, Christopher S. and Sallie B. King, eds. *Engaged Buddhism: Buddhist Liberation Movements in Asia.* Albany: State University of New York Press, 1996.

Quisinsky, Michael. "Jules Isaac." In *Personenlexikon zum Zweiten Vatikanischen Konzil,* edited by Michael Quisinsky and Peter Walter, 139–40. Freiburg i. Br.: Herder, 2012.

Ratzinger, Josef. *Die letzte Sitzungsperiode des Konzils.* Köln: J.P. Bachem, 1966.

Ratzinger, Josef Cardinal. "Das Erbe Abrahams." In *Weggemeinschaft des Glaubens. Kirche als Communio,* 235–38. Augsburg: Sankt Ulrich, 2002. [Available in English as *Pilgrim Fellowship of Faith,* translated by Henry Taylor. San Francisco: Ignatius Press, 2005.]

———. *Die Vielfalt der Religionen und der Eine Bund.* Hagen: Verlag Urfeld, 1998. [Available in English as *Many Religions, One Covenant: Israel, the Church, and the World,* translated by Graham Harrison. San Francisco: Ignatius Press, 2000.]

Recker, Dorothee. *Die Wegbereiter der Judenerklärung des Zweiten Vatikanischen Konzils. Johannes XXIII, Kardinal Bea und Prälat Oesterreicher—eine Darstellung ihrer theologischen Entwicklung.* Paderborn: Bonifatius, 2007.

Riedl, Gerda. *Modell Assisi: christliches Gebet und interreligiöser Dialog in heilsgeschichtlichem Kontext.* Berlin: De Gruyter, 1998.

Rosenthal, Gilbert S. *A Jubilee for All Time: The Copernican Revolution in Jewish-Christian Relations.* Eugene, Ore.: Pickwick Publications, 2014.

Rosenzweig, Franz. *Der Stern der Erlösung III,* 3rd ed. Heidelberg: Schneider, 1950.

Jalal ud-din Rumi. *The Mathnawi of Jalal ud-din Rumi,* translated and edited by Reynold Alleyne Nicholson. Tehran: Research Center of Booteh Publication Co., 1381/2002.

Ruokanen, Miikka. *The Catholic Doctrine of Non-Christian Religions according to the Second Vatican Council.* Leiden; New York: E. J. Brill, 1992.

Rūpagosvāmī, Sri. *Upadeshamrita (The Nectar of Instruction),* translated by Prabhupada. New York: Bhaktivedanta Book Trust, 1975.

Ryan, Thomas. *Interreligious Prayer: A Christian Guide.* Mahwah, N.J.: Paulist Press, 2008.

Sacks, Jonathan. "On Creative Minorities." *First Things* (January 2014).

Safran, A. et al. *Judaisme, anti-judaisme et christianisme: Colloque de l'Université de Fribourg.* Saint-Maurice: Editions Saint-Augustin, 2000.

Salemink, Theo, ed. *You Will Be Called Repairer of the Breach: The Diary of J.G.M. Willebrands 1958–1961.* Leuven: Peeters, 2009.

Saritoprak, Zeki. *Islam's Jesus.* Gainesville: University Press of Florida, 2014.

Schirch, Lisa. *Ritual and Symbol in Peacebuilding.* Bloomfield, CT: Kumarian Press, 2004.

Shannon, Thomas, ed. *The Hidden Ground of Love: The Letters of Thomas Merton on Religious Experience and Social Concerns.* New York: Farrar, Straus and Giroux, 1985.

Sharma, Arvind. *Hinduism as a Missionary Religion*. Albany: State University of New York Press, 2011.

Sherwin, Byron L. and Harold Kazimow, eds. *John Paul II and Interreligious Dialogue*. Maryknoll, N.Y.: Orbis Books, 1999.

Siddiqui, Mona. *Christians, Muslims & Jesus*. New Haven and London: Yale University Press, 2013.

Smock, David, ed. *Interfaith Dialogue and Peacebuilding*. Washington, D.C.: United States Institute of Peace Press, 2002.

Söding, Thomas. "Erwählung—Verstockung—Errettung. Zur Dialektik der paulinischen Israeltheologie in Röm 9-11." In *Communio. Internationale katholische Zeitschrift* 39 (2010): 382–417.

Soloveitchik, Joseph B. "Confrontation," *Tradition: A Journal of Orthodox Thought* 6, no. 2 (1964): 5–29.

Soulen, R. Kendall. *The God of Israel in Christian Theology*. Minneapolis: Fortress Press, 1996.

Steinkerchner, Scott. *Beyond Agreement: Interreligious Dialogue Amid Persistent Differences*. New York: Rowman & Littlefield, 2010.

Stone, Douglas, et al. *Difficult Conversations : how to discuss what matters most*. New York: Viking Press, 1999.

Al-Suyuti, Jalal ad-Din. *Asbab al-Nuzul*. Beirut: Muassisa al-Kutub al-Thaqafiyyah, 2002.

Swearer, Donald K. "The Ecumenical Vision of Buddhadāsa Bhikkhu and His Dialogue with Christianity." In *Buddhist Studies from India to America: Essays in Honor of Charles S. Prebish*, edited by Damien Keown, 270–85. London: Routledge, 2006.

———. "The Hermeneutics of Buddhist Ecology in Contemporary Thailand: Buddhadāsa and Dhammapitaka" In *Buddhism and Ecology: The Interconnection of Dharma and Deeds*, edited by Damien Keown, 21–44. Cambridge, Mass.: Harvard University Press, 1997.

———. *Me and Mine: Selected Essays by Bhikkhu Buddhadasa*. Albany: State University of New York Press, 1989.

Swidler, Leonard, ed. *Towards a Universal Theology of Religions*. Maryknoll, N.Y.: Orbis Books, 1987.

Al-Tabarsi, Ahmad b. Ali al-Fadl. *Majma al-Bayan fi Tafsir al-Quran*. Beirut: Dar al-Murtaza, 2006.

Tanner, SJ, Norman. *The Decrees of the Ecumenical Councils*, vol. 2. Washington, D.C.: Georgetown University Press, 1990.

Tapie, Matthew. *Aquinas on Israel and the Church: The Question of Supersessionism in the Theology of Thomas Aquinas*. Eugene, Ore.: Pickwick, 2014.

Thistlethwaite, Susan Brooks. *Interfaith Just Peacemaking: Jewish, Christian, and Muslim Perspectives on the New Paradigm of Peace and War*. New York: Palgrave Macmillan, 2011.

Tück, Jan-Heiner. "Das Konzil und die Juden. *Nostra aetate*—Bruch mit dem Antijudaismus und Durchbruch zur theologischen Würdigung des nachbiblischen Bundesvolkes." In *Freude an Gott. Auf dem Weg zu einem lebendigen*

Glauben. Festschrift für Kurt Kardinal Koch zum 65 Geburtstag, Zweiter Teil-
band, edited by George Augustin and Markus Schulze, 857–93. Freiburg i.
Br.: Herder, 2015.
———. "Wo war Gott? Der deutsche Papst in Auschwitz—eine theologische
Nachbetrachtung." In *Der Theologenpapst. Eine kritische Würdigung Benedikts
XVI*, edited by Jan-Heiner Tück, 122–34. Freiburg i. Br.: Herder, 2013.
Volf, Miroslav, Ghazi bin Muhammad, and Melissa Yarrington, eds. *A Common
Word: Muslims and Christians on Loving God and Neighbor*. Grand Rapids,
Mich.: William B. Eerdmans, 2010.
Watt, W. Montgomery. *Muhammad: Prophet and Statesman*. London: Oxford Uni-
versity Press, 1961.
Waxman, Mordecai. "Introduction." In Zvia Ginor, *Yakar Le'Mordecai: Jubilee
Volume in Honor of Rabbi Mordecai Waxman*. Great Neck, N.Y.: KTAV Pub-
lishing House, Inc., 1998.
Weigel, George. *Witness to Hope*. New York: Harper, 2001.
Wimberly, Anne Streaty. *Soul Stories: African American Christian Education*, rev. ed.
Nashville: Abingdon, 2005.
Wittgenstein, Ludwig. *On Certainty*, translated by G. E. M. Anscombe and G. H.
von Wright. New York: Harper, 1972.
Al-Zamakhshari, Mahmud b. 'Umar. *Al-Kashshaf*, edited by Adil Ahmad Abd al-
Mawjud and Ali Muhammad Muawwadh. Riyadh: Maktabat al-Abikan,
1998.
Zehner, Joachim. *Der notwendige Dialog: die Weltreligionen in katholischer und evan-
gelischer Sicht*. Gütersloh: G. Mohn, 1992.

Contributors

Anthony Cirelli is Associate Director of the Committee on Ecumenical and Interreligious Affairs of the United States Conference of Catholic Bishops.

Rev. Francis X. Clooney, SJ is the Director of the Center for the Study of World Religions and the Parkman Professor of Divinity and Professor of Comparative Theology at Harvard University.

Rev. John W. Crossin, O.S.F.S. is Executive Director of the Committee on Ecumenical and Interreligious Affairs of the United States Conference of Catholic Bishops.

Anuttama Dasa is International Director of Communications for the International Society for Krishna Consciousness and a member of its Governing Body Commission.

His Eminence Timothy Cardinal Dolan is Archbishop of New York and Co-chair of the National Council of Synagogues-United States Conference of Catholic Bishops Dialogue.

Archbishop Michael L. Fitzgerald, MAfr is President Emeritus of the Pontifical Council for Interreligious Dialogue.

James L. Fredericks is Professor of Theological Studies at Loyola Marymount University in Los Angeles, California.

Ann Garrido is Associate Professor of Homiletics at the Aquinas Institute of Theology in St. Louis, Missouri and a consultant with Triad Consulting Group—a communications firm based in Cambridge, Mass., specializing in healthy dialogue.

John Garvey is President of The Catholic University of America.

Rev. Larry Golemon is Executive Director of the Washington Theological Consortium and an ordained minister in the Presbyterian Church.

Rabbi Irving (Yitz) Greenberg is President Emeritus of the Jewish Life Network/Steinhardt Foundation.

Rev. Sidney H. Griffith is Professor Emeritus of Semitic and Egyptian Languages and Literatures at The Catholic University of America.

Sayed Hassan Akhlaq Hussaini is a researcher from the Center for the Study of Culture and Values on the campus of the Catholic University of America who has taught philosophy in the United States, Iran, and his native Afghanistan.

His Eminence Kurt Cardinal Koch is President of the Pontifical Council for Promoting Christian Unity.

Judi Longdin is Director of Ecumenical and Interfaith Concerns for the Archdiocese of Milwaukee, Wisconsin.

Bishop Denis Madden is Auxiliary Bishop of Baltimore and Chairman Emeritus of the Committee on Ecumenical and Interreligious Affairs of the United States Conference of Catholic Bishops.

Rabbi Noam E. Marans is Director of Interreligious and Intergroup Relations for the American Jewish Committee (AJC).

Very Rev. Mark Morozowich is Associate Professor of Liturgy and Dean of The School of Theology and Religious Studies at The Catholic University of America.

Seyyed Hossein Nasr is University Professor of Islamic Studies at The George Washington University in Washington, D.C.

Michael Root is Ordinary Professor of Systematic Theology at The Catholic University of America and was a drafting member of Catholic-Lutheran *Joint Declaration on the Doctrine of Justification.*

Bishop Mitchell T. Rozanski is the Bishop of the Diocese of Springfield, Massachusetts and the Chair of the Committee on Ecumenical and Interreligious Affairs at the United States Conference of Catholic Bishops.

Rev. Thomas F. Stransky, CSP is the Rector Emeritus of the Tantur Ecumenical Institute for Theological Studies in Jerusalem. He served as one of the original staff members of the Secretariat for Promoting Christian Unity in the Vatican from 1960 to 1970, including the drafting of *Nostra Aetate.*

His Eminence Jean-Louis Cardinal Tauran is President of the Pontifical Council for Interreligious Dialogue.

Wilhelmus (Pim) Valkenberg is Professor of Religion and Culture and the Director of the Institute for Interreligious Study and Dialogue at the School of Theology and Religious Studies at The Catholic University of America.

Index

Abbey of Our Lady of Gethsemani, 44. *See also* Gethsemani Encounters

Abbott, Walter, SJ, 3

'Abd al-Jalīl, Jean Mohammed ben, OFM, 120

'Abdalla, Amr, 231

'Abdel Haleem, M.A.S., 133n3

Abraham, 22, 24, 30, 33, 108, 138, 156, 171, 181-82, 187, 244

Abrahamic faiths, ix, 23, 39, 118, 125, 127, 130, 138, 146, 150, 229, 253, 259

abrogation (*naskh*), 101

abuse, 229

acarya, 81

accountability, 231

Ad Gentes, 20, 66-70

Advanced Institute of Islam (NADEO), 266

Africa, 256; Afro-Asiatic religions, 63

afterlife, 246, 272

Aga Khan, 96

aggiornamento, 45

ahl al-dhimma (protected persons), 137

ahl al-kitāb. See People of the Book

almsgiving, xiii

Al-Alwani Chair, 226

Amaladoss, Michael, 86

American Academy of Religion, 259-60

American Jewish Committee, 208, 214-16, 218-19

American Sikh Council, 249n17

Amici Israel, 8

anatta / anatman. See nonself, teaching of

Anawati, Georges, OP, 16, 24, 120

Angelus Silesius, 106

Anglicans, 31, 258

anti-Catholicism, 201

anti-Christian hostility, 122, 235

Anti-Defamation League, 208

anti-Judaism, 166, 168, 205

anti-Semitism, xvii, 17, 126, 165-68, 185, 201, 205, 212, 220-21; condemnation of, 8, 16, 34, 165, 174, 190, 215-16

apologetics, 118

Areopagus, 22

Arjuna, 78

Arnold, Leo, 3

art, 62

asceticism, 44, 62, 184

Ashoka, 51

Asia, 253, 256; (South-)Asian religions, 41, 249

Asín Palacios, Miguel, 112

assimilation, 179, 188

Atatürk, Mustafa Kemal, 142

Athenagoras, Patriarch, 171

Augustine, 170, 277

Auschwitz, xvii, 166, 172, 209

āyāt (signs, verses, revelations), 135, 137

al-Azhar, 96

Baar Statement, 34

Badaliya, 19

al-Baghdadi, Abu Bakr, 97, 143

baptism, 30, 33, 35, 236

Baptism, Eucharist and Ministry (World Council of Churches), 38

Bar Mitzvah, 211

Barnabas, Epistle of, 167

Basetti Sani, Giulio, OFM, 120

Baum, Gregory, 10, 16

Bea, Cardinal Augustin, 4, 9-10, 14, 16-17, 19, 27, 161-62, 168, 214

believing, 211; without belonging, 212